BLACK IN
SELMA

BLACK IN SELMA

The Uncommon Life of J. L. Chestnut, Jr.

J. L. CHESTNUT, JR.

JULIA CASS

Farrar, Straus and Giroux

NEW YORK

Farrar, Straus and Giroux
19 Union Square West, New York 10003

Distributed in Canada by Douglas & McIntyre Ltd.
Printed in the United States of America
Designed by Victoria Wong
First published in 1990 by Farrar, Straus and Giroux
First Farrar, Straus and Giroux paperback edition, 1999

Library of Congress Cataloging-in-Publication Data
Chestnut, J. L.
    Black in Selma : the uncommon life of J. L. Chestnut, Jr. /
J. L. Chestnut, Jr., and Julia Cass.
        p.   cm.
    ISBN 0-374-52688-5 (pbk)
    1. Chestnut, J. L.   2. Afro-American lawyers—Alabama—
Biography. 3. Civil rights movements—Alabama—Selma—
History. I. Cass, Julia. II. Title.
KF373.C389A3   1990
340'.092—dc20
    [b]   89-77436

WITH LOVE, I dedicate this book to my dear wife, Vivian, my children, my grandchildren, and my parents. I also dedicate this book to the warm memory of John F. Shields, a remarkable and courageous black high school teacher who helped me understand the black predicament and taught me to question leaders. Lastly, I dedicate this book to all who care enough to stand up and be counted.

J. L. CHESTNUT, JR.
November 20, 1989
Selma, Alabama

Contents

Preface

Initially, J. L. Chestnut, Jr., a black attorney in Selma, Alabama, didn't see his life as a book. He wasn't sure his experiences in the boondocks of Alabama would be of national interest, and he was skeptical about whether any publisher up in New York City would be attracted to the story of a black man they'd never heard of.

I thought otherwise.

Chestnut was born in Selma in 1930. He grew up in the era of segregation, when most black people, including his parents, made accommodations to what seemed to be an unchangeable situation. He went to law school at Howard University in Washington, D.C., in the 1950s, when the *Brown* v. *Board of Education* case that struck down school segregation was being decided. In 1958, he returned home to Selma to become the town's first and only black lawyer.

When the civil rights organizations came to Selma in the middle 1960s to launch a voting rights movement, Chestnut represented demonstrators in court and provided valuable information on local values, personalities, and thinking, in part through his unique relationship with the white circuit judge James Hare. He was there beside the Edmund Pettus Bridge when state troopers and local white posse men attacked the civil rights marchers on "Bloody Sunday," March 7, 1965, the event that led to the passage of the Voting Rights Act, a turning point for black America and for Chestnut personally.

Since then, Chestnut has been a leader in the longer march, the process of turning the possibilities opened up in 1965 into real grass-roots change long after the national spotlight and national civil rights leaders had gone elsewhere. He is a trial lawyer, said to have tried more capital cases than any other lawyer in Alabama. He and his law firm—the largest black law firm in Alabama— have filed numerous civil rights lawsuits. He has run for state office; one of his partners is a state senator. He has been in the thick of organizing the black vote locally and statewide. He also is chairman of the board of deacons at Selma's First Baptist Church (the black one), a husband, and the father of six children.

I met J. L. Chestnut—whom his friends call Chess—in the winter of 1984, a month before the Super Tuesday presidential primary. I was then the Southern correspondent for the *Philadelphia Inquirer*, stationed in New Orleans, and my editor asked me to go to Selma to cover a series of racially tinged political developments. I hadn't been in Selma a day before somebody told me I needed to speak with Chess. This is a common occurrence, I would learn, with national reporters who come to Selma.

A lot was happening in Selma that week. Excitement over the candidacy of Jesse Jackson was producing scores of black registered voters, almost matching the number of whites. F. D. Reese, a local black civil rights leader in the 1960s, had declared himself a candidate for mayor against Joe Smitherman, the white man who had been mayor since 1964. Two days before I arrived, Smitherman had orchestrated the firing of black deputy registrars, and blacks had taken the issue to the U.S. Department of Justice.

Chess's analysis of the politics of the firing of the registrars and of the upcoming mayor's race was complex and intriguing. He explained how racial politics are played in Selma and described the personalities and motives of the players. He also predicted that Reese would lose the mayor's race because, he said, Reese had been persuaded by white leaders to adopt a losing strategy. When I asked how that could happen, he shook his head and said, "You really have to know the whole background of the South."

He went on to tell me about an experience in his youth, in-

volving Selma's two leading black ministers, that revealed to him
the compromises black leaders accepted. He then tied that revelation to the contemporary situation. Clearly, Chess had been a
student of power and leadership—who has it and how they got
it—from his earliest days. Though I had been covering the South
for almost two years, I had never heard a more frank or sophisticated analysis of a racial situation. And I knew little of the kinds
of relationships black leaders had with white leaders in the South
in the 1930s and '40s.

I returned to Selma on quite a few occasions after that. Interviewing Chess further, I learned more about his life and began
to see it as representative, spanning the Old South and the New
South in a small Southern town that had played a crucial role in
transforming American politics.

To write this book, I lived in Selma for most of 1988 and part
of 1989, interviewing and tape-recording Chess. I read through
the Selma *Times-Journal* from 1950 to the present, court records
of Chess's cases, previous books about Selma, and accounts of
relevant events appearing in other Alabama and national newspapers. I also interviewed Chess's parents, wife, children, law
partners, and numerous others, black and white, who had been
involved in incidents in his life.

Though the main body of the book is drawn from my interviews
with Chess, the brief introductions that precede the book's five
sections, providing the context of Selma's history and other relevant background to Chess's story, are in my own words.

For the rest of the book, told in Chess's voice, he and I worked
together, using his memory, written records of events in his life—
court documents, newspaper accounts, correspondence—and interviews with others whose memories helped trigger his and added
details he had forgotten or didn't know.

Chess's high school friends described him as the classmate who,
when there was something the students wanted taken up with the
principal, stood out front speaking for the group—a leader. They
also said he was the one they'd see in the schoolyard surrounded
by laughing students—an entertainer. He remains both. He is a
complex person—angry and fun-loving, blunt and kind, suspicious
and generous, skeptical and hopeful.

In some parts of Selma, Chess is a controversial figure. Many whites consider him too radical and combative, though there are white people in Selma who think highly of him. The white community was curious and concerned about the book—white Selma is preoccupied with its image in the world at large—but a number of white people were helpful to me and only a few were hostile.

Black Selma considers Chess one of its first citizens. Each year, the *Times-Journal* asks its readers to send in the names of those they consider leaders, and Chess always comes out at the top. The same day that some middle-aged white women were telling me how controversial Chess is, a sorority of middle-aged black women was honoring him as its Man of the Year.

To me, Chess is an inspiration. He hasn't been afraid to step up, speak out, take the heat, make mistakes, and continue on. His experiences in life and his insights about power and the attitudes of those who have it and those who don't have relevance well beyond the spheres of race and region. I believe readers of any color or sex or from any part of the country will find his story meaningful and will gain a deeper understanding not only of race relations but of human nature and the mechanisms of social change.

Despite his initial skepticism about the project, Chess agreed to spend enough time with me to gather information for a proposal and an outline. When he read the proposal, he realized his life was indeed bookworthy and became excited. He began to see the book as the untold story of the efforts of "grass-roots folk" in Alabama, as opposed to those of famous national leaders.

Chess is an extremely busy man, trying cases, attending meetings, and making speeches all over the state. I found that the best way to squeeze out a chunk of time with him was to ride along on these trips and interview him on the way. Whenever I accompanied him on speechmaking occasions, he always introduced me to the audience and commented with a grin, "You don't know how rough it is being followed around Alabama by a white woman with a notepad and a tape recorder."

The fact that I am white caused him some apprehension. He didn't care for the way it might look—that it took a white person to write a black person's story—and for the message he felt this would send to the black community. Also, he wasn't certain that

I could appreciate or understand all the subtleties of his experiences. He was concerned, too, that I might be turned off by his outspokenness about race and ultimately not want to write a story told from the black perspective.

On the other hand, there I was, pushing for and ready to write a book that he had come to see as important and worthwhile. And Chess loves an audience. When he saw the book proposal, he decided, "What the hell. Let's do it."

JULIA CASS
Philadelphia, Pennsylvania
November 1989

"If there is no struggle, there is no progress. Those who profess to favor freedom yet deprecate agitation are men who want crops without plowing the ground. They want rain without thunder and lightning. They want the ocean without the awful roar of its many waters. The struggle may be a moral one or it may be a physical one or it may be both moral and physical. But it must be a struggle. Power concedes nothing without a demand. It never did and never will . . . Men may not get all they pay for in this world but they must certainly pay for all they get."

FREDERICK DOUGLASS

". . . I must confess that I am not afraid of the word 'tension.' I have earnestly opposed violent tension, but there is a type of constructive, nonviolent tension which is necessary for growth. Just as Socrates felt that it was necessary to create a tension in the mind so that individuals could rise from the bondage of myths and half-truths to the unfettered realm of creative analysis and objective appraisal, so must we see the need for nonviolent gadflies to create the kind of tension in society that will help men rise from the dark depths of prejudice and racism to the majestic heights of understanding and brotherhood.

MARTIN LUTHER KING, JR.
"Letter from a Birmingham Jail"

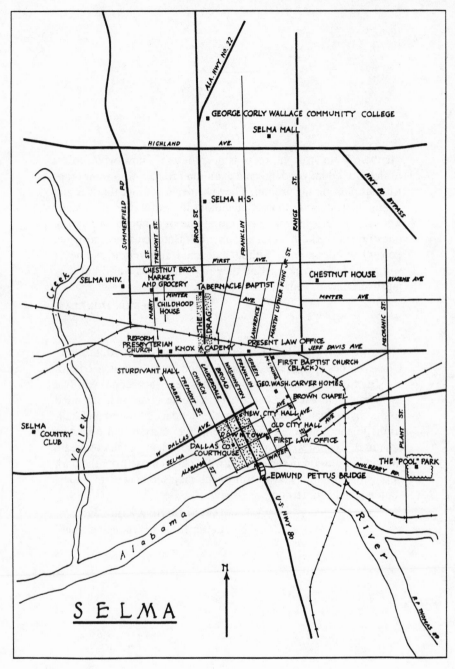

© Robert P. Thomas

PART ONE

1930 - 1958

A steamship picking up cotton at the dock behind Water Avenue in Selma
(Courtesy of the Old Depot Museum, Selma)

Introduction

The city of Selma sits on a bluff overlooking a bend in the Alabama River 160 miles north of the river's mouth in Mobile, 50 miles west of the state capital in Montgomery, and 90 miles southwest of the state's industrial center in Birmingham.

In 1930, the year J. L. Chestnut, Jr., was born, Selma was the business, banking, and transportation hub of Alabama's cotton-plantation region. It was the place where landowners, farmers, and sharecroppers shopped on Saturdays, went to the movies, visited the doctor, stayed in the hospital, sold their cotton, took the train, and banked their money if they had any. A sign outside the city limits proclaimed Selma the fastest-growing and friendliest town in Alabama—the fourth largest in the state, with a population of 18,012; just over half its residents (9,249) were black; 8,763 were white.

The town was founded in 1819, when Alabama was still a territory, by eight men who bought the land on the bluff, divided it into lots, and offered them for sale. Its original white settlers were farmers, most of Scotch-Irish descent, who were leaving the exhausted soil of the piedmont areas of Georgia, the Carolinas, and Virginia for new, rich land on which to grow cotton. The dark-colored soil along a belt across central Alabama proved to be especially suitable for cotton and gave the region its name, the Black Belt.

Selma's original black settlers were African slaves brought from other Southern states to do the hard labor required in planting and picking. The slaves arrived in "large droves, some hundreds daily, . . . brought to [Selma] by men like James Hall, Watson, Willis and Jordan, whose business it was to trade in negroes," Selma resident John Hardy wrote in his 1879 book, Selma: Her Institutions and Her Men. *"Several large buildings were erected in the town especially for the accommodation of negro traders and their property . . . [One was] a three-story wooden building, sufficiently large to accommodate four or five hundred negroes. On the ground floor, a large sitting room was provided for the exhibition of negroes on the market, and from among them could be selected blacksmiths, carpenters, bright mulatto girls and women for seamstresses, field hands, women and children of all ages, sizes and qualities. To have seen the large droves of negroes arriving in the town every week, from about the first of September to the first of April, no one could be surprised that the black population increased in Dallas County, from 1830 to 1840, between twelve and thirteen thousand."*

With this army of slaves and its fertile soil, Dallas County, of which Selma is the seat, produced more cotton than any other county in Alabama in the decades before the Civil War. Selma, with its key position by the river, became the queen city of the Black Belt.

During the Civil War, Selma was a foundry, producing arms and ammunition for the Confederacy. Despite its fortifications and a strenuous defense led by the Confederate general Nathan Bedford Forrest, Selma fell to Union general John Harrison Wilson's raiders on April 2, 1865. In the aftermath, much of the city was burned or looted. Many slaves left the plantations with the coming of freedom, but they lacked money (slaves were forbidden to own or inherit property), education (learning to read and write was punishable by thirty-four lashes), or skills other than farm labor. Many had no choice but to become sharecroppers or tenant farmers for their former masters or other large landowners.

Agriculture remained the basis of Selma's economy in 1930. Laboring in a white man's field was the leading occupation of the black residents of Dallas County, which had a population of

55,094, 40,867 of whom were black. Domestic service was the second leading occupation of black Dallas County residents. Other major employers, primarily of white people, were the Southern Railroad, which maintained a roundhouse in Selma, and a few cotton-seed and cotton-oil mills.

Selma in 1930 was a pretty town. It prided itself on having the finest department stores in the Black Belt, three white and two black hospitals, five banks, three movie theaters, a hotel that replicated the Doge's Palace in Venice, Italy, a minor league baseball team, and a surprising number of grand homes. A cut below these Tara-like mansions were rambling Victorian houses; below them were smaller cottages with large porches on paved streets lined with sprawling live oaks.

The poorer whites lived in east Selma, near the roundhouse of the Southern Railroad. Though some of them lived in poorer circumstances than Selma's middle-class black families—the funeral-home directors, doctors, and dentists—these were very few. White families of even modest means could afford at least one black servant.

A small group of prominent white men—large landowners, bankers, cotton merchants, major businessmen, lawyers, and wholesale grocers who advanced seeds and supplies to the large plantations— dominated Selma's economy and politics. These men sat on the boards of the banks and decided who would receive loans, and they determined who would hold political office. "City Council was a buddy system. It was 'I'll run if you don't,' " according to Edgar Russell, Jr., a retired circuit judge.

During the Reconstruction period, from 1867 to 1877, when an army unit occupied Dallas County and enforced the Fifteenth Amendment giving blacks the vote, Dallas County elected a black U.S. congressman, state senator, criminal court judge, four city councilmen, five county commissioners, a tax assessor, and a coroner. But in 1877, when the federal troops were withdrawn, white Democrats regained control of Alabama politics and every black elected official in Dallas County was driven from office—either by abolishing their elective offices in favor of ones established by the governor or by gerrymandering voting districts to create a white majority. Black people were officially disenfranchised by the 1901

Alabama constitution, which instituted educational and property requirements that would have excluded most black people even if these requirements had been interpreted fairly by local boards of registrars, which they were not.

Like all towns across the Deep South, Selma in 1930 was rigidly segregated in its facilities and its recognitions of status. One white man remembers being punished in school when he announced, "There's a lady here," about a black woman who came into the building. Black people were also excluded from holding most jobs other than manual labor, and a black person holding a job comparable to a white person's received a lower salary. According to the Selma school-board minutes, for example, the salary range for white teachers in 1930 was $900 to $2,300; for black teachers, $400 to $675.

Comparatively speaking, though, Selma had a larger black middle class than did the surrounding towns. It also became a regional center for black education, provided primarily by four church-sponsored institutions—two by Northern white denominations, two by black denominations. Two of the black schools provided some college training—Selma University, founded by the black Alabama Baptist Convention to train black Baptist preachers, and Concordia College, founded by the Missouri Synod Lutheran Church to provide schooling for black children in addition to a college department to train ministers.

In 1930, Selma operated one overcrowded public school for black children, Clark School, which went through the ninth grade. The city operated six public schools, including a high school, for white children. In 1935, when the Reformed Presbyterian Church, a Northern white denomination, found itself financially unable to support Knox Academy, the junior high and high school for black children it had founded in 1874, the church offered to turn it over to the city school system. Selma accepted the offer, and Knox became the public black secondary school going through the tenth grade, extended to twelfth grade a few years later.

At that point, Selma was one of the few cities in the region to provide a full high school education for black children and a full school year. Schools for black children in the country usually ran only from November through March so the children could plant *and pick cotton. Selma also spent comparatively more on black education than the rural counties did. In 1930, the Dallas County school system spent $51 a year for the education of each white child, $7 a year for each black child. The amount the town of Selma spent per student cannot be determined from the school-board minutes, but the proportion appears to be more like 3 to 1.*

White Selmians considered their town a cut above others in race relations. "Selma had a paternalistic pattern I think because this was a slaveholding area and slaves were valued as property," said Sam Earl Hobbs, a retired Selma attorney whose father represented the Selma area in Congress in the 1930s and 1940s. "I was born in 1917, and when I was growing up, race relations were—or anyway, appeared to be—quite amicable."

CHAPTER 1

King of the Drag

Whipping an opponent before a fight was a psychology Muhammad Ali, the prizefighter, mastered, and I've often wondered whether he learned it watching white people in his native Louisville deal with blacks. Both he and the white South sent the message "You don't have a chance. You're crazy to challenge me. You're already beat," to foster a loser psychology in the other fella.

I discovered as a teenage gambler that it's far easier to beat a person who expects to lose than one who came to win because the former will give up somewhere along the line. I also learned that power is most effective when you don't have to use it, when folk just assume you've got it. Every time you have to use it, you lose a little of it, which the white South was to discover during the civil rights struggle. I learned this at a card table when I was fifteen years old.

My favorite uncle, Preston Chestnut, was a professional gambler, one of the best Alabama ever produced. He traveled all over and represented what I thought was success. His money was helping to sustain my father and his other brothers with the farm they operated during my teenage years, the World War II years. Their base was forty acres that my grandfather owned, but with Preston's gambling money, they leased other farmland and pro-

My uncle Preston Chestnut (Courtesy of Clifton Chestnut)

duced a hundred bales of cotton a year when many whites weren't getting fifty on a comparable amount of land. That impressed me.

Also, schoolteachers fell over backwards for Preston. He married a beauty queen named Velberta. He dressed in fine, tailored clothes. He drove a 1941 fluid-drive Dodge in 1941. When I heard Preston's name on "the Drag," the nightlife section of black Selma, it was said with admiration and awe. He was the king.

I talked to Preston at great length about gambling. I'd ask what he was doing, but he was very reserved about what he would tell me. He didn't want me to go down that road. He was pushing me to finish high school and go to college. But I deviled him so much he showed me a few things, and I picked up a little bit here and there watching him and other gamblers on the Drag at night.

During the day I went to school at Knox Academy, Selma's segregated black junior and senior high school. I lived with my father and mother, my adopted sister, and my Aunt Lennie and

Side street off what once was "the Drag." In the 1940s, these buildings were busy clubs, joints, and cafés (© Penny Weaver)

Uncle Frank in a wood-frame house a half block from the corner grocery store and meat market my father and Uncle Frank owned. By black standards, we were a middle-class family, and my mother had middle-class ambitions for me to go to college and make something of myself. At fourteen, though, I knew what I wanted to be: King of the Drag.

Many nights, beginning when I was in the eighth grade, I jumped down from my bedroom window and bicycled over to the three blocks of cafés, upstairs dance halls, backroom gambling dives, and bootleg joints on Broad Street between Tabernacle Baptist Church and Jeff Davis Avenue, the dividing line between black Selma and white Selma.

Always, a few dozen men, at least, were hanging around under the brightly lit marquee of the Roxy Theater where speakers blared out onto the sidewalk the sound track of whatever B movie, black film, or short on black entertainers was playing inside. Next door was the White Dot Café that Charlie Bates, a bootlegger, owned at the zenith of his career and, on the second floor, a VFW club. On the other side of the Roxy was a café called Bro Fields, where you could get hot links and rice for 15 cents, then a barbershop and stairs leading up to a bootleg joint called Jabbo's. Around the corner was Stella Brown's, a chicken-in-the-basket place, and rows of tumbledown wooden houses where you could drink or gamble, usually both.

Objectively, the Drag didn't amount to very much. But to me at that age it was a kind of Harlem, an oasis in oppressive little Selma, with jazz, entertainment, drinking, gambling, chocolate-brown women teasing, and sharply dressed men strutting in zoot suits, narrow pointed shoes, and Big Apple hats—enormous hats turned up behind and down in the front with a long feather pointing upward.

My friends and I hung around with the older fellas, listening, dreaming, lying. Gambling was a major topic and activity. If the men weren't making high/low bets on major league baseball games, they were shooting dice or playing poker, Georgia Skin, Tonk. Being surrounded by it, we got into it. It wasn't the money that interested me; I couldn't buy anything expensive without my mother asking questions. I was attracted by the challenge, the head-on competition. If you were the best gambler, hell, you were the leader, the champion.

I got into the game called Georgia Skin. The dealer sets out the deck. Everybody picks a card. Then the dealer starts to turn cards from the deck and you're betting everybody at the table that his card—queen, ten, whatever—will come up before yours. Preston told me how to nick the face cards by attaching a little piece of sandpaper to your finger with flesh-colored adhesive tape—a nick here on the king, there on the queen. If you practiced enough—and I practiced all the time because I was determined to win—you could run your hands around the deck when you cut the cards and gauge where the high cards were, which improved your odds.

But nicking cards was dangerous. I kept looking for a foolproof way to beat a fool, and I found one: order a case of cards, mark them, then sell the cards to the store that supplied the joints where I was gambling.

I picked one little line in the design on the back of the cards for the king, a different line for the each of the other cards, and widened them subtly with a fine-point pen. You had to know what you were looking for and practice at it to see them. I used the Bunsen burner at Knox Academy at night to open and reseal the cellophane around the cards that was supposed to ensure that they weren't tampered with. Then I sold them for half price to the store on the Drag that supplied most of the joints. I think the owner assumed they were stolen. So I didn't have to do anything when I got to the gambling houses. They were my cards to begin with.

With this system, I really killed them at poker. I was playing grown men—well, adult males pretending to be men—and I found it extremely satisfying to walk in off the street, fifteen years old, and break them.

One night, I was winning in a poker game at the VFW Club —naturally, they were my cards—and a man named Richard "Luvalley" Cole reached across the table and slapped me after losing five hands in a row. Luvalley was a veteran and he couldn't have a little upstart showboat like me embarrass him. He was drinking whiskey and I'd had several beers. I stood up and told him if I found him there when I returned this would be his last night on the planet, which guaranteed he would be there waiting. He couldn't leave and save face.

I got on my bicycle, rode home, and woke my parents. I told them I had a headache and got the key to the grocery store to get a Stanback headache powder. I rode to the store, put all the knives and meat cleavers in a brown paper bag, and rode back to the club.

They were having a dance in the front room. When I hit the top of the stairs, I tripped and all the knives and cleavers fell out of the bag and clattered to the floor. Folk on the dance floor ran over tables and into each other. Luvalley was standing at the bar. He saw me and I saw him. I grabbed a meat cleaver and he started running. I ran behind him and threw the cleaver. It just missed him and struck the wall. My life and his could have been over in that minute. But I was mad, young, reckless.

I dodged the police all night, but the next morning they found me at a shoeshine stand. I was sitting there getting my shoes polished. A policeman came up, stood in front of the stand, and ordered, "Come here, boy."

"He's talking to you," I said to the fella getting his shoes shined next to me.

The policeman pointed at me. "No. I'm talking to *you*, boy."

I said to another fella there, "Hey, he's talking to you."

The policeman planted himself right in front of me and glared. "You, boy, get your ass down." I stepped down as slowly as I dared.

"Yessir."

I discovered that day that being taken to jail didn't frighten me in my bones as it did so many black men. I knew I wasn't in the kind of trouble anybody would kill over. It didn't involve a white woman or a threat to white power. A black bartender had called the police because I had turned out a dance and cost him business. Playing that little game with the policeman in front of other blacks at the shoeshine stand was playing with the limits. But I had been watching the police since I was seven years old, and I thought I knew where the limits were. I also knew the policeman would have to think twice about slapping me around because my father knew white people of some consequence. I got out on bail and paid a fine for disturbing the peace. I caught more hell from my mother.

After a while, it developed that even in a game of poker or Georgia Skin where I didn't have marked cards, it was difficult for some people to beat me. They were overwhelmed by the reputation that J.L. does not lose, so that a fella with a pretty good hand was far more likely to fold when I was on the other side. They were whipped before the game started—by my reputation of invincibility.

I had another psychological edge: I didn't care about the money, so having $100 at stake didn't change my temperature at all. The money I won I loaned to people, gave away, or hid in tin cans under our house because my mother didn't know I was gambling. I bought a ring once and she thought I had taken the money from the cash register at the store. That bothered me. But I saw the power of money—how you could almost buy a person—which gave me insight into the relationships of black people with white employers and the bankers downtown. My Uncle Preston was forever pushing economic development for black people and I think this came from what he learned gambling—that money not only talks, it commands.

The men who ran the gambling joints knew something was wrong, but couldn't figure out what. They'd break open a new deck, figuring I nicked the cards or slipped in some of my own, but I kept winning. I don't think they could conceive of anybody going to the elaborate lengths I did to win. But they didn't want me in their places anymore. Sometimes the betting would stop when I sat down, and this cost them because they took a cut of each hand. Some called the police. "We've got a minor down here, Chestnut, come get him." And the police, who supplemented their salaries with payoffs from these joints, came to protect their financial interests, grabbed up the cards, and took me to the station.

It struck me as illogical that if the house man, a black professional gambler, couldn't figure out what I was doing, he would think the white police could. And the police responded to the call and went through the charade—spreading out the cards, poring over them like Sherlock Holmes—that they could discover something black professional gamblers missed.

Standing in some policeman's little cubbyhole of an office, watching him study the cards, I thought, These people are not that smart. All that presumed superior white brain power is a sham. It was out of this realization that Red Fern, a black cabdriver, and I pulled something over on the police that gave me more satisfaction than all my victories at the card table.

The Drag then was patrolled by a single white policeman who carried himself with an exaggerated swagger, demanding and getting the mass of black men standing on the sidewalk to part like the Red Sea to let him through. We called him Mr. Craw (as in "sticks in your craw"). He was an average-sized man, not imposing physically but striking in his dress, his swagger, and his supreme confidence that he could control hundreds of black people on a Saturday night by himself.

He led with his chin stuck out like Benito Mussolini, and the way he moved his hips drew attention to his pistol hung low in a

Western-style holster. He wore black riding boots and britches and cut the widest possible swath through the crowd of blacks, who peeled off in nervous deference as he strutted straight ahead.

One night, a warm Saturday night when the sidewalks were crowded, one black man—a little fella named Jim Shorty—didn't move when Craw strode up. Shorty was running his mouth to his buddies and feeling his corn whiskey. I was standing on the corner by the Roxy, cracking jokes with my friends, about twenty feet away from Shorty. I was seventeen years old and not yet fully grown. I would never be tall, but at that point I was shorter than Shorty, about 5 feet 5 inches. I was wearing the hip uniform of the day, a sport shirt with an open collar and drapes—pants wide at the knee and tapered at the ankle like the ones Cab Calloway wore in the movie *Stormy Weather*.

Craw shoved Shorty aside, and Shorty mumbled something.

The policeman stopped and glared. "What did you say, nigger?"

"Go fuck yourself," Shorty spat out. The crowd fell silent and froze in place. We heard what Shorty said but didn't quite believe he said it, although if anyone was going to make such a direct challenge to white authority in Selma in the 1940s, it would be somebody like Shorty, whom both whites and blacks would call "crazy."

Shorty was in his thirties, one of a group of young black men, very limited in education, stuck in third-rate jobs that didn't pay enough to buy a home in a lifetime, whose existence centered on raising hell at night. He was in and out of jail regularly for getting drunk or fighting over a woman or trying to whip somebody two times larger than he. I had known Shorty since I was a kid fascinated by him and other black prisoners in striped uniforms who were forever digging massive holes in the dirt streets of black Selma to repair broken water or sewer lines. Some of these prisoners were in chains as well as stripes, and Shorty was almost always one of them.

There was street talk that if you took a policeman's gun and brought it to headquarters, the policeman would be fired. Shorty had that thought in him as well as the whiskey; I also think Shorty had just had enough of bowing and scraping.

Good Samaritan Hospital, 1940s (Courtesy of the Fathers of St. Edmund, Selma)

He grabbed Craw. The policeman threw a punch and missed. Shorty punched him twice and dropped him to the ground. They rolled around on the pavement under the bright lights of the Roxy marquee. Shorty was trying to get the policeman's gun with one hand while hitting him with the other. At some point, Shorty knocked him out. The policeman lay there unconscious and up popped Shorty with the pistol, talking about going down and turning it in at the station.

"You're crazy! Get out of here! They'll kill you!" somebody yelled. Most folk scattered—ran into the White Dot or Bro Fields or around the corner. With all the people driving by rubbernecking, it wouldn't be long before every policeman in Selma would be there. My friends took off, but I stayed. I was curious to see what Shorty was going to do and who was going to help him.

Shorty left the policeman on the ground and ran around the corner to Stella Brown's, the fried-chicken place. I ran behind him. He wasn't two feet inside when folk started waving their arms and shouting, "Don't come in here! Don't come in here!" They about had a fit. I saw desperation in everyone's eyes but Shorty's. He backed out of Stella's, turned, and checked the pistol to see how many bullets were in it. I read that to mean he knew he was dead. The question was how many of them could he take with him.

"Pssssssssst." I got Shorty's attention and gestured to him to come over to my father's jeep, which was parked a little farther down the side street from Stella's. Shorty jumped in, and I drove over to Good Samaritan, the black hospital run by a Catholic mission a couple blocks away. It was a large white wooden house with a big porch. I went in and started up a conversation with the nurse on duty. I often stopped by to tease the nurses or say hello to a friend who was sick, so there wasn't anything strange about me dropping in. When the nurse went off to check on somebody, I unlocked a side door. I snuck Shorty inside, put him in a broom closet, and told him I'd come for him in the morning.

When I got back to the Drag, police were everywhere. Up and down the side streets, flashlight beams bounced around in the darkness as the police searched under houses. Policemen were looking in the drink box in Stella Brown's, cursing. They patted Selma down—bus station, train station, joints. They stopped and questioned every short slender black man they saw. It was only then that it occurred to me how much danger I was in. Then I was scared. I was almost frozen. I knew there were people who would turn me in for a dollar and a white smile if they'd seen me with Shorty.

I found Red, a black man who owned a cab and who looked white. We went to Good Samaritan at about six in the morning, got Shorty out of the closet, and put him in the trunk of Red's cab. Shorty had sobered up and was anxious to get his ass out of Selma. I gave him $50 of my gambling money and Red took him away. There wasn't anything unusual about Red driving out of town to pick up somebody, and once he got away from Selma, everybody would assume he was white.

17

Red took Shorty out on the road between Marion, in Perry County, and Birmingham. When a bus came by, Red flagged it down. He told the driver Shorty was a nigger from off his place who needed to visit a sick relative in Detroit and would the driver be sure Shorty got on the right bus in Birmingham. Even if the driver had heard about Shorty and the incident in Selma, he wouldn't connect that story with a black man being put on his bus by a white man. So Shorty got away.

Red and I had already pulled off something similar, though not quite as dangerous, with three prisoners working in those holes in the street. On each occasion, the prisoner got permission to go to my father's grocery store a block away to get a Coke. I slipped him some of my gambling money, and when no one was watching, he went around the corner and got in the trunk of Red's cab. Red had some used clothes for the men to change into once they got out in the country. Then Red dropped them off at the bus station in Uniontown, thirty miles away.

It fascinated me that the men guarding the prisoners always assumed a woman was involved in the escape. Each time, a guard said something like "He's down there in one of those bitches' houses. She put him up to it. She couldn't wait for him to get out. He's got one on him that long." They seemed to assume no black man would have the nerve to challenge them, which made doing it all the more satisfying because who had pulled it off were a black man and a black boy.

CHAPTER 2

Shotgun Houses

I was born on December 16, 1930, in my grandparents' yellow six-room house on a dirt street in east Selma. The name J.L. was a white banker's, a man my father's mother admired. I suppose she thought she was giving my father a leg up in life by naming him after a successful and popular white man. My grandmother knew the banker only from a distance, though, at the bank where people called him by his initials, like J. P. Morgan. She didn't realize he undoubtedly had a full name. The name Chestnut came from my white great-grandfather.

Until I was seven, my mother and father and I lived on Tremont Street in a wood-frame duplex "shotgun"—three rooms lined up railroad style so that a shot fired in the front door would sail right out the back. Our block had oak and chinaberry trees, wide unpaved sidewalks almost indistinguishable from the dirt front yards, and the highest and lowest of black life—the president of a black college whose family played croquet on their grass lawn and a bootlegger, Miss Becky, who kept a stash of corn whiskey in a hole dug under a fence.

Robert Lynn, the son of the college president, and I played cowboys-and-Indians, climbed trees, spied on Miss Becky and her customers, and nosed around whatever the adults were doing. Once a month, some fellas dug a big hole in the ground in a vacant lot down the street, burned wood to get charcoal, and put

My grandparents' house, where I was born (© Penny Weaver)

a whole hog on a homemade grill over the coals. The men sat around all night long drinking and telling tall tales while the hog barbecued. Robert Lynn and I stayed up as late as we were allowed to listen.

I was especially intrigued by the black prisoners in stripes working in the gigantic holes in the street. The city of Selma worked white prisoners ony in the white cemeteries. Robert and I sat on the dirt, watched the black prisoners dig, and talked to them. We talked about the size of the hole, how they were going to repair the broken water or sewer lines, how long they'd been in jail, and what for. To me at that age, it looked like fun to be down in those muddy holes, and I loved to listen to the men talk about cars and horsepower and Birmingham, the big metropolis ninety miles away. It took about a day to get there.

I was concerned about the prisoners in chains, though. They looked so pitiful shuffling over to the water keg to get a drink on a hot day. I worried about whether they had to wear the chains to bed at night, but I was reluctant to ask. I was afraid the answer would be yes. When I said my nightly prayers—"Now I lay me down to sleep . . ."—and got to the part about God bless this person and that person, I prayed that the men I saw in shackles during the day weren't shackled at night.

Sometimes in stories about white children growing up in the South, the child experiences a rude awakening to the significance of race. A white child and a black child have been playmates. The black child's mother works as a maid in the white child's house, and they see each other every day. They're good buddies. Then when the white child is five or six and is having a birthday party, he or she is told that the black playmate can't come.

I had no such dramatic or abrupt experience. I can't imagine any black child of five in Selma in the 1930s expecting to be invited to a white child's party or allowed to break the code of color in any way. No black parent would have been foolish enough to let his or her child harbor illusions that certainly would lead to disappointment and probably to trouble. If you were black, the significance of race wasn't something you suddenly discovered. It wasn't even something you had to be told. It was something you just grew up knowing, something almost instinctual.

Your place was obvious: black people sat up in the "buzzard roost" at the white movie theaters and the white people sat downstairs. My mother and Aunt Lennie couldn't try on clothes in the department stores or use the restrooms. Only one downtown store, S. H. Kress, had a "colored" restroom. A few of the white cafés had separate little eating rooms for blacks; most just had a window where you placed an order from the sidewalk. Everywhere, black folk had to wait until all the white people were served. Black men and women were never addressed as Mr. or Mrs. Black people lived in smaller houses on unpaved, poorly lit streets and they worked for white people, not the other way around.

Whenever a white person came into my father's grocery store—especially a policeman or a woman—I noticed the atmosphere shift. My father and his friends would be standing around talking about baseball or whose coon dogs were the best, joking and carrying on, and suddenly they'd quiet down and everything would get a little bit edgy and unnatural. It was similar to what you see on the animal shows on public television when the antelope or zebra are grazing on the plain in Africa, the perfect picture of relaxation, and the scent of one lion in the grass changes everything. There's a tenseness. They begin to look and gather and get ready to move in a minute.

I seldom heard my parents or other black people discuss segregation. Certainly they didn't talk about doing anything about it. It was just the way things were, and folk accommodated themselves to it.

My mother was determined to get the very best for her family, and she dealt with white people on that basis. She understood, strategically, that it was better to have a white person on your side than a black person. What could a black person do? She didn't long to be white or consider white people superior. My mother doesn't consider anybody to be superior. She's a person who believes she can move Mt. Everest if she has to, and it never occurs to her she might not be able to do it. I never heard her doubting herself or worrying about failure. She was always full of confidence. Years later, when I was basing an argument in federal court on the message of inferiority sent to black people by segregation and its crippling psychological effect, the judge remarked, "They certainly didn't trim *your* crown, did they?" The attitude that caught the judge's eye came straight from my mother.

One time, for example, she decided that she and my Aunt Lennie would open a little fried-fish joint. She found a white man who would lend her $80 to rent and fix a place, get some tables, and buy the fish. When she discovered they didn't have enough money left to get the electricity cut on, she didn't waste a second worrying. She called the Rockola (jukebox) man and asked him to pay for it. Since he stood to make money, he agreed, as my mother knew he would.

That's how she operated. She sought out white people who would help her and her family, and when they did, she was loyal to them for life. They were her friends. That's what it was all about to her. You didn't bother white people by doing anything they didn't like. You got along and got your family along by cultivating white people who would help you.

Her father, Lewellen Phillips, took care of the horses and drays and did numerous backbreaking jobs for Frank Cothran, a whole-

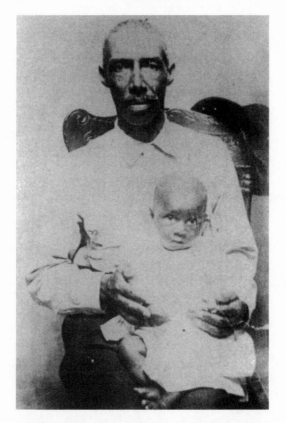

My grandfather Frank Chestnut holding one of my uncles (Courtesy of Mr. and Mrs. J. L. Chestnut, Sr.)

sale grocer who took a classic Southern paternalistic interest in my grandfather and his family. Lewellen and Cothran wore the same size clothes, and Cothran gave my grandfather his used suits. When the Cothrans got a new stove, the Phillipses got the old one. When my mother and her five siblings needed shoes, her father would go to see Cothran and Cothran would give him a note to take to the store. My mother used to brag that she and her sisters could get any type shoes they wanted and Mr. Cothran would pay for it. Cothran lent Lewellen the downpayment for the house where I was born.

Lewellen was a leader of sorts, a deacon at the black First

My maternal grandmother, Johnnie Mae Phillips
(Courtesy of Mr. and Mrs. J. L. Chestnut, Sr.)

Baptist Church. First Baptist, along with Tabernacle Baptist, was the largest, most prominent, most middle-class church in black Selma. We went every Sunday. I often spent the night with Lewellen and my grandmother, and I'd be awakened in the morning by him stomping around the house with his coffee, fussing about something at First Baptist: "That preacher is crazy if he thinks he's going to do that. He doesn't run the church. *We* are the officers."

I understood at a very early age that this was black man's politics. My grandfather and active black men like him engaged

My father and my mother (Courtesy of Mr. and Mrs. J. L. Chestnut, Sr.)

in pitched power struggles in the black church similar to the ones white men carried on over who would be sheriff or probate judge. Church splits were common when I was a boy, part of the factionalization of the black community where all our struggles and arguments were waged against each other.

Like her father, my mother fussed and raised hell—within, of course, the black community. Whenever I told her of a slight or mistreatment by a teacher, or even a principal, she stormed over to the school the next day, if not that afternoon, to straighten them out. She was determined that I would become somebody—preferably a doctor. When I was going into the second grade, the school ran out of spelling books. My mother borrowed somebody's and copied it all by hand. I learned to read and to count at home. She didn't trust the teachers. She went over the next day's lessons with me every night in every subject and fussed and fussed until I got it right, even slapped me out of the chair a few times.

Rubbing Nadinola skin-lightening cream on my face was another nightly ritual she insisted upon, based on her practical recognition that the most successful blacks in Selma—the postman, the doctors, the more prominent preachers—were light-skinned. Nadinola was part of getting ahead, like going to college, and it worked to a point. I'm medium brown and I turned kind of reddish. My mother also made me take 25-cent piano lessons and wear starched short pants and suspenders.

I was her only child and her major preoccupation. Whatever I really wanted she used her considerable powers to get. A few months after I began pestering her for a brother or sister, I came home to find a baby sister. A woman from McWilliams, a little crossroads town forty miles from Selma, had been made pregnant by a white man. She worked for the white man and his wife, and her grandmother was scared for her to stay in the country and have the baby, so she sent her to Selma. She couldn't bring the baby back with her—or so her grandmother thought—and my mother agreed to raise the child. We called her Dimp for her dimples.

My father urged me to be wary of white people. He didn't sit down and give me a lecture. At opportune times, he gave one-liner lessons with the message: "Watch out. Be careful. Keep your distance." He had commercial dealings with white people because this was a necessity, but he was not anxious for me to get close to any of them. He always insisted, "If you can help it, don't work for them. Work for yourself."

My father was a strong believer in independence, though it often eluded him. His father, Frank Chestnut, had been an independent, landowning farmer, and my father grew up in that small farm atmosphere that seems to breed independence and self-reliance.

Frank Chestnut's father—my great-grandfather—was a white

man who owned land and a boardinghouse in Marion Junction, a small community twelve miles west of Selma. Frank Chestnut's mother—my great-grandmother—was a black woman whose father had been a slave. At the turn of the century, Marion Junction was a railroad junction—from Mobile, one train went north to Birmingham, another west to Demopolis—surrounded by large cotton plantations.

My father says many landowners in that area had two families, their white children and their black children. It wasn't anything startling or unusual. My white great-grandfather wasn't married, but he helped support his sisters and their sons, some of whom he sent to medical school. My grandfather lived as a servant with his white cousins, milked the cow, did chores, helped care for them. He didn't go to school. As a teenager, he became a cook and handyman at the boardinghouse.

Frank's father willed his money and property to his white sisters and nephews. But not long before my father was born in 1909, Frank's father became ill, called Frank to his bedside, and gave him a hog, a wooden table painted green, and some money Frank used to buy forty acres near a little town named Beloit. Frank became a successful farmer. He bred horses, sold chickens, turkeys, hogs, cotton, and raised almost everything his large family— eleven children—needed. When they needed clothes or shoes, he brought them to Selma in his surrey and he paid for them.

My father expected to stay on the farm, but when he was fifteen, his father had a stroke and the family moved to Selma, where my grandfather could get medical care. My father and his younger brothers kept the farm going a short while, but it was too much for them. They sold the stock and equipment for $500, moved to Selma, and my father got a job as a "porter" delivering prescriptions by bicycle for a white drugstore for $4 a week. So at sixteen, my father went from driving his father's surrey and living a relatively independent life to bicycling around white Selma and being subjected to "Boy, come here" and "Nigger, do this."

My grandfather lingered, helpless in bed, for three years. He had a $2,000 life insurance policy, and he told my father he wanted him to use it to study to be a doctor. One of my grandfather's white cousins, a doctor, came to see him often while he was ill

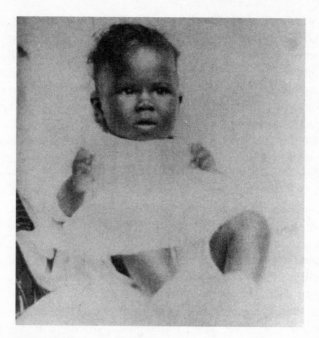

Me as a baby (Courtesy of Mr. and Mrs. J. L. Chestnut, Sr.)

and offered to keep up the payments on the insurance. When my grandfather died in 1928, my grandmother sent her oldest daughter to the doctor's office to get the policy. He ran her off. The family had spent most of the $500 from the sale of the farm stock on my grandfather's medical care, and they had barely enough left to bury him.

My father is a quiet man, not volatile like my mother. He told me this story in an unemotional, matter-of-fact tone, but he was making a point: White smiles and offers of friendship may not be genuine, and if something happens, there's little a black person can do about it. Best to do your own thing and, as much as possible, steer clear of them. This was a lesson in life he was serious about, and he reiterated it in many different forms while I was growing up.

When I was born, he was working as a porter for a meat market owned by Green B. Suttles, who also owned Selma's stockyard. He worked so hard, Suttles taught him how to butcher and hired some of his younger brothers. When Suttles sold the market to concentrate on the stockyard, my father got a job at another place called the Pay 'N Tote. He had his butcher block, served the black customers, and earned $8 a week. A white butcher had his block, served the white customers, and earned $15. My father, like all blacks, accepted the wage differential and the justification that it cost black people less to live. However, one day a black postman, Nat Phillips, came in to buy a rump roast, as he often had when my father worked at Suttles's. The owner of the Pay 'N Tote called my father over and told him the meat he was cutting for Phillips was for white people. He had to sell him the "colored" meat—older meat of a lesser grade. My father whispered to Phillips not to buy it and started looking for other work.

He heard that Frank Cothran, Jr., the son of the wholesaler my mother's father worked for, wanted to rent out the meat part of a grocery store he operated at Minter Avenue and Mabry Street in black Selma. My father went to see him.

"You married Lewellen's daughter, right? Go on over there. You can pay me later," Cothran said. Suttles had equipment left from his market, and my father bought it on credit. This was in 1936. Two years later, my father took over the grocery part, too, and brought in his younger brother, Frank Jr. They called the store Chestnut Brothers Market and Grocery.

A year after my father got the store, we moved to a six-room wooden house on Mabry Street a half block away. Frank, his wife, Lennie, and their two daughters lived with us. It was a nicely furnished place, with a rug on the floor of the living room and a piano. We had a big side yard, really a vacant lot, where my father and Frank raised collard greens, butter beans, and turnips. Between the store and the garden, we had enough to eat during the Depression when so many other folk were going hungry.

I didn't know any white people, but I observed the ones who came into our neighborhood. There were my father's white customers who assumed and received special favors and deference. I noticed they often asked for—and got—the best cuts, and my father let them feel all over the meat, which he didn't allow his black customers to do. There were insurance salesmen selling nickel policies and merchants hawking ironing boards and pots and pans. They were friendly but salesman-phony. There were

Me as a boy (Courtesy of Mr. and Mrs. J. L. Chestnut, Sr.)

white women dropping off their maids and sometimes making a big fuss over the maids' children, usually in a patronizing manner.

Then there were the ever-present police. When I was seven or eight, my mother took me to see the doctor because I kept running to her with wild, exaggerated tales about an arrest: "Mama! Mama! The police just left from down the street! They arrested Miz Becky! She was selling whiskey! They put me in the car and I had to take them and show them where she had the whiskey hid! They was cussin' at me." Dr. Walker told my mother not to worry; I just had a vivid imagination and wanted to call attention to myself. But I don't think that was the reason for my stories. I was trying to spur my mother into doing something about the way the police treated black people. Since she'd blast over to the school if I said a teacher cursed me, I hoped she'd go downtown to straighten out the chief of police or get Reverend D. V. Jem-

In the 1930s and '40s, this building housed the Chestnut Brothers Market and Grocery (© Penny Weaver)

ison, the most powerful black minister in Selma, to go downtown for her.

I was too young to understand the more subtle economic, social, and psychological ways white Selma maintained control over black Selma. But the police were blatant. They were in black Selma deliberately doing things to send messages of fear across the community. They weren't a neutral force enforcing the law. They *were* the law. They acted like despots, slapped black men who didn't say "sir" fast enough, extorted payoffs and information from the bootleggers, lent money at outrageous rates of interest, and pretty much took what they wanted when they wanted it from whoever had it. I heard stories of black men taken to the jail and never seen again.

Hardly a day went by that I didn't see one of Selma's big black police cars cruising around or parked in front of someone's house. Every Friday, beginning at about four o'clock, the chief of police and one of his officers made the rounds of the bootleg houses— openly, in the chief's car. Bootleg corn whiskey was a big thing in black Selma in those days, and most blocks had at least one or two houses you could go in, sit around a little table, and drink shots, or buy a pint or half-pint bottle to take out. You could buy legal liquor at the Alabama state stores, but many black folk couldn't afford or didn't care for it, and there weren't any bars or taverns in black Selma then.

The chief and his man would pull up in front of these places— picture an unpainted shotgun house with a swing on the front porch and two rusty chairs—toot the horn one time, *brrrrump*, and the bootlegger would run out and lean over into the car with his or her $5. Policemen were paid next to nothing, and taking payoffs from bootleggers and lending money to poor blacks—$1 for 25 cents interest—was how they got by.

Sometimes the bootleggers would be leaning into the chief's car for quite a while, which I later learned had to do with information. Black and white Selma were so separate the police had no way of knowing what was going on in black Selma unless a black person told them. After each transaction, the chief's car would pull off and go down the next block. It made me mad that they didn't even bother to get out of the car.

There were four bootleggers in my immediate neighborhood— Miss Becky around the corner, Miss Irene down at the other end of the block, an old man across the street, and Dan Craig two houses away. Their locations were obvious: the people coming and going, the noise, the drunks—and also the police. The only place I never saw a police car around was Dan Craig's, until one day when I was twelve. It was the first time I remember being really frightened.

Dan Craig was a quiet, polite man, someone I knew and liked. He was one of "the club" of about a dozen black men who sat around on produce crates by the potbellied stove in my father's store and argued about hunting and dogs. Craig had a job, but something happened to it and he started to sell bootleg whiskey. A customer, though, could not sit down in Craig's house. His was one of the few places you had to buy a bottle and keep moving because Craig wasn't the kind of man who wanted men drinking and hanging around his wife, who sang in the choir at Morningstar Baptist Church, and his two grade-school-aged daughters.

What drew the attention of the police to his operation probably

The shotgun house where Dan Craig used to live (© Penny Weaver)

was his new car. Until then, Craig apparently had been in business without any arrangement with them, and they hadn't taken note of his place because it was so low-key. Anyway, one day Craig and his wife were in Craig's new Chevy when two policemen pulled up behind them and tooted the horn. They were on Minter Avenue, around the corner from our house and the Craigs' house on Mabry Street, and almost directly in front of my father's store. In the car with the police was a black man nicknamed Big Motor, an informant Mrs. Craig later told me had come in their house and bought a pint earlier in the week.

Craig pulled over. He got out of the car on the driver's side, Mrs. Craig got out on the passenger side, and the two policemen walked up to them. Big Motor stayed in the police car and two friends of the Craigs', who were in the back seat of the Chevy, stayed in that car.

According to Mrs. Craig, one of the policemen made a remark to her husband and hit him in the mouth. Craig grabbed the policeman's shirt collar and asked, "Why did you do that?" The policeman then began hitting Craig with a billy club. Mrs. Craig started to come over toward him, but the other policeman yelled at her, "Get over there and stay over there, you bitch!" Then that policeman turned and joined the other in beating Dan Craig, right there on Minter Street, with billy clubs and a slapstick. They hit him so hard on the head with the slapstick, it broke and the gravel inside it flew out all around.

I heard the sounds of scuffling and moaning and yelling and the half slap, half thud of the billy clubs from my house down the street. *THWAK. THWAK.*

"You goddamn nigger. Where's that whiskey?"

"Leave him alone! Leave him alone!" Mrs. Craig was pleading.

"Shut your damn mouth."

When I got to the corner, the policemen were dragging Craig toward their car. His head was bleeding. There was blood all over his shirt. One of the policemen, a large man with a scowl on his face and a flabby stomach hanging out over his trousers, had his right hand clamped on the back of Craig's shirt collar and was tugging him along like a dog. The other policeman, a smaller man with squinting eyes and tobacco juice dribbling down one side of his mouth, was walking alongside Craig, jabbing him in the side with his long billy club.

"Stand up! Stand up!" he yelled at Craig with each poke. Craig appeared to be only semi-conscious, half walking and half stumbling, as the policemen pushed and pulled him down the dirt street. He was badly beaten. Mrs. Craig later told me that Arthur Pitts, the white attorney she hired to represent her husband (on a charge of resisting arrest), said after seeing Craig, "They don't do a hog like that unless they kill it."

I walked up and stood near Mrs. Craig at the back of the Craigs' car. As the policemen dragged Craig by us, they ordered Mrs. Craig not to move the car. They'd be back for it. They glared at me. When they got to the police car, they had trouble pushing Craig inside and yelled at Big Motor, "Help us. Help us." His black hands reached out to help pull Craig into the car.

Other people on the street heard the beating and were peering out their windows or standing on their porches in the fading light. It was about dusk on a warm spring day. They watched in silence as the policemen pushed Craig into the back seat of the police car. The only sounds were the car doors slamming shut, the engine cranking up, the car roaring off. It headed in the opposite direction from the jail. This was something Selma policemen did often to add the extra scare—to the man arrested and to the black community—that they might be headed to the woods instead of to the jail.

I walked on to the store, passing my father and some of the men who hunted with Craig. They were standing out on the corner. I said, "Son-of-a-bitch!" They just shook their heads and went back inside without saying a word. No sooner had the car pulled away with Dan Craig than black Selma went back to business as usual.

That was what really frightened me—the way my father and the other men removed this from mind, as if it hadn't happened. Their silence, the way they turned their backs without a peep of protest, stood in such painful contrast to the masculine bravado they carried on with each other in the store and their manly fellowship on midnight coon hunts deep in the dark woods.

Inside the store, I tried, but failed, to get a conversation going about the awful thing that had just happened. Everyone was scared even to comment about it. Later, I talked to my father and he said, "What did you want us to do? Commit suicide?" I knew he was right, but goddamn!

When I left the store, I saw the police car in front of the Craigs' house and immediately got apprehensive. I knew they were looking for the whiskey, but I didn't know if Mrs. Craig was there or what might happen to her. I walked over and stood on the porch of their house, listening. Suddenly the policemen came out, the same two who had beaten Craig. They noticed me standing there and stopped dead still. It seemed as if time itself stopped as the big one stood glaring at me.

He looked like he was about to say something on the order of "What the hell are you looking at, boy?" and to be thinking, What am I gonna do with this brazen young nigger here? My reaction then was the same as it would be twenty years later, in the 1960s, when the Lowndes County sheriff held an ax handle poised to strike me in a courtroom where I was defending a black man: I froze in some indescribable combination of fear and confidence. In both cases, the other man blinked and withdrew. Thank God.

After being dragged off, Dan Craig was gone for a while. A

doctor at Good Samaritan, where Craig was taken at some point, told Mrs. Craig that her husband's head needed so many stitches it looked like a map. When Dan came back to Mabry Street, there was hesitation in his speech. His sentences were disjointed and sometimes he'd be talking about one subject and in mid-sentence jump to another. It was sad to see.

At about the same time, I began to understand that something awful was going on with another man in my father's little hunting circle. A policeman, one of the highest-ranking on the force, was involved with the man's wife. He was a fireman on the railroad, and I'd see him walking up the street when he came home from his run down to Mobile. When he got to the corner of Minter Avenue, where the store was, he'd always look down toward his house in the next block. If the policeman's car was parked in front of it, he'd come in the store, drink a Coke, talk about dogs, and wait till the car left. If the car wasn't there, he'd go on home, change his clothes, and come over to the store later. This was such a standard routine that whenever I saw the man in the store in his blue railroad overalls, I would know without even looking that the policeman's car was in front of his house.

The men in the store, the other hunters, said nothing about the situation. The black community readily rationalized it. There was a kind of unspoken consensus that it could happen to anyone, like catching a disease. The irony was, a black man might well kill another black man over his wife. Also, the woman involved would have been looked down on in the church, considered a slut, if the man had been black. But here everybody figured the only kind of hero the husband could be was a dead one and maybe the wife would get a little something extra for her children. I felt sorry for the man and relieved that the policeman wasn't stopping at my house.

There was one group of black men not quite so silent or quick to rationalize—the returning World War II veterans. I noticed a restlessness in these men. They'd be down on the Drag where my friends and I would hang around them. They spoke of the army as a curious institution—in one way an extension of Selma and all its Southern customs with segregated black units doing work like supply and cooking, yet in other ways providing a kind of freedom they never experienced in Alabama.

It seemed that most of them, when they got a leave, made a beeline to Harlem or some other Northern metropolis. There they saw black policemen, black salespeople. They talked about Harlem all the time, and we younger boys were all ears because we thought Harlem was just the ticket. The veterans' attitudes about the South and its way of life obviously had been affected by these experiences. "I'm going out to Selma University on the GI Bill and I'm going to get my diploma and I'm going to get my ass to Detroit," they'd say. "I'm not going to put up with this damn crap here."

The veterans were more willing than my father and other men in his generation to complain openly about the police and other white people. For example, there was one white man who was notorious in black Selma for walking around the black community at night looking for women.

Veterans on the Drag said, "That son-of-a-bitch coming down here running in behind our women. We ought to catch him and whip his ass." They didn't actually get beyond talk, but my group, a little younger, admired them and acted it out. With the older men's encouragement, we chased after the white man. He'd be coming down the street and we'd jump out of the alleys, throw rocks at him, and laugh when he ran.

CHAPTER 3

Play Ball

When I was growing up, the most powerful black man in Selma (or so I thought) was the Reverend D. V. Jemison. Jemison was pastor of Tabernacle Baptist Church, a large prestigious church with white Grecian columns, green stained-glass windows, and solid walnut pews. He also was chairman of the board at Selma University and president of the National Baptist Convention U.S.A. The convention was and is the largest black organization in America. So here was this little black preacher in Selma, Alabama, who had clawed his way to the top position of black Baptists in the United States, which meant a top position in black America.

Jemison lived around the corner from my father's store and passed by at least twice daily on his way to and from the church office. He was a short, stocky man with a big barrel chest who always wore a black suit and a black hat. When he walked down the street, children came running from blocks away. Jemison always carried a pocketful of jingling pennies and gave them to children who remembered the little sermonettes on "Respect your parents" or "Love the world and the world will love you back" that he delivered to us on the street corners in his enormous voice, which could be heard from blocks away on Sundays when he was preaching.

"Now, what did I tell you yesterday? If you tell me, I'll give you three pennies."

"You told us, 'Take a bath three times a week.' "

"Very good. Now, three days ago, I gave you a vital lesson. What was it?" Sometimes it took Jemison two hours to get to Tabernacle from his large house on Lapsley Street seven blocks away.

Occasionally Jemison stopped in the grocery store, and I noticed that my father and the other customers showed him a kind of deference, as if he were white—not quite, but almost. "Morning, Dr. Jemison." The men would touch the brims of their hats. If he came in when they were talking about women or cursing and arguing about dogs, somebody'd say, *"Hush!* It's Dr. Jemison." If a schoolteacher or the principal came in, there would be a change, too. The conversation would get quieter. But when Jemison walked in, it pretty much stopped because if anybody was going to speak while Jemison was there it would be Jemison— the way, in the army, everybody snaps to attention when an officer walks into a room.

"Carry on, gentlemen," Jemison would say in his great big booming voice as he dug down in the drink box to get a Coke.

White people showed uncommon respect for Jemison, too. White Southerners had a tendency at that time to call any black man wearing a suit and necktie "Reverend." But it was not unusual to hear a white man call Jemison "Dr. Jemison." And Jemison had a special relationship with the white establishment. He could get a $15,000 bank loan to remodel his church when other black preachers had trouble getting $1,000. Most fascinating to me, if a black man got arrested for something he did to another black man, Jemison might be able to get him out of jail—almost the same way white employers could. There were even a few occasions, well short of anything involving a white woman, when a black did something to whites, particularly so-called white trash, and Jemison would make a trip downtown and it would all be over with. This was common knowledge in the black community. There were no black lawyers in Selma then, and when black people got in trouble with the law, it was "Go see Dr. Jemison."

Damn, who is this Jemison that he can do this? I wondered. It was obvious he was on a different plane from other black men and I wanted to know how he got there. But all he'd say when I asked how he managed to have some particular person released from police custody was "I talked to some people." So my curiosity about him was pretty much stymied—for a while.

Because Jemison was head of the national black Baptist organization and most black ministers in Selma were Baptist, he was the leader of the large flock of black preachers in town. An exception was Reverend Claude C. Brown, pastor of the Reformed Presbyterian Church, a mission established in black Selma by Northern whites just after the Civil War.

Until Brown, Reformed Presbyterian, a white frame church located about fifteen blocks from Tabernacle Baptist, had been pastored by white ministers from the North. Brown's mother, who was half white, half Indian, and married to a light-skinned black man, was a member of the church and brought her son there regularly when he was growing up. The mission sent him to Knoxville College, a Presbyterian school for blacks in Knoxville, Tennessee, and then to the Reformed Presbyterian seminary in Pittsburgh.

In style, Brown and Jemison could not have been more different. A tall, dignified-looking, light-skinned man who resembled U.S. Supreme Court Justice Thurgood Marshall, Brown dressed as if he were headed for a golf course—in contrast to the stocky, darker-skinned Jemison, who, in his black suit and black hat, always looked like he was on his way to a funeral. Blacks of a certain class thought more of Brown than of Jemison. Brown was better educated. He didn't preach like a black preacher—jumping up and down, hollering and sweating, the way Jemison did. He was more like a white minister, a lecturer giving a lesson.

Because he had the backing of a national white organization, Brown had greater resources than Jemison. Brown gave out clothing donated by Reformed Presbyterians around the country and helped bright young people get scholarships to Knoxville College. All this seemed to be a threat to Jemison, a natural politician who wasn't keen on another black preacher having an independent power base. Brown didn't care for Jemison either, for reasons of social class. He considered Jemison loud and uneducated.

Brown also had relationships in the white community and he, like Jemison, could intercede for a black person in trouble. But he was a much quieter, behind-the-scenes man than Jemison, and I didn't hear that much about Brown or pay him that much attention until some friends and I wanted to play baseball on Sundays.

Selma at that time had a minor league baseball club, the Selma Cloverleafs, which my friends and I followed as closely as the white boys in town and imitated in our own games. There were three youth baseball teams in black Selma. Brown had the Junior Herd, part of his Ralph Bunche Club. Another competitor for black souls, the Fathers of St. Edmund, had a baseball team as part of its Don Bosco Club.

The Fathers, an order based in Vermont, had started a mission in Selma in 1937 and by the mid-1940s were running the hospital in black Selma and building a large complex that literally surrounded Tabernacle Baptist. One of the priests, Father Ziter, took a big interest in young people. He started the Don Bosco Club, built a basketball court, and took black children on camping trips. James Robinson, one of my best friends growing up, was recruited through baseball and basketball into the Catholic Church and today is a priest in Detroit. Both Jemison and Brown denounced the Fathers. They'd be in the store repeating something they heard from whites downtown about the Catholics being Communists, which intrigued me because I'd never before heard either minister say anything negative about a white person.

I didn't play baseball with the Junior Herd or the Bosco Club. I managed and played shortstop for a team called the Rinky-dinks—basically a group of boys from school who got together to play. The spring I was in tenth grade, we decided it would be nice to play on Sunday afternoons. Sundays would be the best time to draw a crowd to watch the game, especially the girls because on Saturdays they helped their mothers around the house.

At that time, the baseball diamond where the black teams usually played was in a city-owned park called "the pool"—a large, dug-out area like a fishpond without water located in the black community. No one had been playing on Sundays and I was told that, if the Rinkydinks were planning to do that, we'd have to go to City Hall and get permission from the chief of police.

Four other boys and I went downtown to police headquarters on the second floor of City Hall. I told the man in the foyer we were there to see the chief. The chief's door was open, and he invited us into his office, a small, plain room with an institutional desk. There were law-enforcement magazines around and one book, *The White Man's Burden*, on the windowsill. I was intrigued by the title.

The chief, a big, burly man who looked the part, was chewing tobacco and spitting it into a bucket alongside the desk. I expected him to act impatient and dismiss us, but he didn't. He seemed fascinated that a group of black youngsters had the nerve to come down to City Hall, to the jail, to face the chief of police. Not many black adults would. He asked what we wanted.

"We want to play ball in the pool on Sundays," I said. "Is it all right?"

"If it's all right with Dr. Jemison, it's all right with me," the chief answered.

This worried me because Jemison disapproved of dancing and playing cards and most anything that was fun. "You know Dr. Jemison's a preacher and he's against everything," I said.

The chief laughed, but I persisted. "If you tell us we can play, you know Dr. Jemison will go along with it."

The chief said, "I just told you, if it's all right with Dr. Jemison, it is all right with me." So that was that with the chief. We thanked him and said goodbye.

Goddamn! Jemison is everywhere, I thought as we left. What's he got to do with this?

Our entourage went from there to Tabernacle and found Jemison in his small office in the church basement cluttered with stacks of religious periodicals.

"Come in! Come in! What can I do for you?" Jemison said in his big voice. He looked at one of the boys. "My, look at that suit!" We told him the Rinkydinks wanted to play in the pool on Sunday afternoons.

"The chief said it was all right but we should talk to you," I told him.

"Nope, nope, nope! It just isn't right, boys. The answer is no."

"But, Dr. Jemison, *why?*"

"You need to be in church on Sunday. It's the Lord's Day."

"But we're talking about *after* church. At one o'clock."

"You boys know very well you ought to be in BYTU." This was the Baptist Youth Training Union, a late-afternoon Sunday school with Bible classes and training for junior deacons.

"That's at five. We'll be done playing by then, Dr. Jemison." We pleaded but he didn't relent.

"You ought to be at home getting ready for it. We're just not going to play any baseball on the Lord's Day."

We stayed there for a while trying in a respectful way to persuade him, but didn't get to first base. Jemison suggested that if we didn't have enough to do on Sundays, we could try cleaning up the neighborhood. We finally gave up, but I was hot about it. I didn't think we should have to get permission from a preacher to play ball in a public park.

The next day I went to my civics teacher, John Shields. Shields was a highly unusual teacher. Way, way ahead of the times, he was teaching black history, and he was bluntly critical of Selma's black leaders, especially preachers. One of Shields's favorite lessons was the competition among the three religions. He talked about it a lot, aiming at the boys in the Don Bosco Club and the Junior Herd and Jemison's crowd, telling them these churches and ministers were standing in the way of black progress.

"Why are you looking up to these preachers? Don't you see how they're running errands for whites?" This was the way Shields talked, so it was natural for me to take the situation with Jemison to him and ask him what to do.

"That's obvious," Shields said. "Go to Claude Brown."

This answer really got me confused. The Rinkydinks were talking about a ball field owned by the city and here we were being sent from one black preacher to another. Shields wouldn't explain his advice, just said, "Do it and you'll see. You'll be able to play."

So I went to Brown's neat, uncluttered office in the parsonage next to Reformed Presbyterian. I told him what had gone on with the police chief and Jemison, and he said, "I don't see a thing wrong with you boys playing baseball. I'd much rather have you playing baseball than out there in some devilment."

Brown picked up the telephone and called the mayor. It was

John Shields with three of his students. I'm on the right
(Courtesy of Vivian Burke)

the first time in my life I heard a black man call the mayor—the first time, in fact, I heard anybody call the mayor. I sat in Brown's office as he told the mayor some boys wanted to play baseball on Sunday afternoons in the pool and he didn't see anything wrong with it. But for some reason, the chief of police and Jemison had vetoed the idea. The mayor obviously told Brown he didn't give a damn what Jemison and the police chief said. Brown hung up the telephone and told me the Rinkydinks could play on Sundays.

I went back to Shields and told him what had happened. Shields laughed and said, "I told you."

Right there, I saw the hard cold truth of power in Selma: the white community picked the black community's leaders. It had been a mystery why everybody looked up so to Jemison. Why was he so unique? I'd seen but never thought about the fact that when blacks got white approval this added to their stature in the black community.

I saw in this incident that a major source of Jemison's power was the damn police chief. Whites—through the chief—let Jemison decide whether some kids could play baseball on Sunday. That gave Jemison power in the black community. They let him intercede for some black who got involved in incidents whites didn't care much about. Brown had connections with a different group of whites, the Presbyterians, the mayor, and they gave him favors to dispense.

I began to understand, too, the other side of the power equation. Shields had been saying how, for little crumbs of power, black preachers and other leaders could be counted on "to keep the natives in line"—to cool off potential uprisings and to preach that blacks should clean up their own back yards rather than challenge the system. By their own example, these black leaders sent the message that to get along you go along.

Any black leader who started criticizing the status quo would find no more morsels of power thrown his way by white Selma, and this, in turn, would cut down his influence in black Selma. This was the awful dilemma of black leadership in Selma—and in America—and I saw it for the first time in the baseball incident. It was a revelation. Shields had been talking about it, but here I had a chance to peep on the inside for myself. I saw and understood the nakedness of black leaders.

The way some of my friends collected around Father Ziter or Jemison or Brown or Andrew Durgan, the most popular teacher at Knox Academy, I latched on to John F. Shields. He was dealing with issues that interested me and was willing to talk frankly. He didn't dress anything up or talk in vague generalities. Shields had come to Selma from South Carolina. He went to Shaw University, one of the better colleges for blacks in the South. When I was in school, few black teachers had a college education other than some summer courses at Alabama State College, an underfunded black college in Montgomery.

Shields never said much about his background, so we knew little about him. He was a loner and an outsider—a peculiar man. All the years he lived in Selma, I never knew him to have a woman or a friend. He looked as if he might have been part Indian, and he wore his hair cut in an odd way, without sideburns. I think he put a bowl on his head and cut his own hair. When he wasn't in the school, he was by himself all the time. He lived in a wood-frame house on Broad Street—a junky place, crammed with books, the place of a man who lived alone.

Shields had discovered something that seemed to free him from fear of white power. I don't know what it was; he didn't believe in God. But there was no doubt he was prepared to die. If the police or the Klan had come to get him, they would have had to bring him out feet first. It would be another twenty years—until 1965 when I saw John Lewis, president of the Student Nonviolent Coordinating Committee (SNCC), eyeball to eyeball with Sheriff Jim Clark—before I would see another black man in Selma as unafraid as John Shields.

Everybody at school was surprised he wasn't run out of town. I later learned that the federal government was paying part of his salary through some New Deal program. But somehow he survived in the Selma school system until he died in his back yard in the 1950s. What the man taught was remarkable for his place and time. In that black school in Selma, Alabama, in the 1940s, he denounced white people, attacked the church, and criticized most black leaders in town.

Shields tore into the central underpinning of the South. He taught that segregation was not natural. It was not a system ordained by God or established in nature whereby the superior and benevolent white race exercised dominion over the inferior black race. It was an unnatural system devised by men, white men, to exploit the black race for their labor.

Unlike other black adults, Shields questioned the "Southern way of life" and challenged us to question it. I had noted the differences between white and black Selma, but the significance of the difference didn't fully register until Shields made it clear. He taught that the white people who lived in the fine houses misused black people, worked them ten, twelve hours a day in their homes or fields, and paid them barely enough to support their families.

"Why is it because they're white they ought to have that and just because we're Negro we ought to have less?" Shields would ask.

"Well, maybe they're smarter," I once answered.

Shields persisted: "On what basis do you say that?"

When I answered, "Well, they've got better houses and more money," Shields pointed out that I was thinking in a vicious circle.

Shields also talked about Knox Academy itself, the school the

A girlfriend and I on the Knox Academy campus (Courtesy of Henry Mayfield)

Presbyterians built in 1881. The top floor of the three-story brick building had been condemned as unsafe when my mother was a student. When I got there, it was still boarded up. Big two-by-fours were nailed across the staircases leading up to the third floor, and sometimes plaster would fall down onto students in classrooms on the second floor. I had seen schools out in the country, little one-room shacks, and I thought Knox Academy had a very nice campus. It certainly was far above average for blacks in Alabama at that time.

Shields's comparison was not with other black schools but with the white one, Parrish High School, which was newer, nicer, larger, had a gymnasium, tennis courts, better-equipped science labs, a well-manicured campus. Why was that? he asked.

Shields expanded my view of the police. I'd originally thought they were different from other whites, a separate breed, because there were white people in Selma I couldn't imagine beating up a black person. Shields taught that the police weren't out there on their own. They were the "overseers of the Selma plantation," doing the dirty work to keep the system going. I started to make the connection between all of white Selma and the conditions that existed in the black community and became suspicious of whites of goodwill. Their goodwill was inconsistent with the gross inequities.

In Shields's teaching, most leaders in black Selma were not doing anything to change the situation. Were any of these leaders trying to do something about the falling plaster at Knox Academy? Were they using their connections with the police chief and the mayor to do anything about the way the police beat up black people? Other than hand out clothes and help a few individuals, were they doing anything to help black people rise out of poverty?

"Look around!" he challenged us. "If your leaders are leading, *where* are they leading?"

Shields went even further. Not only were black leaders not helping, they were part of the problem. They were playing a role in the exploitation and repression of their own people. He said Jemison and Brown were like the straw bosses in the black settlements in slavery times who helped the masters keep the black people subservient and reconciled to slavery while the straw boss got a little authority and a few other scraps from the white man's table.

One spring, the body of a black man who'd gotten himself into some kind of trouble with white people was brought into town tied to the running board of a car like a dead cow. I didn't see this but I heard people in my father's store saying that the car was driven right down a main street and parked in the vicinity of the courthouse with the dead man on the running board in full and grisly view. Shields pointed out that no black leaders said peep about this and, when questioned, told folk the situation was being "taken care of downtown."

Black teachers and preachers taught "Count your blessings. Get an education." The bootleggers operated as informants for the police. The wealthiest black people, the funeral directors and the doctors, had their connections with the white power structure. If a black person got killed, the police chief could turn the body over to whichever funeral home he wanted. So the funeral directors were always sending a turkey to the chief or the mayor on their birthdays. None of them was trying to work any changes for the black race.

This was what infuriated Shields. He told us black leaders were selling us out—and the worst were the ministers. He despised what they were preaching in the pulpits—that their congregations would get their reward in the afterlife. "We'd be better off if all the preachers were run out of Selma today," he declared. I thought Shields was too harsh on Jemison and Brown. But I came to the disturbing conclusion that Shields ultimately was correct—that despite their good intentions and good deeds to individuals, black leaders were helping to maintain a status quo that was detrimental to the people they were supposed to be leading.

Not long after the baseball incident, I wrote as much in a paper in an English class and produced a minor uproar at Knox Academy. The assignment was: Pick an authentic American hero and explain the choice. I attacked the standards by which heroes were selected. The essence of my argument was that the people the black community looked up to as leaders did not deserve to be followed.

I started out with Booker T. Washington, eased up to Jemison, and then landed on the school principal. I wrote that Booker T. had tried to control everything in black America, that he said everything Henry Ford and the white Southern politicians wanted to hear so they would contribute money to Tuskegee Institute and thus to Booker T.'s station in life. I went on: "Now we have all these Booker T.'s in Selma."

I wrote that Jemison, while well-intentioned, was not his own man. His limitations were critical and there was a serious question as to whether the good he did cost too much. Then I lit into the principal, Roy Stone. I was still mad that the Rinkydinks had to go see preachers to play baseball in a public park, and I thought the principal should have stepped in and said we could play. He was the principal and he should have stood up for us. "But he doesn't have what it takes to do that," I wrote. "So what good is it for him to have prestige and to be walking around talking about he's the principal?"

The English teacher was outraged. "What in the world possessed you to write such a paper?" she demanded. She was offended by what I had written about Jemison, "one of the finest men in Selma," and she thought I was doing a great disservice to black people by attacking our heroes. She was especially infuriated by what I'd written about the principal.

"You have slandered Mr. Stone. Now you go and apologize to him," she ordered. She had told other teachers about the paper and word had gotten out about what I'd written.

"I don't know," I said. "I believe in what I wrote."

"Well, you think about it and I'll talk to you after recess."

During recess, of course, I went straight to Shields. "Screw 'em. Don't apologize" was Shields's advice. "If you do, it will do nothing but make a bigger situation out of it."

So I didn't apologize, though I later realized I was wrong about Roy Stone. Principals were put on such a pedestal in the black community that my view of his power was inflated. I also learned more about Roy Stone. He never wore a hat, for instance, so he wouldn't have to tip it to white men. And he continued to insist to the school board that they build a new black high school, finally succeeding the year after I graduated.

At the time, though, I followed Shields's advice, said no when the English teacher asked, "Well, did you make up your mind? You gonna apologize?" She glared at me, said "Hmmmm," and let it go—just as Shields had predicted. This reinforced my admiration for Shields as a man who could analyze a situation better than any other black adult in Selma. Many of the concepts Shields taught at Knox Academy became part of the framework through which I have looked at life ever since.

His primary theme was: "Individual progress is a dead end," which was the opposite of what our parents taught. Just as white Southerners rationalized their institutional racism against blacks as a group by focusing on their close relationships with individual black people, black Southerners had learned to live with the desperate reality of our position as a group and to concentrate instead on individual progress.

Shields said the individualistic approach was pointless. "The only choice is being a prisoner with money or a prisoner without it, and that's no choice. Look at Dr. Walker. He's got all that money, but when he goes into town, he's just as colored as you, has to get in the same line at the bank, has to drink from the colored water fountain. Don't you see it's not far that you can get by yourself?" He constantly told us we had to find a way to bring other people with us, to uplift the group. The whole race had to get together to overthrow the system. Shields was the first person to tell me I ought to consider studying law. He said, "Go get yourself a law degree and fight the system. *Evil* damn system."

All these lessons about power and leadership were underlined for me the summer before I graduated from high school, when I drove C. J. Adams, Selma's "race man"—black civic activist— away from Selma for the last time.

Adams, like Shields, was an unusual man for his time and place. He had been an army officer, one of the very few black officers in World War I. He then was a mail clerk on the railroad, which gave him an economic independence from local whites few other blacks enjoyed. He was a smart man, too, who bought real estate. When he retired from the railroad, he spent most of his time helping black people. He became a notary public and the closest thing black Selma had to a lawyer in the 1930s and '40s.

Adams was well aware of government policies, and he got the necessary documents together for veterans and others to receive benefits. Roosevelt was pushing through Congress a whole series of programs to help poor people, but in the South that often meant poor whites because many blacks were not aware of the programs and didn't know how to apply for them. Adams went from family to family and used his education and knowledge to help people who were desperately poor get in on some of the benefits.

Adams also started a chapter of the NAACP in Selma—or, rather, tried to start one. Actually, Adams pretty much *was* the NAACP in Selma at that time because others were not inclined to join. It was dangerous business. It would call attention to you, and who knew where that would lead. In addition, he founded the Dallas County Voters League, an organization of a handful of black people who were interested in voting.

C. J. Adams owned the building that housed Chestnut Brothers

Shields often spoke of the contrast between the fine houses on paved streets in white west Selma . . . (© Penny Weaver)

. . . and the shacks on unpaved streets in black east Selma (Courtesy of the City of Selma)

Market and Grocery, and he was a friend of my parents. One time when my mother wanted to borrow $200 to buy an insurance policy for my college education, Adams said he would sign for it at the loan company. She and Adams went to the loan company, and the man told him, "If I were you, I wouldn't sign it." Adams said, "I'm going to sign it"—and did. That was typical of his attitude.

He acted the way a white Southerner might expect a black man from up North to act. He clearly wasn't one of *their* Negroes and he wanted that understood by them and by blacks. When Adams walked into a store downtown, his manner was such that the white storekeepers wouldn't be laughing and smiling and calling him "Uncle." He was no-nonsense and white people were very uncomfortable around him.

Some black people were, too. I noticed that when Adams came in our store, a few of the men sitting around on produce crates would get up and leave. Adams was not a loner like Shields—he was much more out and about in the community, and the way he carried himself called into question the daily accommodations other blacks made to the humiliations of segregation.

Adams was jailed several times, charged with notorizing false birth certificates and other documents. My father thinks Adams may well have falsified some documents. But everyone in black Selma believed Adams was prosecuted because the white man didn't like him.

He was getting out from a term in the penitentiary the summer before I graduated from high school. Old, sick, tired, Adams had had enough of Selma. He wanted to go to Detroit, where he had family, to live out his remaining years, and my father asked me to drive him. It was hot in the car, and the old man was sick. He had asthma and I had to stop often along the road so he could give himself a shot. During the long ride, Adams talked about the enormous reach of white power. He said that by the time he got to the prison, word had come down from the judge or somebody that he was to have special treatment, that he was a nigger who needed to be broken. So his time was very hard to make.

He described his situation as a double prison where, inside one set of walls, he was surrounded by another—a wall of silence.

Nobody would have anything to do with him. He worried that maybe the guards had told the prisoners he was a snitch. At some point, though, he figured out it wasn't that. The other prisoners heard he was a race man and didn't want to bring problems on themselves by associating with him.

Sick as he was, though, his spirit was still there. He told me, "Don't give an inch. Never let them break your spirit." But at his age, he simply couldn't take any more of Selma. He knew had he stayed on he wouldn't have a minute's peace.

As I drove Adams out of Selma, I watched him look back at the town and saw a strange expression on his face. There were tears in his eyes, but also a kind of satisfaction. I think he knew he would never be back, but he also knew he had left his mark. I was glad to be able to drive him away. I felt better for Adams when we pulled up to his relative's house in Detroit.

"Well, old man, they can't bother you here," I said.

C. J. Adams said he was beyond being bothered.

CHAPTER 4

My Dreams

When I was in the eleventh grade, Edwin Moss, the older brother of my best friend, James, came back from the war, picked a group of us off the street, and changed our nighttime interests from mischief to music. He organized a band, the Masters of Rhythm, and wrote arrangements for us.

Edwin was into jazz. He'd gone to Alabama State College and played with Erskine Hawkins's band. In those days, black state colleges didn't get sufficient appropriations. One of the ways they stayed afloat was by having touring jazz bands. Hawkins headed the one at Alabama State. After college, Edwin played piano for a while with the Ray Shep Band.

Jazz and showbiz had excited me as far back as I can remember. Every year around Halloween, two black minstrel shows—Silas Green and Earl D. Backus—came to Selma, and I was overjoyed just seeing the first truck in the caravan pull into town. I'd rush over to the vacant lot about three blocks from my house to see Green's or Backus's people erect a huge tent, spread sawdust on the ground, and put out rows of metal folding chairs. The stage was the flatbed of a truck with some extensions. It had curtains, scenery, and a live jazz band down front like a Broadway theater.

I watched everything. These were show people, and I liked the proud way they walked, the sharp way they dressed, the confident way they talked. The first five rows were reserved for whites, but at eight o'clock, when the band kicked off the show with a hot jazz number, I was in the sixth row, spellbound.

The band built and teased musically until the atmosphere was one of almost unrestrained joy. Then an articulate and professional voice, unseen, announced simply, "Ladies and gentlemen, Silas Green from New Orleans." The crowd roared as the curtains slowly moved back to reveal, center stage, the character Silas Green in baggy pants, large suspenders, oversized shirt that nowhere touched his neck, loud green tie, black black face, enormous white lips, hands outstretched.

Silas grinned wildly and went into an hysterical dance. He was limber as a dishrag and literally floated to the floor. Meanwhile, from both sides of the stage, dancing and kicking high, came a line of beautiful brown women with skimpy outfits, high high heels, and shapely legs. The audience hooted and stomped on the sawdust.

Watching Silas manipulate the crowd, hearing live jazz, seeing those long-stem women gave me a feeling that is hard to describe. I hadn't run into much else in life that seemed so satisfying. Though both shows were owned by whites and all the jokes were on us, they were a black thing. Everyone involved was black— the performers, the band, the dancers, the men who sold and took the tickets and handled the money. The white people who filled up the front rows—deliverymen, railroad people, that class—seemed superfluous. These minstrels were events as black as the black church, and they gave me, there on a dirt street in Alabama, a sense of belonging to a culture that was more than positive; it was thrilling.

When I was nine or ten, I set up two boxes in my back yard in front of a place where two or three planks of the fence had rotted. I got Aunt Lennie's daughters, Yvonne and Baby Sister, to be showgirls. I hid behind the fence on the neighbor's side while Yvonne and Baby Sister kicked up their legs and one of my friends beat on a bucket with a stick. When Yvonne said, "Ladies and gentlemen, the star of our show, Silas Green!" I popped through the hole in the fence with my hands out, and the audience, my friends, clapped. They'd been to Silas Green and knew when to applaud. I told jokes and looked around to see if my mother was watching because some of Silas's jokes were filthy.

When Edwin started the Masters of Rhythm, I persuaded my mother to buy me a saxophone. But I had to promise I wouldn't become a professional jazz musician. She didn't want me to live that life—traveling from town to town messing with whiskey and women and running the risks of the road. I made the promise, thinking that in time she'd give in, because that's what I wanted to be. I loved jazz and saw it as an enjoyable ticket out of Selma that could take me to the top of Harlem, which was the top of the world. I could make something of myself and not have to deal with white domination.

I phased out gambling and practiced on my saxophone every day. In the summertime, James Moss and I would sometimes go from eight in the morning till ten at night. When we weren't playing, James and I would be trying to write music for the Masters of Rhythm. We played for schools and clubs all around Alabama. Once, we played at the Selma Country Club for a graduation dance of kids at Parrish High, and I saw how certain whites lived. I'd never seen a patio before or the blue water of a swimming pool.

The great jazz bands—Count Basie, Duke Ellington, Lionel Hampton—played one-night stands in Selma, usually at the Elks Rest, on their way from Birmingham to Mobile. The Elks Rest was a big dance hall over a poolroom and beauty parlor. I'd go upstairs and station myself in front of the band when the musicians were tuning up. They played two or three hours with a thirty-minute break. I'd stand in that one spot until the last note was played.

Like Edwin, James was a gifted natural musician. If he heard something, he could play it. I wasn't at that level. What James could pick up instantly would take me hours or days to learn, but eventually I understood it better than he did. I had to understand it to play it. I sat for hours with a record next to the piano figuring out a piece of music, and in time, I could listen to Basie or Ellington and know pretty much where they were, what they were doing, how they got there, and where they were going next. I have found in life that you can more than compensate for lack of natural talent with sweat and devotion, and I was determined not to be outdone. I thought it far more likely that a man with James's enormous talents would wind up working for someone like me than vice versa.

Also, though I never would be a top-flight saxophone player, I found I had other talents that could be useful to a bandleader. At dances, there invariably was a raffle for a door prize when the band took a break. The practice was for a local person to reach in the box and draw out the lucky ticket. It wasn't long before I took over that part of the show. I created a personal version of what I'd seen Silas Green do—pick a well-known local person and tell wildly exaggerated stories about their lack of prowess with women or their incapacity to hold alcohol.

I had no doubt that one day I would arrive in Harlem and take it over. I had three or four different girlfriends at different times when I was in high school. We'd sit up in the VFW Club or Elks Rest and I'd spin out my dreams. I was going straight to New York and put together a group nobody could touch. We would sell records, millions of them, because I had ideas of what the public wanted to hear and how to put it together musically. My girlfriends listened and dreamed along with me.

In the meantime, when I was in the twelfth grade, my father lost his store. Two state sales-tax agents came in one day with a large unpaid tax bill for thousands of dollars' worth of meat they said was slaughtered under my father's permit during the war. I wasn't in the store when they came but there were anxious discussions at home that night between my parents and Aunt Lennie and Uncle Frank.

The next day, my father went to the stockyard to see Suttles, the man who'd taught him to butcher and who had helped set him up in the store. When the war came and meat was rationed, butchers applied for and were issued permits to have meat slaughtered. You couldn't sell meat unless you had a permit; the government also established the ceiling price. Inspectors came by stores that had permits to be certain they weren't overcharging.

Suttles helped my father apply for the permit. At some point during the war, he told my father he had some meat he could sell if he could get it slaughtered. He said he wanted to help a couple white markets that couldn't get permits because they weren't selling meat before the war. So my father let him slaughter extra meat on his permit.

My father told Suttles about the state agents' visit. He came home and told us Suttles said he didn't know anything about it— he ran a stockyard; he didn't sell meat retail. He said that if my father thought some white merchants sold meat under his permit, he should go see them about the tax problem. My father told the tax agents the whole story, and they said it was his permit and his responsibility.

To settle the tax bill, my father auctioned off the contents of the store—scales, counter, freezer, food. Four years earlier, my mother and Aunt Lennie had started teaching in the Dallas County school system, and the state now attached their salaries. On Saturdays, teachers went to the bank and lined up to get their checks. When my mother got up to the card table where the checks were distributed, hers wasn't there. The woman said her pay and Lennie's had been garnisheed. My mother was so embarrassed she walked home through the alleys. She and Lennie didn't get checks for three months.

My father didn't complain or cry. He knew he had no recourse, legal or otherwise. But he became a quieter man and his routine changed—no more hunting or long enjoyable conversations about dogs for a while. He applied for a meat cutter's job in a new supermarket in Montgomery after seeing a want ad in the paper. He needed a recommendation from someone who knew his skills as a butcher, so he went to Suttles, who wrote him a nice letter. Later, Suttles became ill, called for my father, held his hand, and told him he loved him.

My father didn't get the supermarket job. When the manager saw he was black, he said they couldn't hire him because they couldn't have a black man working behind closed doors with a white woman. So my father went to work scrubbing floors, straightening up tables, and emptying the garbage at Craig Field, an air base six miles outside Selma. His experience quickened my determination to get the hell out of Alabama and the South.

All this came up as my parents were about to send me off to college. My mother cried when the state took her savings, but she didn't miss a beat. She and Lennie worked extra hours in a cigar factory that summer. She got some money from Preston and borrowed some from a white man downtown who admired her determination and her ambitions for me. Her boy was going to college. I would have preferred going straight to Harlem, but how could I disappoint her?

So, in the fall of 1948, I showed up at Talladega College, a small black Harvard in north Alabama, with my saxophone and two lapel-less suits like Dizzy Gillespie and the bebop crowd wore. I could not have been more out of place or more miserable.

Talladega was founded by the Freedmen's Bureau and the American Missionary Association right after the Civil War. Its original purpose was to educate black teachers, who then would go out to teach the thousands of uneducated freed slaves. By the late 1940s, however, the institution had evolved into an exclusive, academically renowned, black liberal-arts college, financed by the Congregational Church. Its president and most of the faculty were white Northerners, and it attracted a select group of upper-class blacks.

I'd never heard of Talladega College until Shields brought it up. He said the best education possible was available there, and he could pull strings to get me accepted. All through high school, Shields had been on my case about gambling and drinking. "There's nothing down there for you," he said of the Drag. "If you go off to college and come back, the same fools will be running around in the same dives." Though he continued pressing me to consider the law, he didn't try to dissuade me from becoming Count Basie II. He just insisted I go to college first.

At Talladega, I found myself one of the few blacks from Alabama and one of the darkest-skinned people there. Most of the students were bright, well-educated, light-skinned blacks whose fathers were doctors, lawyers, or pastors of large prominent churches in Chicago, New York, Detroit, Los Angeles. For example, Adam Clayton Powell's nephew was a student at Talladega.

The Talladega campus is a pretty, restful place with oak trees, green grass, and old-fashioned brick buildings. But I felt as alien as I would have at the all-white University of Alabama. I had little in common with my schoolmates, who had lived fairly sheltered lives in Sugar Hill in Harlem or Nob Hill in Chicago, or other enclaves of the black urban elite. They looked almost white and acted white, and they had a kind of built-in prejudice against Southern blacks. They laughed at the way I said "New Yok" and at my black Southern expressions.

When I walked into the dining hall, I got the same feeling I experienced when, as a boy, I walked into a white establishment to do something for my father. The inflections of the voices, the subject matter were similar, and I sensed the same critical eyes on me: What's *he* doing here? It seemed to me their great desire was to divorce themselves as much from the black experience and the black community as this society would let them. I thought they were a bunch of phonies living in a make-believe world in which their light skin and family connections made them different from the rest of us. In Selma, there was a club of light-skinned blacks who held parties and prided themselves on being the Negro elite. To me, it was a fairy tale to think their status amounted to a hill of beans. As Shields pointed out, they drank at the same black water fountains.

I made friends with some black folk in the town who were more my type. I also sought out a black Missionary Baptist church and attended services there instead of at the chapel at the college. The chapel was more like a white church—very sophisticated music and, to me, very cold. Somebody got up and lectured every Sunday. He didn't preach. It wasn't a hell of a lot different from going to class. I ignored the requirement to attend chapel and went instead to the Baptist church where they sang and preached and I left feeling like I'd been to church.

As Shields had said, the professors were good. The best thing I heard the whole year was a lecture given by my sociology teacher about the Dixiecrat rebellion. The fall I arrived at Talladega, the Southern Democrats, led by Strom Thurmond of South Carolina, walked out of the Democratic National Convention when the party nominated Harry Truman, who had integrated the armed forces and pushed other modest civil rights proposals. The Southerners then met in Birmingham, formed the States' Rights Party, and nominated Thurmond, who told the nation, "We believe that there are not enough troops in the Army to force Southern people to admit the Negroes into our theaters, swimming pools and homes." Everybody called the new party the Dixiecrats, but the sociology teacher called them the "Dixierats."

But most of the time I stayed in the dormitory and played my saxophone. I hardly went to class. I was eighteen years old, and instead of standing out like a sore thumb, my instinct was to stay away and do my own thing. I understood that the dominant culture requires some assimilation as the price of even moderate success. But at Talladega the question was whether they were giving up the black ship altogether.

"Why the hell would you arrange to get me into Talladega?" I asked Shields when I came home for Christmas. "It's the antithesis of everything I believe in and everything I thought you believed in." He said Talladega was the best of the lot academically. "If you can cope with white Southerners, you damn sure can cope with Negroes trying to be white. You should take advantage of what it has to offer."

But I couldn't. It was painful to sit in a classroom and listen to a black student try to sound white. To me, this wasn't consistent with education. This was some kind of miseducation. It's hard to put my finger on it, but I went to Talladega to better myself only to find a group of black people who appeared to be ashamed of themselves and of the black race. It seemed to me they weren't so much trying to better themselves as to change into something they weren't and never could be. Since these were the blacks who would go back to Chicago, New York, and elsewhere to become the professionals, the presidents of black colleges, the preachers in important black pulpits, the leaders of the race, it's not surprising black America is so fucked up and far behind.

A Talladega professor, a Creole from New Orleans, told me about Dillard University. He said it was middle-class and I might find it more to my liking. The minute he said it was in New Orleans, firecrackers went off in my head—the whole jazz scene. I don't think I passed a single course at Talladega, but my mother didn't lose faith. I called her near the end of my freshman year and told her I wanted to go to Dillard. She said, "Great. We'll send you."

Instantly, I felt a part of Dillard. Here were students and professors who looked and talked like me. Like Talladega, it was financed by the Congregational Church, but its atmosphere was more like regular folk. And I fell in love with New Orleans. Where I had been peculiar playing the saxophone all day at Talladega, nothing was more natural in New Orleans, and I helped pay for my education by playing and emceeing at nightclubs.

I majored in business administration. A jazz orchestra leader needed to know business, and my Uncle Preston was encouraging me to learn business so I could help in an enterprise he had in mind. My uncles' farming business had collapsed after the war because Frank, who was doing most of the farming, fell out with Preston, who was providing most of the financing. Not long before I went to college, Preston became a traveling salesman for the E. F. Young Company, a black-owned cosmetics firm. He went all over Alabama with Young's pomades and hair straighteners. This dovetailed with gambling, because he was so good he had to be on the move or he couldn't get a play.

Preston was a man of many ideas when it came to making money, and the plan he began pushing when I went to college was a black grocery cooperative across the Black Belt. The new supermarkets were killing the Mom and Pops, and centralized purchasing would help them compete. On the road with Young's products, he stopped and talked to grocers and to black leaders about the idea.

He also stopped to see me regularly at Talladega and Dillard. He wanted me to learn accounting, inventory, and marketing. He said black grocers had the same problems all over, and if we could get this thing going in one place, there was no telling how big it could get, how much money we could make, and how much good we could do. I considered economic unity the route to black independence and freedom, and I thought if anybody could bring it off, Preston could. I figured once we got the system set up, we'd hire people to run it, so I could do that and be a bandleader, too.

At Dillard, I wrote a paper on the problems of black leadership that aroused as much controversy as the one I had written at Knox Academy. I questioned what Talladega, Dillard, and other black colleges were teaching potential leaders. Talladega had the upper class, the so-called cream of the crop, and was teaching them to do as their parents had done—run black America under the dictates of white America. What was Dillard teaching middle-class blacks?

My argument was: Both colleges taught accommodation and didn't dare teach anything else because they were financed from the same pocket—white America. The Congregational Church with Dillard and Talladega, the Rockefellers with Spelman College, Henry Ford with Tuskegee Institute, and the U.S. government with Howard University set up these institutions so blacks could have doctors, teachers, preachers, even lawyers. But did they create these schools to teach blacks they could hold equal responsibility or authority with whites? Obviously not. If not, what did they have in mind?

I said Dillard was teaching a different fantasy of black leadership than Talladega, but a fantasy no less. It was a fantasy I could live with. It was what I was used to, what my mother taught. Both colleges said, in so many words, "Don't lead black America where white America doesn't want it to go. Keep your place and work hard." They were fooling themselves if they thought they were teaching bona fide leadership.

The paper was the talk of the campus. Some of the faculty felt it was a personal attack on everything they represented. What was the alternative? I had my sophomoric answers. Why couldn't the black upper class finance a black college that would be controlled by black people?

Several professors at Dillard encouraged me to study law because I constantly raised questions that were legal in nature and wanted to debate every issue. Benjamin Quarles, a noted black historian who taught at Dillard, and Daniel Thompson, a sociologist, arranged for me to go to Howard University Law School in Washington, D.C.

Naturally, my mother was all for it. So was Preston. By the time I graduated from Dillard, his thinking about the grocery cooperative had grown beyond joint buying for a group of merchants. He was talking about a chain of supermarkets owned and operated by the black community. We would create a corporation, sell shares across the Black Belt, and absorb the Mom and Pops

My Vivian (Courtesy of Henry Mayfield)

by giving shares to the owners. If I was a lawyer, so much the better.

While I was at Dillard, I married Vivian Davis, a Selma girl four years younger than I. I knew Vivian's mother, Inez, before I met Vivian because Inez was helping support the two of them by selling a little bootleg whiskey. They were alone in the world. But Inez did all she could to keep her daughter apart from that life. She dressed Vivian like a little doll in starched short dresses that stood out like a ballerina's. At Knox, I'd catch Vivian on campus and just hold her by the arms. She had a fit. "Let me go! Let me go!" I'd just hold her there and tease her.

One of my friends was going with a girl who lived next door

to Vivian. I went with him one day to see his girlfriend and discovered that was where this little cute girl lived. I went strutting over there and got run off. Inez didn't want a gambler and drinker like me messing up her precious daughter. So I didn't have much of a relationship with Vivian while I was in high school. But before I went to Talladega, I told her I would write and asked if she would answer. At first she said no, but I think she was a little bit impressed that this senior who was going off to college was talking about writing to her. She finally agreed. I wrote and proposed that she get rid of the little fella she was going with. She wrote back that she couldn't do that. I persisted in my campaign, and when she broke up with him, I asked her to marry me.

Inez wasn't too pleased, though she'd softened some since I was a college man. My mother was upset because she thought marriage—and, inevitably, children—at that point would get in the way of my pursuit of a professional degree. We ignored both of them and went ahead and got married. We had two children, Ronnie and Inetta Geraldine, by 1953 when we moved to Washington so I could learn to be a lawyer.

CHAPTER 5

Rumblings

I arrived at Howard Law School in the midst of preparation for arguments before the U.S. Supreme Court in the *Brown v. Board of Education of Topeka* case challenging segregation in the public schools. Thurgood Marshall and the other lawyers for the NAACP Legal Defense Fund, which filed the lawsuit, had already made oral arguments to the Court in December 1952, but the Court delivered a set of questions to the attorneys on both sides and called them back for their responses a year later.

Two months after I got to Howard in the fall of 1953, the law school and the NAACP brought in noted black legal thinkers from around the country to go over the questions with Marshall and the NAACP legal team. These sessions took place in the basement of the Howard University library, the location of the law school. You couldn't keep me and the other law students away. These were *the* black lawyers—Thurgood Marshall, Wiley Branton, Herbert Reed, James Naibreth, Robert Carter. We'd read about them in *Ebony* and *Jet* and, lo and behold, here we were in the same room with them.

The Justices' questions centered on the Fourteenth Amendment (equal protection under the law). The other side had argued that if public schools were equal, separation was irrelevant constitutionally. Our side had argued that separation on the basis of skin color was *per se* a denial of equal protection because it sent a message of inferiority to black children and separated the black race from the mainstream of American life. Ours was the uphill battle, since a ruling on our behalf would mean not only uprooting fifty years of legal precedent, established in 1896 in the *Plessy* v. *Ferguson* case, but overturning numerous legislative programs passed by Congress in recognition of *Plessy's* separate but equal doctrine.

In discussing how responses ought to be shaped, the lawyers at Howard got into nuances of language. A few felt the Court was not going to outlaw school segregation in a single opinion. Such a far-reaching decree was one we'd have to work toward by stages. They didn't want the legal team to foreclose some lesser ruling by arguing it has to be this or nothing else. At best at this point, we might be able to make equal a reality.

Most of the others, particularly Marshall, argued that the Court's opinions in similar, recent cases and the fact that the Justices were calling them back indicated that if they put the question to the Court properly, now was the time to get the ruling we sought. I was of the first opinion when I came into the sessions—that a Court that upheld segregation for fifty years wasn't going to overturn it—but Marshall was so damn confident and persuasive I eventually accepted his point of view.

Everybody, though, was apprehensive about how a desegregation ruling, if it came, would be enforced. In conversations between sessions, one professor kept raising the point that even if the Supreme Court did reverse itself, we were not likely to get a President to enforce the ruling or a Congress to impeach him for failing to do so. I found this statement striking because of my own lack of faith in the white people who ran America. I didn't think a popularly elected President would stand up on behalf of a despised minority who couldn't even vote against his own people who could.

In January 1954, after one semester at Howard, I was drafted into the army. Various people at Howard had advised me to move my draft registration from Selma to Washington. "You know those damn white Southerners don't want a black man going to law school," they said. I neglected to take their advice, and at the end of the semester, the draft board in Selma revoked my deferment and ordered me to appear before them within a matter of weeks.

That's how I met Congressman Adam Clayton Powell, Jr., from Harlem. I wanted to keep my deferment, if possible, and, if not, at least avoid having to travel back to Selma just to go into the army. There was no point in seeking help from the congressmen from Alabama. It was their people on the draft board, and they weren't going to intercede on behalf of a black man unless I had a powerful white sponsor. So even though I wasn't from Harlem, I contacted Adam. He'd been saying for years that he represented the black nation, and this was true. Almost any Southern black who needed something from Washington had a better shot at it through Adam than through the white congressmen representing his state.

Adam treated me as one of his constituents. He couldn't keep me out of the army. That would have been unfair, I guess, since men were dying in Korea. But I didn't have to go back to Selma, and after basic training, the army stationed me at the Aberdeen Proving Grounds in Maryland, less than a hundred miles from Washington.

At that time, Truman's executive order integrating the armed forces was six years old, and the pressure was on from the NAACP to move some blacks into higher positions. When I got there, the army was desperately looking for black officer material—meaning, in the army's way of thinking, black college graduates. I wasn't at Aberdeen long before my company commander called me into his office to talk about officer candidate school, which would have doubled my enlistment time. He said that, with integration, a black person could go somewhere in the army; it was a good opportunity. I said that might be true, but I had other plans. I'd gone to one semester of law school. I wanted to serve my two years and go back to complete my degree.

"Well, whether you like it or not, we've sent in your name," he said. I immediately telephoned Adam and he said he'd do what he could. The commanding officer was trying to get orders cut for me to go to officer candidate school. The orders twice got to the Pentagon, then something happened. They never went through, and I was stationed for the duration of my two years at Aberdeen, teaching ammunition supply and escaping to Harlem every chance I got. Through Adam's intercession, the army released me two months early so I could resume law school when the semester began in January 1956.

I was still in the army when the Supreme Court declared school segregation unconstitutional, agreeing with the NAACP's argument that separate was inherently unequal. My reaction was "I'll be damned!" Like most blacks, though, my excitement was tempered by a strong dose of caution because in issuing its historic decision on May 17, 1954, the Court put off deciding how and when it would be enforced.

In hearings eleven months later, lawyers for the Southern states argued that dismantling their dual systems and mixing the races would be difficult, if not impossible, to do quickly. They asked the High Court not to fix a deadline for desegregation and to leave the details of how it should be accomplished to local school boards under the supervision of local U.S. district courts. The NAACP lawyers argued that an unconstitutional system should not be allowed to persist and that wavering on enforcement would give aid and comfort to the forces of resistance. They asked the High Court to order segregation ended by the fall of 1956.

The Court accepted the white South's position. In May 1955, it declared that desegregation should proceed "with all deliberate speed," but then left it up to the lower courts to decide whether individual school boards were making a prompt and reasonable effort, allowing these courts to take "local conditions" into account in gauging progress.

Everyone at Howard Law School was apprehensive because, as a practical matter, "all deliberate speed" probably meant just the opposite. Placing enforcement in the hands of the lower courts and opening the issue of local conditions meant that individual lawsuits would have to be filed against each and every school district that remained segregated. This would be time-consuming and expensive, and it looked as if the Legal Defense Fund would have to fight and finance all the cases. President Eisenhower had backed away from the Court's ruling, so we weren't going to get any help from the U.S. Department of Justice. The law students at Howard thought we'd be lucky if we pulled off desegregation in our lifetimes.

While I was at Aberdeen, Vivian and I had another child, Rosalind. Back in Washington, I worked nights washing cars in a hotel, then got a job as a disc jockey on a radio station, WOOK, that had just changed over to black programming. I played jazz and clowned around on my afternoon show—like putting on a Lawrence Welk record as if by accident, saying, "How the hell did that get in here?" and breaking it, *bap*, on the air. Then I'd play the most Negroid, down-in-the-gutter blues number I could find and grunt over it with great satisfaction. I called myself "The Little One"—a nickname I got at the Howard Theater, a Washington version of the Apollo, where I emceed on occasion. I'm small and somebody asked, "Where's 'the little one'?" and the name stuck.

I made money promoting clubs and booking acts. For a percentage, I'd appear myself. I'd announce on the air, "Watch out. The Little One will be there." I did stunts like renting a hearse and casket and getting four or five friends to be pallbearers. We pulled up to the club, the pallbearers brought the casket in, and who was lying up inside it but The Little One with a cigar.

I also wrote some speeches for Adam Clayton Powell. I went by to thank him for his help and started spending time around his office. He was the most influential black man in America, and I wanted to learn from him. Though he looked white and had the elite background of the students at Talladega, he embraced being black. He liked to talk street slang like "Keep the faith, baby." I was walking down the hall of the House office building with him one day when he said that to a congressman from Mississippi, then deliberately and coolly blew smoke in the congressman's red face from one of the long, thin cigars he smoked.

He was a remarkable individual. Here was a preacher who was not ministerial in any way—a playboy, handsome and debonair, absolutely in love with pretty women, money, and booze, who made no bones about it at any time. Also, here was a man who strongly believed in the rights of black people and was prepared to take on white America by himself—in fact, wanted to take on white America by himself. He didn't want anybody else out there with him. That was a flaw. In every session of Congress from the late 1940s on, he introduced a far-reaching civil rights bill and made a rousing speech on the floor of the House, then went down to Bimini with one of his many female friends. Organizing was not his forte.

Adam thought his speeches were sometimes too shallow for a

congressman. They didn't have enough facts and figures. So I wrote some for him. He wanted me to come to Harlem after I graduated to practice law and work with him. I thought that was a splendid idea. I wanted to help Preston, but I'd dreamed about Harlem all my life, and Vivian said she wanted no part of a little town or the South.

In the meantime, up popped Martin Luther King, Jr. The first time I saw King was not long after I came back from the army. I was passing the chapel at Howard, saw a crowd of undergraduates milling around and going inside, and asked what was happening. They said Martin Luther King, Jr., was speaking. I'd heard about the bus boycott in Montgomery in detail from Preston, and I went in.

There at the podium was a man one year older than I whose voice was not unlike mine, quite deep and Southern. I was very much at home listening to him. It was like a piece of Alabama had been brought to Washington, D.C., and deposited there on the campus. He talked about the boycott and about forming a national organization to fight for freedom. I was ecstatic that a group of black people had brought the bus company to its knees in the cradle of the Confederacy, just fifty miles from Selma. What impressed me most was the unity. I had never known blacks to stand together on anything where whites were on the other side.

Something else happened while I was up North that aroused my interest in coming home to Alabama—a rape trial in Selma that rallied the black community as it had never been rallied before. One night in March 1953, the young white wife of an airman at Craig Field called the police and reported that a black man had come in through her window, jumped on her, and raped her. She could see only his eyes—the rest of his face was hidden by a mask—and the knife he held at her neck. Then, a month later, the mayor's daughter, a young married woman, reported that she had awakened to find a black man sitting on her and holding a knife. She struggled and fought until she wrested the knife from him and he fled.

The town just went wild. I wasn't there, but Preston called regularly to tell me what was going on. The police were getting five or six calls a night—"There's a nigger in my house! I saw him! I saw him!"—from white women all over Selma. White men bought burglar bars and guns and began nighttime patrols. Black men were almost afraid to leave their homes, and black women feared for their husbands and sons. The police were arbitrarily rounding up black men for questioning and filling the jail.

One night a few months later, two white men stopped a black man walking down an alley on the border of the white community. They called the police. The man's name was William Earl Fikes. He lived in Marion, forty miles away, was married with four children, and worked in a gas station. He was almost inarticulate, possibly mentally retarded. The police took him to a prison in Montgomery—for his protection, they said—and wouldn't allow his father or anybody to see him. They questioned him for twelve, fifteen hours at a time and after several days came out with what they called a confession.

Fikes was charged with raping the airman's wife and attempting to rape the mayor's daughter. Both were capital crimes in Alabama—a punishment used in rape cases almost exclusively for black men convicted of raping white women. Two white attorneys were appointed to represent Fikes in the alleged rape of the airman's wife. She testified she had identified a man at the prison by his eyes and voice as her attacker, and she pointed to Fikes as the man. She admitted, though, that he was the only man brought for identification.

With her testimony and Fikes's "confession," everyone anticipated a quick guilty verdict and the death penalty. The jury—like all Alabama juries then, twelve white men—did find Fikes guilty, but imposed a sentence of 99 years in prison. It turned out that one of the jurors didn't believe in capital punishment. White Selma was infuriated that Fikes wasn't ordered put to death. What surprised and interested me, watching from afar, was the reaction of the black community. Instead of turning their backs and accepting the situation the way they had when Dan Craig was beaten, they came to Fikes's defense.

The way Preston read it, white Selma had gone too far with its indiscriminate arrests and calls for the electric chair. Also, some black leaders knew the Fikes family and had doubts about whether he was the rapist. Most significant of all, black Selma had a determined race man, Sam Boynton, who had succeeded C. J. Adams and who made the Fikes case a cause. Boynton had come to Dallas County in 1928 as a U.S. agricultural extension agent to work with black farmers. Both he and his wife, Amelia, the black home-economics extension agent, were graduates of Tuskegee Institute. Boynton often talked about their shock at the slave-like dependency of black sharecroppers and tenant farmers in Dallas County.

Boynton held a strong belief in economic advancement as the way out of oppression. He was always trying to find financial resources for black people who wanted to get off white people's land and buy their own. Being a farm agent, he knew all the government programs. He also knew A. G. Gaston, a black millionaire in Birmingham, and other people in Atlanta and New York to call to help blacks who wanted to help themselves. His other theme was voting. More blacks needed to go down to the courthouse to try to get registered. Being kept out of the political process undermined what we could do.

His agenda was similar to C. J. Adams's, and Boynton was the old man's protégé. He shared an office with Adams for a while and took over as Selma's black notary public and as head of the Voters League after Adams was jailed and I drove him to Detroit. In the early 1950s, when the national NAACP was pushing for members, possible plaintiffs, and money for its impending attack on school segregation, Boynton, along with two World War II veterans, J. D. Hunter and Ernest Doyle, revived Selma's almost dormant NAACP chapter.

The rape uproar and Fikes's arrest gave their drive momentum, a concrete injustice to organize around. Boynton started a fund-raising campaign for Fikes's defense in the black churches. Then he arranged for the NAACP Legal Defense Fund to send two black lawyers from Birmingham, Peter Hall and Orzell Billingsley, to represent Fikes in his trial for attempting to rape the mayor's daughter.

Peter and Orzell were the first black lawyers ever to try a case in a Dallas County courtroom. This fact alone stirred up great excitement in black Selma and in me. I came home specifically to watch the trial. I'd already heard about Peter Hall. He and an older Birmingham lawyer, Arthur Shores, were trying cases in Alabama for the NAACP Legal Defense Fund that Thurgood Marshall would pick up and argue before the Supreme Court on appeal. So I was very interested in meeting him.

The day before the trial, I saw Peter at the Elks Club. He was sitting at the long mirror-tiled bar, drinking whiskey and looking for respectable, educated blacks to testify that they had never been called to serve on a jury. He intended to challenge the systematic exclusion of blacks. He said something I've never forgotten that would become my approach to the practice of law: "I don't know if Fikes is guilty, but it's damn sure the system is. I intend to try the system while the circuit solicitor is trying Fikes."

The trial was held in the Dallas County Courthouse, in a typical small-town courtroom—large and drafty, tall windows, poor acoustics, a scratched wooden floor. There was an enormous raised desk for the judge, a rail separating the audience from the lawyers, twelve uncomfortable cane-bottom chairs for the jury, and long wooden benches for the spectators—one side for whites, the other for "colored." The benches were filled the day the trial began and Selma got its first look at Peter Hall, black attorney.

His appearance was striking. Whites and blacks in Selma rarely saw a black man in a suit other than the standard black ones preachers and undertakers wore. Peter was wearing not only a suit but an expensive, tailored one. He was movie-handsome—tall, light skin, mustache—and sophisticated. He carried himself in a way that suggested Duke Ellington or Billy Eckstine. Though he was raised in Birmingham, he went to law school at De Paul University in Chicago and he didn't speak with a Southern accent. He spoke very formal English, referring to Fikes as the "defendaunt."

I was sitting in the audience when he came in. He was a little late, probably for effect. He walked with a slight limp—he had a cork leg—at a determined but unhurried pace up to the bench, where he planted that cork leg and started arguing a flurry of pre-trial motions.

From that moment, it was obvious that Peter Hall was the smoothest, most competent lawyer in the room—and that Peter Hall knew it. He dominated the white judge, the white lawyers.

Orzell was impressive, too, as a researcher in that trial. While Peter would be making a legal point, Orzell would be flipping the pages of a law book and would have it open to just the right citation when Peter turned around and reached for it.

Peter's first move was to ask the judge to quash the indictment against Fikes and dismiss the pool of jurors on the ground that blacks were systematically excluded from juries, thus violating Fikes's right to a trial by his peers. Blacks who packed into the courtroom watched with delight as Peter questioned white county officials—the circuit solicitor, the circuit clerk, the jury commissioners, and others—in a polished, polite way that masked the aggressiveness of what he was doing.

The officials testified that, indeed, no blacks had served on juries in Dallas County in modern times, but that didn't mean they were being systematically excluded. A few had been in the pool of potential jurors over the years, they said, but black people had to be more carefully screened than whites because of their higher percentage of illiteracy, venereal disease, and felony convictions.

Peter then put on the stand a dozen highly educated and respectable blacks, among them Sam Boynton, to inquire whether they had ever been called for jury duty or knew any black person who had. Though blacks sometimes were witnesses in criminal trials, taking the witness stand on an issue that challenged the system was a provocative act in Selma in 1953 and contributed to the excitement the trial aroused in the black community.

Peter's mode of defense—or offense—was new to me and I'd watched a lot of trials in the same courtroom with the best defense attorneys in town. When I was home from Dillard, I used to run by the courthouse to watch the show. There would be these towering battles between James Hare, the prosecutor, and defense attorneys like McLean Pitts and Tom Gayle. Sometimes the trials would last almost a week over some black who had slit another black's throat in some joint. Yet here were these powerful white men arguing for days before an all-white male jury I didn't think gave a damn anyway. I used to wonder why.

I later concluded it was part of the old Southern tradition of a plantation owner looking out for "his" black to get him a lawyer when he killed some other black. The accused usually was a good worker, but on Friday night to Sunday he'd be in the black community raising hell. One of the reasons he felt free to raise hell was "I work for Mr. So-and-So and I can do what I want down here." Now, if the fella who got cut or killed worked for a different powerful white, if all of a sudden this white man and his family were deprived of a man who'd been working for them for years, the children loved him, the wife relied on him, the white man would be down at the police station and courthouse demanding that the perpetrator be arrested.

Hare would argue that black people had to be punished like children. He genuinely believed it was in our genes to mess up in joints on Saturday night, and we needed to be slapped hard when we got out of line. His style was to go to the jury, paint the defendant as worthless, and put the issue on an economic basis. "If this nigra can kill with immunity, no nigra is safe," implying to the jurors "yours or yours or yours."

Pitts and Gayle would argue, "Well, you can do nothin' to bring back the dead nigra. He's gone. But now you're going to deprive Mr. So-and-So by putting his nigra in the penitentiary at the public's expense."

They really went at it because all of them—Hare, Pitts, Gayle—loved the combat. It was a contest to them, like a football game. What Peter Hall was doing was completely different. He certainly wasn't representing some white man's nigger. He wasn't engaged in showing off his legal prowess. He wasn't even, really, defending an individual. As he said that day in the Elks, he was prosecuting the system.

Naturally, Peter did not succeed in getting a white judge in Selma to allow any blacks on the jury. This was an argument geared for appeal to higher courts outside Alabama. The judge also denied Peter's motion to prevent the prosecution from using Fikes's confession on the ground that it was obtained by "Gestapo-like tactics."

The trial lasted three days. Since the mayor's daughter said her attacker had had a towel over his head and she couldn't identify him, the principal evidence was the confession and the testimony of the airman's wife that Fikes was the man who'd raped her. The defense presented many character witnesses, including the white owner of the filling station. The jury was out just forty minutes before returning the verdict—guilty, sentenced to death.

There was no outburst from the packed courtroom. Everyone expected that verdict and it scarcely diminished the excitement in black Selma. Peter Hall's defense of Fikes had an effect on the black community similar to the effect of Jesse Jackson's campaign thirty-five years later. Black Americans in 1988 didn't expect Jesse to win the nomination and black Selmians in 1953 didn't expect Peter Hall to win with an all-white jury. How could he win? But what a hell of a fight! Folk brought their children to the courtroom to see black men who weren't bowing or Uncle Tom-ing in the presence of important white people. Boynton got maybe a hundred new NAACP members.

Peter's motions, though, did save Fikes's life. The conviction was overturned by the U.S. Supreme Court on the basis that the confession was not voluntary, given Fikes's limited mental and verbal capacity, his isolation for nearly a week, and the highly suggestive questioning by the police. The case made new law that the totality of the circumstances of a confession—not just evidence of beatings or other physical coercion—could be used to determine its voluntariness.

The prosecutor chose not to retry the case because the confession was basically all he had, and Fikes was in jail for 99 years in the rape of the airman's wife. Peter had to make an awful choice. The same illegal confession had been used in the trial for that rape and unquestionably the court would strike down that conviction, too. But dare they ask? Although the airman's wife had identified Fikes only by his voice, he might well be convicted again without the confession and without a juror holding out against the death penalty. So to save his life, the defense chose to allow Fikes to remain in jail on a sentence almost certainly based on an unconstitutional conviction.

The Supreme Court's decision came in 1957, a year before I finished law school. The fact that a case from my hometown was making law for the nation added to my motivation to go back to Selma. The rumblings of change were coming from the South, and I was losing interest in Harlem by the minute. Between Martin Luther King and Peter Hall, Alabama was where the action was. Forget New York. Dixie, here I come!

PART TWO

1958 - 1962

Black downtown Selma on a busy Saturday. My first law office was in the second building from the corner (Courtesy of the Food Service Training School, Selma)

Introduction

While J. L. Chestnut, Jr., was up North studying law and serving in the army, white Alabama was organizing resistance to the Supreme Court's decision on school desegregation.

White Selma's initial reaction to the ruling was opposition, disbelief, and a hopeful expectation that, as then-school-board member Carl Morgan put it, "it really wasn't going to apply to us. A ruling had been made but there were no guidelines as to how it was going to be interpreted, and it seemed like a bad dream. We did not anticipate the overreaction of the federal government. Our initial thought was: Well, that's what they decided in Washington, but it may not affect us that much."

The chairman of the school board told the Selma Times-Journal *he was going to wait and see what action the state took on the issue—and it was clear that the state was gearing up for massive resistance. At least once a week, the* Times-Journal *carried a story describing the latest legislative ploy in Montgomery—passing a law declaring the Supreme Court's ruling not binding on Alabama, discussing a bill to allow public funds to be spent on private schools, appropriating more money for the attorney general's office to "litigate this thing for generations, if that's what it takes," as one senator put it.*

In the meantime, the Selma school board continued business as usual, breaking ground for a new white elementary school and a

*new black elementary school a year after the Supreme Court ruled
separate schools unconstitutional. Stating that "since the school
buildings are owned by the City of Selma, I feel I should voice my
opinion regarding segregation in our schools," Selma's mayor,
Chris Heinz, read a letter to the City Council shortly after the
groundbreakings:*

> *Under our present system, each race is free from social discrim-
> ination, free from any ill-feeling that would exist if our system were
> to be changed. . . . I feel I speak for all of the thinking citizens of
> our community, both whites and colored, when I say to you I am
> sure there will be no integration of white pupils in colored schools
> and no integration of colored pupils in white schools in the City of
> Selma.*

*To make certain, a White Citizens' Council was organized in
Dallas County. The Citizens' Council movement, a reaction to the
Supreme Court decision, began in Mississippi in the summer of
1954, then spread to other Southern states. The one formed on
November 29 in the auditorium of Selma's white junior high school
was the first and largest in Alabama.*

The Times-Journal *counted 1,100 to 1,200 "Black Belt farmers,
merchants, bankers, professional men and public officeholders"
overflowing the auditorium "to learn the plans for applying stern
economic pressure on Negro advocates of integration." About six
hundred of them paid three dollars to join after a Mississippi leg-
islator warned of the dangers of "race mixing."*

*The day before the meeting, an unnamed Selma attorney ex-
plained the purpose of the new organization to the newspaper:
"The white population in this county controls the money and this
is an advantage that the Council will use in a fight to legally maintain
complete segregation of the races. We intend to make it difficult if
not impossible for any Negro who advocates desegregation to find
and hold a job, get credit, or renew a mortgage."*

*The attorney made a point of differentiating the council from the
Ku Klux Klan. "We are not anti-Negro. We only want segregation
maintained. And we are not vigilantes. We will operate openly and
violence is the furtherest thing from the minds of the Council mem-*

bers. We have lived with Negroes all of these years without trouble and it is our utmost desire to continue this happy relationship but on a segregated basis. We have no hatred for the race. In fact I believe we have love for the Negro and have his welfare far more at heart than the NAACP."

The White Citizens' Council was mainstream—middle-class and predominantly white-collar. Its members were landowners, merchants, doctors, lawyers, and virtually all the elected officials in the county. Always onstage at council rallies were Bernard Reynolds, the Dallas County probate judge; Chris Heinz, mayor of Selma; James Hare, the circuit judge; and Walter Givhan, the state senator for Dallas and several other Black Belt counties. In fact, the mayor of Selma and the Dallas County probate judge made the nominations for the council's board of directors. Its first chairman was M. Alston Keith, a prominent attorney and chairman of the Dallas County Democratic Executive Committee.

The council's rallies generally were held at the city-owned Municipal Stadium. Barbecue was served, and often the Parrish High School band played. There were family memberships, a Junior Citizens' Council at the white high school, and an annual essay contest. One year, the choice of subjects was "Why I Believe in the Social Separation of the Races," "Subversives in Racial Unrest," "The Importance of Preserving States' Rights," and "Why Separate Schools Should Be Maintained." The prize was $50 and the judges were two officers from the Craig air base.

Every meeting reported by the Times-Journal *included an invocation by a minister assuring those present that the separation of the races was God's will and quoting Scripture to prove it: "Some shall be rulers over many and some over few." "God created three races and ordered the bounds of their habituations." The speeches conveyed fear and urgency: "The goal of the NAACP is to open the bedroom doors of our white women to Negro men . . . This is white man's country. It always has been and always will be," Senator Givhan said at one rally. Warned McLean Pitts, Selma's city attorney, "We intend to maintain segregation and do so without violence. But I know the first time a Negro tries to enter any white school in Selma, blood may be spilled on the campus."*

Those present and those speaking saw their cause as a righteous one. *One speaker used the famous quotation from Edmund Burke, "The only thing necessary for the triumph of evil is for good men to do nothing," in urging a staunch defense of segregation.*

Not everyone in white Selma joined the Citizens' Council or approved its methods, and many who paid their dues and attended rallies did no more than that. Certainly not everyone who joined participated in the delegations that pressured employers and banks to fire or refuse credit to black people who the council thought were getting out of line. But the organization drew a tight net of conformity around white Selma, too. If an employer balked, the council leaders would spread the word "nigger-lover" and, if the employer was a merchant, threaten to boycott his business. "There were decent good white people who didn't believe that was the way to go, who thought there should be open communication between black and white leaders to discuss the situation," recalls Kathryn Windham, a Selma writer. "These people were pressured and there was bitter conflict—friendships broken and economic suffering." Two Jewish merchants broke up a partnership over the issue—one partner insisting they had to join; the other refusing. The partner who didn't join left town.

For anyone with political ambitions, active participation in the Citizens' Council was a must, according to Joe Smitherman, then an appliance salesman, who would become a city councilman in 1960 and mayor of Selma in 1964. "There was a guy who had a little café with an old black woman waiting on tables. She'd done something the council was against, and they wanted me to go down there and tell him to 'get rid of the nigger.' I didn't like pressuring another merchant, but I did it." Those who disapproved of the council at most refused to join themselves. There was no organized opposition and nobody criticized the council's goal of maintaining segregation.

The first targets of the council's economic reprisals were black parents who petitioned the Selma school board in the fall of 1955 to integrate the public schools. This was part of a national NAACP effort to find out what to expect from the Supreme Court decision. It was anticipated that some communities might voluntarily desegregate if blacks presented a united request. For others, litigation would be necessary.

Twenty-nine parents, buoyed by the Supreme Court ruling and

Peter Hall's vigorous defense of William Fikes the year before, signed the petition. Within a week, all but a handful had called or written letters to the board asking for their names to be withdrawn.

As reported by the Times-Journal: *Kemp M. Stallworth, an insurance agent, said, "I didn't know I was signing a petition for Negro children to go to white schools." Sadie May Washington, employed at the Bayuk Cigar Company, denied she was a member of the NAACP. Minnie Bell Harris, a maid, said she thought she was signing a petition for "better living." Joe Vann, Sr., a civilian employee at Craig Field, said, "I am not now and never have been in favor of white and colored attending the same school. I signed the petition thinking it was for better schools." Isaac Rhodes, a painter, said, "I just want my name withdrawn with no comment." Of the twenty-nine who signed the petition, sixteen lost their jobs within a month.*

Two local NAACP leaders, J. D. Hunter and Ernest Doyle, refused to withdraw their names. Doyle recalled, "The Citizens' Council had a black man bring the message, a guy who worked at the Albert Hotel. He told me I had to live with these people and I should take my name off. I was a paperhanger with 95 percent of my business in white homes. The Citizens' Council blacklisted me, and I didn't make another white dollar for twenty years." Hunter's job was secure—he worked for a black insurance agency— but he had trouble getting credit. The reprisals and the failure of the petition—the school board ignored it—deflated the enthusiasm for civil rights activism, and black Selma sank back into resignation.

J. L. Chestnut, Sr., who'd gotten a job as night foreman at Cloverleaf Creamery, was present when another petitioner was fired. "The boss men told him Sam Boynton must have pressured him to sign it. They said if he took his name off, he could keep his job. They really wanted him to stay because he was a good worker. But he refused to do it. He had to leave Selma to get another job."

J.L. Sr. didn't sign the petition. He had no children in school and, anyway, considered it "a waste of time" that would only get him in trouble. He had no way of knowing that three years later, when his son returned to Selma to be its first and only black lawyer, the boss men would have a conversation with him.

CHAPTER 6

Outside the Rail

When my car crested over the hump of the Edmund Pettus Bridge on a warm night in June 1958, there was Selma, the same old Selma. I drove through town on Broad Street, past the stores closed for the day and the white teenagers hanging around Carter Drug and the Wilby Theater. I headed for the Drag to see who I might bump into. It looked the same, too—the Roxy Theater all lit up, people eating and drinking in the White Dot Café, men standing around on the curb watching the cars and the girls go by.

I stopped and yelled out at some familiar faces. I heard no talk about boycotts or school integration or the other civil rights issues being hotly debated in Washington and at Howard. Just the usual gossip—whose husband was chasing whose wife, what preacher was in a mess—that had been going on when I left. I went in the direction of my parents' home, where Vivian and the children had come several months earlier, down the familiar unpaved streets past the familiar rows of tumbledown houses.

I felt glad to be back among family and friends, privileged and proud that I was about to take on some of my people's and the community's problems and saddened a little that a life that might have been spent in Harlem, around the corner from Count Basie, Duke Ellington, and the Apollo Theater, had led instead back to the boondocks of Alabama.

Though so much was the same, Selma was different in atmosphere. Just as I anticipated more developments along the lines of the Montgomery bus boycott, so did white Alabama. There was a tension in the air that had not been present when I left for college, and a different sort of nervousness in the white community from the panic over the rapes.

Some things whites would have overlooked in 1948—a black woman making a smart remark to a policeman, for example—were less likely to be overlooked in 1958. When a group of black deacons went to the bank for a loan to repair the roof of their church, they were more likely in 1958 to get into a review from the loan officer of the pastor—"How's he coming along?"—and other questions probing whether he was preaching the party line. Remember, a young Baptist preacher, Martin Luther King, Jr., had led the boycott fifty miles away. Comments were made to black maids, handymen, and other employees about Montgomery and school integration and outside agitators stirring up trouble trying to mix the races. "We get along fine between the races, don't we? We're not going to have that mess here." I read about meetings of the White Citizens' Council in the *Times-Journal* and its efforts to keep black people cowed though, in reality, nothing as concrete as a civil rights movement had developed in black Selma. Far from it.

There were five black lawyers in Alabama then—Arthur Shores, Peter Hall, and Orzell Billingsley in Birmingham, Fred Gray in Montgomery, and Vernon Crawford in Mobile. When I and three classmates from Howard—Richard "Icewater" Pearson from Birmingham and Solomon Seay, Jr., and Calvin Pryor from Montgomery—passed the bar exam that summer, we brought the total to nine.

What I had in mind, starting out, was building a garden-variety practice to help black people with legal problems and represent them in the courthouse. I wasn't marching in with NAACP cases. But being the first and only black lawyer in a small, segregated town in 1958 was a challenge, in itself, to the established order. Selma had black professionals—two doctors, three dentists, teachers, preachers, principals, and the presidents of Concordia College and Selma University. But they worked in a black world.

My first law office was on the second floor in this building, above what is now Randy's (© Penny Weaver)

There weren't two court systems, though, so I was about to go to work as a black professional in the white world. With the exception of janitors, everyone working in the Dallas County Courthouse and Selma City Hall was white. Lawyers were not only white; they were the upper-class whites.

A few days after I opened my office, I was summoned to the courthouse by Bernard Reynolds, the probate judge. In Alabama, a probate judge—who may or may not be a lawyer—is chairman of the county commission and also handles estates, deeds, wills, lunacy hearings, and auto, fishing, and hunting licenses. When I got to the probate office, about ten white women were standing in the outer room by the secretaries' desks and Reynolds, a short, somewhat stocky man, came out and stood in front of them. He seemed fidgety and nervous, and I didn't know what was going on.

"I want to get one thing straight with you now," Reynolds declared. "I want you to be respectful of and treat accordingly each of the ladies in my office. I will not tolerate any abuse of them in the slightest. Do you understand?"

I said, "I understand exactly what you're saying. What I don't understand is why you're saying it." Here was the highest official in the county government dressing me down about abusing white women when I hadn't even spoken to any—and not merely saying it but carrying on a performance. I was angry. I told him, "I have never been disrespectful of a lady in my life, and unlike you, I also respect black women."

Reynolds told me to get out of his office before he lost control of himself.

The next Sunday, Lawrence Danzy, chairman of the deacon board at First Baptist, rushed up to me in church. "What are you doing down there sassing white women at the courthouse? Judge Reynolds told me he had to straighten you out." I told Danzy I'd had no words with any white woman, let alone trouble, and the only thing I knew was that Reynolds had called me in and made a silly speech.

"Well, somebody must be telling him something because Judge Reynolds wouldn't make that up out of whole cloth. You better control yourself," the deacon insisted.

Danzy was a man who loved and believed in white people. So I didn't argue with him. But that's the way the system worked. Reynolds came on with it first. Then he got a pillar of the black community to follow through on it, lock it in.

The manager at Cloverleaf Creamery questioned my father shortly after I came home. He wanted to know why I had studied law. My father said something noncommittal like "Well, I don't know. I reckon 'cause he wanted to be a lawyer." A few months later, a boy who cleaned the front office overheard the bosses talking about me and told my father. The bosses said the NAACP had sent me back to Selma and it wouldn't be good for the "other niggers" at the creamery for my father to be working there. My father came home and told my mother his days were numbered at Cloverleaf. When school let out that spring, reducing the creamery's milk business, the night shift was laid off. My father was the only worker not recalled.

The George Washington Carver Homes, where we lived when we came back from Washington, D.C. (© Penny Weaver)

I learned years later that the Dallas County Bar Association passed a resolution for one of its members to talk to the banks to make sure I wouldn't get a loan to set up a practice. The white lawyer who revealed this said the bar's opposition wasn't related to anything in particular its members thought or feared I would do. Just as they didn't want to drink at the same fountain with a black person, they didn't want a black lawyer in the same courtroom with them.

The resolution made no difference because I had no intention of asking for a loan. I had no collateral—I'd blown all the money I made in Washington—and I would not ask my parents to mortgage their home on something as risky as opening a black law practice in Selma.

Vivian and I and the children had moved into a three-bedroom apartment in the George Washington Carver housing project, a complex of brick buildings lined up like army barracks on a treeless block across the street from Brown AME Chapel. Vivian's

Edwin Moss in his Exalted Ruler regalia (© *Selma Times-Journal*, Selma, Alabama)

mother, Inez, lived with us to help with the children. Though it was not her preference, Vivian accepted our move back to Selma. She felt it probably was temporary, I'd get my fill soon, and we could move on to a larger city. I was not sure she was wrong.

I intended to practice out of the projects until I made some money to open an office. It turned out, though, that I did get a loan from the Elks Federal Credit Union, a new institution that had sprung up in black Selma while I was gone. It was started by the Fathers of St. Edmund as another outreach in the black community, though the man who ran it and made it go was Edwin Moss, and he's the one who offered me a loan.

While I was in Washington, Edwin, the jazz musician, had gone to work for the Fathers. He was in charge of their begging operation that sent letters to Catholics around the country. This was one of the best-paid jobs in black Selma, and the president of the Chamber of Commerce visited the Fathers to tell them they were paying Edwin too much. Edwin also had gotten himself elected Exalted Ruler of the Pride of Alabama chapter of the Independent and Benevolent Protective Order of Elks of the World, the largest black middle-class organization in Selma. The Fathers and the Elks gave Edwin a power base different from that of black preachers and school principals, and he began playing a unique leadership role in Selma.

He wasn't a race man in the sense of C. J. Adams or Sam Boynton. He wasn't pushing voting or the NAACP or any challenge to the system. But he wasn't downtown selling out black people in the Uncle Tom sense. He worked with the white leaders and within the system to do what he could for blacks and for himself. He was Selma's moderate black leader. Many times over the years, he and I would not see eye to eye. Yet he always helped me.

The Fathers' idea of a black credit union had a lot of appeal to Edwin. Running in essence a bank would extend his influence, and Edwin was interested in doing something so that no black person would lose his house when he had only $500 left to pay on it. Starting a black financial institution was difficult, though. The Catholics had to persuade a U.S. senator to intercede in getting a federal charter because some white moneylenders tried to block it. Also, some black folk didn't trust a black institution to handle their money or thought a little credit union was low-class. Preston was having similar problems selling shares in our Colored Merchants Association. Edwin showed up everywhere seeking deposits, even after poker games at the Elks, and he had the credit union off the ground by the time he offered me the loan and an office on the second floor of the Elks building.

The Elks building was a three-story red brick structure on Franklin Street in the main black business section downtown. On Saturdays, the sidewalks would be jammed with black people from the farms doing their weekly shopping. My office was on the second floor, along with a black dentist's. Upstairs was the Elks' bar and ballroom and, on the ground floor, a barbershop and beauty-supply business. On the same block were two funeral parlors, another dentist, a café and bar, and Sam Boynton's office.

It was a perfect location for me. Across the street was City Hall, a yellow brick building that housed the city and county jails and the police court. Next to it was a black community center where the farm folk hung out once they'd finished shopping. It was built in 1939 with federal money through the persistent efforts of C. J. Adams, Boynton, and a white Episcopalian minister, E. W. Gamble, who persuaded the city to donate the land. Until then, the country people had no place to go to the bathroom, nurse their babies, or get shelter in bad weather.

My first clients were people steered to me by Preston, mostly for wills and divorces, but there were also the drunks and petty thieves from the jail across the street. One serious consequence of being the only black lawyer was not having an experienced lawyer to attach myself to and learn from. I confined myself to the police and the Dallas County courts because they handled only misdemeanors that could always be appealed, so I could learn without doing anybody too much harm.

I was concerned about my inexperience and about how much a black lawyer could do for black people in the white courts. I was more willing to fight for them than most white lawyers were, but would this make a difference? Would they be better off with a white lawyer pleading their case? These were unanswered questions. I was breaking new ground.

My early cases involved only blacks and presented no threat to the status quo. Still, Hugh Mallory, the judge of the Dallas County court, was openly hostile. He'd snap at me and make little speeches: "I'm going to overrule you. No lawyer would come in here and even propose that," implying that I was only a sort of notary public.

The city court judge, Edgar Russell, Jr., knew my family. His father-in-law managed money for white widows and lent it, or part of it, to black people. My mother borrowed from him for the house and some of the money that sent me to school. Russell worked with his father-in-law, and he liked my mother and she liked him. He used to tell me all the time how much he admired her gumption. He was always bringing venison or fish to put in

PART TWO: 1958–1962

The famous Dallas County Courthouse (© Penny Weaver)

my parents' freezer. For years I wasn't my mother's lawyer; Russell was. She'd call him for legal advice.

In these black-on-black cases, Judge Russell treated me the same as he treated white lawyers with black clients. If I was representing someone proved guilty, Russell found him guilty. If I was representing someone who got arrested because he was black, without any real evidence against him, Russell often dismissed the case, usually with some explanation that allowed the prosecutor and the white arresting police officer to save face. "Well, it's a close call, but this time I'm going to find him not guilty."

In court, the lawyers stood around or sat at tables inside the wooden rail at the front of the room. The defendants and witnesses sat on wooden benches in the audience waiting for their cases to come up. There weren't any colored or white signs, but the blacks sat on the right side and the whites on the left. Since most of the accused and the witnesses were black, the right side always got full and blacks would start to fill up the back of the left section, always leaving at least two rows empty between them and the few white people even if that meant some of them had to stand.

At first, I didn't sit with the other lawyers inside the rail. I stayed with my client outside the rail until the judge called his case. I knew this made a bad situation worse. It emphasized I was different—not quite a real lawyer—and underlined the message judges sent by calling me "J.L." and the white lawyers "Mr." I also was aware that my prestige and practice would get a boost if I went up there where the white lawyers were. But I was afraid this would provoke a lot of needless trouble—an argument with a judge, possibly some kind of contempt charge that would have to be appealed and cost a fortune and probably be a losing battle anyway. That was an attack on segregation, and it wasn't worth it to me. I just didn't see sitting inside that railing with a bunch of Selma white lawyers as any great boon.

The majority of them looked on me as an unwelcome curiosity, some kind of pathetic notary-public joke. Representing people? A nigra? How's he gonna win a case? Nobody said that, but it was in their expressions and attitudes. Most were cold and kept their distance, but a few were not unfriendly. Harry Gamble, Sr., the son of the Episcopal minister who'd helped Boynton and Adams get the black community center, stopped me on the street to ask about my practice and give tips on legal procedure. He also gave me an outdated copy of the Alabama Code, my first law book.

I had long—and sometimes drunken—conversations about the law with T. G. Gayle, one of the defense attorneys I'd watched as a teenager. His wife had been burned to death in a fire at the country club. I don't think Gayle ever fully recovered. Many nights he'd be at a bootleg and barbecue joint run by a woman named Jelly. She was a cousin of Vivian's mother and her house was a clean, nicely furnished double shotgun by the railroad tracks. Gayle was as racist as any white Southerner but for some reason—I think because he loved talking about the law—he gave me all kinds of advice when I came in there.

We'd sit up talking till one in the morning, drinking whiskey and eating barbecue, and he'd say, "Well, in time they'll get used to you if you let them. But you've got to know how to act, and don't push too damn much." Other times he'd say, sadly, that he couldn't understand why it was so important that I practice law in Selma. What could I do around here anyway?

Gayle's advice about not pushing went right out the window when Peter Hall came back to Selma and tried a few cases. Just as Orzell Billingsley was his sidekick in Birmingham, I became his sidekick in Selma. I'd watch him, carry his books. It is really from Peter Hall that I learned how to try a case. He learned from Arthur Shores, of Birmingham, the first black trial lawyer in Alabama.

Peter showed me the crucial importance of dominating the courtroom. He was a master at that. No way was he going to sit quietly in the audience. He'd be inside the rail, damn near in the witness box, and would be insulted if anyone suggested he sit anyplace else. He wasn't about to wait his turn either. He'd walk up and ask the judge, "Where's my case on the docket?" If this was the city or Dallas County court, there might be fifty cases and Peter's might be number thirty-five.

"Well, Judge, I have to be back in Birmingham," he'd say. "You need to move this up." And they'd do it. Watching him taught me a whole lot about being aggressive, that if you take the step and take it with authority, more often than not those who want to oppose it are uncertain. If not given time to think, they'll likely back away.

White people respected Peter I think because of his ability and sheer arrogance. In his aggressiveness and mannerisms he had somehow risen above being black. I watched him talking with the judges, and it wasn't the condescending conversation—white judge to black lawyer—they had with me. It was two esteemed members of the bar speaking. Sometimes Peter would be talking about "those people," meaning black people. This bothered me, and I'd tell him, "Damn, Peter. You're acting like you're white." He'd tell me in some smooth words to go fuck myself. He knew what he was doing.

I ultimately came to the conclusion that this wasn't any Talladega bullshit of thinking white was superior. Peter basically didn't like anybody, black or white. He thought the whole human race was beneath him, a bunch of selfish, lazy connivers. He had no tolerance at all for human failings; if you were late or made

Peter Hall (© *Birmingham News*, Birmingham, Alabama)

a mistake, you were in for it. His standards transcended all standards. Though the white judges and lawyers treated him almost as if he were white, he wasn't that, or black either, but a third race of which he was the only member.

I think this sense of superiority was Peter's way of dealing with the predicament we were in. Anyway, he was the meanest man and the best trial lawyer I've ever known. He could discourse learnedly on the law and also tear some policeman's ass into small pieces in streetwise cross-examination. This was risky business in 1958. Often the witness against your client would be a policeman, and classically in the South, policemen were rednecks. The big thing they had going was being superior to blacks. The white lawyers, being from the country-club class, could attack their credibility. But if a black man did that, what would be their reaction and the reaction of the jury? Peter would come in on them in such a sophisticated way they wouldn't know what hit them.

Here's how far Peter transcended color in Selma, Alabama:

One night we'd been to the Chicken Shack, a little nightclub with food, liquor, a jukebox, and dancing. When we left and headed for the Elks, Peter was drunk and driving with his hat pulled down over his ears, so he could hardly see. Two blocks from the police station, he hit a fire hydrant. Water shot up in the air and firemen and police came running. When they recognized Peter, they just fixed the hydrant and hushed up the incident, the same way they would have had Tom Gayle been involved. Peter made no effort to hide what had happened and drove around the rest of the week with his front grille busted out.

I thought, Damn! Why have I been walking on cotton, afraid the sky's gonna fall in?

That was the end of my sitting outside the rail. Peter made clear that sitting inside was more than a matter of professional prestige or being where the white lawyers were. It was a matter of being where the *lawyers* were. It added to your stature and dominance and helped you get a jump on the other fella. It was strategically and tactically part of being a good trial lawyer. And nothing happened the day I did it, which reinforced Peter's lesson that aggressive acts almost always leave the opposition trying to figure out what to do.

From working with Peter and arguing cases half decently, I began to get a reputation as a fighter, someone not afraid of the police and judges. I was growing all the time, learning more about what was possible and not possible, wise and unwise. White lawyers began to show a grudging recognition that maybe I wasn't just a notary public. Also, I hadn't done anything yet to shake the foundations of the system, and their worst paranoid fears about me hadn't materialized.

My new status became obvious in a later conversation with Probate Judge Reynolds when he was being challenged for re-election by a lawyer from one of Selma's old families. Reynolds was the first probate judge in Dallas County who wasn't a member of the traditional ruling class and wasn't an attorney. This time he invited me into his inner office. "I really could use your help," he said, and named some of the handful of blacks, about 150 or so, who were registered to vote in Dallas County. He didn't say a word about our previous conversation or even acknowledge that it had taken place, and I sat there thinking about the arrogance of white men and the greediness of politicians. I told the judge that, frankly, I was more interested in his defeat.

"But why?" Reynolds asked. "My opponent is nothing but rich trash."

I responded that his opponent probably wouldn't go around making gratuitous assumptions that I would insult ladies, black or white. Reynolds looked perplexed and finally said, "Oh! You're going back to that old thing. Well, J.L., you were a colored lawyer coming in here and I didn't know you. I didn't know what kind of New York nonsense you were bringing here, and I wanted to avoid any problems for me or for you. The women here were nervous and I felt it was necessary to make them feel secure. But I didn't have anything against you. Since you've been here, all I have heard is that you conduct yourself as a gentleman. So far as I'm concerned, that old incident is history." He went on to name four or five blacks he wanted me to talk to on his behalf.

I said, "I don't think so, Judge," but he kept pushing. "Well, at least give me the courtesy"—that's the word he used—"that you will think about it." I made a beeline to the people he named and begged them not to vote for him. But he squeaked in and won.

The tense and dangerous reality of being a black lawyer in Selma didn't come home to me until I was faced with two desperate situations about a year after I came back. Two black people needed help in the worst way and their problems were brought to me, a brand-new black lawyer, because there was nowhere else to take them. Both situations involved black men, white women, and sex.

One afternoon, Reverend Charles A. Lett, pastor of the Green Street Baptist Church, and two of his Masonic brothers met me coming out of the courthouse. They'd been to my office with urgent business and the secretary had directed them there. They couldn't wait. One of Lett's parishioners and a fellow Mason was in terrible trouble, and they wanted my advice and help. The man's name was Johnson, and he worked as a chauffeur and handyman for a white merchant. He drove the man and his wife to the store, parties, business, wherever they wanted to go. The white fella was a lush, so when the black fella got him home, he'd sometimes have to undress him and put him in bed. Over time, a pattern developed where he and the man's wife would tuck the fella in, then go down the hall to her room and get in bed together. A few weeks earlier, the white fella either was playing drunk or wasn't as drunk as they thought. He surprised them and called the police.

The woman insisted she wasn't raped. Despite all the pressures on a white woman in this situation to claim rape, she refused to do it. So the police were in a quandary. Here they had an angry white husband who'd found his wife in bed with a black man. But the woman wasn't cooperating. Their response was to put Johnson in jail, allegedly for his protection.

Two or three weeks went by. Johnson remained in the city jail—not charged with anything, still "for his own protection." Wilson Baker had been speaking with the woman, trying to convince her to change her story. Baker, a police captain I first met one of the times I was taken to police headquarters with my fixed cards, had resigned a short time earlier to run for sheriff, but I guess had been brought back to question the woman; he was known for having a persuasive way with people. He apparently had been holding off the husband and others by arguing it would be best to run the man through the courts and let him go to the electric chair.

"Attorney Chestnut, can you help us? We're afraid Mr. Johnson won't make it through the night," Lett said. Through certain preachers and bootleggers who had a direct line to Baker, word was out that Baker had given up on the woman. Also, a group of men Lett said looked like Klansmen had gathered in front of the white merchant's store earlier that day. Lett and the Masons were certain something was going to happen.

Baker's efforts having failed, we were afraid he would turn Johnson over to Jim Clark, the sheriff of Dallas County, and get himself out of the way. In our minds, this would be the equivalent of giving Johnson to the Klan because it was widely believed that some of Clark's deputies were associated with the Klan, if not card-carrying members. I told Lett we needed to get his man out of jail that night.

As Lett and I were standing on the steps talking, Sheriff Clark drove up in his car. As always, he was dressed like General Patton—short haircut, spotless shoes, creases in his pants, pearl-handled pistols, dark glasses. I brought Lett over and introduced him to Clark as Johnson's pastor. I pointed out that Johnson wasn't charged with anything and told Clark that Lett and these men would like to get him out of jail.

"What are you going to do with him?" Clark asked.

"Send him someplace where he can find himself," Lett said.

Clark asked how we were going to protect him, and I said he couldn't be in any more danger with us than he was in the jail.

Clark shrugged—"Have it your way"—and walked on into the sheriff's office.

I had a feeling he'd rather pass on this one. With the woman unwilling to prosecute, it was an ugly and embarrassing situation. If Johnson was released while in Baker's custody, Clark could blame Baker—and they were bitter political enemies. Baker had just challenged Clark in the sheriff's race, and Clark barely won. Baker was smarter, better-educated, and supported by the older families and business people in Selma. But he got so hungry for votes he made a campaign appearance at a Klan rally outside town and lost the handful of black votes, along with the Jewish and Catholic vote. This was ironic because Baker, by Southern standards, was a moderate.

Lett and I and the Masonic brothers went immediately to the jail on the second floor of City Hall and told Baker we wanted to take Johnson out that night. I said we'd talked to Sheriff Clark and he'd said he had no problem with that. I was reasonably certain that Baker wanted to deal with Johnson lawfully—let the courts execute him—or not at all. By talking to the sheriff first, I hoped I was giving him an out to use with the husband: "Well, the sheriff didn't want him. He said it was my problem and I'm just going by the law." During Baker's years as police captain, though, black men had been shot and killed in the jail, so I didn't trust him to protect black interests in a situation where white passions were high. I told Baker—and Clark, too—that "people in New York" were taking an interest in the situation. I wanted them to think the NAACP was watching. Baker said we could take him. There was some question as to when would be the best time to do it. Our group went off into a little session among ourselves and decided on midnight, figuring there wouldn't be as many people around. That shows how inexperienced I was. Witnesses were what we needed.

That evening, Lett rounded up more Masonic brothers, about a dozen, and brought them to my office. We had a long, nervous wait until midnight—looking at our watches every two minutes, staring out the window at the jail, walking down to the corner to see if there was anything out of the ordinary going on outside. I hoped I'd provided both Baker and Clark with a way to blame each other. But I was gambling. I didn't know for certain what either one would do or whether someone else—some policeman or deputy sheriff—would get wind of the plan and tell the Klan.

At about quarter to twelve, Lett, the Masons, and I walked across the street and up the stairs to the jail. It was so quiet you could have heard a mouse sneeze. About four policemen were there. They went back to the cell block and brought Johnson out. We had five cars. Lett and I got in the first car with Johnson and one of the Masons. We were getting ready to lead the procession when somebody suggested we ought to be in the second car. So we moved back in the procession and headed to Montgomery across the Edmund Pettus Bridge and out Highway 80, the same route the civil rights march from Selma to Montgomery took six years later.

It was the darkest night, the loneliest night. I was more frightened than ever before in my life. All of us had guns except Lett, who came armed only with a Bible. I was wearing a pistol so large I had to sit sideways in the car. We had to go through Lowndes County—Klan territory. I half-expected some kind of shootout.

Every time we came to a curve or a hill, I had my hand on my pistol. Would the Klan be on the other side? But we got to Montgomery without incident and put Johnson on the bus for Detroit. It was twenty-five years later before I saw him again, one day when he stopped by my office to say hello. He said he just wanted to see Selma once more.

He was lucky to have lived to see anything. One word from the woman and he would have been electrocuted.

The second desperate situation occurred about a month later, when a pregnant, heavyset woman from the country came into my office so wrought up she didn't even sit down before she started talking. Her name was Mary Aaron.

"Mr. Chestnut, I don't have any money and cain't get anybody to help me. They're claiming my husband raped a white woman, and I know he didn't do it. He's not the type." She said she didn't even know where they'd taken him. She called the county jail and he wasn't there. She told me all the places she'd already gone for help—other lawyers, the Montgomery NAACP. She said if she couldn't get some help she didn't know what she'd do. She was afraid they were going to kill her husband outright in jail.

I tried to calm her, told her to slow down. She was talking fast and I was trying to get what facts she knew. But she wasn't even sure where the alleged rape had occurred, except it was in Montgomery in the area where her husband, Drewey, worked driving a truck for a quarry. I told her I'd take the case. If she hadn't been so desperate, I wouldn't have jumped in like that. I would have looked into it first. I didn't know whether the judge would be willing to appoint me if Drewey was declared indigent or how I would finance the case. It obviously would take up all kinds of time. It wasn't in Dallas County, where I was somewhat familiar with the system, but in Montgomery, where the aftermath of the bus boycott was lingering in the air. And I was just one year out of law school and hadn't tried but one or two minor cases before a jury. This was a capital crime involving the white South's racial obsession.

But it was obvious I was her last shot. I told Mrs. Aaron I wanted to get in touch with Solomon Seay, Jr., because we were going to need somebody who knew his way around the Montgomery courts. She told me she'd gone to Solomon and he said he was tied up. But he didn't hesitate when I called. I drove out to see Mrs. Aaron the next day—she lived in a shack in Lowndes County—to tell her Solomon and I were going to try the case together.

We found Drewey in a state prison. They'd moved him from the less protected county jail because men with guns started gathering outside. He said he didn't do it, said he was downtown trying to cash a check at the time the woman, a nurse, was raped. He was a large and quiet man who seemed mature beyond his years.

It was going to take money to track down witnesses and leads, and Solomon and I were getting just a pittance from the court. We thought we might be able to get help from the Montgomery Improvement Association since Solomon's father was a minister high up in that organization. Through him, we arranged a meeting with Martin Luther King, Jr., and Ralph Abernathy at the association's office.

We laid out what we knew about the facts: The victim had just come home from work and was out watering the lawn. She told the police she went back in the house, opened the closet in the nursery where her baby was sleeping, and a black man grabbed her and pulled her inside. A terrific struggle took place that broke out the wallboards of the closet. They fell on the floor of the nursery and wrestled some more until the woman became exhausted and he raped her. She called the police. Bloodhounds were sent out, but they lost the scent of the assailant.

Drewey was arrested in his truck a short distance away. The nurse was unable to identify him in a lineup, but a few days later they brought her to the prison and made Drewey repeat, over and over, the words the attacker had used during the struggle. That's when she identified Drewey as the man who had raped her. The police said Drewey had particles of wallboard in his trousers when he was arrested and scratches on his ankles.

Abernathy asked whether or not Drewey was guilty. I said I didn't think so but we really didn't know. "He says he's innocent, and if he is, we're gonna have a hell of a time proving it without funds." Of course, they knew the importance of a good defense went beyond guilt or innocence. King had led a demonstration in Montgomery a year earlier protesting the pattern of injustice against blacks in the courts. Solomon and I said the point was fighting for this man's life. Both Abernathy and King thought it unwise for the Improvement Association to involve itself in a criminal case. We couldn't raise money or interest from the NAACP either. Peter was too booked up to get involved, and we made the mistake of not presenting the case as one that raised larger constitutional issues. So Drewey Aaron wound up being represented by two green attorneys without a quarter, hardly, to build a defense.

But we went at it, and I learned what a traumatic experience a major trial is. It's a test of your knowledge and mettle, and the outcome means everything to your client. There was Mrs. Aaron, whose belief in Drewey's innocence never wavered, sitting behind him with their three young sons. There was the all-white male jury, the white judge.

For any objection we made, no matter how routine, the judge would ask for an explanation so the district attorney could oppose it. At one point, the DA and I got into a kind of parry and response. I had objected to something. The DA explained his basis. I came back and attacked that; then he came back and I came back until it became a battle of wits. The objection was now secondary. He was going to have the last word, to drive it to a point where I would be left without any response. I was determined this white lawyer was not going to do that to me. I didn't think his mind was quick enough or his tongue sharp enough. And I had the last word and won it.

My attitude was: "You white boy, you're no match for me. I won't even have to work up a sweat." And I didn't. Whether I'm immodest or not, it was clear in the opening arguments that he didn't have the verbal facility I do. Had I been white, he would have sought to avoid a confrontation. But because I was black, he couldn't admit I had any abilities superior to his, and he came right out with a direct challenge. So it delighted me to whip his white ass.

I learned something about white jurors, too—that a serious problem was their fascination with the novelty of a black lawyer. They tended to concentrate on Solomon and me more than on what we were saying. A black lawyer? Arguing with these white lawyers here? Cross-examining a white woman? I kept seeing frowns and expressions of disbelief. How do you communicate to them? I started drawing on my nightclub act—mother-in-law jokes or my wife this, or some kind of joke about myself that might humanize me in their eyes. "What a way to make a living! I could have been a teacher, better yet a preacher."

But that trial confirmed to me that all-white male juries simply were not compatible with justice where black people were concerned. Certain things they just would not listen to. A black person's word didn't carry the weight of a white person's. We put on several black alibi witnesses, people unrelated to Drewey who had no reason to lie and were mistaken at worst. One of the jurors literally turned his back on them and the others wore expressions of great disdain.

The jury was out about two hours. There wasn't any suspense for Solomon and me. We fully anticipated the verdict—guilty, sentenced to the electric chair—and were already planning our appeal during the deliberations. The basic fact of life for a black trial lawyer in Alabama in 1959 was the almost virtual certainty of losing at the trial-court level in any case involving race. There were black students in the 1950s who decided against going into law because they didn't have the temperament to always lose or the patience to wait for appeals.

That's where our chance was. Things were getting better all the time on the appellate level, with the Supreme Court breaking new ground. I knew not to envision the trial as the whole ball game. The hard part was explaining this to the defendant's family and making sure you got into the record at the trial the things you needed to build your appeal.

Solomon and I left the courthouse after the jury verdict and went to a bar called the Top Hat. Our routine that night did not vary one bit from what it had been on other nights. We knew what had to be done and were committed to doing our damnedest to pull it off. We'd made mistakes, but we'd given Drewey Aaron a decent defense. Solomon was a detail man, and we raised so many points in a series of appeals that the case was still undecided when the U.S. Supreme Court threw out Alabama's existing death penalty.

So we saved Drewey's life. And through that trial, I got a sense of what it was like in the Alabama courts, what the prosecutors and judges were really all about, and I was ready to take them on.

CHAPTER 7

Roadshow

In the early 1960s, Orzell Billingsley and I made forays into the rural Black Belt to try cases financed by the NAACP Legal Defense Fund. We'd go out there, argue a case, and raise a whole lot of hell—carry on for a week, file motions, and make statements unheard of in the little country courthouses. Our agenda was to have the kind of impact in the rural counties that Peter and Orzell had in Selma with the Fikes case. We were trying to put some brakes on the white powers, build backbone in the black community, and raise legal issues that might make law on appeal. With Orzell's fearlessness and my showmanship, we developed a reputation that anything might happen when we rolled into town in Orzell's light green Lincoln.

Most of our cases were criminal ones with a racial angle—a black man accused of some crime against a white person. There weren't yet the civil rights statutes of the mid-1960s—the Civil Rights Act of 1964, the Voting Rights Act of 1965—that provided the basis for many legal actions on civil rights since then. In the 1950s and early 1960s, the Legal Defense Fund raised civil rights and constitutional issues primarily in the context of criminal cases, and the Alabama Black Belt was fertile territory.

Even run-of-the-mill cases were pregnant with the possibility of making law. Policemen, sheriffs, deputy sheriffs were untrained and, when it came to black people, often unrestrained. So the

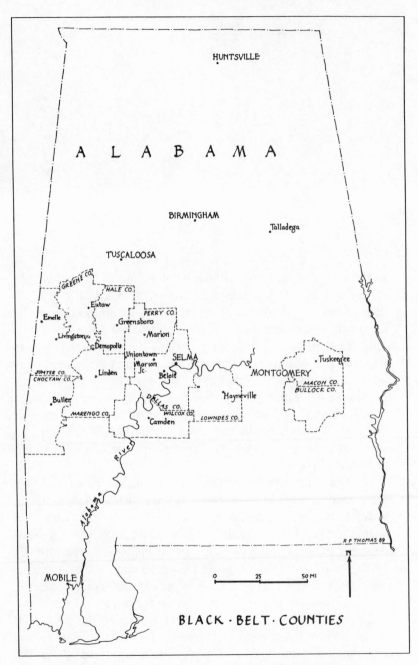

Map of Alabama showing the Black Belt counties (© Robert P. Thomas)

Orzell Billingsley (© *Birmingham News*, Birmingham, Alabama)

constitutionality of confessions, arrests, or searches and seizures could be questioned. Even without beatings or physical intimidation, the basic situation—the utter vulnerability of a black person brought in for questioning by a white sheriff—itself raised a doubt as to whether a statement or a confession was made voluntarily.

With my long-time interest in curbing the police, I took up this issue with great enthusiasm. Orzell and I and other NAACP lawyers throughout the South sent up a barrage of appeals based on arrests and confessions, trying to push the Supreme Court toward the decision it ultimately made in the *Miranda* case.

It also was obvious, from the Court's decisions against segregation in public education and transportation, that all-white male juries were on their way out. So the systematic exclusion of blacks from juries was a standard element in the trial and appeal of criminal cases financed by the NAACP. This was something black lawyers had a personal stake in seeing changed. You get damn sick of losing all the time and having to question whether your clients or potential clients would be better off with almost any white lawyer, even one who didn't know his way to the courthouse bathroom.

Peter had the contacts with the Defense Fund in New York but no interest in going out into the boondocks. He was as urbane as Duke Ellington. He'd stay in Birmingham, give advice, send in time sheets, and collect the money while Orzell and I went on the road and tried the cases. This wasn't an everyday thing. There were only so many cases the NAACP was going to finance, and it took a brave person or a desperate person to be willing to bring in the NAACP—not to mention two wild young men like Orzell and me, who were sure to maximize not minimize the case. But the brave and the desperate were out there, and about twice a month Orzell would swing through Selma and we'd head out to Perry, Greene, Wilcox, Lowndes, or Sumter County.

The Black Belt is beautiful country. The land has a gentle roll, lush and fragrant in the spring, with honeysuckle, wild plums, and berries; lazy and hot in the summertime, with blazing fields of cotton and soybeans, cows lying out under big shade trees, dragonflies flitting over fishing ponds and swimming holes, cicadas buzzing in the twilight. I liked to stop to pick wild plums—and also to go back into the woods to the hidden stills for corn whiskey so strong you could use it in your cigarette lighter.

The desperate human landscape, however, undermined our appreciation of the natural beauty. The days of picking cotton by hand were pretty much over, and many farms had switched from cotton to soybeans and cattle. But quite a few black people continued to live in falling-down sharecroppers' shacks on the edge of the white man's field—two or three rooms, cardboard in the windows, no plumbing—where a man and his wife, probably his mother-in-law, and six to ten children were crowded together.

All along the road, also, were little churches with all-day Sunday services and Wednesday-night prayer meetings. I've often thought these prayer meetings were in vogue in black churches

Children picking cotton in Dallas County (Courtesy of the Fathers of St. Edmund)

because living conditions were so hard we couldn't get enough relief on a Sunday to last until the next Sunday. We had to come back mid-week to refuel. Driving by these country churches at 6:30 Wednesday nights you'd think it was Sunday. Raggedy trucks, old smoky cars, and a few wagons would be parked outside, and we could hear the people singing and praying for the white man without calling his name: "Bless my enemies."

Of the county seats—Linden, Marion, Greensboro, Livingston, Hayneville, Camden—not one had a population over 6,000. Selma was progressive by contrast. These places had no Selma University or Concordia College, no Sam Boynton or C. J. Adams, no Voters League, no air base. They were typical-looking sleepy Southern towns—white community on one side of the tracks and black community on the other, in sections with names like Rabbit Yard or Foggy Bottom. All had some version of a courthouse square, with stores surrounding a courthouse that invariably had white columns and a monument to the Confederate dead.

When we drove up, we'd deliberately park the Lincoln in the sheriff's space and sit there awhile before we went in the court-house. Black people on the square would pass by, look, and it would lift them up a little bit. This not only sent a message to the black community, it was demoralizing and confusing to the sheriff. He'd figure, "Damn niggers pull up here in my spot. They're eager for a fight. That's flat NAACP. They're trying to set up something," and he'd be leery of making a move.

You'd hardly see a black person in the courthouse in those days. Those who were there paying taxes or buying auto tags would be looking down and speaking quietly, as if they were in a hospital. Orzell and I would come in loud, make an entrance almost like actors. This was something we'd picked up watching Peter, but we put our own twist on it. We were a lot more pro-vocative than Peter ever was. I'd carry on almost a nightclub routine with whatever black folk were in the hallway. "You mar-ried? To him? What you want with that ugly man?" If a judge or district attorney started lecturing me, I'd sometimes cut them off. "I don't care what you say. I'm gonna appeal anyway." Orzell was even more blunt. He'd tell a sheriff, "Kiss my ass."

Where Peter gave the impression of a sophisticated jazzman, Orzell's persona was more like that of a blues singer, earthy and direct. He was shorter, darker-skinned, and Negroid all the way. He'd graduated five or six years ahead of me at Howard. There was something fierce about Orzell's manner around white people, an intensity that made them uncomfortable. His very presence would be saying, "You racist son-of-a-bitch. You give me a chance and I'll fix you good." He was one of very few blacks then—or now—who would say to white people's faces exactly what he'd say about them in the company of only blacks.

Orzell would not be talking with white lawyers and judges about the law as Peter did, and he wouldn't be trading jokes with them as I did with Judge Russell and other white people with whom I had daily dealings. I don't think you could find a white person in the Black Belt who ever had an easy conversation with Orzell Billingsley. Yet the moment we'd cross the railroad tracks into the black community, a change would come over him. He'd relax. Around black people, he was easy to laugh, easy to smile, easy to know. Unlike Peter, he genuinely liked people.

Perry County, just west of Selma, was where we started and where we tried the most cases—from representing a kid accused of shoplifting at a white store to defending the owner of a black club who caught the white Coca-Cola deliveryman in bed with his wife and shot and killed him. But the case that excited us the most—the one we thought had the most potential for putting the system on trial—involved a white voodoo doctor folk called Doc Jones and a young black man named Lucius.

Doc Jones lived in a trailer in the rural part of Dallas County. He made his living sneaking onto the plantations in the Black Belt, presenting himself as a kind of witch doctor, and selling potions and spells to black country people. He would go down by the Alabama River, gather weeds and herbs, grind them up, and sell them as cures. He had a reputation for being very interested in young black girls. The white landowners didn't want him around, and some had threatened to fix him for good if they caught him back on their land bothering "my niggers."

Lucius grew up in a little house on a white man's land with his father, who was a sharecropper, his mother, and a younger sister. When he was about eighteen, his father died and Lucius did what many young men from rural Alabama were doing in that era. He went North, to Columbus, Ohio. He got a job in a rubber plant and saved his money to come back and get his mother and sister, who still lived in the little house in the white man's pasture in Perry County.

He decided to surprise them and showed up without notice, to find his eleven-year-old sister gone. His mother said the girl had been complaining of cramps in her stomach and Doc Jones, who'd happened by in his old truck, had taken her away to perform some ritual to get rid of the snakes and demons that were causing the problem. Lucius set out immediately to bring her home. He was angry. He found the trailer in Dallas County, banged on the door, and said he'd come for his sister. Doc Jones came to the door with a shotgun and ordered him off the place.

Lucius then went to the Dallas County sheriff's office to report what was going on. Jim Clark or a deputy told him he should have come to them first. It wasn't his damn business to be going around telling white men what to do. He'd best get his smart ass back to Columbus and they would see that the girl was brought back home that day. They put him on a Greyhound bus in Selma to go back to Ohio, but he got off the bus when it stopped in Marion, the seat of Perry County. He hid somewhere near his mother's house, waiting for the sheriff to bring his sister home so he could take her and his mother to Columbus.

Apparently, though, all the sheriff or deputy did was call Doc Jones and tell him to take the girl home. It was Doc who showed up with the sister while Lucius was hiding in the woods. Lucius was so outraged he jumped on Jones and beat the hell out of him. He had a rope and might have choked him to death if his mama hadn't been crying and begging him to stop.

Doc Jones drove straight to the Perry County sheriff's office and they came out and arrested Lucius. Lucius's mother went to the white landowner, who told the sheriff to let Lucius go without bond. He would guarantee the boy's presence at the trial. The sheriff agreed. This was a big landowner. The landowner told Lucius to go back to Columbus until his mother contacted him. He told the mother not to worry, he'd protect her boy. She just needed to be sure he came home for the trial.

What I found utterly fascinating when I learned of these events was the fact that the mother now refused to go with Lucius to Columbus. She wouldn't leave because she'd promised the white man her boy would come back to Perry County, and her staying would guarantee that. It made much more sense for Lucius to grab up his mother and sister, go North, and stay there, the way Shorty had when we put him on the bus to Detroit. If he didn't come back, Alabama was not going to spend a quarter or a stamp to get him extradited. But if he returned, his chance of getting a fair hearing before an all-white Perry County jury was as remote as Orzell's and my chance of winning a case there.

But Lucius's mother believed so implicitly in the landowner she couldn't see this. Undoubtedly, he had sent for the doctor when someone in the family was ill, probably got them clothes, maybe buried the husband. Large landowners generally worked their black families for a lifetime and the black families almost always died penniless. But the landowners would protect "their blacks" from the excesses of everyone but themselves, and folk like Lucius's mother relied totally on them.

A teacher in Perry County who knew and liked Lucius came to my office to discuss the situation. Unlike the mother, he was worried about leaving the boy's fate in the hands of the white landowner. He thought Lucius needed legal representation. Clearly, the landowner felt some obligation to the mother and didn't like Doc Jones. But how far he would or could go to protect Lucius was open to question, and it was conceivable that the boy would end up in the penitentiary. Here was a black man who'd whipped a white man and, in Alabama in 1960, that routinely took precedence over everything.

To Orzell and me, Lucius's predicament represented a chance to strike at the common practice in the South of selective prosecution—of seeing nothing but black wrongs. Time and time again, in situations involving black and white where both could be considered wrong, only the black was prosecuted.

We were prepared to argue, in Lucius's case, that he was denied the equal protection guaranteed by the Fourteenth Amendment. A white man had abducted a minor black child—no telling what he was doing with her in his trailer—and law enforcement refused to do anything except make a phone call and raise hell with the child's brother for trying to protect her. Then, when the black man got mad and whipped the white man, he was charged with assault and attempted murder. If Lucius had been white or Doc Jones black, everybody in Perry County, including the sheriff, would have thought Doc Jones got what was coming to him. And, of course, if a black man had taken off with an eleven-year-old white girl, there would have been hell to pay.

For our motion on unequal protection, I subpoenaed the clerk of the court to bring the records of any case in Perry County in the previous twenty-five years where a white man had been prosecuted for trying to protect a white female from a black aggressor. The clerk said there were none. I asked, then, if there were any cases where whites had been prosecuted or convicted of any crime against blacks. He was able to name about three prosecutions but no convictions.

The state put Doc Jones on the stand and read the statements Lucius and his mother had given the sheriff. Our defense was "irresistible compulsion." This is a concept in Alabama law that says a person is not responsible for an act if his mind snaps and he cannot resist the urge to commit the wrong. This provided a perfect mesh of defending an individual and trying the system because the very same circumstances—Doc Jones's reputation with young black girls, his taking the eleven-year-old sister to his trailer, the Dallas County sheriff doing practically nothing about it—supported both our scenario that Lucius snapped and our argument of unfair racial application of the law.

The courtroom in Perry County is a large, wide room with wooden seats for the audience that bank upward on a gradual incline as in a theater. There are entrances on both sides about halfway back in the seating section, which was nearly filled, as the trial progressed, by black people. I had never seen that many black people in the Perry County courthouse. They'd heard about us and were curious. Also, I think they figured coming to a trial involving a white man that powerful white men didn't like wouldn't get them in trouble with Mr. Charlie.

Partway through our case, just as everybody was returning from a break, I heard loud sounds coming from one of the entrances. I was at the counsel table and looked over to see Orzell standing in the door saying something obscene to the chief deputy—something to the effect that Doc Jones needed his damn white ass whipped and the sheriff and deputy needed their white asses whipped, too, and he, Orzell, was prepared to do it. The deputy said something profane back—"smart goddamn nigger"—and they kept at it. It was a big ruckus. All the folk there, especially the black spectators, were electrified.

Some of the jurors heard the argument and, on this basis, the judge declared a mistrial. I suspected he and the other white powers didn't like the ramifications of our case and were relieved to have a reason to stop it. The whole thing was having an effect on blacks different from what they had anticipated. Orzell had just told off the chief deputy and nothing happened to him. It was telling to me that the prosecutor never retried the case, which was a victory for Lucius but a big disappointment to Orzell and me. We wanted to put it all out there, appeal it, carry it as far as it could go.

So the Lucius case made no new law, but it did have local

impact. Several years later, when the civil rights movement spread out from Selma into the Black Belt, it took root first in Perry County. In my opinion, our cases helped create the atmosphere for this. The example of two black men walking around the courthouse without fear had to mitigate against the utter hopelessness that so engulfed black life. It also gave a presence to the NAACP Legal Defense Fund. It let black people know: You don't have to take *every* damn thing. Even down there in those fields, isolated, apparently at the mercy of white landowners, there is somebody else you can call on and, damn it, they will come.

Our intention also was to put white powers on notice that they could and would be challenged on at least some of their excesses. Our roadshow stirred them up, too. When we hit a courthouse for the first time and stopped in an office to look up records or a deed, we could be certain that within ten minutes some big, red-faced, tobacco-chewing sheriff would be there. He might or might not say anything, might just stand there and look while we went about our business with the expression: What are you niggers looking for? Who are you? Or he might ask. Often he'd follow us out of his county.

But the South is a peculiar place, full of contradictions, and there were all these personal relationships across racial lines. In Marengo County, the sheriff marched in while we were in the probate office searching records and told us, "We don't want no troublemakers in this county. We don't need no niggers like you here. I want you to get out of this county *now* and I don't ever want to see you here again."

Orzell and I said we had a right to search the records and we intended to do just that. The sheriff was stunned. We later learned he ran to the judge, who told him he couldn't do anything unless we broke the law but asked him to watch us. Who were we? The sheriff then spread out across the county, trying to find out what he could, and went to a black man he knew and trusted. I think they grew up together. This man knew my father, told the sheriff I was J.L.'s son, I was a decent fella.

Next time we were in Marengo, the sheriff told me, "The Dobys know you. I guess you all right." And his attitude changed. He wasn't exactly friendly. He was still the white sheriff and we were still blacks and, on top of that, lawyers. But he treated us with condescending acceptance and, in things noncontroversial, was even helpful. Here was a sheriff so racist he couldn't stand to have a black man down there searching the records. But there's another black man who could change his attitude by telling him, "He's all right. I know him." That's the South for you.

This didn't make us feel safer. In fact, these kinds of relationships added to my fears. For $25 or less, there was always some black out there, half crazy, who could come up and blow your brains out. Orzell and I were acutely aware that there were blacks in Alabama who felt they owed their very souls to white people and didn't owe any black anything, especially a black who whites didn't like. This was hard to guard against—somebody who might be laughing in your face one minute and shooting you in the second minute.

Alabama was extremely tense. In 1961, when we were riding around the Black Belt in Orzell's Lincoln, trying cases, the Freedom Riders were traveling Greyhound and Trailways through the Deep South to force compliance with a court ruling that outlawed segregation in bus terminals. In Alabama, they were met by vicious white mobs everywhere they went. Someone put a bomb on a bus in Anniston, and the injured were refused treatment in the local hospital. "Bull" Connor, the police commissioner in Birmingham, allowed the Klan fifteen minutes to beat up the Freedom Riders before his police force arrived at the terminal. It was Mother's Day, and he said his men had been visiting their mothers.

Our little cases were about the only civil rights things going in Marion or Eutaw or Livingston, and these were Alabama's citadels of racism. These were places the black majority would control if ever allowed to exercise equal power. The white minority knew what was at stake. So we went out there with a sense, always, that anything might happen.

We'd be coming out of the courthouse in the late afternoon. Often a bunch of rednecks would be standing there with the sheriff, who'd roll his eyes as we walked by. Were they the Klan? Would they follow? I wanted a pack of cigarettes, but was it wise to stop in this white-owned country store?

I carried a German pistol, which had been modified to a .38 when I was in the army, in a shoulder holster made at a shoe shop in Washington. Orzell had a .38, too, and we lived with a sense that each day could be our last. We weren't gripped by fear, though. It didn't consume us. Orzell was not the kind of man who frightened easily or panicked. His attitude was: What I'm doing is right and I'm not going to give an inch. He exuded confidence. And, going back to my gambling arrests, I experienced fear, but it wasn't immobilizing. We were uptight, yes, but our fear was sublimated by anger and there was excitement in what we were doing. It was an adventure. We were young men, we were shaking things up, and we were drinking a lot of whiskey and having fun in the process.

Sometimes we'd give the impression we'd left town, but actually we'd circle back to some schoolteacher's house. Every place we went, we'd meet a few teachers and other young people we felt we could trust and who wanted to party. To them, we were an event—black lawyers who rolled up in a Lincoln and were the nervous talk of the town. We brought a sense of excitement that broke the routine of everyday life in a small Southern town, and there were always some female teachers who wanted to be part of that excitement so long as there wasn't too much risk.

Schoolteachers were the most educated black people around, but were as vulnerable as sharecroppers since their jobs were in the hands of the white school board. At that time, their future was uncertain. If and when the schools were desegregated, where would they be? The governor and other white leaders were going around telling black teachers they were going to lose out if integration came. And they were isolated. The older teachers were so much a part of the system they were part of the problem. The younger ones had been exposed to different ideas at college and also to fraternity and sorority life. Then, suddenly, they're back in little old Hayneville or Eutaw. Orzell and I provided a kind of relief for them, as they provided relief for us.

These teachers had nice houses—carpeting on the floor, immaculately clean, and, invariably, a piano. Somebody would bring a bottle of whiskey, and we'd play some music, sit around, drink, and have a lot of fun. Sometimes the conversation would get serious. There'd be talk about the Freedom Rides, sit-ins, and other things going on in the cities, and a discussion would begin on whether black people would have to get guns and kill some people. Then somebody would go play the piano or change the subject because the talk was affecting the whole mood.

It was not unusual for Orzell to leave with one of the teachers. He had a considerable appreciation of female beauty, and the Black Belt had plenty of that. Perry County, in particular, was known for its beautiful women—meaning, in that era, light-skinned women. Coretta Scott King, Andrew Young's wife, Jean, and Ralph Abernathy's wife, Juanita, grew up in Perry County. When I was young, boys were always trying to hitch a ride to Uniontown or Marion to go see the "pretty girls." I don't know why there were so many light-skinned women in that county except, obviously, a hell of a lot of miscegenation went on there, going back to the days when the plantation owners had relationships with their favored house slaves.

I could take it or leave it and, mostly, I left it. To go into a town, meet a woman I'd probably never see again, pile up, sweat, did not appeal to me. I would much rather find a joint where folk were drinking, and sit around and trade lies. But not Orzell. If somebody was on our tail when we left town, it was as likely to be an irate husband as the sheriff or the Klan.

Orzell had traveled the back roads of the Black Belt so often he could go from county to county almost without emerging from the woods. He knew all the cow paths. And he could sense danger. On more than one occasion, I'd suggest we stop at Big Ed's or some other bootleg joint on the way back to Selma and Orzell would agree. But when we got there, he'd say, "Well, I think not." The next day we'd learn the place had been raided or somebody had been there looking for us. I learned to respect Orzell's warnings that "We ought to leave now" and "Let's not stop there" and, about some seemingly friendly black, "I don't trust that son-of-a-bitch at all."

But if I'd had only Orzell and myself to rely on, I don't think I would have taken so many chances. I was relying on God. It wasn't that I rode around having profound religious thoughts about the Lord seeing me through. But that is what I sincerely believed. All around me all my life black folk have held on because of an unshakable faith that things will work out, give the Lord time. This faith provided strength in what appeared to be a hopeless situation, and black life was full of accidents and coincidences that could not be explained. You can't live around that and not be affected. I reached a point where I was not interested in any rational approach to God because I saw what faith could do. I saw a whole folk sustain themselves with nothing more, hardly, than that, and this gave me courage. I felt that when the time came and I was face to face with death, I'd be in God's hands one way or another.

That time came, not surprisingly, in Lowndes County. The civil rights workers who came to Alabama a few years later considered Lowndes and neighboring Wilcox County the most resistant and violent in the state. Viola Liuzzo, a white Detroit housewife, would be shot to death in Lowndes County after the Selma to Montgomery march, and Jonathan Daniels, a young white Episcopal seminary student from New Hampshire, would be killed in Lowndes County while helping with black voter registration. That was the climate.

My client that particular day was a black sharecropper. He had wanted a place of his own as he got older, and the white man whose land he worked had sold him a little parcel, two or three acres, and deducted so much out of his portion of the yield to pay for it. That had been going on for a number of years, but the sharecropper never got a deed. Then the white man died. His son took over the farming operation and gave the sharecropper so many days to vacate because he wanted to use the land as pasture. The old man had built a little shack on the property, his family lived there, and he was scared to death. He came to my office, crying, and I filed a lawsuit. The case had no NAACP issues and wasn't complicated legally so I didn't get Orzell down from Birmingham.

The sharecropper gave me the names of black people who knew about his arrangement with the deceased white man, and I had a subpoena issued to about ten of them. The sheriff's office issues subpoenas, and a deputy went out and delivered them. Right on his heels was the sheriff, who told my witnesses they didn't have to come to court and he didn't want them there. My client told me what was going on, so I went around to each of these blacks' little shacks the day before the trial and told them they had to be there. They were telling me what the high sheriff said, and they were scared. I was telling them they'd been subpoenaed and the judge would put them in jail if they didn't show up.

My father decided to come with me to the trial. He said he wanted to watch, but I think he was concerned about my safety. We picked up about half the witnesses. The others we couldn't find. Then we drove on into Hayneville to the courthouse, a decaying white building with the inevitable columns that sat on one side of a grassy square with the inevitable Confederate monument.

The courtroom was straight out of *To Kill a Mockingbird*— plank floors, tall windows, and a cage across one corner where they put prisoners awaiting arraignments. The windows were kept open in the summertime because there wasn't any air conditioning, and sometimes insects would come in and bite the jurors or birds would fly in and circle around the high tin ceiling.

An unusual number of people were around that day because county health officers were inoculating dogs for rabies behind the courthouse. My father stopped to see if there were any coon dogs he could buy cheap. My client, the witnesses, and I went on into the courtroom. The sheriff walked right up to me with a scowl on his face. He was a typical-looking Alabama sheriff—big man, paunch hanging over his pants, star on his shirt, Western hat.

"Once I tell my niggers they don't have to come to court, I don't want no other niggers goin' round tellin' em they have to come," he said.

A criminal case had just been tried in the courtroom and an ax handle used as an exhibit was lying on the prosecutor's table. When I started complaining to the judge that the sheriff had been telling my witnesses to ignore subpoenas, a clear violation of law, the sheriff grabbed the ax handle, said, "You son-of-a-bitch!" and drew it back. I froze in fear and anger. I knew if I made one step back or forward he was going to knock the hell out of me.

My father walked in to see this frozen scene: The sheriff standing with the ax handle drawn back and glaring at me. Me staring at the sheriff, unblinking. The judge smiling uncomfortably from the bench. The audience sitting motionless and silent. The only sound in the stunned courtroom was the yelping and barking of the dogs outside. My father stopped in the doorway, and a split second later, the sheriff lowered the ax handle and moved back two steps. It looked as if he'd lost his nerve. He walked out cursing, almost dragging the ax handle on the floor.

I expected to have to appeal, but I won the case right there in that little county courtroom. The blacks who had come to testify did so without hesitation and left the courtroom walking tall. I guess everyone around the courthouse that day heard what had happened because when we came out, a crowd of black people were standing in the little park in front of the Confederate monument. They clustered nervously around us, seemed like they wanted to hug us and clap.

With the attention we aroused with the legal cases, Orzell tried to fuel his larger agenda. Everywhere we went, he talked about organizing and a new day. He wasn't speaking in terms of massive demonstrations or marches. His interests were economic development and politics.

All through the Black Belt there were concentrations of black people in villages that were not incorporated. By incorporating as towns, they could establish their own little governments, get a share of state money for water lines and sewers, and, in the later 1960s, federal grants. As the lawyer handling the incorporations, Orzell made money. The people in these little towns— Forkland, Roosevelt City, Bogue Chitta, White Hall, Memphis— got running water and some power over their lives. Some of the first black elected officials in Alabama were mayors of the all-black towns Orzell incorporated.

Orzell also was a founder and president of the first statewide black political organization in Alabama. In this, as in so much else, he was ahead of his time because this organization came into being before the Voting Rights Act. In 1960, Louis Martin, a black newspaper publisher active in the Kennedy campaign, organized a caucus of Southern black leaders in Atlanta to talk about what they could do to help the Kennedy–Johnson ticket. The Kennedys figured black people would not be likely to vote for the Republicans, and Martin's trip was part of their effort to promote black voter registration. Other Democratic candidates had sought the black vote but hadn't sought to increase it. The Kennedys were hungry for every vote they could get.

The caucus in Atlanta was one of the first times in the South that whites expressed anything positive about blacks getting involved in the political process. The Alabama delegation was Orzell, Peter, and Arthur Shores from Birmingham, C. G. Gomillion, chairman of the political science department at Tuskegee Institute, and Rufus Lewis, a businessman in Montgomery. Martin asked each state's delegation to do what it could to get more blacks registered and to the polls to vote for Kennedy.

Of all the states involved, Alabama's delegation not only took up Martin's charge but formed the Alabama Democratic Conference (ADC), a statewide network of local voters leagues and improvement associations that lasted beyond the Kennedy election. After the Voting Rights Act was passed and thousands of blacks got registered, ADC gave the black vote in Alabama an organized impact, and it became the most powerful statewide black political organization in the country.

While I was running around with Orzell and Peter in the early sixties, the ADC's stronghold was Birmingham. I'd go to meetings and come in contact with the shrewdest black leadership in Alabama. A few white Democrats sometimes met with us to promote certain candidates. This was striking to me—white men talking politics with black men. Birmingham, for all its racism, was distinctly different from Selma and the Black Belt.

Out on the road in the Black Belt, Orzell was always promoting ADC. "You need to form a chapter. You need to go after the vote." This was part of the new day he talked about. He wasn't bringing this so much to the schoolteachers as to the poor, uneducated folk in overalls. Though he was a lawyer, he was genuinely at ease with them. He'd talk at length and at their level without an ounce of arrogance or condescension, and they'd respond in kind. Orzell's weakness was that he didn't follow through. But I was learning something about my region and my people—how you build a law practice, how you become a politician, how you sell blacks on a cooperative venture, and how you motivate and lead people on the bottom rung of a despised minority.

Most blacks who went to college and came back weren't trying to relate to this group, as they aren't today. The middle class is here and the underclass is there. Orzell was going in the opposite direction, and the importance of that, even now, is apparent. He was putting into practice, in 1960, what Shields had said: "You will never rise by yourself. You've got to bring the group with you."

CHAPTER 8

Sinking Pretty Low

George Wallace was the first judge to call me "Mr." in a courtroom. This was in Barbour County in late 1958, when Wallace was circuit judge. I was helping Peter Hall represent a group of poor black cotton farmers who had been fleeced by one of the largest cotton-oil-processing companies in the South. The company brought several smooth big city lawyers down from Birmingham who were not only eager to use subtle racist ridicule on us and our clients but sought to overwhelm us with the technicalities of the law.

One of the Birmingham lawyers had a particularly disgusting and scornful way of referring to our black clients as "these people." Every time he used that phrase, Wallace got red in the face and looked with some sympathy toward our clients and us. Finally, he told the lawyer, "Please refer to Mr. Hall's and Mr. Chestnut's clients as the plaintiffs or don't refer to them at all." His voice was ice cold.

We won every case. Wallace was sitting as judge and jury, and he awarded our clients more money than we had asked for. George Wallace was for the little man, no doubt about it. But what he wanted more than anything else was to be governor. When he ran in 1962, campaigning on Segregation Now! Segregation Tomorrow! Segregation Forever! and vowing to stand in the schoolhouse door, I considered him a dangerous and unprincipled opportunist, willing to destroy Alabama to promote himself.

Wallace reinvigorated white Alabama's resistance. Each September since I'd been back, another school system in the South had been forced to desegregate—Little Rock, Richmond, New Orleans. Wallace was elected the fall the courts ordered the University of Mississippi to admit James Meredith, when riots broke out and the Kennedys sent in the National Guard. The walls of Jericho were beginning to crumble and up stepped Wallace saying, "Don't worry, folks. We'll hold the line. I am the man to do it." These claims stiffened white resolve, and the atmosphere became more tense and the potential for violence a notch greater.

In Selma, the Wallace phenomenon was clearly in evidence. Sheriff Clark put out a call for able-bodied white men to help him deal with so-called emergencies. Three hundred showed up to be part of his posse. Country men with horses became the "mounted posse"; others were the "walking posse." Though some professionals and landowners belonged, the posse men for the most part were of a lower class than the White Citizens' Council. Clark and the posse would show up at sites of civil rights activity— Oxford, Mississippi, when James Meredith enrolled; Birmingham when Martin Luther King was there—to support the forces of white resistance.

From my vantage point, the white community in Selma was reacting to phantoms and in every way oversensitive because there was no counter-development I could see in the black community. It seemed to me they were engaged in a paranoid obsession similar to their belief that white women were in danger from black men. When I looked at the black community, I didn't detect any threat to white women or to segregation. The posse was organized to head off an assault that wasn't developing in black Selma any damn way.

In Selma in 1962, no black institution or organization, with the exception of the little Dallas County Voters League, was promoting civil rights or organizing black people around any goal except going to heaven, providing a decent education, or having a good time—not the clubs or fraternities, not the churches, not Selma University, not the black teachers' association. The

Selma's black elite in the 1950s (© E. W. Williams)

NAACP was banned statewide, and the local chapter already was demoralized by the fallout from the unsuccessful petition to integrate the schools.

At the bootleg houses, the clubs, the Elks, Selma University, we would occasionally discuss the public issues of the day. It was frustrating to listen to the pessimistic theme song: "These folk here won't get together. They won't take a chance." In a way, it was more difficult arguing about oppression with black people than it was with white people—and a whole lot more discouraging.

My favorite hangout at that time was James Porter's, a white frame house in east Selma. It was much smaller than the Elks club—a modest-sized living room with two couches, a television, and a piano, and a smaller room off to the side with booths where people played cards. It wasn't a dive. On Wednesday afternoons, when Selma's shops and offices closed, you could find one hundred years of college education out at Porter's place. Folk enjoyed Porter, a slender black man with a deliberately refined way of

The house on Eugene Street where we lived in the 1960s and early 1970s
(© Penny Weaver)

Formerly, the Chicken Shack, one of my favorite hangouts (© Penny Weaver)

speaking who was known for singing "Danny Boy" in an Irish tremolo. I liked him because he didn't hesitate to speak his mind. He was a character.

Sometimes I would argue a point as hard at Porter's as I would in court. I would be trying to prove that while some particular case—like those that outlawed the all-white Democratic primary in Texas—had been decided elsewhere, the court's decision opened a door nationally. "I don't know about Texas, but I don't see any doors opening in Selma. Do you?" That's what I'd hear. Many black people in Selma thought and talked only in terms of what George Wallace or white people in Selma were going to permit. They thought the state of Alabama was more powerful than the federal government. I'd say, "In the ultimate analysis, it's not so much what George Wallace will accept as what Washington will put on his ass."

My concern was whether federal power would be exercised against Southern whites on behalf of blacks, and on this score, in 1962, I was only slightly less pessimistic than the people I was arguing with. I was glad Kennedy was President instead of Richard Nixon, but both Jack and Bobby seemed far more interested in appeasing powerful Southern senators than in pressing the cause of black people. I didn't think anything of great consequence would come out of the White House or the Justice Department.

My pitch was how we could improve our own lot economically and any other way that was reasonably open. How long were we going to sit down here in this unreal, degrading, insulting society and do nothing except have annual dances and picnics?

Preston and I had hopes that the student sit-ins and boycotts elsewhere would raise the consciousness of blacks in Selma—give some sense of how important their dollar was and how they could make it speak for them. We saw economic development as a natural consequence. It was all right to argue with a white man over whether you could buy a twenty-five-cent hamburger from him, but a better response was to prop up black businessmen and buy hamburgers from them. We were very concerned that not one of the black cab companies that sprang up in Montgomery during the bus boycott survived after seating on the buses was integrated.

We'd go to the Elks, church meetings, Selma University, trying to sell people on economic development: Invest in shares in our black grocery association. Let's put together a black department store, black supermarket, black whatever. By then, Preston had given up gambling and had become a deacon in the Green Street Baptist Church. He said he concluded that money ill-gotten never served any useful purpose since everything he'd won in his years of gambling had come almost to naught. He still worked for the E. F. Young cosmetics company, but because he wasn't gambling anymore, he was anxious to start an enterprise in or near Selma and not have to spend so much time on the road.

At that point, we'd had a setback in our grocery association plan because we hadn't cleared it with the state securities commission. We had to start all over selling shares, and this made black people more skeptical about black enterprise than they already were. We couldn't get anything moving.

When I came back to Selma, I didn't expect or want to be part of the white world. But I hadn't anticipated I wouldn't be quite part of the black world either. It wasn't that I was an outsider. There was a quiet pride in the fact that a black lawyer was in Selma, and this was enhanced by the fact I was from Selma and my family was here. It wasn't that I didn't enjoy the company of friends or they mine. When I got into theatrics, making jokes, recalling funny incidents at Payne School or Knox Academy, I would be the center of attention. A lot of blacks delighted in having these kinds of conversations with me. The whole Elks membership were people I could kid around with and have fun.

But this was somewhat superficial. In order to feel at home and at ease, I had to stay away from certain subjects. It's not a total but a deadly sort of isolation when your values are different from those around you. I didn't give a damn about hunting or how the local football and basketball teams were doing, and I was bored to death with pussy conversations. Talking about who was screwing whom was a primary pastime at places where black men got together. How many times can you seduce Ella May and how long will it remain news when she has screwed practically everybody in Selma?

Now and then someone would tell me, "I'm with you come

Sam and Amelia Boynton and their two sons (in the
1930s) (Courtesy of Amelia Boynton Robinson)

hell or high water. You stand up." But this was bar talk. Nobody
wanted to get into a conversation about actually doing something.
Whenever I pursued meaningful discussions, I made people uncomfortable and nervous. Some were job protecting, had relationships with white people, or didn't want to talk about anything
controversial because they didn't know what other blacks would
report back to white people. Besides, they'd gone to the Elks or
wherever else to have a good time. The upshot was, I felt lonely
in my own hometown.

The sole headquarters for civil-rights-type activities in Selma
was Sam Boynton's office, and in the early 1960s I moved my law
practice over there. It made sense to share a secretary and be at
the hub, such as it was, of progressive black activity. The office

was narrow, long, and unremarkable. In the front, a receptionist's desk faced the door. There was a book rack filled with dusty magazines, farm publications, and NAACP bulletins along one wall between the reception desk and the door. Along the wall on the other side was a small couch. I used a desk in the middle section, separated from the reception area by a divider that went halfway up to the ceiling. The largest portion of the office was a separate back room that had a desk, a big table, and a number of chairs. This was where the Dallas County Voters League met. Cheap linoleum covered the floors, and the place was hot as hell in the summer.

Boynton had retired as agricultural extension agent. He and his wife had three or four businesses going, including selling insurance for a black company and buying and selling real estate. Boynton had more outside contacts than any other black in Selma. Besides his business and NAACP connections, anthropologists studying black folk culture would stop by his office for leads to the country folk and Tuskegee often sent Africans who were visiting America to learn new farming methods over to see Boynton in Selma.

By the time I moved in, Boynton had curtailed many of his activities. He had high blood pressure and had suffered a series of strokes. He liked to sit up in the front, on the couch, to look at the people walking by and talk to those who stuck their heads in the door to say hello. Sometimes I'd sit up there with him and he'd reflect on his life. He talked about first coming to Dallas County, going about his job, and how white people wanted him to be what he wasn't and never would be. He said he realized early on that, much as he liked Selma, it was going to be a troublesome place for him. And it turned out that way.

As with C. J. Adams, Boynton's dignified manner was considered "uppity" and drew hatred from the white side. One time—I wasn't there—a white insurance agent, an old man who sold a lot of policies in the black community, came in and started beating him with a walking stick. Mrs. Boynton fought the man off and became the talk of the town. Also like Adams, Boynton was indicted—for fraud involving a bankrupt insurance company in Texas. He never was brought to trial, but the indictment was reported in the newspaper and caused him considerable embarrassment. He was aggressive in business and the owner of quite a bit of property, so all sorts of rumors and jealousies about him and money circulated in black Selma.

He wasn't dissatisfied with his life, though. He had helped blacks where they were—on the farm. Some who had been sharecropping now owned land because of him. Others now owned a few head of cattle or hogs. But he was sad that so little progress had been made in bringing black people out of our subhuman status.

Though ill, Boynton remained president of the Dallas County Voters League. In my view, the league was little more than a forum where a handful of people would discuss the importance of getting more black people registered to vote, debate various ideas about how to accomplish this, and then go home. It was a confidence builder more than anything else where people came together and agreed not to give up the ship. About 150 blacks were registered voters and 10 to 15 came regularly to meetings of the Voters League.

The legal requirement for becoming a registered voter in 1962 involved passing a test on the U.S. Constitution and Alabama law, but the surest way for a black person to get registered was to have a voucher. At least half the black registered voters in Dallas County and half the Voters League membership had been vouched for by a white person—the school superintendent, a banker, an employer—or a certain select black. This meant these blacks were considered no problem by the white community, which became a problem for the Voters League. Though they weren't for giving up the ship, they weren't for rocking the boat. Their suggestions centered on which white people might vouch for a few more of us.

A half dozen younger people, along with Boynton and his wife, were more aggressive. They were Ernest Doyle and J. D. Hunter, the veterans who'd been involved in the NAACP; James Gildersleeve and Ulysses Blackman, brothers-in-law who taught at Concordia College; Marie Foster, a dental hygienist; and Frederick Reese, a science teacher at Hudson High School, the school built to replace Knox the year after I graduated. Why these particular individuals—and not others—became the ad hoc civil rights leaders is hard to say. With the exception of Reese, the one thing they had in common were incomes less dependent on white Selma than most other black people.

Reese was my age. He had attended Knox Academy and Alabama State University. He was a serious young man with leadership abilities, and when he returned to Selma to teach, he quickly became president of the black teachers' organization. He really pushed the teachers to register to vote. I think John Shields, with his talk about the absurdity of teaching civics and being unable to vote, put a burning on Reese's ass the same as mine. Reese was and is a proud man, and he took personally the denials and degradations of segregation, especially when they were directed at intelligent black people with education. He was very sensitive to the situation captured in the joke: What do you call a colored man with a Ph.D.? Answer: A nigger.

The one action of the Voters League during this period was Marie Foster's citizenship class, which illustrated our problems and the hopeful persistence of Marie in forging ahead anyway. Marie was and is an absolutely determined woman, fiery, willing to take on the whole structure whether it made sense tactically or not, absolutely bitter toward white leaders at the courthouse, and emotionally and personally involved in registering black people. It deeply angered Marie that married black women like her mother were not addressed as "Mrs." in person or in the newspaper or telephone directory. To her, this was humiliating, denying black women the dignity and protection of marital status. I considered this practice more disgusting than humiliating. It reflected more on the newspaper and on white people than on Vivian, my mother, or Aunt Lennie. I was interested in being called "Mr." by a judge for tactical reasons since juries often look to a judge for a signal of his preference and being J.L. when the opposing lawyer was Mr. put me on a lower level. Otherwise I couldn't have cared less.

Marie was a widow with three children. She worked as a hygienist for her brother, Sullivan Jackson, a dentist whose office was over Boynton's. Through her day-to-day associations with the Boyntons, she got interested in voting and the Voters League.

For almost ten years, she took the registration test and always "failed one or more pertinent questions," as the rejection form read. But she's the sort of person who never gives up. She kept taking the test again and kept coming to the Voters League meetings with yet another plan about how to increase voter registration.

Marie correctly diagnosed a serious problem—that few black people in Dallas County were even attempting to get registered. Many were afraid and were skeptical about the importance of the vote anyway. But even folk who recognized its importance felt hopeless about passing and some were embarrassed about failing. Grading was so arbitrary that some teachers with master's degrees failed while some barely literate blacks with vouchers passed, along with nearly all the whites. This embarrassed some teachers so much that if they attempted to register at all they tended to keep this a secret until they passed.

I had gone down to the registrar's office soon after I returned home in 1958. My intention, really, was not to get registered but to get turned down. In my somewhat naïve, gung-ho-ness as a new black lawyer, I saw myself as a perfect test case—a law-school graduate who knew a lot more about the Constitution than the people giving the test. Here was something to put my name on the map in a hurry, help me build a clientele. So I purposely dressed down—wore khaki pants, an old T-shirt, tennis shoes, and a baseball cap.

When I went in, this old fella—who I later saw on every other jury; they called damn near the same group of white men as jurors every time—gave me a questionnaire and a look of curious disdain. I was delighted with his attitude. I thought, This ignorant old coot will make the best possible witness. Hell, he may become the unwitting father of black voting in Dallas County. On the space for employment on the application blank, I wrote *Soon*. I didn't have an office yet. I completed the written questionnaire pertaining to government. Then the old fella asked me some questions about the Constitution. The one I remember is: "How are the constitutions of the United States and Alabama the same?"

I said, "They both remain unenforced and floating in the same sea of hypocrisy." I think he liked the roll of the words. He looked at me and smiled, "Professor, you qualify." I was so taken aback and dejected I didn't know what to do.

Such casualness was out by 1962. The hold-the-line mode of white Selma meant the tests were harder and the registrants watched more closely. In this atmosphere, fewer blacks than ever went to the courthouse to even give it a shot, which was Marie's concern.

The Voters League had copies of some of the written tests, which were changed monthly. Marie thought if the league sponsored a series of citizenship classes where people could see the tests and practice taking them, they'd be more willing to go to the courthouse and give it a try. We all said, "Great idea," when she proposed this at a league meeting. The next Sunday, she drove around to all the major black churches in Dallas County to announce the first class—and exactly one person showed up. He was an old man, Major Washington, who couldn't read or write. It is an example of Marie's indomitable spirit that she stayed with him until ten o'clock, taught him to write his name, and continued to hold the classes.

Boynton was always talking about a lawsuit to challenge the practice of vouchers and discrimination on the test. This was going to take money and expertise we didn't have, but he finally persuaded the Justice Department to file one. U.S. District Judge Daniel Thomas in Mobile took it under advisement—his standard response to civil rights litigation—and the case languished.

Every so often somebody in the Voters League would suggest going door-to-door, but nobody actually did because it was pretty much a useless activity. The meetings were kind of unreal. We would sit there and discuss plans as if we were going to go out and implement them, as if they had some chance of success. Everybody had to understand—though nobody said it—that this was wishful thinking. I thought it rather remarkable that these people could keep on meeting faithfully once a month to discuss the impossible.

If anyone had told me then that this little group sitting around that dingy office, debating how to add a couple more names to the voter rolls, was in a sense the genesis of a movement that would win the right to vote for blacks all over America, I would have said not just "You're dreaming" but "You're crazy." I did not foresee that at all, though I attended virtually every meeting.

In fact, I saw little on the horizon in Selma. When I first came back, I was looking forward and had some hope. In 1962, I knew the landscape. I'd tried this and tried that and my efforts weren't amounting to much. Even Martin Luther King was a disappointment. I'd been so excited about him busting loose in Montgomery, but he moved back home to Atlanta. I thought, Goddamn! It was an awfully frustrating period.

By 1962, the roadshow was slowing down. The constant tension of not knowing what would happen next and the worries of Vivian and my mother were getting to me. We now had a fourth child, a son, Terry, born in 1959. Vivian was concerned that something awful would happen to me or us. She asked me to try to be, in her words, "normal" and play the crusading down. My mother constantly questioned whether a particular trip or case was necessary, then she debated why it wasn't necessary or why somebody else ought to do it instead of me. She told me she was afraid when the telephone rang that somebody at the other end would say I was dead. I later went through similar agony with one of my sons.

Meaningful cases were hard to come by. With the lines drawn more tightly, blacks getting in trouble with whites were even less willing to hire a black lawyer and make a civil rights issue out of it. They and I were concerned that white jurors might feel it more necessary than ever to demonstrate which side they were on. The best thing, many blacks felt, and probably rightly in a narrow sense, was to get some white lawyer to go downtown, minimize the situation, and get into some sort of damage control. I began to think I might have been able to make more of a difference in Harlem.

My practice was pretty much wills, deeds, minor criminal cases, and divorces. Alabama at that time was a quickie divorce state. I had contact with lawyers in New York, where divorces were hard to get. A number of Alabama lawyers were doing quickie divorce work until the newspapers raised a stink and the legislature changed the law. I could have made big money in the divorce business had I been interested. But I didn't find anything fulfilling in that. Since I was faced with the necessity of making a living and feeding my family, I did enough to make some money. Then I'd leave the office and go over to the Elks or Porter's. It got so I'd work about three days a week. The rest of the time, I got drunk.

Sometimes I'd go flying with Dr. Bill Dinkins, whose father was president of Selma University and whose mother gave me those twenty-five-cent piano lessons. He was a medical doctor, three years older than I, who had an office upstairs over Boynton's. Doc loved gadgets. He started out with a shortwave-radio thing and built it up until his house was virtually a radio station— great big antennae on his roof, looked like a network hookup. In connection with that mania, he went out and bought an airplane, a Piper Cub, that he kept at the airport in Montgomery.

Wednesday afternoons, when Selma closed down, we'd go to the liquor store across the alley to replenish the inventory in his plane. Then Doc put on his flying clothes and we'd head to Montgomery. He had an outfit like a World War I flying ace: leather helmet, old-fashioned goggles, and a white silk scarf. He was short, with straight hair and a thin mustache, and he reminded me of Captain Midnight. We'd load up the whiskey and get in the plane. It was tiny—one seat in the front and one in the back.

Off we'd go down the runway, Doc's scarf flapping in the air. Most times we went nowhere in particular. He might fly over to Georgia or up to Tennessee. Usually he'd fly over Selma on our way back, buzz over his friends' houses, and radio down to his wife at his house to see if dinner was ready: "Piper 2100 to home. What's cookin?"

One Saturday we flew up to Nashville and landed on the football field at Tennessee State University at halftime—two drunks and whiskey bottles rolling out on the fifty-yard line. We stood up and took an elaborate bow. The people in the stands went wild. Then we took off again, circled the football field, and headed back to Montgomery.

Doc flew by road signs. He'd say, "Look out there and find Highway 14." If I couldn't, we were lost. Often we didn't know exactly where we were. We were grounded by the FAA when we accidentally got in the commercial lanes at the Montgomery airport. Doc was calling for his location and the tower radioed back, "Do you know where you are?" Doc said, "No, that's why I'm checking with you."

"You're in the commercial lane. Get out of there! Look back!" We looked back and there was this big jet, looked like the Empire State Building floating through the air. It was moving faster than sound so we didn't hear a thing. It glided silently over us. After a few minutes, the sound came along in a roar and turned our little plane bottom up. That's when Doc lost his license.

The other young black doctor in Selma, Dr. Edwin Maddox, bought a yacht. This was his response to Dr. Dinkins's airplane. He had his outfit, too—a navy-blue and white suit that looked like an admiral's, with braids and epaulets on the double-breasted jacket and "scrambled eggs" on the bill of the official-looking cap.

To shake Dr. Dinkins up—this was before he lost his license— I told him I would no longer be flying with him on Wednesdays. "I'm moving from the air force to the navy." Doc couldn't stand that. If I went with Dr. Maddox the next Wednesday, he said, he'd land on the deck and make an aircraft carrier out of Dr. Maddox's boat. So that Wednesday, there I was, on the deck of a yacht with one medical doctor dressed like an admiral standing at the wheel and another medical doctor in a Red Baron costume flying right behind us in a ten-foot-long airplane, ducking and dodging all the way down the Alabama River to Cahaba. It was funny as hell. But sad. We'd come back to Selma to be useful, to make a worthwhile contribution. Feeling frustrated in this, we'd gone to the opposite extreme and become almost like characters in a comic opera.

Dr. Maddox later drank himself to death, almost literally. Dr. Dinkins wound up serving time in the penitentiary for writing fraudulent prescriptions for drugs. Almost all Selma's black doctors and dentists of my generation—educated in the fifties and beginning their practices about when I began mine—had a terrible time and either left or ended in some awful condition.

This was not the case with N. D. Walker, the leading black doctor when I was growing up. He was able to practice in Selma all his life without feeling the kind of frustration experienced by

Dr. Maddox and Dr. Dinkins. He was of my father's generation, when the expectations of blacks were so low as to be pathetic. He didn't anticipate change. His generation didn't think in terms of group progress. They thought about survival, and Dr. Walker survived. Dr. Dinkins and Dr. Maddox studied medicine in an era that foresaw change, but once in Selma, they were as discouraged, personally and professionally, as I was.

There must have been 50,000 black people in the region, most of them poor, who needed medical care. Runny-eyed, poorly nourished black children were a common, depressing sight. Selma's two white hospitals weren't integrated until the 1970s, when Medicaid required it. Good Samaritan, the hospital built by the Fathers of St. Edmund, was much better than the norm of black hospitals in the South but not on a par with white hospitals. Dr. Dinkins and Dr. Maddox were viewed not as doctors but as *black* doctors and were looked down on by people with far fewer skills than they had. They were no more a part of the medical establishment of Selma than I was of the bar association. And some of the people they came to help were still in the Dark Ages, buying cures from the likes of Doc Jones.

Add it all up—isolation, racism, the enormity of the problems we had come home to address—then throw in booze and you've got three black professionals playing outrageous games in a yacht and an airplane. That was our escape, but it wasn't the only one. Other blacks got tied up in prayer meetings, the Elks, fraternities and sororities.

Compared with what Martin Luther King or the Freedom Riders were doing at that time, you might say we were blowing it. But their situations were different from living at the grass roots— not easier or less dangerous, but less relentless. They came and went. We faced the problems without letup. When King went to the boondocks, he'd stay a few days, then fly off to Atlanta, Washington, or Los Angeles where he was around people who appreciated and understood what he was doing. The Freedom Riders had each other, and they often went to Atlanta to recharge. We were sunk, by ourselves, in Selma.

I was sinking pretty low. I'd be out at the Elks or Porter's or the Chicken Shack until two in the morning, come home, and everybody'd be asleep. It was very important to Vivian, with her image of what a family should be, that the man handle the finances and pay the bills. Sometimes I didn't leave her enough money, or she needed to get something for the children and she didn't know where I was. When the water bill or phone bill came, she'd give it to me; I'd put it in my pocket and forget about it. They'd be around threatening to cut off service, and where was I? She'd check with the office and often they didn't know. So she'd have to come to some joint, and there I'd be, sitting in a room with a bunch of drunks.

By that time, we had four children—two girls, two boys—and had moved into a house on Eugene Street. It was a one-story, three-bedroom wood-frame house similar in design to the one on Mabry Street where I was raised. It was in dilapidated condition—not nearly as nice as the housing project where we had been living. But Vivian wanted her own home in a real neighborhood, and we couldn't afford a better one with me working only three days a week and blowing some of that in the clubs and joints. This move turned out to be an awful mistake because the neighborhood was pretty bad and one of our sons later got into serious trouble there. But Vivian was happy with the house. She did a wonderful job fixing up the rooms and making the place a home without much to work with.

She didn't have me to help her with the house or the children. My mother reared me. Aunt Lennie reared her and Frank's children. My father didn't deal with me on a daily basis as my mother did, and that's how I viewed the man's role. I'd see the children as I came and went, but I didn't sit down and have conversations with them. I didn't give a second thought to leaving the rearing of our children entirely up to Vivian.

When she couldn't find me, Vivian would go to my mother to borrow money to buy groceries or keep the lights from being shut off. My mother got so exasperated, she told Vivian to leave me. My own mother! She said to Vivian, in my presence, "He's not going to straighten up. I'm sorry. You bring those children over here and we'll raise them. Forget about him." Vivian didn't say anything, didn't leave, didn't consider leaving. Her children, her family were everything. She is a person who dearly loves home.

As one who had an incomplete family, no father around, no brothers or sisters, no close-knit extended family, she wanted to keep her own family together at all costs. She might be disgusted and angry, but if my mother or anyone else criticized me, she would automatically get defensive. "Well, he's not that bad." She's also that way about her children.

My father almost gave up on me, too. After losing his job at Cloverleaf, he started working as a bartender at the Elks and then opened a little joint with Edwin Moss called the Flower Club. Many nights, he'd watch me spill beer on myself and careen out the door. I didn't drink a lot, but one beer or glass of whiskey and I'd be high. Edwin kept saying, "Give Chess time. He'll be all right." My father was skeptical, told Edwin, "I hope I live to see it."

Sometimes the police picked me up walking along the street or driving my car. For a while, they'd take me to my parents' house until my father told them, "Next time carry him to the jail." Since the Elks was right across from the jail, sometimes I wouldn't wait to be arrested. I'd go across the street and ask, "You got an empty bed?" They'd say, "Yeah, go on back there."

When you've really been drunk and wake up, you can't remember the night before. Sometimes I'd wake up, see the bars, and start raising hell about my constitutional rights. The jailer would respond, "We didn't arrest you. The door isn't even locked. Push it." I'd be so embarrassed.

One afternoon, my father saw me staggering across the railroad tracks behind Jeff Davis Avenue. He stopped to ask if I wanted a ride. I don't remember this, but my father told me I looked up at him and mumbled, "I cain't do it by myself." He took this to mean the whole civil rights, racial progress thing, and he had no interest in getting involved in that. He got back in his little white truck and drove off.

PART THREE

1963 - 1965

Memorial service at Brown Chapel in February 1965 for Jimmie Lee Jackson, a young black man killed by a state trooper at a voting rights march (© *Selma Times-Journal*)

Introduction

On a map on a wall at the headquarters of the Student Nonviolent Coordinating Committee (SNCC) in Atlanta, a big X was drawn over Selma. Because of Selma's location in the heart of the blackest section of Alabama, SNCC had sent a worker to check it out as a possible site for community organizing. He came back and reported that Selma was too backward. There was too much fear in the black community and there were too many Uncle Toms. The whites would lock up SNCC workers in a minute and nobody would be out demonstrating in the streets for them.

This was in the fall of 1962, when SNCC received money from the Southern Regional Council, a biracial group in Atlanta, for black voter education and registration. The money came, in part, from a foundation over which the Kennedys had influence. The idea was to channel some of the energy of the young people in SNCC from "direct action"—Freedom Rides, sit-ins, boycotts, and other confrontations that made the Kennedys and white leaders uncomfortable—into voter registration.

Obviously, the Kennedys—and the national Democratic Party— would benefit from any success in registering more black voters. But failure could be useful, too. The Justice Department was filing lawsuits against voter discrimination in the South. The more black people who tried and failed to get registered, the more evidence there would be of denial and interference.

Direct action, however, was SNCC's stock-in-trade, and some of its leaders considered voter registration tame. But they were a group of students, out of school and broke. Nobody was giving money for boycotts and sit-ins. Most SNCC workers had been involved in the Freedom Rides and other dramatic confrontations, and the question within the ranks was whether or not to go conservative and do voter registration. It didn't take long to find out that a serious, organized drive for black voter registration in the Deep South was about as hot a direct action as you could get.

It was through this voter registration program that Bernard Lafayette, a young black divinity student and former Freedom Rider, came to play a brief but significant role in Selma. He was taking time off from the American Baptist Theological Seminary in Nashville, at that time a breeding ground for student civil rights leaders. Nashville had three black colleges—the seminary, Fisk University, Meharry Medical College—and Nashville students organized some of the earliest sit-ins in the late fifties. Guiding lights were the Reverend Kelly Miller Smith, head of the Nashville Christian Leadership Council, and James Lawson, a pacifist and theology student who'd spent time in India studying nonviolence. While attending the seminary, Lafayette, who grew up in Tampa, Florida, went to Lawson's workshops on nonviolent resistance at a Nashville church. So did other future civil rights leaders—John Lewis, who would become chairman of SNCC, and James Bevel and C. T. Vivian of King's Southern Christian Leadership Conference (SCLC).

Lawson taught the philosophical and spiritual underpinnings of nonviolence, devised mock confrontations because nonviolence is not a natural human reaction to taunts and attack, and described strategies for community organizing. The latter would be especially relevant for Lafayette's mission in Selma. No civil rights organizer could expect to walk into a black community in a small town in the Deep South and get an immediate following like some pied piper. As Lafayette put it, the first struggle would be against black fear, not against white resistance.

From Lawson and Martin Luther King, Jr., Lafayette learned the process—in theory—of consciousness-raising. The first step is awareness: realization of oppression. The second stage is internal conflict: seeing the injustice and how one's own behavior has conformed to it. This was what the mass meetings in churches were all about—the speeches on oppression from civil rights leaders, the freedom songs, the testimonials of local people who overcame their fears and were standing up for justice. The next step is making an outward demonstration of internal change by confronting the system—marching, being jailed—which makes the injustice more visible and more people aware. Going to jail, something that produced terror in the hearts of most black people, was a striking way of overcoming deep personal fears. The final stage, reconciliation, looked forward to the day when the change in black people would produce a change in white people and the world would be like the one King envisioned in his dream.

Leaving college and Nashville, Lafayette joined the Freedom Riders in 1961 and, in the early fall of 1962, was up North raising money for SNCC. When he completed that assignment and returned to Atlanta to join in the voter registration program, all the sites SNCC had selected were taken except Selma. James Forman, then chairman of SNCC, told Lafayette he could join another worker in Georgia, but Lafayette wanted a place of his own. Forman explained why the X was drawn over Selma, but said Lafayette could go check it out for himself if he wanted to.

In a brief visit in November, Lafayette's experiences were consistent with the other worker's assessment of Selma as a town of black fear and Uncle Toms. He wasn't there thirty minutes, he said, before the police knew of his presence and came to check him out—and a black person had told them because only black people knew who he was and that he was there. When he met with the alliance of black ministers, the head of the organization declared, with scarcely a hint of sarcasm, that they didn't have any racial problems. "We know how to get what we want from white people. You just have to know how to ask." The minister fell to his knees and held out his hat.

Lafayette said that his most encouraging meeting was with the Voters League. At least there were a few stand-up folks—the Boyntons, Marie Foster, Ernest Doyle, F. D. Reese, and J. L. Chestnut, Jr. He went back to Atlanta and told Forman he was going to give Selma a try. So in February 1963, two weeks after George Wallace's

*inauguration as governor of Alabama, twenty-two-year-old Ber-
nard Lafayette, armed with real-life training in nonviolence from
facing vicious mobs as a Freedom Rider and theoretical training
in community organizing, drove to Selma in a 1948 Chevrolet to
build a movement.*

CHAPTER 9

Something Altogether New

Bernard Lafayette knew Selma would be a hard nut to crack. But he didn't appreciate how hard until he got here. Just finding him a place to live and a church where he could hold a mass meeting were problems. Churches and houses were being bombed ninety miles away in Birmingham, and folk were wary of having any close association with "the Freedom Rider," as Bernard became known.

The only people Bernard had solidly in his corner at the start were the half-dozen younger members of the Voters League. Marie Foster and Amelia Boynton found him a place to live. The rest of us were willing to do whatever we could—introduce him to people, endorse his efforts, help him get a church. We were very glad to see him although none of us knew just what he was going to do—or could do.

Bernard was a slender young man, unimposing in appearance, voice, and manner. He struck me, and others who met him, as a nice, likable fella. He laughed easily but was obviously dedicated—prepared to work eighteen, twenty-four hours a day, whatever it took. Our major concern when he arrived was for his safety. We urged him to be careful where he went, keep someone with him at all times, and stay off the streets after dark.

Bernard made Boynton's office his headquarters, so I saw him often. We had many discussions about what needed to be done

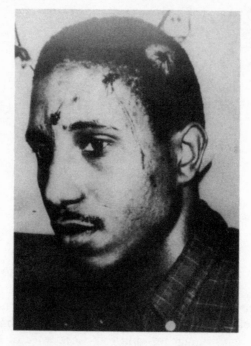

Bernard Lafayette after he was attacked by two
white men (Courtesy of Bernard Lafayette)

and how to go about doing it. His approach to the Voters League
was: "You people have been working to get more people registered. I'm here to help you." It was clear to me, though, that
SNCC hadn't sent a field organizer to Selma to get another twenty-
five people registered. Bernard didn't detail any ambitious plan,
but he obviously had more in mind than the little things the league
had been doing. He talked at length about the psychology of
fear. This was one of his favorite subjects. "What is the limit of
the number of black people they'll allow to register to vote? You
don't know if that limit has been reached because fear has kept
you from testing it. We need to find where the line of tolerance is."

I thought the line of tolerance was damn clear. People had been
trying to get registered for years. The board passed the few it
chose and failed the rest. Then there was this business of having

a white person or a select black vouch for your residency and character. I'd quote Frederick Douglass: "Power concedes nothing." "Except what it must," Bernard would add. His view was that we would never find the line of tolerance by sending two or three isolated people to the courthouse every month. What would happen if obviously qualified black people went to the courthouse often and in large numbers? It was possible that white Southerners were more resilient than I gave them credit for being. They might go ahead and register a hundred obviously qualified blacks rather than risk a lawsuit exposing their discriminatory practices. We needed to focus more pressure on the registration board, get the attention of more people in the community, get them interested in the process. Bernard spoke of having a mass meeting right away to kick off a voter registration campaign. However, that turned out to be a whole lot more difficult than he thought.

At Bernard's request, I took him around and introduced him to various black leaders and groups. He felt certain that the right to vote was something intelligent blacks in leadership positions, particularly in the field of education, would join him in supporting. Certainly they could be persuaded to try to become registered voters themselves.

I got Bernard on the agenda at the next Elks meeting and introduced him to the middle-class black men sitting on chairs in the ballroom. He gave a nice talk about the importance of the vote—"A people without a vote is a people without a voice and at the mercy of those in control of the system"—and said that together we ought to be able to do something about the situation. Edwin Moss then made a speech agreeing with everything Bernard said. Bernard was encouraged, but I wasn't. Preston and I had talked to that crowd many times. I told him the Elks weren't going to do a damn thing, and they didn't.

I also took Bernard to Selma University. That's where his first breakthrough came. Benny Tucker, Willie C. Robertson, and a few other students joined him without reservation or hesitation. They became almost his assistants and helped him recruit more students. But J. H. Owens, the president of the university, was dead against it. "You can't go around walking in the face of white people one day and then beg them the next day to donate money to your school," he said. "You're not going anywhere in this world without the help of white people and you might as well face it." He threatened to expel students if they participated in meetings and demonstrations. He told them, "Don't get involved. You'll hurt the school."

But Bernard was serious and methodical in making contact with people like Owens, and that impressed me. It was like the Voters League meeting for years to discuss the impossible. He had more patience than any young person I've ever met. He'd stop on Washington Street and talk at length to Eddie Ferguson, who owned several of the most profitable businesses in black Selma, even though there wasn't the slightest chance of recruiting Eddie for anything.

Bernard also had long philosophical conversations with the older Dr. Dinkins, the retired president of Selma University, who was solidly of the old school. I think Bernard genuinely believed so much in his cause that just discussing the subject reinforced him. His approach wasn't argumentative. He'd make his points by posing alternatives rather than saying, "That's the biggest Uncle Tom crap I ever heard," which I was likely to say. He always was careful to tell people only the good things others said about them to try to minimize the jealousy and competition.

However, reaching way back to Shields and to that revelation of Claude Brown's and D. V. Jemison's relationships with the white powers, I knew Bernard would strike out with most of the preachers, the teachers, the middle class. In theory, these would be the very persons who would lead and staff a voter registration effort. But the ties they had to the white ruling hierarchy—the ties that established them as leaders—made them the least likely group of all to become involved. They had the most—the best jobs, the largest homes, the most prestige—and therefore the most to lose.

"It's nothing but mess. That boy ought to go home. He's gonna get the white people all stirred up, then he'll run back to Atlanta and we'll be picking up the pieces." This was my mother. She wasn't going to risk her job, her paycheck. "Look here," she told me. "It was your meat and bread. It got you where you are. It helped you get through college." Also, she didn't want to offend the superintendent of schools, whom she considered her friend. Every time I went over to my parents' house, she warned me to "stay away from that mess. You can get yourself killed." When my mother wasn't present, my father spoke with a determined militancy that left no doubt where his sentiments lay, though he didn't get involved.

I heard defeatism in the barbershops: "It's not gonna come to a damn thing. Somebody'll get their brains blown out. Somebody'll lose their job, and they're not gonna get anybody to register anyway. Remember what happened to those folk who signed the petition to integrate the schools? Got run out of town and nothin' came of it."

Though I had no hope in the middle class, I thought other, less-compromised people might be reachable. All that winter, I tried to counteract the negative conversations, though I wasn't entirely positive myself. I found I had a hard time selling voting unless I could somehow tie it to the price of pork chops or a better job. The right to vote was an abstraction to people who were convinced that white people weren't going to give up enough power to make much difference in any case. I believed that myself to a large extent.

In my view, white power was invincible. I thought blacks could make some accommodations around the edges, economically and so forth, and use the appeals courts to blunt some of the worst injustices. I could look at Northern cities where blacks could vote. The white powers let blacks have some power and influence so long as it was kept on the south side of Chicago or Harlem in New York. At best, I thought we might make some sort of arrangement like that in the South. But as far as envisioning black people sitting on county commissions or city councils making decisions that affected white people, that was fantasyland. I thought only some modest progress could be made and, hell, it beat doing nothing.

Going around Selma asking people to join the Voters League or to come to one of Marie's citizenship classes or a mass meeting, I was hit constantly with questions I wasn't sure, deep down, I could answer satisfactorily: Why do you want me to go out there and risk my family's welfare? Why should I do that?

Everybody understood that law enforcement would be taking names and auto tag numbers at any mass meeting and turning them over to the White Citizens' Council. So deciding whether to come to a meeting involved weighing your own welfare against what you wanted to contribute to group progress. The possibility of losing your job was real, and you had to consider whether or not you could do without it. Not all the professional civil rights workers who came to Selma fully appreciated how much greater the risk was for the local people. As my mother pointed out, they could always go home to Atlanta. My own tolerance, though, stopped short of black Selma's so-called leaders, who I thought should be willing to take a risk and lead—not hide.

What I emphasized to regular folk wasn't voting but unity— sticking together, pooling our resources, helping each other. About voting, I usually said we might be able to register enough people to get some black policemen like they had in Harlem. In my book that alone was worth almost any sacrifice. When Bernard and others, or I myself, talked about freedom, I always envisioned getting white policemen out of black Selma.

Often, in the evenings, I went to see Claude Brown. He was black Selma's most persuasive critic of the civil rights movement, not of its goals but of its means—mass meetings, demonstrations, confrontation with white power. I really wanted to win him over. His views were heartfelt and his contributions were such that I couldn't dismiss him as an Uncle Tom as I did some "leaders" I felt were just making arguments to avoid risking their necks or losing their perks.

My opinion of Claude Brown had risen substantially since I blasted him and other black leaders in that high school paper. I couldn't help but be impressed by his dedication to black Selma and its institutions. His Ralph Bunche Club had become Selma's black YMCA, and though he was a Reformed Presbyterian, he did more for Selma University than we black Baptists who owned and ran it. Unaccredited though it was, Selma University provided the only college education many local black people could afford, and some of Claude's loans to the school really were gifts because he never tried to collect. Many of the books in its library came from him.

In fact, a few years later, after the Civil Rights Act outlawed segregation in public facilities, Claude used Selma University in a slick move to get my support for a new black Y building. I was against building a separate black facility. Claude's view was that, segregated or not, the black children needed it and the board at the white Y was willing to help finance it as a branch of their Y, which I saw as a front to forestall integration. He said my opposition was hurting his effort to get seed money in the black community and was making the Y board nervous about a lawsuit. So when the leadership of Selma University asked Claude to sign another note, he told them he would if they got me off his case about a segregated Y. Three Baptist preachers came to my office and advised me in very certain language to shut up or they were going to lose the school.

"You got me," I told Claude. He grinned from ear to ear. I admired his skill in reaching back and sawing the limb off under my ass. That was a nice touch.

Throughout the civil rights period, Claude and I sat around and debated for hours in his office in the parsonage of Reformed Presbyterian. He'd be at his desk near the window, legs crossed, leaning back in his chair. I'd be leaning forward in a chair beside the desk, smoking cigarettes and arguing with him.

"Lawyer, have you heard about burning down the barn to kill the rats?"

"Of course I have. It's a foolish proposition."

"Well, that is exactly what is being advocated on the streets of this city."

Claude was committed to the proposition that we could not rise by ourselves. We were lacking in resources, education, and skills because we had been denied certain opportunities to develop. In his view, we needed white people to help us advance. He'd talk about black progress: We came here as slaves from the jungles of Africa. Now we owned land, businesses, insurance companies. We had Duke Ellington, Howard University, doctors, numerous fine churches, even black lawyers. "Not one black college would exist had it not been for white people and they didn't do that because they hated us," he argued. "They did it because they were Christian and felt for all people. To jump up now and de-

INNER DIRECTED

Claude Brown (Courtesy of Mrs. Claude Brown)

nounce white people as racists is to ignore a hundred years of help and support." He thought it was fundamentally wrong and self-defeating to confront and alienate the very people who had the resources to help in order to pursue a fictitious pot of gold at the end of some so-called rainbow.

"Damn it, Claude, you're just rationalizing because you don't want to face white people regarding anything unpleasant," I'd say. "It's too important to you to have these people think highly of you as a leader."

He'd fire back: "It's easy to blame others for our own shortcomings. None of you will do anything on behalf of Selma University. You should go around to the PTA and see how many parents show up. And that's the future of the race. You and Bernard and the integrationists evidently believe in some sort of magic wand. You're going to have some demonstrations, confront some people, upset a town, and whiff, equality is going to come."

One of his favorite statements was: "You cannot free an ignorant, unskilled man because just as soon as you remove the
shackles, somebody else will come along and place new shackles
on him." Who would control the votes of the blacks on the large
farms if they got registered? Were black voters going to be more
discerning than white voters had been all these years? Progress
would take time and education.

"I recognize these problems," I'd say. "But we have to start
somewhere." My position was like Martin Luther King's in his
"Letter from the Birmingham Jail"—that "wait" meant "never,"
that gradualism didn't work. The white South had refused to share
any measure of power with the black race for the hundred years
since slavery, and the "creation of tension," as King put it, was
necessary to even open the doors to meaningful negotiation.

There was no denying that some of what blacks had achieved
up to that point, colleges and other institutions, had come pre-
cisely in the manner Claude was advocating—through people like
him sitting down and reasoning with white people. What was being
proposed by the civil rights movement was something altogether
new—full citizenship and equality rather than this hat-in-hand
dependence.

"We can't temporize forever. We can't take a whole race and
relegate it to the contacts you and Edwin Moss can unofficially
make with the mayor and police chief in our behalf. Hell, this is
America! This is a democracy. We need to take the risk. We need
to bite the bullet. America needs to bite the bullet." We'd really
go at it, argue like hell, sometimes till three in the morning. Of
course, we had no way of knowing which of us events would prove
correct.

For all Claude's deep reservations, though, he couldn't turn
his back on anything that involved black people. He slipped Bernard some money, and he wasn't one of those ministers who
looked the other way or crossed the street when they saw the
SNCC worker, afraid to reveal they even knew him. But he wasn't
above confronting Bernard in front of my office across from City
Hall and letting the mayor see him shaking his finger at the "Freedom Rider," giving him a lecture.

Bernard gradually became convinced that he wasn't going to

make any sizable dent at the adult level. If any adults were going to be moved—and there weren't going to be many—it would be through me and Voters League people like Mrs. Boynton and Marie Foster, who by then had twenty to twenty-five people coming to her citizenship classes. Bernard didn't give up, though. He more or less left the adults to us and intensified his efforts with young people.

Recruit the children—and their parents will follow. That became Bernard's strategy. King's organization, SCLC, was using the same strategy, very successfully, in Birmingham that same spring. When the Birmingham demonstrations lost supporters while King was in jail, SCLC workers went to the black schools and recruited hundreds of children. They emptied the classrooms and filled the ranks of the marches. When "Bull" Connor, the infamous police commissioner, sprayed them with fire hoses and herded them off to jail, their parents and other adults got mad and got involved.

The young people in Selma were ready to act. They didn't have jobs, houses, mortgages, or ties with the white power structure. They didn't necessarily want to go to school anyway. The movement gave them a chance to rebel against parents and teachers and rewarded them for knocking authority—the natural bent of teenagers. We are paying a price for that now. A generation of blacks has grown up with their concept and appreciation of authority undermined—the family's, the law's, society's. But we had no choice. For us to progress, some generation was going to have to break with authority.

Being young himself, Bernard had a knack with young people. To them, he was a sort of hero, a celebrity—a Freedom Rider! He recruited them on the street and in their homes, and he slipped onto the campus at Selma University and Hudson High School. Joe Yelder, the principal at Hudson, threatened to call the police on Bernard, but that didn't stop the recruiting effort. Students he'd already recruited would recruit others. Bernard's wife, Colia, had joined him, and she worked with the young people, too.

In early May, Sam Boynton died. As he lay gravely ill during the last few months of his life, Bernard often visited him at night, though Boynton was no longer conversant. Bernard told me that sitting by the bedside of the dying race man filled him with thoughts of the torch being passed between generations. He and the younger generation were carrying on the mission of their elders, who had gone as far as they could go. Boynton's death became the occasion for Selma's first mass meeting—a combination memorial and voter registration rally. Ironically, this meeting was held at Tabernacle Baptist, the church Jemison pastored when I was a boy, the most influential and accommodationist congregation in black Selma.

Ever since Bernard arrived, we'd been speaking with various pastors about using their churches for a meeting. Most of them pushed the decision off on their deacons, who nervously told us their church buildings weren't fully insured and they couldn't take responsibility for risking what folk built up nickel by nickel. Preston's pastor, Reverend Charles Lett, told Preston and me flatly, "I'm not interested in civil rights. That's not my field." This was the same Reverend Lett who'd asked me and his Masonic brothers to help him rescue his parishioner from jail, a man capable of bravery when one of his own was in danger but unwilling to confront the system on behalf of a possibly losing cause.

His attitude was typical of black pastors. Martin Luther King, Jr., Ralph Abernathy, Andrew Young, that group of civil rights preachers were unusual. Not criticizing civil authority, not stirring up political controversy was deeply ingrained in the black ministry. It went back to slavery, when the plantation owner built the slaves a little shack for a church and made sure the guy preaching wasn't fomenting rebellion. King once told me that everywhere he went, the first opposition came not from whites but from black preachers. Paradoxically, the church has both sustained and shackled black people.

Almost without anybody asking, though, Reverend Lewis Lloyd Anderson jumped into the fray and made Tabernacle available. He was regularly denouncing the white South from the pulpit, and he was anxious to help the cause—no matter what his deacons thought.

The incongruity of L. L. Anderson pastoring Tabernacle Baptist was striking and unintentional. The middle-class congregation didn't know they were getting a firebrand when they brought

Tabernacle Baptist Church (© Penny Weaver)

Anderson to Selma in the mid-1950s after Jemison died. Like Jemison, Anderson was—and is—a dynamic preacher. That's what got him hired. Though not a big man, Anderson has a large barrel chest and an extremely deep voice. He fully articulates each word and speaks with such poetic phrasing that people say words fall at his feet and beg to be used. He can move people, move them up out of the pews.

Many in the congregation were shocked and disturbed by the message Anderson began delivering upon his arrival in Selma. "Are we to be, for-e-vah, second-class citizens in this land? Have we not felled the trees, built the bridges, picked the cotton, and given suck to the babies?" Anderson grew up in Pittsburgh, briefly pastored a church in Montgomery, and knew Martin Luther King. When the bus boycott started, he often returned to Montgomery to make speeches. With all the white watchfulness of that era, the Citizens' Council network, word soon got back to Selma. I did not see for myself but would bet my life that some bankers or businessmen, the probate judge, or some other powerful white had conversations with the trustees and deacons along the lines of: "We don't want those agitators tearing up our town like they're doing in Montgomery. We hear that new preacher of yours is one of them. What do you want with him?"

Anyway, a group of the deacons led a campaign to run Anderson out of the church, got an injunction to bar him from the sanctuary, and showed up with a letter written by a woman in Montgomery claiming Anderson had fathered her child. But they had no proof of this claim. The group of deacons couldn't get enough votes to remove him, so Tabernacle split in two. About thirty-five influential members of the congregation left and formed another church.

Shortly after that, just as I was returning from law school, Anderson was in a car accident that killed a black pedestrian. He was convicted of manslaughter and sentenced to ten years in prison. Peter, Orzell, and Fred Gray, a black lawyer from Montgomery, represented him and appealed the case all the way to the U.S. Supreme Court, which overturned the conviction. With all this in the background, it's not surprising Anderson offered his church for a mass meeting. He didn't even consult with his deacons, and they were upset and fearful. The elder Dr. Dinkins, a member of Anderson's deacon board and his future father-in-law, begged him to change his mind.

Anderson had to make a painful choice. Dinkins and the other deacons were the church leaders who stuck by him during the split. How could he now turn his back on them? Such moments of betrayal, or accusations of betrayal, were part of the process of change—Benny Tucker and the Selma University students "ruining" their school, Anderson forsaking his loyal deacons, children disobeying their parents, hell, me going against the wishes of my mother. Of course, I'd been doing that for years.

Anderson didn't budge. If he couldn't use the church, he informed the deacons, he'd hold the mass meeting on the sidewalk outside and, with a loudspeaker, tell the public the officers were too scared to open the doors. Anderson told me Dr. Dinkins literally broke down and cried, told him, "You are deserting your friends and going with strangers."

I arrived early and found the church filling up with people

almost an hour before the meeting was scheduled to begin. It was a balmy spring evening, light and pleasant, very much at odds with the serious, apprehensive mood of the people entering the church. Police and sheriff department cars circled the block; other policemen and deputies stood outside the church and across the street.

Just before the meeting started, Sheriff Clark came bustling inside the church with four or five deputies and a court order from James Hare, the circuit judge, citing their right to be in the church to maintain public safety. Ernest Doyle, a Voters League officer, asked them to at least leave their weapons outside, but Clark didn't respond. He and his deputies stood around the back, huddling and whispering, then fanned out along the walls.

I was sitting up on the podium along with Bernard, James Forman, SNCC's chairman who'd come over from Atlanta, Reverend Anderson, and Reverend C. C. Hunter, one of the older members of the Voters League. Hunter gave the opening prayer, a very cautious one to the effect of "Love thy neighbor and let God fight your battles."

Tabernacle has a round sanctuary with a balcony extending halfway around the circle and a dome above. I was amazed at how many people came—about 350. Maybe two-thirds of the crowd were teenagers and students; the remainder were adults. Everyone was tense and silent.

Looking out at the audience, I thought about how this event had not occurred during Boynton's lifetime but so close after his death. I tried to fathom what C. J. Adams's reaction would have been—in Tabernacle Church, of all places. Also, I was not unmindful of the fact that we were just a block and a half from Shields's house and the back yard in which he fell dead.

Forman's style was quite different from Bernard's—more earthy, bold, and outrageous. He talked about what black people were sick and tired of taking at the hands of the white man, and he told the black folk in the audience to come out in the open with their views on freedom and get themselves down to the registration office the next week to hasten the day of reckoning. It was a provocative speech, delivered in the face of the sheriff. People were shouting "Amen" and "Say it!"

When Forman sat down, up popped Reverend Hunter, who gave a kind of rebuttal. His theme was: We shouldn't put all the blame on the white man, because we had a lot to do with our problems ourselves. We were irresponsible. We drank in joints. We let our children run wild. We had a long way to go to improve ourselves before getting into voting or any of the other things Forman was talking about.

[handwritten marginalia: i ntrw Ftml / r v i Sn]

Most of this was standard fare, preached a thousand times by a thousand black preachers, but the audience that night was having none of it. Their reaction was ice cold. I would have thought a man who made a living in the pulpit manipulating black attitudes would have sensed the rejection and moved on. But either Hunter didn't or was so conditioned against displeasing white people he couldn't help himself. He kept trying to justify the points he was making, shooting desperate glances at the sheriff and the reporter for the *Times-Journal*, but he only succeeded in digging a deeper hole for himself.

Why doesn't this fool give up the ghost and sit down? I thought. Though some of his arguments were the same as Claude Brown's, Hunter had not sought to build black institutions or used his white contacts for the benefit of black people. To me, he was just another preacher trying to please white people for whatever advantage that would bring him personally, a classic Uncle Tom.

The story in the newspaper the next day led off with Hunter's remarks. Throughout the civil rights period, the *Times-Journal* sought out and quoted black people whose views the editors endorsed, one of the white community's means of trying to pick the black community's leaders. The story did not boost Hunter's prestige, as it might have in times past. He clung to his viewpoint, and as black public opinion changed, he lost hold of his church.

As we left Tabernacle, law-enforcement people made a show of getting tag numbers and looking hard at us. A group of white men were standing across the street, glaring with threatening looks. My conclusion in looking at the crowd's reaction to this display of white displeasure was that the intended intimidation might keep additional people from coming to other meetings, but it wasn't working on this group.

This first mass meeting gave Bernard's presence wide circulation. On June 12, one day after George Wallace made his stand in the "schoolhouse door" at the University of Alabama, Bernard was attacked. It happened at night as he pulled up to the house where he was staying. Two white men got out of a car parked across the street, told him their car had stalled, and asked if he'd give them a push. Bernard immediately agreed, parked his car behind theirs, and got out to check whether the bumpers on the two cars were at the same height. As he leaned over, one of the men hit him on the head with the butt of a rifle. Bernard fell and got up; the man raised the rifle and struck him again, also in the head, and again. Then a man in Bernard's building heard Bernard yelling and came out with a rifle. The white men drove off.

This was the same night Medgar Evers was killed in Mississippi, and Bernard later was told the attack on him was part of a Klan conspiracy to murder him, Evers, and another civil rights leader in Louisiana that night. I saw him the next day on Washington Street, his eyes all swollen, face bruised, blood all over his shirt.

"You need to go clean yourself up," I said.

"No way," he told me. "This is the symbol we need."

He wore that T-shirt with caked-up blood for two or three weeks, and this was a sort of turning point in terms of public sympathy in black Selma. Even the blacks who were most apprehensive about him couldn't help but respect his commitment and courage, and they damn sure didn't go for anybody beating him. People were impressed that he didn't leave town.

Other efforts were made to discourage Bernard and his activities. He was arrested for vagrancy. Some of the people who went to the meetings lost their jobs, though many adults who attended were unemployed or self-employed. One night, people came out of a meeting to find their taillights smashed. Then, on their way home, they were arrested for driving without them. An interesting development was the extent to which this white pressure was backfiring. It made some blacks angry who might not have gotten involved, and a few more churches, including my church, First Baptist, opened their doors for meetings.

Bernard kept weekly mass meetings going with different speakers. One week he'd bring in a group of independent black farmers from some little crossroads like Bogue Chitto to talk about their

ASK YOURSELF THIS
IMPORTANT QUESTION:
What have I personally done to
Maintain Segregation?

If the answer disturbs you, probe deeper and decide what you are willing to do to preserve racial harmony in Selma and Dallas County.

Is it worth four dollars to prevent a "Birmingham" here? That's what it costs to be a member of your Citizens Council, whose efforts are not thwarted by courts which give sit-in demonstrators legal immunity, prevent school boards from expelling students who participate in mob activities and would place federal referees at the board of voter registrars.

Law enforcement can be called only after these things occur, but your Citizens Council prevents them from happening.

Why else did only 350 Negroes attend a so-called mass voter registration meeting that outside agitators worked 60 days to organize in Selma?

Gov. Wallace told a state meeting of the council three weeks ago: "You are doing a wonderful job, but you should speak with the united voice of 100,000 persons. Go back home and get more members."

Gov. Wallace stands in the University doorway next Tuesday facing possible ten years imprisonment for violating a federal injunction.

Is it worth four dollars to you to prevent sit-ins, mob marches and wholesale Negro voter registration efforts in Selma?

If so, prove your dedication by joining and supporting the work of the Dallas County Citizens Council today. Six dollars will make both you and your wife members of an organization which has already given Selma nine years of Racial Harmony since "Black Monday."

Send Your Check To
THE DALLAS COUNTY
Citizens Council
SELMA, ALABAMA
YOUR MEMBERSHIP IS GOOD FOR 12 MONTHS

Advertisement in the *Selma Times-Journal* on June 9, 1963, three weeks after the first mass meeting (© *Selma Times-Journal*)

efforts to get registered. The underlying message here was: Hey, you Selma sophisticates. These folk in overalls are doing more than you are. People from Birmingham, where the movement was in full swing and all over the television news, were frequent speakers. At every meeting, people who'd gone to the registration office would stand and be applauded. Not many of them were succeeding in getting registered—I proved to be correct about the line of tolerance—but more people were going down to the courthouse to put the pressure on.

167

When Bernard left in midsummer to go back to college, Selma had a few more black registered voters and a hardcore of mostly young civil rights activists. He had not succeeded in enlisting the middle class, but it had become more difficult for them to speak flatly against civil rights activities. Bernard had a way of challenging you without challenging you, of seeing clean through you.

He had that effect on me one night when I showed up half high at a mass meeting at First Baptist. I was jumping up, mimicking the way Clark pronounced the word "nigra," and calling him and his deputies the Gestapo. The deputies glared at me, obviously trying to decide what to do. Bernard always attempted to keep the meetings fairly responsible and not let them get out of hand. He had to come over and tell me to cool it. I went out the back of the church, jumped the fence, and went home, embarrassed.

Bernard's departure led to a big shake-up in the Voters League between the older heads, who welcomed the cessation of activities, and the Young Turks, who wanted to create more tension. No longer were Marie, Mrs. Boynton, Reese, Doyle, and the other more active members willing to sit around debating the impossible. We wanted to keep the momentum going and proposed writing a letter to invite Martin Luther King to come to Selma.

The older members argued at several heated meetings that inviting King, who regularly was denounced as a rabble-rouser in the newspaper, would destroy the organization.

"Well, what the hell," we younger folk retorted. "We've been meeting for years and only 150 black people are registered. What kind of a Voters League doesn't have any voters, anyway?"

Reese quoted Frederick Douglass about people who want rain without thunder and lightning. He had ambitions and leadership skills and, from watching Birmingham, saw some possibilities as far as who was going to be running the show here. A compromise finally was reached that we would send a letter to King as a separate "steering committee" of the league. Reese became president of the committee, which soon became, in effect, the league.

As it happened, the next civil rights leader to show up in Selma wasn't King but Worth Long, a staff coordinator for SNCC who arrived in September, the day after the Sixteenth Street Baptist

Church in Birmingham was bombed and the four little black girls killed. Worth organized six weeks of almost daily demonstrations at the courthouse and there were massive arrests. Kids left school to participate. The black principal, the white superintendent, their parents couldn't stop them. SNCC had succeeded in making going to jail an honor, not a crisis.

Ronnie, my oldest child, then thirteen, participated in the demonstrations that fall and the sit-ins downtown the next spring. My daughters Rosalind and Inetta Geraldine, whom we call Gerald, were less involved because they were younger. Also, just the thought of her little girls in the back of a police vehicle was almost more than Vivian could stand, and she actively discouraged the girls from participating. On several occasions, though, I saw Gerald and Rosalind at afternoon mass meetings. I winked at them. They knew I wouldn't say a word to Vivian. Vivian put less pressure on Ronnie because he was older and male, though she didn't like him missing school.

Many of the demonstrators lined up at the courthouse were too young to vote. But that wasn't the point. The registrars weren't going to register many black people anyway. The strategy was to attract media attention by demonstrating—with long lines—that black people in Dallas County wanted to register to vote and were being denied this right. Sheriff Clark had a local photographer take pictures of everyone in the line, and he went from adult to adult asking how their employers would react when they saw the photos.

More than four hundred people went to jail that fall for parading without a permit and unlawful assembly. I was so busy some days I didn't have time to drink or think—appearing in court, calling all over begging bond money, dealing with worried, irate parents.

I remained skeptical of what could be accomplished, but my hopes were beginning to rise. I was surrounded for the first time since I'd returned home by people who were thinking and acting on a level that excited me—not only SNCC workers but celebrities like Dick Gregory, the comedian, and James Baldwin, the author, who sort of adopted Selma and hung out in my office.

SNCC proved to be correct in its theory that when young people got arrested, their parents would get involved—if only to come to a mass meeting for information. Once there, they would be treated to some outrageous speeches. It was awesome for people conditioned to an almost deathly fear of the police to watch Dick Gregory get up in a church, make fun of the sheriff and police to their faces, and not get arrested, much less lynched.

The most dramatic mass meeting that fall, though, featured not some celebrity but James Porter. This was a meeting at Tabernacle at which Bruce Boynton was the speaker. He'd been invited not only because he was Sam and Amelia's son but because he was well known as the defendant in a famous case ordering integration of interstate transportation facilities. He was coming home to Selma from Howard in 1958—he was a year behind me in law school—and sat down for a hamburger at the white café in the bus terminal in Richmond, Virginia, because the accommodations for blacks looked unsanitary. He was arrested, and the court decision in his case led to the Freedom Riders, who were testing racial discrimination in bus facilities.

The afternoon of the meeting, Bruce stopped by Porter's place when he got in from Chattanooga, Tennessee, where he was living and practicing law because Alabama used his arrest in Richmond to prevent him from being admitted to its bar. He mentioned he was in town to be the guest speaker at the mass meeting, and someone asked what he was going to talk about.

"Exodus," he said.

"Hey, isn't there a song about that?" Porter asked. This led to a decision that Porter, Clyde Jones, Cleophus Olds, and W. J. Anderson, Jr., who were sitting there drinking, would come to the meeting and sing that old Negro spiritual "Go Down, Moses." All of them had musical talent. Clyde was a professional piano player.

This meeting, like the first, was at Tabernacle. The pews were full. The balcony was packed. Sheriff Clark and a few deputies were standing near the door. I was there to introduce Bruce. Before he spoke, the quartet from Porter's came forward. Clyde, seeing the sheriff's glare, ducked out, but the others started the song: "Go down, Moses,/ Way down in Egypt land." When they reached the chorus, something got into Porter—maybe gin. Instead of singing, he shouted it out and pointed at Sheriff Clark:

Tell old Pharaoh
TO LET MY PEOPLE GO!

It was electrifying. As the song continued, W.J. and Cleophus would drop out when the chorus came so Porter could shout it a cappella—LET MY PEOPLE GO!—and point at Clark with his long, skinny arm. Clark changed color, tried a phony smile, fidgeted, walked here, walked there. The audience was deathly quiet, as if everyone was holding his breath. I think Porter did a couple extra choruses, each time pointing at Clark, until the sheriff turned and left the church and his deputies followed. Porter got a standing ovation, sat down, and had to get up for a second one. The church just roared.

One thing was now clear to me. The meetings were a success. We wouldn't have too much trouble getting people down there for that kind of drama if we could sustain it. The people in that church were really into it and having a ball. It ran in the face of three hundred years of history.

Judge in a Nutshell

One afternoon in early July 1964, the circuit clerk called and asked if I was coming to the courthouse that day. "Judge Hare wants to see you," she said. I had many cases before Judge James A. Hare, whose circuit included Dallas and four other Black Belt counties, and the clerk's call didn't signal anything unusual. In fact, it was something of a nuisance.

I left my office to walk to the county courthouse six blocks away. It was a hot, sticky afternoon and I wasn't in any hurry. On Washington Street, I stepped inside the musty coolness of the Liston and Clay Lounge to talk to Wranch Pettway, who'd called me that morning in great distress.

Wranch said he'd been approached by an Alabama Beverage Control agent and a Selma policeman about spying on the movement and mass meetings. Though nobody had made an outright threat, the clear implication was: Cooperate or lose your liquor license. Wranch was worried. Typical of black businessmen, he wasn't involved in the movement and didn't want to be. He wanted to avoid alienating the police, the civil rights workers, his customers, his suppliers, and everyone else.

"Hell, come on to a meeting," I said. "We'll give you some half-truths to take back that won't amount to anything." I had a couple beers with Wranch before walking out in the hot sun again to see what Judge Hare wanted.

Circuit Judge James Hare (© *Selma Times-Journal*)

Hare was sitting at his desk in his office on the second floor of the courthouse. He gave me a thin smile as I came in and sat down. He wasn't a physically imposing man—about my height (five foot seven), average build, wide hips, a narrow face, sandy-colored hair. But when excited, he had that intensity of expression you see on evangelists and ideologues convinced they have a patent on truth. That day, his eyes were flashing.

"If these unsanitary, unbathed ruffians think we are going to lie down and give Selma over to them, they have another thought coming," he declared. "I am not going to sit idly by while they destroy this city."

Racial tension and violence had erupted in Selma that week, though I disagreed with Judge Hare that the city was on the brink of destruction. President Johnson had just signed into law the Civil Rights Act integrating public accommodations. Cafés and drugstore fountains already were being tested by SNCC and by Selma's young activists. With the law's passage, their activity heightened. On the Fourth of July, blacks began sitting in the downstairs section of the Wilby Theater. A group of white men approached the ticket window and shouted, "There's niggers in the Wilby!" Crowds gathered and Sheriff Clark closed the theater.

When four black youngsters tried to get served at the Thirsty Boy, a short-order place, Clark arrested them for trespassing and used a cattle prod on one of them. Some white teenagers got treated for cuts after a bottle was thrown through their car window, presumably by blacks. A melee broke out after a mass meeting—a shot was fired, bricks and bottles were hurled through the air. Sheriff Clark and his mounted posse charged with nightsticks and tear gas into the black crowd. I was still in the church with some other people. We heard shouts and ran outside—into a haze of tear gas. A day later, Clark arrested about fifty blacks in the voter registration line at the courthouse.

Hare read me a copy of the injunction he said he was filing that afternoon. It prohibited fifty specifically named blacks and fifteen black organizations—he also threw in the Klan to give the appearance of fairness—from holding public meetings of more than three people. He said he called me to his office because he wanted to let me know personally that I was one of the individuals named. He didn't want me to find out when the sheriff delivered the injunction to my office. It is significant that he did not so inform the other forty-nine people named. He considered notifying me a courtesy due a member of the bar, and more importantly, he knew me.

I wasn't one of the outside agitators. I was from Selma. I'd been corrupted at Howard University—that is, by Thurgood Marshall, Eleanor Roosevelt—but my blood was good. I was an unruly black, but I was *his* unruly black who, though misled, could be reclaimed. Hare was incapable of believing that any black from Dallas County—especially an educated black—would, on his own, be in favor of integration or the wholesale registration of black people.

"Snick [SNCC] and Slick [SCLC] will not reach Claude Brown. He is more educated than they are," Hare often told me. He was very fond of Claude. In Hare's rationalizing mind, the reason many educated local blacks weren't demonstrating was because they knew better, not because they had better jobs and more to lose.

Hare said he was reluctant to name me in the injunction, but some people insisted on it. "Anyway," he commented with a wry grin, "it'll be good for your practice." It would make my name stand out, boost my status with the NAACP, surely bring me some business. A black lawyer enjoined in Selma, Alabama, could make some Yankee money. I didn't need Hare to enhance me with black people and didn't appreciate being named, but I had no doubt that, in his twisted and misguided way, he meant to be helpful.

This was the judge in a nutshell: absolutely willing to use and abuse the law—subvert the U.S. Constitution if necessary—to maintain segregation and the Southern way of life, totally convinced that J. L. Chestnut, a Selma "nigra," wasn't really in favor of civil rights, and completely sincere in wanting to help my law practice while blocking my whole race from redressing our grievances.

I said, "Judge, your injunction is not worth toilet paper. The governor hasn't even declared a state of emergency. You can't ban folk from meeting. You won't even be sustained in Mobile," meaning not even Daniel Thomas, the federal judge, Hare's soul brother, would be able to uphold such an obvious violation of the First Amendment.

As usual, Hare didn't listen. He puffed away on a cigarette and talked about drastic situations calling for drastic solutions. He couldn't see why any self-respecting black would want to sit in the Thirsty Boy. Self-respecting whites didn't go there. The view in the Wilby Theater was no better or worse upstairs or downstairs. Qualified blacks could vote. These demonstrators talking about changing the South were pawns of Moscow. They weren't interested in voting. Half the people in line at the courthouse weren't from Selma or were too young to vote. They wanted to stir up trouble and mix the races.

He had it on good authority—J. Edgar Hoover—that the NAACP was a Communist front. "I know you're involved with that outfit for your practice, but you're being duped, James. You'll find that out." He always called me James. That was his name and I guess he liked it. I'd tell him, "My name is J.L." He'd say, "Yes, yes, James," and go on talking.

The Department of Justice filed a motion to get the injunction dissolved, but Judge Thomas sat on it. Meanwhile, there were no civil rights meetings in the black community except for secret meetings of the Voters League Steering Committee at Mrs. Boynton's house. The injunction wasn't broken until January, when King set up shop in Selma, and Thomas eventually dissolved it legally. But Hare succeeded in suspending the First Amendment in Selma for six months.

Though big, burly Jim Clark became the symbol of white resistance in Selma, Judge Hare was the power behind the scenes. Clark looked the part and played it well. He was a hothead. But he wasn't his own boss. He was subservient to Judge Hare both by law and by social class. Clark wasn't out there on his own authority ordering the marchers away from the courthouse and arresting them en masse. Clark had a temper, and he added jabs, shoves, and slaps of his own. But the orders came directly from Hare. James A. Hare was the commander in chief of the forces of white resistance in Selma, and I was his favorite "nigra."

When I had controversial cases before him, Hare would end court early so I wouldn't have to go home after dark. He was concerned about my safety. He appointed me to represent indigent defendants where most white judges gave all that business to white lawyers. In fact, I could hardly lose in Hare's court in non-jury cases where no black/white matters were involved.

Some white lawyers used to ask me to represent their black clients in divorces and in civil suits involving other blacks, saying we'd split the fee, because they knew I'd win before Judge Hare. He didn't give a damn about the evidence. If two ordinary blacks with no white connections were involved, it was a Mickey Mouse case to him. Sometimes I wouldn't have a shred of evidence, but I'd make my argument and Hare would say, "I agree with James."

Our relationship was peculiarly Southern and bursting with contradictions. Judge Hare genuinely liked me—within a certain very narrow context. He didn't want to sit down and eat with me. He wasn't going to invite me to his home. He didn't consider me his equal. But within all these serious limitations, the man liked me. I'm not sure, though, that "like" is the right word. Hare saw what he wanted to see, and I don't think he ever saw or wanted to see the real me. But the James Chestnut he saw, he liked. He got a kick out of ruling for me against white lawyers. I think it did something for his conscience and helped him rationalize many things. Hare was a great rationalizer.

I didn't dislike Hare, though it would be misleading to say I liked him. He was a man of remarkable tenacity and intellect. I was struck by his shrewd observations about life, the law, and people. Hare was up-front, direct, and didn't mind stating his honest views on the whole business of race. Other white Southerners were indirect and often untruthful about their feelings. He and I never became angry with each other personally, though our positions and sometimes our words were confrontational. We had an unspoken understanding that we didn't want to fall out with each other. If he used me to ease his conscience, I used him to help my practice, my clients, and the civil rights movement. Hell, he was the judge. And our hours of conversation and debate gave me an invaluable, fascinating peep at the mindset of the white South and the power arrangements on the white side.

Hare was a blueblood, raised in the country west of Selma. Whether his family's property would be more appropriately called a farm or a plantation I don't know, but their land holdings were quite extensive. He studied law at the University of Alabama, represented Dallas County in the Alabama legislature, worked as an assistant state attorney general, then was appointed circuit solicitor to fill an unexpired term.

That's when I first saw him—as the overzealous prosecutor going head to head with defense attorneys in black-on-black criminal trials. When the circuit judge died in 1954, Hare was appointed, then won re-election every four years after that. His wasn't an unusual career. These positions—circuit solicitor, judge—were traditionally passed out to or won by members of the old, established families.

Hare was married and had several children, though he never talked about his personal life with me, a black man. That was taboo. In my presence, he referred to his wife as "Mrs. Hare," and he seemed uncomfortable when she came into his office while I was there. He looked as if he wanted to hug or touch her, but didn't. I could sense his awkwardness. He must have reintroduced

Mrs. Hare to me fifty times. Every time she happened to show up and I was in the office, he'd go through the ritual. "This is Mrs. Hare. This is James."

Hare did not believe in equality. Hierarchy was the natural order, with the white man at the pinnacle. "If it's not ordained, James, why is it universal all over the world?" He talked about the nigra people in Africa in the trees, with bows and arrows, killing and eating each other when the missionaries came and brought Christianity to them, put them in clothes, and educated them. "They've never built a civilization." Hare hated this business of some Africans having more than one wife. He thought blacks were sexually unrestrained and full of venereal diseases.

Hare considered himself an expert on Africa and owned many books on the subject. You might have guessed his office to be a professor's. There were books stacked on the floor, in built-in cabinets, in a large revolving bookcase, book after book on Hare's big interests—the law, Southern history, anthropology, sociology, and white supremacy.

I was getting an opposite reading of African history from James Baldwin at the same time. Amazingly enough, in my little town of Selma, Alabama, in the mid-1960s, I was hearing about Africa almost daily from a white judge in the courthouse and a black writer in my office.

Whenever Baldwin was in Selma, he liked to sit on the couch in the front of my office, drink Scotch, and talk. He said civilization originated along the Nile in Africa and kingdoms flourished on that continent before the white man came out of the caves in Europe. While there was some tribal warfare in Africa before the white man came, war for the sake of exploitation and imperialism was purely an invention of white people, who brought syphilis and other diseases with them. The Europeans conquered Africa not because they were superior but because they were more ruthless. To Baldwin, Christianity was basically a way of getting in the door. He said, "Whenever the missionaries came, J. D. Rockefeller and J. P. Morgan were not far behind."

Judge Hare claimed to know where the various African tribes lived on the continent and where they were settled in America. He had a globe next to his desk, and he was always calling me over to point out the homeland of this or that tribe.

178

"Now, right here, James, is where the Ibos come from."

He believed that many black people in Dallas County were descendants of the Ibos and Congolese, two of the "most backward" tribes that were brought to America. He was convinced that he could look at a black person, identify his tribal origin, and, from that, know his disposition. He would take reporters from big Northern newspapers over to his window and, pointing at the demonstrators lined up below, identify which tribe each came from by the coloration of their gums, the size of their lips, or their protruding heels. He said Ibos had protruding heels.

He was trying to persuade the reporters that the situation was complex, that the rebellion in Selma wasn't a matter of civil rights but of tribal characteristics and weaknesses being exploited by the mulattos, the commissars, the Popes, and the Yankees. There were tribes in Africa who were farmers, he said, and they were well suited to agriculture. But other tribes were warlike. That was in their blood, and it was a mistake to bring them over here in the first place. "You will not be able to domesticate them any more than you can get a zebra to pull a plow or an Apache to pick cotton." In Hare's theory, the Ibos, though not genetically perfect for agriculture, were capable of domestication and had been somewhat civilized by a century of close white supervision. But they were of low intelligence and were easily influenced by the mulattos from New York.

"Look at Adam Clayton Powell and Thurgood Marshall. They're half white and have no home. They're mixed up. Whites don't want them, nigras don't want them, and they're mad at everybody. That's why they're running around with the NAACP trying to undermine law and order. That's what happens when you mix the races. Thurgood Marshall will not be satisfied until he has wrecked the United States and mongrelized the white race. You're not a mongrel, James. You have a home. What are you doing mixed up with them?" Hare considered me, Claude Brown, and obviously intelligent blacks like Booker T. Washington exceptions to the ignorant black mass. It was interesting that Hare would rant about Marshall's mixed blood to Claude, who was half white and resembled Marshall.

Hare's tribal nonsense obviously was degrading, but frankly, it sometimes made me laugh. He'd go off on the Ibos, hear me chuckling, and look up with a frown. "Nothing is sacred to you, James."

"Oh yes it is."

James Hare was an intelligent, well-read man. But where race and the South were involved, he was obsessed, irrational, almost crazy. I'm sure he had seen some awful things in his life—had to have as the circuit solicitor around the jails. Being as intelligent as he was and, in a way, sensitive, he needed to justify all the horrors, the patent unfairness, and the suffering hidden behind the magnolia trees. As the civil rights movement challenged white power and assumptions, his rationalizations became more elaborate and absurd. He became a warped, exaggerated, tragic caricature of a racist Southern judge. I'd hear white lawyers say he was around the bend—though, significantly, nobody seriously challenged him for re-election. It got so we couldn't get divorce decrees signed without him launching into his racial theories or reading a passage from a book he'd just gotten in the mail.

I happened into his office the day he received a copy of Daniel Moynihan's report on the black family. He was on the telephone trying to place a call to Harvard to offer Moynihan his congratulations. He was thrilled that a Northern liberal had "proved" that black people were not the equal of white people.

As usual, Hare saw in Moynihan's report what he wanted to see. Yet ironically, Hare was the person who pointed out to me the importance of being a skillful listener. It started by my jumping up in court and objecting to something that on closer examination was not quite what the other side had said. Hare used to tell me I'd made an eloquent argument but it was almost irrelevant. I had a certain concept as to what some case was all about, and even though the evidence told a different story, I continued to litigate my mindset.

He was a complex man. On one occasion in the late 1950s, I told Edwin Moss I'd get Hare to kick off the oratorical contest at a statewide convention of black Elks being hosted in Selma by the Pride of Alabama chapter. Edwin was pushing to be Exalted Ruler over the whole state, and I knew it would help his chances and be impressive as hell to the Elks from Birmingham and Mobile to have a circuit judge speak at the convention. In that era, when black people didn't have the vote, you rarely had mayors or judges or any white officials except the school superintendent appearing before black groups.

I never had any doubt that Hare would agree. All I had to do was ask. He made the standard speech white school superintendents gave to blacks. It was almost identical to what you would get from my mother and the black middle class: Work hard. Go beyond the call of duty. The only limitation on you is you. Shoot for the sky. Imagine this coming from Hare, with all the limitations he placed on the black race! But he stood up there and honestly said that to the young oratorical contestants.

Hare thought a black person ought to have pride as a black in a black's place. He was all for black people developing businesses and institutions, but the ultimate responsibility for society was held by whites. Blacks were not meant to run anything involving whites but should be encouraged to be thrifty and responsible and to be good teachers, good athletes, and good musicians—all within a segregated society.

Part of his fondness for me was his genuine respect for people who persevere. Hare was impressed that a black fella from Selma had graduated from law school and passed the bar. Also, Hare loved the combat of a trial. A few times his vigilance on race lapsed when I really lit into a white person with a shrewd cross-examination. Hare would sit there enjoying that until it dawned on him this was a black/white thing. I could see on his face the moment he awakened to that reality and put on a frown.

Other times when I was addressing a jury and turned a phrase well, he would have an expression of almost ecstasy. Often on Mondays he'd poke his head out the door of his office when he heard my voice in the hallway. "James, come in a minute." He wanted to tell me what his pastor had said at church, some particularly flowery passage that made some point. Hare would remember it damn near word for word. He'd lay it out there for me and we'd both admire it. I'd poke my head in his office when I had a good joke—not bawdy—or a story I knew would make him laugh.

Our relationship was par for the course in Selma. White Southerners have always had warm feelings—even a kind of love—for black individuals while having a morbid fear—even hatred—of blacks as a group. I've gone to black funerals and seen white people there crying. Once, when Orzell and I were on the road, we saw my uncle Frank Chestnut out hunting with Harmon Carter, a wealthy and utterly conservative white man who owned the Carter Drugstore. Frank is a contractor and he took care of Carter's properties. Orzell and I rounded a bend and there were Carter and Frank on horseback, with a black man who worked for Carter running along on foot opening gates so Frank and Carter could ride through and follow the dogs.

The week integrated public accommodations became law, Carter removed the lunch counter at his drugstore rather than serve black people—including, presumably, my Uncle Frank. He made a ceremony of it. But he liked Frank, would hardly go hunting without him. Frank was his man. Frank was riding on a horse the same as Carter while another black man on foot ran ahead and opened gates for both of them. It's crazy.

But these were ties that bind, and they came into play in the civil rights era. Relationships across racial lines were not relationships between equals—almost always, a job was at stake. But for maids, cooks, drivers who had been "a member of the family," as white people like to say, kind feelings and loyalty also were involved. Those who participated in demonstrations often reported that, like Judge Hare, their employer/"friends" assumed they didn't really mean it. "What have those agitators been doing to you?"

This was Southern white arrogance that they knew "their" blacks, though nothing was further from the truth. When black people in some numbers stopped telling white people what white people wanted to hear and started expressing their real views, it was a shock. The civil rights movement exposed as a rationalization the white South's refrain that their blacks were happy, didn't want to vote, weren't interested in integration. There they were, hundreds of them, lined up at the courthouse. And there I was, a Selma black man, representing marchers and filing motions in Hare's court, speaking freely about civil rights. Hare couldn't face the truth, so he convinced himself I was a puppet of the NAACP. He was blinded by his self-serving rationalization of what I was, even though, right before his eyes, it was obvious I wasn't that.

That Hare "liked" me and I "liked" him in no way tempered my involvement in the civil rights movement. It was better that he liked rather than disliked me—it made my work easier—but having a personal relationship with a white person wasn't what I was all about. I considered these relationships a dead end—a patronizing cover that hid the truth, the reality of the awful, unforgivable manner in which the total group was systematically treated.

Still, it's difficult to interact daily with people, especially those in power, and not be influenced. When you're dealing one-on-one and a Judge Hare or even a Jim Clark turns you some kind of small favor, this can affect you because you're human. When important people sit down and talk to you, not quite as equals but with a kind of acceptance not given to most blacks, that can easily go to your head. You can become intoxicated with the thought that you are special and different. If you're not exposed to anything else, you can lose perspective and start thinking, Well, things aren't that bad. These people are all right. I wasn't in any danger of forgetting I was black or deserting the cause. It was a matter of losing the edge, and you need an edge to go out and confront resistance every day. So it was very important for me to go to the mass meetings even when I wasn't giving a speech or a report.

To hear of brutality by Jim Clark or his posse—slapping a woman, chasing a group of children with cattle prods—made real the consequences of Hare's scheming upstairs in the courthouse, seemingly away from it all. To hear a mother describe how she'd lost her job, and knew she would lose it, but considered marching worth the sacrifice was inspiring. To see young students willing to get their heads whipped gave a depth of meaning to the Constitution I could never feel in the sterile atmosphere of the courtroom. The sermons, speeches, and singing inspired in me, as in others, a feeling of togetherness.

I'd leave the church remembering Shields: "When Dr. Walker goes to the bank with all his money, he has to stand in the black line." You're not *that* damn special.

Worth Long, the staff coordinator of SNCC, told me after a court hearing one day that he wouldn't be able to play a role like mine—being a lawyer involved in the civil rights struggle while maintaining relationships with the opposition in the courthouse. He said he'd suffer "role confusion." I found my situation complex but not confusing. I have known who and what I was and the situation I was in since I was ten years old. I've never had a doubt about who and what the opposition was. My instinct has always been to try to use and not be used.

In the early stages of the movement, getting enough bond money was a serious problem and I could sometimes get Hare to release people on their own recognizance. Just as there were reasons for wanting masses of people to go to jail, there were reasons for wanting to get them out. You can stall a movement if too many people get stuck in jail for too long. As the movement grew and waves and waves of demonstrators were arrested, I could persuade Hare to expedite hearings and not force expensive appeals in the case of every single marcher.

"Damn it, Judge, we're going to be here all day. If we can't work something out, I'm leaving this to someone else." Hare didn't want to deal with some mulatto from Atlanta or New York and, depending on the mood he was in, often agreed to hurry things along. I was in a unique position to get him to do this.

I'm convinced Hare would have been even more extreme except for some of the conversations he had with me and with Peter Hall, who spent a lot of time in Selma representing marchers, as I did. We kept telling Hare that, like it or not, King was the undisputed leader of the movement. An attack on King wasn't going to hurt our cause and it damn sure wasn't going to help his. We also kept pushing him to pay closer attention to what Claude Brown and other moderate blacks were saying and quit denouncing every call for change as a far-left import from Moscow.

Often when Claude was in the courthouse, he'd stop by to see Hare. On certain matters, they concurred Both had no time for the Fathers of St. Edmund, whom Hare called "the Popes." One of the younger priests, Father Ouellette, was the only white person in Selma to openly support the civil rights movement. He was a handsome man who wore gold cuff links. Claude was accustomed to competing with the Catholics in terms of boys' clubs and scholarships. In fact, he could use the Catholics' activities to persuade the Reformed Presbyterian hierarchy to jack up his budget. But Father Ouellette was changing the rules of the game with his political activism, which was the last thing Claude wanted to engage in. Hare considered Catholics race mixers, un-American, Roman poison.

But Claude did not agree with Hare that everything was great for black people in Dallas County. He often said that the black schools weren't what they ought to be, that people ought not be insulted just going into a store trying to buy a pair of shoes, that the situation needed some correcting—and Claude certainly was not a radical.

I especially valued my relationship with Hare for giving me a front-row seat to his relationship with Jim Clark. Judge Hare was a sort of 1960s version of an 1860s plantation owner. Jim Clark was his overseer, the lower-class white man who ran the fields and controlled the slaves. Hare told Clark many times, in my presence, that he, Judge Hare, was in charge. The courthouse was his jurisdiction. Clark showed more deference for Hare than I did. When he went into Hare's office it was: "Yessir, Judge," and he'd jump to it.

The judge had upper-class contempt for "white trash." He once told me, "Mongrelization would improve some of these people." He thought something was wrong with a man, especially a white man, who couldn't make it in America. He was capable of throwing the book at a poor white thief and giving a black thief a light sentence. One day as a skinny, scraggly-looking young white man was being led out of Hare's courtroom, Hare seriously commented to me, "I don't know why you're pushing integration. You're going to have to be with them."

Hare sometimes came down hard on Clark. "You have to draw that man a picture. You have to keep him on a leash," he'd complain when Clark did something on his own that Hare disapproved of.

I took great delight in going to the sheriff's office one afternoon and seeing Clark on the telephone almost crying. He was talking to Judge Thomas in Mobile. This was at the height of the demonstrations in January 1965, and Judge Thomas had just issued an order barring Selma and Dallas County officials, including Clark and Hare, from hindering voter registration applicants.

As soon as I learned of the order, I went to the courthouse to find out Hare's reaction and plans. He was chain-smoking, pacing back and forth in his office, declaring, "I don't care what Judge Thomas ordered. If there are any demonstrators in front of this courthouse while my court is in session, I have ordered the sheriff to put them in jail." I made a beeline down the stairs to Clark's office on the first floor. I knew his ass was in trouble, and I wanted to see how he was going to handle the dilemma. Two judges, two members of the country-club elite, had issued conflicting orders. Now he was in a position where he had to alienate one or the other.

Clark was sitting at a secretary's desk in the front room of the sheriff's offices. It's a congested area with two desks, a bank of filing cabinets, and four or five chairs for people to sit. This was a Saturday and the secretaries weren't there. The sheriff had on his usual regalia—a military-style shirt with three pleats down the back, well-pressed pants, shiny black shoes. His cap, like a general's with all that braid on the bill, was on the desk next to the phone. You could always spot Clark—big, robust, immaculately dressed—in a mass of posse men or state troopers as he swaggered down the street with his nightstick and cattle prod.

But there he was on the telephone, whining, moisture in his eyes. "Y'all don't treat me right. All I'm tryin' to do is enforce the law and y'all have put me in the middle. I'm not gettin' the consideration you are givin' the niggers. What am I supposed to do?"

I couldn't hear what Thomas said. As he listened, Clark tried without success to interrupt, "But, but, but," and finally, with a dejected, defeated sigh, said, "All right, Your Honor. Thank you," and hung up.

I was standing there with a smirk on my face. I said, "Hell, you might as well be a Negro."

He glared at me. "You might as well get the hell out of my office!"

It tickled me all over. I left laughing. I laughed all the way back to my office where I told Peter Hall what had happened. I'd never seen Peter so pleased. We laughed until our sides ached. Peter almost fell out of his chair laughing.

CHAPTER 11

In the Middle

The summer Judge Hare issued the injunction against public gatherings, I dreaded getting up in the morning. I dreaded the routine and anything new the day might bring. I had burned out. I'd been back in Selma six years and gone through a helluva period without letup, relief, or, at that point, tangible progress. Most of my legal work that summer was mop-up from the fall's demonstrations and July's sit-ins. A week of demonstrations resulted in months of litigation. From the fall alone, there were over five hundred cases. Each had to be tried or settled in some fashion and then the bond money returned to the individual or organization that had paid it. It was a numbing routine day in and day out.

Judge Hare's injunction stopped further demonstrations and arrests, a relief in a way. But the cessation of civil rights activity raised the question of what we had accomplished. Over a year of mass meetings, citizenship classes, demonstrations, and federal lawsuits had produced about 150 additional black registered voters, and Selma was almost as segregated as ever.

Through a friend, I got a job that fall, 1964, teaching business administration at Mississippi Valley State University (then College) in Itta Bena. I wasn't planning to stay beyond a year. I just wanted to get out of Selma for a while. Vivian was glad that the daily pressures and dangers would be over, or at least reduced, and she thought she and the children would see more of me.

Being on a campus and dealing with young people made me feel better. A piano player from Detroit was teaching there, and we played together. It was so different from what I'd been going through, so much less anxiety. This respite was cut short, though, when SCLC set up shop in Selma in January 1965. I spent more time in Alabama than in Mississippi, burned up my car going back and forth, and broke my promise to Vivian to spend more time with her and the children.

The summer before I went to Itta Bena, Orzell and I had driven to Atlanta, to SCLC's headquarters on Auburn Avenue, to try to sell King on coming to the Black Belt, using Selma as the hub. We knew, everyone knew, that once the public accommodations law was signed, the next civil rights offensive would be voting— and voting was what we'd been demonstrating about in Selma all the while.

King, Ralph Abernathy, Hosea Williams, and two or three staff people were there, sitting on cane-bottom chairs in a small conference room. It was a Saturday afternoon and everybody was wearing casual sport clothes. Orzell and I got the impression that SCLC was definitely looking at Alabama but was undecided between Birmingham and the Black Belt.

Orzell argued that a voting drive in the Black Belt would have more impact. These counties were majority-black, and if we could get black people registered, we could win control of some governments. It wasn't clear then that blacks could do this in Birmingham. I pointed out that the gentry in the Black Belt—not U.S. Steel in Birmingham—had run Alabama politics for a hundred years. If you pulled the rug out from under these people, Alabama as we knew it would change drastically.

King expressed concern about the difficulty of achieving togetherness in what he called the "open spaces" of the Black Belt. Birmingham was compact and more organized. SCLC had already been there. He was very probing. This obviously was a matter in which he had deep interest. It was almost as if he were thinking out loud and arguing with himself rather than with us.

"You have neglected to pursue one of your strongest arguments," he said. "Sheriff Clark." SCLC had learned that for a protest to draw national attention and support, white violence was a crucial element. In Birmingham, the outrage of Bull Connor's police dogs and fire hoses produced the Civil Rights Act. In Albany, Georgia, where conditions were just as bad, SCLC's campaign fizzled. Its police chief, while jailing the protestors, was restrained in his actions and speech so racism's ugliest face remained hidden from the national audience.

SCLC had a report on Jim Clark—his excessive actions during the SNCC demonstrations and the sit-ins. They saw in him another Bull Connor. But King foresaw a potential problem for SCLC's next campaign. If it wasn't lost on SCLC that Bull Connor was the "father" of the Civil Rights Act, it probably wasn't lost on U.S. Steel in Birmingham or powerful whites elsewhere in the South, including Selma. U.S. Steel likely would rein in Bull Connor if SCLC returned. King wanted our assessment of whether or what Jim Clark had learned.

I said Jim Clark wasn't the issue. The question was what James Hare and his class would do. "I think I know Judge Hare, and he's going to push Clark out there because he's embarked on a holy crusade to save the South and the white race." I underlined that we didn't have big national companies like U.S. Steel and predicted that the bluebloods who owned Selma wouldn't stop Hare. "In my view," I said, "Selma's your ticket."

The matter was left unresolved, but Orzell and I went away feeling we'd made some headway. I don't know what ultimately decided SCLC on Selma. The Voters League Steering Committee, through Mrs. Boynton, kept in contact all that fall and sent a formal letter inviting King and SCLC to help them. By late December, the decision was made that King would come to Selma—and break Judge Hare's injunction—on January 2, 1965, one hundred and two years and one day after Abraham Lincoln signed the Emancipation Proclamation.

All that winter, I'd spend a couple days in Mississippi, get a call from Reese or even from King, and tear over in my Chrysler station wagon. There were marches almost daily from Brown Chapel to the courthouse—hundreds of arrests—and much more legal work than Peter, Orzell, and I could possibly get to. My existence consisted of the Dallas County Courthouse, the jails, Brown Chapel, the Voters League and SCLC office, my parents' house, and, of course, Porter's.

The first thing I did each morning, if I had time, was check the

Wilson Baker, Selma's Director of Public Safety, and a line of demonstrators
(Courtesy of The Bettman Archive)

city and county jails and Camp Selma, a road camp outside town
where they kept the jail overflow. I wanted to know who was
there and make certain they were all right. I went from cell to
cell, delivered messages from husbands, wives, parents, and made
arrangements to get anybody out who was ill or couldn't take it
anymore. The dingy cells were enlivened by the singing and laughter of these willing inmates.

I was always very nervous about the young women in Camp
Selma because some of the jailers were real lowlifes who considered black people animals. This was a dormitory-type place, built
for male convicts who repaired the public highways, so there was
no privacy, no separate restroom for women. The guards didn't
want to put up a blanket or partition because, I suspected, they
wanted to watch. I had a constant battle going about that.

Next, I went to the Voters League and SCLC office—a one-
story brick building near Hudson High—to find out from Reese

what was on tap and call the Legal Defense Fund in New York to let them know what I knew. Then on to the courthouse. It was important for one of us—me, Peter, or Orzell—to be around at the demonstrations to keep track of how many people were going to jail, how many bonds, how much money we had in hand to make bonds, and if that wasn't enough, to get in touch with the Defense Fund and others for additional money.

Deciding how many people to bond out immediately and how many to let stay in jail was a strategic matter that required discussion. It obviously put a strain on the other side to feed and house prisoners, and numbers were symbolically important. When King was jailed, he wrote in a letter to *The New York Times: This is Selma, Alabama. There are more Negroes in jail with me than there are on the voting rolls.* But we couldn't deplete the troops for further marches, and there always were some individuals who wanted the hell out.

From this came many trials. After a full day, I'd sit in the Sunday-school room at Brown Chapel or in the SCLC office with Reese, Doyle, Gildersleeve, Blackman, Marie Foster, Mrs. Boynton, some of the SCLC staff, sometimes King himself, assessing what had occurred that day, what to do the next, how to respond to some new offer from City Hall or the courthouse, and a myriad of other possibilities. Should we start a boycott? Have a night march?

It was very instructive to me the way King handled meetings. Invariably he was the last speaker, even when a meeting lasted four hours. He sat quietly and said nothing as everybody else debated up, down, and any other way. But his presence was felt. People tempered and shaped what they were saying in order to appeal to him. His face betrayed only concentration so it was hard to tell which way he was leaning. You knew a meeting was coming to an end when he stood and summed up the preceding hours. He could remember all the various speakers and the several different points each made. His summaries could take thirty minutes. He logically analyzed and looked at the pros and the cons of each proposal and how it related to our objectives. Finally, he would declare, quietly, which proposal he favored and begin to lay out the next move. King was not only a great orator but one hell of a field general. I came to the conclusion that no one else could have unified the collection of ministers, gangsters, self-seekers, students, prima donnas, and devoted, high-minded people we had in Selma that winter.

By midnight, I'd generally be out at Porter's or the Elks. Sometimes I got a call to come back to the office or go over to Dr. Jackson's house, Marie's brother, the dentist, where King stayed when he was in Selma.

Smelling the whiskey on my breath, King would give me a bemused and somewhat disapproving look. "How can I run a movement when the lawyer won't leave the hard stuff alone? You know that's wrong. Help me." I would agree to help him and ignore his other remarks.

But King kept calling because I had detailed knowledge of Selma. My relationship with Hare gave me an inside track at the courthouse, and I was familiar with all strata of black Selma—from the preachers and undertakers to the crooks and bootleggers. Whenever he was planning some move, King liked to try it out on me, get my opinion of how it would "play in Peoria," as he put it. I think he also saw me as a person born and bred in Selma, loving Selma, with great potential for helping not only in the movement but after it was over.

As a lawyer representing the NAACP Legal Defense Fund in the midst of a street protest movement, I was stretched between competing philosophies and egos, and my own beliefs were challenged. King's philosophy that we had a moral right to disobey unjust laws ran counter to my legal training. Though I understood the limitations of the judicial system—white men in black robes had upheld Jim Crow for almost a century—I was trained to believe that you changed the system through the system. You didn't go out and break the law. You went to court.

King persuaded me we had no better choice. If the movement were to follow the legalistic view I was advancing, it would be reduced to the whims of Judge Thomas and Judge Hare and whether we could find some white judge a few years later willing to overrule them. You couldn't take a people's movement and reduce it to that. I had to agree. Hell, that's right. But as a lawyer, I still worried over the fact that we were deciding on our own which laws were just or unjust.

Also, I was being paid by the Legal Defense Fund, which was dedicated to solving racial problems in America through litigation, not street demonstrations. Its strategy was test cases: Send four or five obviously qualified people to the registration office. If their constitutional rights are denied, file a lawsuit. King, by sending five hundred, was repudiating this concept—then calling on the organization to provide legal services and bail money.

The Sunday-school room at Brown Chapel is a long, plain room with a dozen tables and chairs and the inevitable picture of a blue-eyed, blond-haired Jesus holding a little white lamb on the wall. At meetings there of SCLC staff—Andrew Young, James Bevel, Hosea Williams—I sometimes advanced the position of the Legal Defense Fund, which I came less and less to share. If one of them advocated a march the next day to keep attention focused on the registration office, I'd say the focus wouldn't decrease if they didn't march. We had demonstrators coming up for trial in a few days. One time King said to me, "J.L., that's not the point. We're trying to win the right to vote and we have to focus the attention of the world on that. We can't do that making legal cases. We have to make the case in the court of public opinion."

When I called the Defense Fund about bond and trial money, they encouraged me to go back and try to get SCLC to cut down the number of marchers. I'd tell them there was no way I or anybody was going to convince these people to have a representative march. That's not their emphasis. Sometimes I'd get: "If that's their emphasis, let them pay for it."

The Voters League clashed with SCLC, too. At one point, Judge Thomas ordered the Dallas County registrars to process a hundred applications each registration day—that is, twice a month—and to provide an "appearance book" for people to sign on other days that would give them precedence. As a sign of so-called good faith, the registrars agreed to provide the book sooner than Thomas's order required. From a local perspective that looked like progress, and the Voters League was leaning toward going along with it. But SCLC boycotted the book and kept on lining up outside the courthouse. They weren't in Selma to get a few hundred more people registered in Dallas County.

"But this is *our* movement. You are *our* guests," Reese and others said. I was the Voters League's legal advisor and often had to rush over from Mississippi or get on the phone with Reese to prevent an explosion. Added to this was SNCC's anger that SCLC was stealing the thunder. They had come to Selma first, but King was getting all the credit and benefits. He was the one who could go to Los Angeles, make a speech, and raise money. Within the Voters League, you had people who were pro-SCLC, others who were pro-SNCC, and a third group who were just pro-Selma. It's amazing it all held together.

Meanwhile, there was division on the white side that affected our strategy. White Selma for the first time was dealing with a situation where "their" Negroes were not in charge, and it seemed to leave white leaders with a feeling of confusion. I had predicted correctly that Sheriff Clark, backed by Hare, would follow the Bull Connor mode of "The only way to stop 'em is to stop 'em." I hadn't calculated, though, that Wilson Baker, the city's top law-enforcement officer, would be just as actively pushing for restraint. His strategy was more like the police chief's in Albany, Georgia: "Let 'em march and it'll peter out."

Baker was far more shrewd, far-sighted, and open-minded than Clark. He clearly had political ambitions and, early on, anticipated that blacks in at least some numbers would be voting. He also knew that a more intelligent and moderate approach would appeal to Selma's aristocrats and to the younger bankers and business people who wanted to present a decent image to lure industry. Clark was ambitious, too, but couldn't see beyond the don't-give-an-inch rhetoric of his posse and the White Citizens' Council.

The marches started at Brown Chapel, then proceeded on the city's sidewalks to the county courthouse. Baker would tell Clark he was in charge of the situation. He had talked with Andrew Young and worked out some type of arrangement to allow the march. Clark would tell Baker, "I'm in charge. I'm sheriff of the county and the city is in the county and these people are violating the law."

At one point, an agreement was struck whereby Baker had jurisdiction over the marchers as they walked to the courthouse

Mayor Joe Smitherman with Sheriff Jim Clark, who is wearing his NEVER button
(Courtesy of George H. Braxton)

and Clark had jurisdiction once they got there. But this never worked smoothly. Joe Smitherman, the new mayor, would go along with Baker's strategy for a while, then veer over to favor Clark's. He fired Baker every other day for about fifteen minutes.

Smitherman was the city's first mayor who wasn't a blueblood. Far from it. He was a washing machine and refrigerator salesman from the wrong side of the tracks—widowed mother on welfare, no college education. He had worked for a guy named Pop Gillis, a political character around Selma who gathered the lower-class white vote and worked with the big shots. Pop owned Selma Appliance, and Smitherman was a great salesman. He has the gift of gab. Through Pop, he got involved in politics and was elected to the City Council in 1960. He was skinny, jug-eared, ambitious, personable. I didn't take note of him until he ran for mayor. I had no inkling he was going to be a central figure in Selma's life, and mine, for a long time to come.

Smitherman was backed in the mayor's race by a group of young men called the Committee of One Hundred. This was a postwar phenomenon on the white side—younger men finding themselves frozen out of power if they weren't sons of the select few. They wanted economic growth and a piece of the action, but they couldn't get anything going because the city fathers who controlled Selma's economy and dominated the Chamber of Commerce were uninterested in industrial expansion or any type of change. Joe campaigned on a platform of paving streets, recruiting industry, and serving *all* citizens—meaning all whites.

Chris Heinz, who'd been mayor for a decade, was the in-crowd's man. This election—in 1964—was the first time in my experience that whites were out really trying to hustle up those three hundred black votes—going around asking blacks with influence to use it on behalf of their candidate. It was interesting to watch this group from the country club publicly displaying its sense of superiority over whites of Joe Smitherman's class.

"That man has never seen the inside of a university and wouldn't know what to do if you took him to one," Judge Hare told me. "He has no more business being mayor of this city than you do."

I didn't even vote in that election because I had no enthusiasm for either candidate. Both Smitherman and Heinz were toeing the line with the White Citizens' Council; in fact, Heinz became its president after he lost the election. When Benny Tucker and a few other Selma University students had gone to see Smitherman as a councilman about desegregating city facilities, he'd chased them out with a baseball bat.

Smitherman squeaked in, and three months later, King showed up. Baker had gone off to teach law enforcement at the University of Alabama after Clark defeated him for sheriff. Smitherman brought him back to Selma to be the city's Director of Public Safety.

When the movement broke, Smitherman's constituency was

split on which tactics were best, Clark's or Baker's. In Clark's camp were the poor whites—Smitherman's people, they voted for him—and the loud, emotional group in the Citizens' Council. Baker had a number of the bluebloods who'd campaigned against Smitherman, but also the younger businessmen and bankers who'd been for him. So Smitherman was in the middle, playing both sides to stay alive politically.

One day the Citizens' Council would be on him: "We can't let these niggers take over our city." He'd push Baker to arrest the marchers, fire him if he refused, or request state troopers from George Wallace. Then the bankers and so-called moderates would call him over for a midnight meeting: "Goddamn it, you're playing right in their hands. They want to be arrested." Andrew Young had regular contact with Smitherman and Baker so we were aware of these strains. I later thought it very fitting that Andy became an ambassador. That was his role in Selma.

Claude Brown talked to the moderates occasionally and told me how much they decried Clark's brutality and bemoaned the situation. I didn't sympathize. The moderates were not interested in our objectives. They wanted peace in the streets so they could return to business as usual. I think a few were genuinely willing to see some small changes in Selma—if they could have found a way to do it without any exposure on their part. At best, they'd have a secret meeting and then be worried to death that word of the meeting would leak out.

By confining Clark to the courthouse and being a moderating influence on Smitherman, Baker was useful. Remove Baker from the situation and we might have had the same volatile problem at City Hall that we had at the courthouse and the whole thing might have exploded with more violence than it did. But Baker also was a serious problem. He was very slick. One day, a big group of demonstrators, maybe a hundred people, marched to the courthouse, ready for a major confrontation. Baker persuaded the state troopers and Clark to allow four or five blacks in at a time, which would have eliminated the confrontation had we agreed. On another occasion, Clark and the troopers declared, "No marches." Then Baker came to Brown Chapel and said he'd negotiated for us to hold a limited march down a particular street.

And since he'd helped us there, how about going along with him and having just one march a day? He was forever maneuvering and manipulating.

Each time, there'd be discussion and disagreement on our side, because some people would favor the compromise. Hell, the man was meeting us halfway. But King reminded us to keep our eyes on the prize: This movement was about winning citizenship for black people in America, not about having a march in Selma.

Judge Hare was so emotional on the subject of race, he couldn't think in terms of smart tactics. He kept pushing Clark out there. In this, he deserted his class, many of whom were aligned with Baker's more subtle strategy. "There are whites right here in this city who don't understand our whole culture, our whole existence is under threat here," the judge told me.

I think Hare and the loudmouths in the White Citizens' Council became victims of their own rationalizations. At stake was white womanhood, the purity of the white race, the protection of America from Communism, so there was no room to sit down and reach rational compromises. In their self-serving blindness, they helped produce the Voting Rights Act.

Around black Selma that winter I began to see a transformation, a subtle revision of the power arrangement revealed to me by Shields and the baseball incident when I was a boy: black public opinion began to hold a little weight. Heretofore, you could do almost anything to black Selma, whether you were white or black, and escape without punishment—hardly even any talk. In 1965, for the first time, black people, especially leaders, had to be concerned not only with how they were thought of downtown but with how they were thought of in black Selma. Suddenly preachers and middle-class blacks began saying, "I'm my own man," instead of bragging about their contacts with the mayor or the police chief. Leaders like Reverend Lett and Edwin Moss had to move closer to the movement to retain credibility. In 1963, when SNCC started Selma's first demonstrations, Edwin and a few black businessmen and pastors had created something called the Dallas County Improvement Association and declared publicly that they were against the marches. At the same time, they asked white businesses to ease up on segregation and provide jobs to blacks—classic Ed Moss moderation in going along with the white powers but asking for some *quid pro quo*. By 1965, Edwin wasn't knocking marches. He was marching and financing bonds for demonstrators.

At the bootleg joints, I'd hear fellas say, "Why do we have to be nonviolent? What these people need is some violence." Black people had always been so careful of what they said to each other for fear someone would take it downtown. Now they were talking about violence in a bootlegger's house—a bootlegger who has all kinds of contact with the police or he couldn't be selling whiskey.

I'd go in the Elks and, lo and behold, run into a long discussion about what we could do with the vote, maybe get some blacks on the City Council, put some brakes on the police. My God! A miracle. I'd sit there trying to analyze how it happened, but couldn't. So much was involved.

I think Bernard Lafayette and the other SNCC people, plus Dick Gregory, James Baldwin, and the successes elsewhere of the civil rights struggle, had a cumulative impact. King gave the movement in Selma more legitimacy and raised the confidence factor. If he was in, powerful white people in Washington would be watching. Also, sad to say, the white excess required to shock white America into coming to the aid of black Southerners was required to move some black people right in Selma. Every time Sheriff Clark went to extremes—shoved Mrs. Boynton, used cattle prods on children—more local blacks said, "That's it. I'm marching."

Then there was SCLC's answer to the White Citizens' Council, its gangster element threatening to start a black boycott of black businessmen who didn't line up with the movement. One or two SCLC workers weren't above going into homes and embarrassing men in front of their wives and children by calling them cowards or telling an Uncle Tom, "If you don't knock off that crap, you're gonna wish you had, and I'm not kidding." I saw this and had mixed feelings. How much were Selma people going to be asked to sacrifice? Black businessmen already had a precarious existence, and I didn't think it would help black Selma in the long run for them to be run out of business. But white Selma had so much power over black Selma, I came to the conclusion some of this was necessary.

I knew things were really changing when the schoolteachers,

of all people, marched. Reese organized it, gave a speech at the black teachers' association saying teachers ought not let their students and the working-class people do for them what they should be doing for themselves. He asked how many would be willing to march to the courthouse the next Friday afternoon, and wrote down names. He told them to bring a toothbrush in case they were jailed and promised to get them bailed out by the beginning of the school day Monday.

I was upstairs in court when they arrived and a deputy came in to report a demonstration outside. I ran downstairs and looked out the door. Over a hundred teachers were standing on the sidewalk, bundled up in the cold. Reese and Andrew Durgan, a teacher, were in the front. I was surprised to see Joe Yelder, the principal of Hudson High who'd threatened to call the police on Bernard two years earlier. Reese later told me that Yelder had been away at a convention of black principals and had been hoping the march would already have taken place by the time he returned. He was sorry he had come back so soon—but he rose to the occasion and marched.

At the top of the stairs, with their backs to me as I looked out, were Sheriff Clark; Joe Pickard, the superintendent of schools; and Edgar Stewart, president of the school board.

"What do you want?" Clark asked.

"We came to get registered," Reese said. He said he'd sent a letter to the board of registrars saying the teachers would be there.

Stewart told Reese they'd made their point. They knew the registration office wasn't open.

As citizens they were going into the courthouse, Reese declared, and he, Durgan, and a few others walked to the top of the stairs and stood face to face with the sheriff and their bosses. Clark had it then, said they were making a mockery of the courthouse. He and his deputies got out billy clubs and jabbed at the teachers as they pushed them down the stairs. This happened two or three times, up and down, until Pickard and Stewart grabbed Clark's shirt and pulled him inside. The news media were shooting film of the whole thing, and they knew how it would look to arrest a bunch of teachers.

When Reese realized they weren't going to be arrested, he led the teachers to Brown Chapel. I left and went with them. It was dusk, and when they reached the Carver Homes, people came out of their houses to see them—my God! the teachers are marching!—and clapped. A group of students were in Brown Chapel at a mass meeting, and they gave their teachers a standing ovation. I was elated. It was a real breakthrough, and in the week that followed, there was an undertakers' march and a black businessmen's march. Part of this, though, were the threats: If you don't march, we'll put your black ass out of business.

I couldn't wait to get home to tell my mother that some of her colleagues were at the courthouse trying to get arrested. She said, "Well, I don't believe in that, but now, I do believe in voting." Not long afterward, I looked around at a meeting at Brown Chapel and there was my mother! She'd come with my sister Dimp, who marched and demonstrated all the time. My mother later told me that she agreed with what was said at the meeting, but she didn't go again. She said they weren't her type people and she didn't know the songs. My father didn't come to a meeting or demonstration, but he eagerly expressed his support of the movement in the barbershops, clubs, and wherever else he went in the black community.

Vivian and the children stayed in Mississippi. But during the height of activities that February, Vivian came back to Selma with me on many occasions, bringing the children along. She hated sitting in Mississippi glued to the TV set trying to see me. She participated in several marches, but without much enthusiasm. Deep down, Vivian believed that men, not women and children, ought to be in the front ranks being cattle-prodded and going to jail. Black men ought to be doing that on behalf of black women and children. But Vivian thought the sun rose and set with King, and if King said women ought to be involved, then Vivian would get out there. She never felt right about it, however.

The changes that winter were not easy for some black preachers and leaders whose arrangements and life-styles were geared to the old format. Claude Brown was so torn. The leaders in the white community expected him to be on their side. Yet he knew he had a role of leadership in the black community and blacks needed him. It almost killed him—the torment of not being able to be what everyone expected him to be and being unsure what he really should be. He was straddling two eras, uncertain as to what was right.

We continued to discuss and debate in his office. He was very disturbed about the movement's using children, taking them out of school to march. He saw education as the way up for black people, and he foresaw problems in teaching children civil disobedience.

He was deeply saddened that race relations in Selma were being smashed to smithereens. I thought race relations were going to have to be worse before they'd ever get better, that what he was dealing with was superficial, anyway. But Claude believed deeply in the innate goodness of people, particularly white people, and he thought we should be appealing to their good side. I said I didn't think innate goodness was applicable in this situation. We were dealing with group psychology. There was almost as much fear on the white side as on the black side. All they had to do was call somebody a nigger-lover. Sometimes I'd repeat to Claude what King often preached: that by freeing ourselves, black people would be freeing white people, too.

For all his deep reservations about what was happening to Selma, Claude couldn't turn his back on the movement and remain the kind of leader he wanted to be. So he provided the mobile van that King used on the march to Montgomery, and he financed bonds under the table. He was constantly finding out what was being talked about at City Hall or among the white people he knew. Then he would make suggestions to me or directly to King.

It was not so much out of guilt that Claude supplied the van and bond money as it was a recognition that King might be right, might be onto something. He understood the importance of the vote and the dignity tied up in it. He was not sure, couldn't be, that his way would ever bring that about, certainly not any time soon. He was discouraged that Selma's white political leaders refused to even meet with black leaders. He knew that enough pressure and disruption in Selma was bound to bring some concessions and improvements. But whether these would be worth the cost he didn't know—or what the cost would be.

By the time Claude died in 1975, he and I had come full circle. He'd always been begging me to quit drinking; I wound up begging him. He started serious drinking in 1965. He wanted to be a responsible man and do right in the eyes of God. He wanted to be respected by blacks and whites. Yet he was being called an Uncle Tom in the black community and ineffective in the white community.

The one redeeming thing for him was the young people he helped. One night when we were sitting in his office talking and he was really blue, a young man came by to visit. The young man had grown up in a run-down shack in east Selma. Claude had helped the whole family with food and clothes, and had gotten the boy a scholarship to Knoxville College. The young man came in wearing a uniform to show Claude. He was a lieutenant on the Chicago police force. Claude was so happy to see him. He took infinite delight and satisfaction in this young man's success.

CHAPTER 12

Born Again

On the day that became known as "Bloody Sunday," March 7, 1965, the civil rights leaders, as always, walked a tightrope. They often talked, privately, about the necessity of a Jim Clark, of visible white brutality. But how did you get optimum benefit from that and minimize harm to your people at the same time—and was that possible?

I had driven over from Mississippi that Wednesday and had been trying for days to get back. But indecision and confusion over whether there would be a march to Montgomery kept me hanging around. Jim Clark, George Wallace, Judge Hare had made it clear they'd had all the damn demonstrations they would permit. Baker played his usual role behind the scenes, telling black leaders a march would be a mistake. Folk could get hurt. You ought to call it off. Some leaders in SCLC were saying a march at that point was not important enough to risk King, and some people in SNCC were saying, "Good, we don't need him, anyway." Then SNCC decided to bow out.

Tension was high. The idea of going to Montgomery arose following a violent attack on civil rights marchers in Marion, in Perry County, two weeks earlier. A young black man named Jimmie Lee Jackson was shot to death by a state trooper, and at his funeral, people started saying, "Goddamn it, we ought to carry his body over to George Wallace in Montgomery." This

Marchers stopped by state troopers on Bloody Sunday, March 7, 1965 (Courtesy of The Bettman Archive)

evolved into a plan to walk to Montgomery to petition Wallace for our right to vote.

The decision to march wasn't made until the eleventh hour—by King, who stayed in Atlanta to preach at his church. I think Andrew Young and a few others persuaded King they couldn't cancel the march. Hundreds of people were standing around outside Brown Chapel. Mrs. Boynton, Marie Foster, Reese, a group from Marion, were determined there was going to be a march if there wasn't anybody out there but them.

I walked over to the Montgomery side of the Edmund Pettus Bridge before everybody else and stationed myself at the side of the highway. State troopers and Clark's posse were standing in the road and along the side in front of several stores. We were about two blocks beyond the foot of the bridge.

I had earlier tried to find out what the authorities intended to do but couldn't get a definitive answer. Wallace had been declaring all week that the marchers would be stopped, but didn't say how. Later, he claimed he didn't issue orders to attack, and I think that's true. He wanted to be President of the United States, and he purposely gave vague instructions so he could capitalize on anything good and run from anything negative.

The Legal Defense Fund, as usual, was very anxious for information, and I found a pay phone so I could keep them posted as events developed. The marchers knew they weren't going to get far and carried no provisions for a fifty-mile hike. The question was whether they'd be arrested or attacked. I frankly hoped neither would happen—that the marchers, after a short, symbolic walk, would go back to the church so I could go back to my family and job in Mississippi.

It was a cool day but the sun was out. I was standing on a flatbed truck at the edge of the highway waiting. I could hear Sheriff Clark and Colonel Al Lingo, the troopers' commander, arguing about who was in charge. Soon the first pair of marchers crested over the hump in the middle of the bridge. They were: John Lewis, chairman of SNCC, with Hosea Williams of SCLC in the front row; Albert Turner and Robert Mants, activists from Perry and Lowndes Counties, in the second row; Mrs. Boynton and Marie Foster in the third row. As the column moved forward, I saw Reese and other teachers, Reverend Anderson, teenagers from Hudson High. They knelt briefly and prayed before they moved on toward us.

I wondered what feelings they had looking down at the rows of troopers in blue uniforms and white helmets stretched across the highway, the posse men in khaki uniforms carrying nightsticks big as baseball bats and mounted on fidgety horses, the large contingent of media people with cameras and microphones skirting between the marchers and the troopers, and the jeering crowd of rednecks waving Confederate flags on both sides of the highway.

As John Lewis and Hosea Williams came within a few yards of the troopers, I was on the phone with the Defense Fund in New York. I didn't catch the whole conversation, just a trooper saying over a bullhorn: "Disperse and go back to your church." The marchers stood in silence. I turned away for a moment, then heard something that sounded like a gun—must have been a tear-gas canister hitting the pavement.

The troopers rushed forward in a flying wedge. I saw the column

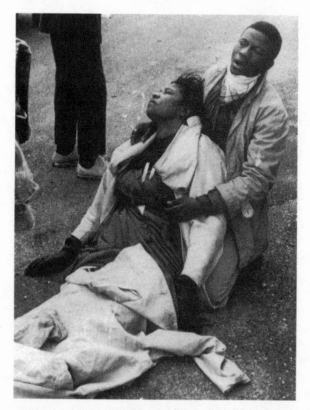

Tear-gassed black youth holds unconscious woman on Bloody Sunday (Courtesy of The Bettman Archive)

of marchers bend to the charge, then topple in sudden clusters. Some lay on the ground, moaning. Others ran, chased by the posse. More tear gas, galloping horses, flying nightsticks, screaming women and children, shrieking white spectators. "Git 'em! Git 'em!" Through the haze of tear gas, I saw a posse man raise his club and smash it down on a woman's head as if he were splitting a watermelon.

I said, "My God!" New York was asking, "What's going on? What's going on?" I described the scene and hung up. Once the troopers lit into the marchers, many ran back to Selma, with the posse in pursuit. Nobody was headed toward Montgomery after that. I made my way toward the bridge, pulled a woman with an injured ankle off the road, and helped Ace Anderson, a black funeral director, and Dr. Dinkins put people in Ace's black hearse, which doubled as an ambulance. Ace rode back and forth across the bridge with his siren going, picking up the injured. He loved that. He was important that day. John Lewis's head was cracked open, bleeding. He had a concussion. They took him to Good Samaritan. There was utter confusion, blood, people lying down. It looked like a battlefield.

My eyes were stinging and my head hurt. I had hoped violence would not occur, but I really was not surprised. It reaffirmed in my mind that a culture geared to deal first with slave insurrections, then with maintaining rigid segregation was prepared to do whatever was necessary to keep its foot in the black man's face. The white South was ready and felt a righteousness about its cause many black people did not feel about ours. To me, what happened on the bridge was nothing new. It shocked the nation because most Americans, including many white Southerners, weren't witnesses to the routine brutality in "niggertowns" all over the South.

Walking across the bridge into Selma, I thought, Here I am from Howard University Law School, an officer in the white man's court, debating with Martin Luther King about the supremacy of law. And here are representatives of the law trampling on the law, on the Constitution, and somehow that's not quite wrong because black folk are not quite people. Am I fooling myself? Wasting my time? What is all this about the Constitution and the law? Black people. My God! We will never be Americans.

I was very surprised by the avalanche of support for our cause from many quarters. Hundreds of people from all parts of the country poured into Selma. King was always talking about "public opinion" and the power of the media to move it in our favor, but until then, I couldn't see it. Being from Selma, I wasn't focused on the national impact. As far as I could tell, the press wasn't having any impact on Jim Clark or Judge Hare or Al Lingo. Law enforcement was out there beating people in broad daylight in the middle of a public highway with the cameras rolling, so what's this about the power of the press?

Everybody in Selma was amazed by the influx of concerned

whites. I think most white Selmians rationalized the attack on the bridge the same way Hare did: "They were asking for it. They provoked it." White Selma didn't expect any more than I did that the aborted march and King's call to the nation would inspire busloads of white nuns and planeloads of white professors and white ministers to come to our little town.

Some of the professors and ministers went to the courthouse and talked to Judge Hare. Hare would get out his dog-eared copy of the Moynihan report to show the alleged inferiority of black people. Hare's spiel was that any qualified Negro who wants to vote can vote, but most of the qualified Negroes don't even want to. "They have lived close to us for year and years. They're used to us taking care of these things. They don't want to be bothered with all that. Sometimes I wish I didn't have to be bothered. They've got the best end of it." Then he'd go into his Africa bag.

The visitors were polite. Some would take issue with Hare. Others would sit and say nothing, but you could see their disbelief. Hare wasn't looking for any real communication. It had a therapeutic effect on him to go through that performance. He had a genuine dislike of Northern white people. He honestly felt that they had ruined the South for economic gain, that slavery was just a cover. They killed the South with differentials in freight rates, reduced it to an agrarian economy to feed the Northern manufacturers. Hare maintained, though, that the federal government in the end would be forced to side with the white people of the South because non-Southern whites would demand it. In the end, a white man is a white man.

I had that view myself. So did George Wallace. He ran for President on it and got a hell of a lot of Northern votes. Despite all of King's beautiful rhetoric about "moving America," I figured white America would move only just so far for black people. I did not anticipate that white Americans would be so sickened by the unrestrained excesses against black Americans as to rearrange the face of the South and transform American politics.

But the fact was, all these white people, many hundreds, came to Selma to march. They faced the possibility of being shot, beaten, or ridiculed, but they were willing to risk it. That was a revelation. It's one thing to sit in New York and send a check.

It's another to come South and lock arms with a black person and say, "We shall overcome." I thought, What the hell is this? A number of these people were young; a few were of questionable character. But no way could you call most of them riffraff, as Judge Hare did. They were the cream of the crop—Governor Peabody of Massachusetts, his seventy-year-old mother, rabbis, nuns, congressmen. So it was reassessment time for J. L. Chestnut.

Until then, the majority of people who came to Selma to participate in the demonstrations had been black. The influx of large numbers of whites couldn't help but activate the old Southern obsession with interracial sex. Hare and other white men talked incessantly about the black and white demonstrators at Brown Chapel engaging in some sort of "sex carnival." The judge told me one day these white girls had come all the way down from Ivy League colleges expressly to have wild, illicit interracial sex. "It's an experience, James," he said. He was so sad. That was cutting his insides out. If the marches didn't ruin the country, miscegenation would.

A different challenge to Southern sexual mores made some white men in law enforcement very uncomfortable. What should a white Southern gentleman do with black female marchers? Policemen had been sending a message to the black community for years by whipping black men publicly. But what about black women who threatened the order and got arrogant about it? Could you just slap them down? Is this Southern? Is this the way we act?

I first noticed this discomfort in the reaction of H. H. Mosely, the old warden at the Dallas County Jail, to the arrest of a group of young black women who participated in a march led by Dick Gregory's pregnant wife. Mosely was very apprehensive about the women being in his jail. He was pushing me hard to obtain some bonds and get the women out in a hurry. Though Jim Clark was his boss, Mosely clearly had reservations about the way Clark sometimes treated black women—pushing them in the registration line if they got smart with him. That was out of the question for Mosely. And he definitely disapproved of the lowlife jailers at Camp Selma peeping at the female prisoners. They were black but they were also women and the South put women on pedestals. "You got to help me, J.L. I can't be responsible. I'm not here twenty-four hours a day. Get them out!" I thought the man was going to have a heart attack. I capitalized on his concern, increased it by referring to the black women in his jail as "these mothers" and "these wives."

Blanchard McLeod, the only circuit solicitor I ever knew who came to court wearing a big pistol on his hip, was very sensitive on this female thing, too. I used it to throw off his equilibrium in the courtroom and also to try to get something done about the Camp Selma situation. I was forever arguing about something that had allegedly happened to some black girl out there—she was felt up or they reached under her dress. Sometimes it wouldn't even be true. I'd make it up. McLeod would get very nervous and excited: "Produce the girl! Produce the girl!"

Within a week of Bloody Sunday, James Reeb, a white minister from Boston, was attacked on Washington Street by a group of white thugs. He was taken to Good Samaritan Hospital, where Dr. Dinkins was the attending physician. Doc himself escorted the ambulance taking Reeb to a better hospital in Birmingham. The ambulance blew a recap tire, then had some other mechanical problem along the way. Doc later told me how frightened he was during the long drive.

Reeb died a few days later, which magnified the national furor and brought more planeloads of people to Selma. White Selma also took Reeb's death seriously. The courthouse was extremely tense and conversation seemed muffled. Judge Hare was not nearly as talkative as usual. I expected the usual tirade about "it's unfortunate but he should have expected trouble, coming down here meddling in a situation he doesn't understand and trying to tell us how to live." But I couldn't hardly get any conversation over it.

So much happened within two short weeks. Big glaciers of ice were melting. I found myself assessing, reassessing, and reassessing my reassessments. One day I'd be so encouraged. But anytime I got too optimistic, my instinctual skepticism—developed in thirty-five years as a black man in America—would reassert itself and I'd draw back: "Well now, I don't know. Don't get too excited here." I was at Porter's the night President Johnson gave his famous "We shall overcome" speech to a joint session of Congress. About six of us were there, sitting on the couches in the front room looking at the television. While we were waiting, somebody said, "I wonder if he's going to say anything about Selma." Somebody else said, "He certainly can't ignore Selma after what's happened here."

Johnson came on and talked directly about Selma—an outrage, an American tragedy. He said he was sending Congress a bill to strike down all the restrictions used to deny people the right to vote. When he concluded his speech with the movement's refrain, "We shall overcome," a loud cheer went up in the room, like at a basketball game when your team has just scored.

Once again, I thought, Good God, this thing is moving faster than I ever imagined. It hadn't been long before, less than two years, that the Voters League and Bernard Lafayette and I had had trouble getting a discussion going about voting. Now I was sitting at Porter's and the President of the United States was on television talking about these things and folk were jumping up and cheering.

I later read that King had tears in his eyes when the President said, "We shall overcome." That honestly was not my reaction. I was happy at the moment but, on reflection, I became uncomfortable. It suddenly dawned on me that King was no longer the number-one civil rights leader in America; Lyndon Johnson was. I was afraid we'd been outfoxed and were in danger of being co-opted. Johnson, and Kennedy before him, were always advocating gradualism. "Don't march. Don't push too hard." This was the same Lyndon Johnson who had told King just a month or so earlier, "Go back home. I can't get you a voting rights bill now. I just got you a public accommodations bill."

Johnson made his "We shall overcome" speech and sent up the Voting Rights Bill only because we had ignored him. If he became recognized as the man responsible for our civil rights victories and allowed to set our agenda, did this mean the end of the movement?

Then came the high of the fifty-mile, five-day march from Selma to Montgomery. Thousands upon thousands of people filled the

Martin Luther King, Jr., and others on the Edmund Pettus Bridge at the beginning of our triumphant march to Montgomery, March 21, 1965 (© *Selma Times-Journal*)

street in front of the capitol on March 25, when the marchers reached Montgomery, more people than I'd seen together in one place in my life.

The impressive thing to me was that no white person had decided there would be a march or where or how far it would go. Those were black decisions. A white judge said, "Well, okay, it's legal," and a white President federalized the National Guard, but they were reacting to a situation created by black people. Blacks were in charge, and there were whites in the march who clearly agreed with this arrangement and were there to play a supporting role. The march to Montgomery was the first enterprise I'd ever seen involving black and white people where the black people set the agenda and ran the show.

All of this had even greater significance because of a prior revelation which changed me forever. This had happened several

months earlier when I came out of the federal building one afternoon to witness a remarkable confrontation between SNCC president John Lewis and Sheriff Clark. The federal building is directly
across the street from the county courthouse. I had been inside
arguing motions before Judge Thomas and wasn't even aware a
march was planned. I came out on the steps and there in the
street below was an awesome line of state troopers—blue uniforms shoulder to shoulder at parade rest, stretching two blocks
in each direction. Standing in front of the troopers in the middle
of the street were Jim Clark and four or five deputies. Facing
Clark was John Lewis and a ragtag group of about twenty marchers. Clark said, "This is as far as you can go. Turn around and
go back. You are *not* going in the courthouse today."

John said, "The courthouse is a public place and we have a
right to go inside. We will not be turned around."

A moment passed. "Did you hear what I said?" Clark demanded. "Turn around and go back." He got right up in John's
face and glared at him, eyeball to eyeball. He was gripping his
billy club, one hand at each end, twisting hard. The tension was
almost unbearable.

"Did you hear what *I* said?" John replied. "We are *not* going
back." He stood his ground, staring directly at Clark with his
usual impassive all-business expression. Marie Foster was standing next to him wearing her usual expression of defiance.

I could feel my heart pound in my head. This boy is crazy, I
thought. A few days earlier Clark had hit an SCLC leader, Reverend C. T. Vivian, in the mouth and knocked him flat a few feet
from where Clark and John were standing. I just knew John was
going to be hurt. Everything I'd seen in my lifetime in Selma told
me so.

I waited there nervously for two minutes that seemed like two
hours as the big, burly white man and the rather short, small black
man faced off in the middle of Alabama Avenue. Then Clark
blinked and backed away. "Goddamn it, go on in," he said, and
the blue line of troopers parted like the Red Sea—exactly the
opposite of all those Saturday nights on the Drag when black folk
moved aside for Mr. Craw.

I was stunned. "I'll be damned. I'll be *damned*! The establishment has blinked!" In that moment I saw that the white South

was not invincible. What I had thought was power in numbers and weapons I began to see as a kind of weakness. If ever I was born again, I was born again right there on the courthouse steps. It was a kind of conversion. It changed my whole outlook.

I understood for the first time some of the things King had been saying. Up until that point, my view was: King went to college. So did I. We were almost the same age. He studied theology and he had his agenda. I studied law and I had mine. What he was doing out there was moving the masses, but I thought I knew how far this thing could go. I didn't really pay attention to him talking about moral right being superior to temporal power or saying, "If there's nothing for which you are willing to die, you are not fit to live." That was oratory for the masses. I thought nonviolence was aimed at the street people, too. I saw no need for me, a middle-class, angry, but educated lawyer, to stop wearing my pistol even though King was on my case about it, calling me a "man of little faith."

John Lewis demonstrated to me that King was not bullshitting about any of this. There was no way Lewis could not have been scared to death. But he stood his ground and won. And he didn't have any pistols. He didn't have any troops. He just had about twenty resolute folk there in a little line. Yet he stood face to face with the power of Alabama and refused on moral grounds to give in—and Alabama blinked.

I thought, To hell with Hare. To hell with Judge Thomas. I have spied your nakedness. All my life I believed that white power could and would draw the line whenever and wherever it wanted, and there was absolutely nothing black people could do about it. The civil rights movement would force some concessions. But there was a limit to how much accommodation the white South would make, and when it decided it was over, it would be over. John Lewis demonstrated this wasn't necessarily true. If you stood up to it, you could prevail.

That gave me a new lease on life. The white South did not own this whole ballpark to do with as it pleased. I saw a future with more possibility than I'd ever imagined. And I didn't worry nearly so much about who was going to get killed or injured in the next march. Fears that had followed me almost from day one of my life were just gone.

Demonstrators (John Lewis on far left) face Sheriff Clark (right) in front of the Dallas County Courthouse. The federal building is in the background (*Selma Times-Journal*)

Come Bloody Sunday, when John Lewis again faced white power and it gave him a concussion, I had some reassessing to do. But even there, the actions of the state of Alabama revealed desperation more than strength. With this blatant use of power, they were losing power. Never again would I go back to the proposition that the white South was invincible. Those pillars of impenetrable strength had moved before my eyes. I realized: I don't have to be wearing a gun. I don't have to be drinking. Maybe we can overcome.

PART FOUR

1965 - 1985

Me in the library of our law firm (Courtesy of J. L. Chestnut, Jr.)

Introduction

White Selma was deeply stung when portrayed internationally as Hate City, USA. That just wasn't true! Their friends and neighbors were nice people. They had cordial relations with local blacks, who hadn't been complaining about their treatment. The marchers were outsiders. Martin Luther King, Jr., was using Selma as a backdrop to get national publicity and money. The Northern media had blown everything out of proportion and given the false impression that if you walked down a street in Selma some white person would be beating up a black person.

The fact that King employed tactics and used the media was considered by many white Selmians as evidence of insincerity and deviousness. The strategy of the civil rights movement—based on the unfortunate reality that it took mass arrests and physical violence against nonviolent blacks, recorded by television, to move white America on behalf of black people—was in white Selma thought to mean that the demonstrators wanted *to go to jail. They* wanted *to be attacked. They asked for it. They were doing it for the cameras.*

On Bloody Sunday, when the marchers ran back into Selma chased by the mounted posse, B. Frank Wilson, then an officer of People's Bank, was standing on Broad Street near the foot of the bridge. He remembers the day well: "Sheriff Clark rode by on a big horse, and a good friend of mine, who was standing there with

*me, yelled out to Clark, 'Good way!' Many people I considered
friends—really good, decent people—thought the demonstrators got
what they deserved. My soul just cried. What a sad thing it was,
what a horrible thing for Selma, Alabama."*

*Wilson was a member of an unofficial group that had been meet-
ing secretly for about six months trying to prevent what happened
on the bridge—violence and bad publicity. This group of about a
dozen men included the presidents of some Selma banks and a few
wealthy businessmen and prominent lawyers. Compared with others in the white community, they were moderate in their viewpoint.
"Nobody was advocating integration," said Sam Earl Hobbs, a
white attorney and bank officer. "But we thought some accommodation would have to be made with the black community and
we thought Clark was promoting violence."*

*Just prior to King's arrival, Ralph Smeltzer, a Church of the
Brethren minister who had spent six months in Selma trying to
mediate a peaceful resolution between the races, detailed SCLC's
plans to the "moderate" group and warned of the potential for
violence and federal intervention. He suggested that the businessmen promote some concessions—a less stringent application of
voting regulations and compliance with the 1964 Civil Rights Act
requiring integration of public facilities—to head off a confrontation.*

*At this point, Probate Judge Reynolds had removed the COL-
ORED and WHITE signs on the drinking fountains in the Dallas
County Courthouse and put out paper cups. But he balked at
integrating the restrooms. He wasn't going to expose white people
to venereal disease, he said. The city closed the municipal swimming pool rather than integrate it. Some Selma restaurateurs had
opened their doors to black people, but others were putting off
compliance in the hope that the Act would be struck down in the
courts.*

*The only public facility in Selma to be integrated voluntarily,
before the law required it, was the library. This was done quietly
in May 1963 because the new director, Pat Blalock, believed
strongly that everyone should be able to come inside, read, and
check out books. (Previously, black people had knocked on the
back door and the library's maid checked out books for them.)*

For a while, all the chairs were removed, then quietly returned.
Smeltzer argued to the businessmen that if they convinced city
and county officials and business owners to comply with the law—
which they were going to have to do, anyway—and persuaded the
Board of Registrars to modify the registration process, King might
take his campaign elsewhere. The businessmen listened but took
no action.

As demonstrators and newsmen filled the streets, the moderates
met at night, usually in the board room at People's Bank. The
group called Clark to one meeting. "He told us to go to hell,"
Hobbs said. They were unpersuasive with Judge Hare, too, and
Smitherman was unpredictable. A serious problem seems to have
been that they were afraid to say anything publicly, though they
didn't put it that way to themselves.

"We felt we could be more effective behind the scenes instead of
being shouted down and have our friends and neighbors and cus-
tomers against us," Wilson said. "We were trying to calm, not
inflame, passions, to reach a peaceful resolution. We were in a
minority, and I don't see how we could have expanded the group
much if we had spoken out publicly. Though others felt as we did,
they wouldn't have joined us because of what their friends would
think about a group that was willing to sit down and negotiate with
black people." So absolute resistance—symbolized by the NEVER!
buttons worn by Sheriff Clark, his posse and supporters—was the
only position with public expression of support in white Selma in
the winter of 1965.

The white churches in Selma were mute about the situation in
the streets, though they were wrestling with the race issue. In the
early 1960s, many national denominations were passing canons or
other internal decrees stating that people of all colors should be
able to worship in their churches. Congregations in Selma and
elsewhere in the South had to decide whether to go along or break
with their national organizations.

St. Paul's Episcopal Church, whose congregation included many
prominent Selma families, among them Hobbs and Judge Hare,
was bitterly divided over whether to approve such a canon. The
vestry voted by a narrow margin to uphold it. But when a racially
mixed group of civil rights workers came to St. Paul's for a "kneel-

in," a group of members turned them away at the door, saying they weren't really coming to worship. This action made a different set of members mad, and when another group came to kneel-in several weeks later, they were allowed inside.

The pastor of the First Presbyterian Church took a strong stand against blocking anybody from worshipping in the church. Some long-standing members left the congregation. A Methodist church split. Selma's largest church, First Baptist (white), established a "sidewalk committee" of men to stand outside during services to make sure no black person came inside. All of Selma's white congregations resented the ministers from the North who came to town for the Selma-to-Montgomery march, and no white church in Selma was willing to hold a memorial service for James Reeb when he was killed.

The first moderates to speak out publicly were a Buick dealer named Arthur Lewis and his wife, Muriel. Lewis was wealthy, having made money in the cigar factory where Chestnut's mother and aunt worked for several summers and in other enterprises around Selma since moving South in the 1940s. He was Jewish, Yale-educated, and an avid Selma booster. At one point, he was president of the Kiwanis Club. Though Lewis was as moderate on race as they came in white Selma, he was good friends with Clark and Smitherman.

"One day the president of a black college came in Art's show-room and my husband held out his hand. The black man stood there with his mouth open and finally said, 'You know, you're the first white man who ever shook my hand.' That really got to Art," Mrs. Lewis said. *"But we were Yankees and Jewish, so we stayed on the sidelines"—until Bloody Sunday.*

After the violence on the bridge, Mrs. Lewis fired off a letter to Time *magazine in which she wrote that local moderates had been too quiet but were working for peace and obedience to the law, including the Civil Rights Act. Locally, the Lewises sent a letter expressing their feelings to close friends and relatives. The White Citizens' Council got a copy of the letter, duplicated it, and sent copies around town. One copy was read publicly on the courthouse steps.*

"The Citizens' Council was run by some of the most respected

people in Selma, but they tried to ruin us," Mrs. Lewis said. A racist poster was put in their yard. They got a flood of hate mail and phone calls. People were told to boycott the dealership, friends gave them the cold shoulder, and Lewis was no longer welcome in the offices of Clark or Smitherman.

This opposition only stiffened their resolve. In early April, Lewis called the group of moderate businessmen to his house and tried to persuade them to sign a mild public statement calling for negotiation and communications that he intended to send to the Times-Journal. *The businessmen refused. They told the Lewises their letter had made them too controversial to be effective and asked the couple to stop discussing the race issue, Mrs. Lewis recalled.*

The same week, the state Chamber of Commerce, upset at Alabama's worsening national image, adopted a moderate civil rights statement and invited local chambers to sign it. It supported obedience to all laws, the right to vote for all "qualified" citizens, upgraded education, improved communication, and an expanding economy. The Selma-Dallas County Chamber voted against endorsing the statement, which was signed by seventeen of the largest chambers in Alabama and published in The Wall Street Journal *and other national as well as Alabama newspapers.*

Infamous Selma was conspicuous in its absence. Top executives of the Hammermill Company, which had just announced its plan to open a $30 million paper mill in Selma, and of the Dan River Company and other Dallas County industries with national markets, placed concerned phone calls to the mayor and business leaders. The companies were taking a lot of flak, and civil rights groups were threatening to boycott their products. The SCLC was picketing Hammermill's headquarters in Erie, Pennsylvania.

With this selling point, the group of moderate businessmen went to work to get the chamber to reconsider, gathering signatures from people they thought would be sympathetic. The publisher of the Times-Journal *got behind the effort, too. Unlike newspapers in many small Southern towns, the* Times-Journal *did report on civil rights events and its editorial position was more moderate than some—denouncing King as a "Judas Goat," a "controversial darky" and "the most notorious liar in the country," but also taking*

Clark and his posse to task for chasing a group of young demonstrators through the woods with cattle prods.

At a heated, two-hour chamber meeting, one faction argued that the chamber shouldn't cave in, and another argued that the community stood to lose Hammermill and Dan River. In the end, the chamber voted to endorse the statement, and Hammermill and the other industries helped pay to run the ad. "It was something we had to do because of economic pressure," Mayor Smitherman said years later. "A dollar bill will change a lot of people's positions." Publication of the ad and signatures in late April 1965 was the first public statement of any position other than diehard resistance.

CHAPTER 13

Picking Up
the Pieces

After the march to Montgomery, most everybody went home—
except, of course, we local folk. We were at home. As soon as
the school year was over at Mississippi Valley State, I packed up
Vivian and the children and we returned to Selma, to Eugene
Street. Vivian had mixed emotions—glad to be leaving Mississippi
but sorry to be moving back to Selma. My parents were pleased.

Tensions had lowered somewhat, but Selma remained un-
nerved. There were sporadic marches to the courthouse. The
police looked on, trailed the marchers, but made no arrests. A
boycott of white merchants begun earlier continued unabated.

Black Selma was tired, and many folk felt relieved that the
army was gone. To the young people, though, it was as if a circus
had packed up and left—only worse. In February and March
they'd been civil rights marchers changing the nation. Now they
were just children in school. That was a big letdown. My mother
said her students didn't listen or pay attention the rest of the year.
Everyone waited and watched to see what would happen next.

I began to notice a shift in white Selma—from don't-give-an-
inch to something more like damage control. They had been held
up to ridicule around the world. It was clear there were limits to
what Washington and black people would accept. Major voting
rights legislation was coming. If Selma was going to be a viable

city instead of a municipal disgrace, some accommodation was necessary.

Judge Hare, Jim Clark, and the White Citizens' Council were still yelling "Never!" But thinking white people were trying to devise the least amount of accommodation while maintaining as much of their way of life as they could. In effect, the Yankees had won again. But a hundred years earlier, the South had stolen the victory. Could they do that once more?

The Chamber of Commerce, the moderates who came forward, were not advocating a restructuring of the South on an integrated basis where blacks would be their equals. They were trying to determine how much they would have to give up to get the Yankees off their back and bring the marches to a halt. Not long after the march to Montgomery, Mayor Smitherman and some councilmen starting having biracial meetings with F. D. Reese, Ernest Doyle, Edwin Moss, Marie Foster, and Claude Brown. Our boycott of local merchants and the national picketing of Hammermill and Dan River were having an impact, and the businessmen put pressure on Smitherman and the City Council to show a little flexibility. Reese went in with a long list: jobs for blacks in city government and downtown stores, appointment of blacks to city boards, integration of city recreation facilities, paving of streets in black neighborhoods, and official adoption of titles of respect— Mr., Miss, Mrs.—for black people.

I refused to participate because I thought the meetings were a mistake. The white leaders were buying time, and time was on their side. They knew maintaining tension and sustaining the boycott would take leadership and constant reinforcement, and local black folk were tired and vulnerable. They'd sit around a table and talk to a few blacks while the juice ran out of the protests. Meanwhile, they'd be signaling to Washington and the national media: Hey, we're meeting. We're making progress here.

We had heated discussions in the Voters League, which had grown from twelve to about forty active people. A few of us argued we shouldn't rest on our laurels or allow biracial meetings to divert our energies. The mass meetings were dying. We needed to breathe life into them. We needed to bolster the boycott. Then we'd be in a position to negotiate from strength. On several occasions, Preston and I made arrangements with black merchants in Montgomery for volume discounts and organized shopping caravans of twenty-five to thirty cars. The intention was to help the Montgomery merchants and lay the foundation for developing more black businesses in Selma. We tried to get the Voters League involved, but they weren't all that interested.

Some people in the league seemed to believe the world was going to be transformed damn near overnight, that between the impending black vote and the might of the federal government, the white South would throw in the towel and everything would be made equal. I think this rosy notion came out of the excitement of the march to Montgomery. The news media, the Northerners who came down to participate, were full of talk of "changing history." They projected a kind of happily-ever-after I knew was unrealistic. It was such a damn appealing idea, though, that folk temporarily basked in it.

Reese and Doyle didn't go quite that far. But they believed they could negotiate democracy into Selma. I was still with Frederick Douglass: "Power concedes nothing without a demand." The white powers conceded nothing to King. How the hell was Reese going to negotiate? It didn't make sense, and if Reese hadn't been up on cloud nine, he would have been better able to assess the situation.

Every time you looked for Reese that spring, he was off making a speech at Harvard or at fund-raising gatherings on the Upper East Side in New York. It was heady stuff for a black science teacher from Selma to be sitting around David Susskind's living room with chic liberals and coming away with $5,000. Then he'd be off to Washington where everybody was talking about passing a voting rights bill on the basis of a movement he helped lead. In this situation, you can easily start reading your own press clippings. Hell, you can handle a little mayor and City Council in Selma.

In tasting the big time, Reese, I think, lost enthusiasm for the grass roots of civil rights protest—demonstrations, boycotts, going to jail. He was letting the protests die while messing around with biracial meetings, thinking he could negotiate change on the basis of his personal skills. My view was that this wasn't a matter of personal skill. I realized later that he and Doyle were beginning a transformation from civil rights leaders to politicians, from outside protestors to inside manipulators. This was premature in 1965; we didn't yet have enough clout to manipulate.

One of my major concerns was maintaining independent black leadership. For the first time, black leaders in Selma had a base of power that wasn't dependent on white people; black folk would march in the streets if the leaders asked. Smitherman was maneuvering to preempt their independence by sucking them into his agenda.

Smitherman offered to put five blacks on the fifteen-member board of the new antipoverty program and let Reese argue him up to seven. This was an empty offer since the federal government required black participation, anyway. Smitherman also offered to arrange a meeting between black leaders and the county Board of Registrars. Surely these concessions should be enough for the blacks to call off the boycott and quit harassing Dan River and Hammermill. Reese didn't fall for this ruse, but that's how the meetings went. Black leaders were maneuvered into reacting to Smitherman's smokescreens instead of forcing the white powers to react to our agenda.

As black people drifted back to the stores, the merchants let up on their pressure. Pretty soon, Reese and the others would go to a meeting and Smitherman would be in Montgomery or someplace. After two or three months, Smitherman stopped calling the meetings. He didn't need them anymore. A few times, Reese threatened to fill the streets if the black grievances were not addressed. He'd call a mass meeting at Brown Chapel and only thirty people would show up.

The unprecedented unity among people conditioned not to rely on each other was dying by degrees. Long-standing jealousies and competitions rose to the surface, especially when food, clothing, and money began pouring into town after the march to Montgomery was over. People who came down to march saw the poverty and talked to local folk who lost their jobs for demonstrating. "What can we do when we get home?" they asked. Voters League people and a character named William Ezra Greer told them, "Send food. Send clothing. Send money."

Greer showed up in Selma right after Bloody Sunday, dressed like a bishop in a cutaway coat. He was slick, oily, worldly, and fast-talking. He claimed he worked—or had worked—for SCLC. He told the Voters League officers they needed him to keep SCLC from walking off with all the money and donations raised in the name of Selma. He talked the league into founding the Selma Emergency Relief Fund (SERF) and letting him be in charge of distribution. Neither I nor the SCLC staff who remained in Selma could persuade the leaders of the Voters League that Greer was trouble.

The basement of my church became SERF headquarters. It looked like a huge flea market and was a first-class continuing mess. There were all kinds of arguments and inequities. Some people who needed help the most were left out. Various local leaders squabbled over who had the authority to dispense what. Hustling preachers trying to ingratiate themselves with their congregations walked off with piles of clothes. Some people apparently were selling stuff. It would have taken a master bureaucracy to set up criteria and make a dispensation of everything in a fair manner. The Voters League people had no administrative experience and left it up to Greer, who they thought did.

Preston and I had not forgotten Montgomery. We had not forgotten that when the bus boycott ended, black-owned taxicabs that had recently sprung up went out of business. We wanted to find a way to capitalize on the movement to strengthen black Selma economically. The boycott was only part of the answer. To bypass the white grocery wholesalers, we had to go to Montgomery. All the black Mom and Pops in Selma bought from the wholesalers on Water Avenue, and there was no point in boycotting white retail merchants while enriching the white wholesalers.

Preston met with King four or five times about a variation on our old supermarket-chain idea. Preston had been selling shares of stock for several years, but we were a long way from the capitalization we needed. He proposed to King that SCLC help finance a black-owned flagship supermarket in Selma that would be part of IGA, a chain of independent grocers. Preston's pitch was: The black community was spending millions in white supermarkets. With our own store, we could employ and train black people and use the profits to establish other stores. By being part of IGA, we could compete with supermarket prices. The IGA bought in volume directly from farms and slaughterhouses, like the A&P did, and we'd bypass Water Avenue completely. Preston had spoken with IGA and they were all for it. They told us, You put up X dollars and we're ready.

King was sensitive to local criticism of SCLC raising so much money off Selma. He thought the supermarket was a great idea. He called a meeting of local black businessmen and leaders to discuss the proposal, form a group, and work out plans. He had people who were going to put up some of the money; the rest would be raised selling stock to blacks in Dallas County.

Edwin Moss, of course, was there, being the head of the black credit union and Exalted Ruler of the Elks. Edwin and the black establishment knew whoever headed the supermarket would be the economic boss of black Dallas County. They persuaded King to funnel the money through the credit union, which was a logical thing to do. But this put Edwin instead of Preston in the driver's seat. Edwin had a good track record in handling other people's money, and I'm sure King saw him as more reliable than Preston, a hair-care-products salesman with a shady past as a gambler.

Edwin, though, never really understood or took an interest in the IGA connection. He and his group didn't make the distinction between a supermarket and a big grocery store. All they thought about was a large store that would create jobs. Once he lost control, Preston refused to sit down with Edwin, his people, and King to make them see the crucial importance of centralized buying. No way. Edwin and King could kiss his ass. The sons-of-bitches had taken our idea.

I went to some of the supermarket planning meetings and insisted they couldn't compete if they bought from those damn wholesalers on Water Avenue. Edwin and his group didn't want to hear it. The wholesalers were prominent white people, Edwin had relationships with them and they were pushing to maintain the business. All I was doing, in Edwin's view, was making some civil rights speech. He thought if the store sold enough in volume it would make money.

They built the supermarket—named B&P for Business & Professional—in the heart of the black community. It was a pretty building in a good location, but it was basically a big Mom and Pop. Because it was new and it was ours, black people were loyal customers for a while. But the prices were just too high and people started going back to the supermarkets. B&P went out of business in two years.

In the meantime, a rumor was circulating in black Selma that Reese was making money off the movement. People who had fallen out with him, or were jealous of his position or angry at his stubbornness, fanned the flames of the rumor, if they didn't start the fire. Wilson Baker heard the talk and cultivated black people he thought might give him information on which to base an arrest. Some talked to him and encouraged his investigation.

Baker and Blanchard McLeod, the circuit solicitor, then dispatched investigators to California, New York, New Jersey, Pennsylvania, Ohio to ask donors whether their contributions were intended for Reese personally or for the league. They tracked down bank accounts. They were anxious to discredit the number-one local civil rights leader. The authorities didn't hide their activities, and we anticipated indictments. As the lawyer for the Voters League, I called SCLC in Atlanta to explore where they stood and whether they'd help finance the defense of any league people who got indicted. The person I spoke with was ambivalent. "Well, we've got to look into it. We can't condone stealing. Let's see what happens."

This was worrisome. It was no secret that SCLC and Reese were on the outs. They had the same problem with him I did—that he wasn't taking care of business at ground zero. Also, the SERF scandal embarrassed SCLC because SCLC was the organization associated with Selma in the public mind. I was afraid SCLC might decide to let Reese fall, even encourage it. A few people in SCLC showed little restraint in pursuit of a desired objective, and I didn't put it past them to whisper in someone's ear, "If Reese goes, you can be the leader."

I called Orzell to ask him to help. I didn't know what we were up against or which way black public opinion would go. I had known F. D. Reese all his life and mine, and there'd been nothing before then—or since—to suggest the man was a crook. I enlisted Orzell because I knew he would defend Reese and wouldn't care who liked it or disliked it.

We called SCLC in Atlanta several times. We said we were not going to be left picking up the pieces by ourselves in Selma. If SCLC didn't stand behind Reese, the black community would be further split and no one would step forward as a black leader in Selma for a long, long time. Orzell and I said we might try to subpoena SCLC's financial records to provide a full picture of Voters League finances since the league was an affiliate of SCLC. We knew SCLC wouldn't want to open its records because this could drive contributors away.

In early July, Reese was charged with embezzling Voters League funds for his personal use. That night, Ralph Abernathy came over from Atlanta to speak at a mass meeting in Brown Chapel. "I don't see Wilson Baker putting any money in the plate," Abernathy said. "It's our money. If Reese needs it, we'll give it to him." Orzell and I were greatly relieved.

The next day, Baker and Smitherman held a press conference, a big hypocritical show of concern for an organization they'd repeatedly denounced. Baker said the investigation began only after black people affiliated with the movement came to him with complaints of leaders dipping into the till. He displayed copies of checks made out to the Voters League and deposited in a bank of Montgomery in an account in Reese's name. He also had copies of three checks, totaling about $1,800, that Reese had drawn on the account to make his house and furniture payments and to buy clothing. The legal point was whether Reese had the permission of the other officers to use league funds. He said he did, and I believed him. There wasn't a vote or formal resolution authorizing him to open an account in his name—the Voters League wasn't a formal-type organization—but it was understood he could take care of his living expenses. His contract wasn't renewed by the school system that spring and he was working full-time for the league, personally raising much of the money. He said he used a Montgomery bank because the White Citizens' Council snooped on accounts in Selma banks.

Orzell and I talked to the officers and they said Reese was

authorized to cover his expenses. I never knew if some of them told Baker and McLeod a different story or if McLeod, on the basis of the rumors, the checks, and the league's poor accounting, assumed the officers would help convict Reese when he got them under oath on the witness stand.

At Reese's trial in March of 1966, two league officers were put on the stand. They testified that Reese had approval to use the money. McLeod seemed surprised. He threw up his hands and moved to dismiss the case. We walked out of the courtroom about three hours after we walked in. Reese's stock had reached its lowest level, but the trial revived it. A black man had taken on the Dallas County judicial establishment and won.

The Reese case, being about money, underlined the importance of economics to our struggle. On this front, we blew it in Selma. We marched for months, caught the attention of the world, and came out of it, economically, with nothing but a supermarket that lasted about as long as Pat stayed in the army.

Like everyone else, I hitched my wagon to the vote. Whereas before I thought we wouldn't be able to do much politically but we might be able to improve our lot economically, I now saw the possibility of our running some of the Black Belt counties and being a political force statewide. I thought—or hoped—this could solve many of our economic problems.

I was pleased that, in drafting the Voting Rights Act, Congress listened to black leaders' warnings that local white authorities in the Deep South states surely would delay, intimidate, gerrymander district lines, switch polling places or registration times, and do anything else they could to skirt whatever law was passed. Unless the legislation mandated some ongoing mechanisms to prevent and deal quickly with non-compliance, we'd get a repeat of *Brown* v. *Board of Education* and have to spend a decade filing lawsuits from county to county to get black people registered.

We won some significant provisions—banning of literacy tests and poll taxes, federal registrars in the short run to bypass local registration boards, federal oversight of local elections, and a requirement that any change in election procedures in the Deep South states be pre-cleared with the U.S. Department of Justice.

Federal registrars set up shop in Selma literally within a week

233

of the passage of the Voting Rights Act on August 6, 1965. The Administration in Washington made this a top priority. Johnson and the national Democrats knew that almost every black registered would vote for the Democratic Party. This would help offset the problems they now had in the white South, so the word was: "Get 'em registered."

Many of the registrars were black postmen given a leave of absence from their regular jobs. In Selma, Nathaniel Phillips, Jr., a black postman and friend, and two other federal employees took over an office on the third floor of the federal building, across the street from the county courthouse, and registered people eight hours a day, five days a week, for months.

The Voters League pushed full speed ahead. Marie Foster and many other local and SCLC people went door-to-door throughout the county, telling folk their rights under the new law, motivating them to get registered, driving those who didn't have transportation. Voting had not been high on the agenda a few years earlier, but a massive change had come about. People had been told and now believed they could become captains of their own destiny through the ballot.

County officials did what they could to keep the numbers down, eliminating any newly registered black who'd been convicted of selling bootleg whiskey as far back as 1921, or who hadn't paid the county road tax or the city street tax. Also, the usual subtle intimidation by white employers and businessmen continued. A black man came to my office to tell me about a conversation he and his wife had with a bank officer about getting a loan to reroof their house. The officer first asked whether they had been marching and they said no. He told them how proud he was that they hadn't gotten involved in that and he certainly hoped they wouldn't get caught up in the disgrace that was going on now— trying to flood the voting rolls with people who were not qualified, weren't even interested in voting, were just being hauled to the registrars by the agitators and radicals. The man who came to see me was the manager of a black insurance agency and the banker's statement had less impact than it might on someone with less training and independence. But he wanted me to know about it.

Still, within six months, close to 9,000 black people registered to vote in Dallas County. To say I was impressed would be an understatement. I was beside myself. These were people who'd been told for generations that voting is white folks' business, stay away from the courthouse, don't antagonize white people. We came from nowhere to somewhere in an awfully short period of time. A voteless, hopeless people had moved in a matter of months to a position of almost being able to elect our own leaders, to govern ourselves. I don't know whether there was any precedent for this in human history. This was a monumental achievement, and Selma couldn't be the same again.

After centuries of ducking and dodging, black people had come out of the closet—and they liked the air. Folk still were concerned for their jobs, their mortgages and bank loans, but the blanket fear of upsetting anybody white was lifting. The reign of terror was over. That was very important, much more so than a supermarket. That's what America is all about—freedom to breathe, freedom from fear. That was fundamental. King often said, "The vote is not the ball game, but it gets you inside the ballpark." That's where we were at the end of 1965. We had gotten into the ballpark. Now we had to learn to play the game.

Inside the Ballpark

One afternoon in the spring of 1966, Wilson Baker stopped me on the street and told me he'd nearly gotten into a fight with Jim Clark the day before in the *Times-Journal* office. Baker was running against Clark for sheriff and both were in the newspaper office buying space for political ads. Clark told the people in the *Times-Journal* that he, Clark, was the white man's candidate and Baker was the niggers' candidate. Baker said he called Clark a liar, Clark offered to go outside and fight, but Baker told him, "We don't have to go outside. I will whip your ass here." Both were huge men; weighed at least 250 pounds apiece. There was some shoving, but people at the newspaper pulled them apart.

Baker was anxious to emphasize to me that he had no objections to being called the blacks' candidate. He was proud of that. But he considered himself just as Southern and proud of his white heritage as Clark, and he wasn't going to let Clark take that away from him. He had white votes, too. He told me, "J.L., you can be of great help to me. We're gonna clean Clark out of the courthouse and y'all need to go to work."

For a while, we'd considered running a black candidate. One person pushing this idea was Stokely Carmichael. He and some other SNCC people stayed on in Lowndes County after the march to Montgomery and organized the Lowndes Freedom Organization, whose symbol was a black panther. There was nowhere

An Open Letter To The People of Dallas County:

Friends,

WE HAVE NOT BEEN OVERCOME

I, in qualifying for my candidacy for Sheriff in the past primary, pledged to support the nominees of the Democratic Party in the General Election, but I did not pledge to support the nominee of Katzenbach, John Doar, and Martin Luther King, therefore, due to the insistence of my friends, my name will be submitted to the voters as a write-in for Sheriff in the November General Election.

I refuse to support the Democratic candidate that stated to the New York Times in Atlanta, Georgia: "The Honorable Judge James Hare's Injunction against demonstrations in Selma, Alabama was not worth the paper it was written on."

—Stated to newspaper reporters in Point Clear, Alabama that he did not observe any mis-conduct among the demonstrators and beatniks that invaded Selma.

Who in 1966 openly solicited Negro votes and did receive the endorsement of Martin Luther King.

—Issued a parade permit as Public Safety Director of the City of Selma to the Dallas County Voters League for permission for 500 adults to parade on a designated route. Wh... Count, over 1700 Participants ... Comment was; "I never could count higher than 500."

As your candidate for Sheriff I pledge to you, the people of Selma and Dallas County, that the Office of Sheriff, or Jim Clark —your Sheriff, will NEVER Be Overcome by Khrushchev, L.B.J., Katzenbach, King or Baker Nor any man quoting the Communist slogan; "We Shall Overcome."

James G. (Jim) Clark, Jr.

Plan Now To Attend The
"JIM CLARK DAY"
Rally—To Be Held Wednesday, Oct. 26—8 p.m.
At The New National Guard Armory—Selma.

SHOW YOUR "NEVER" BUTTON

Jim Clark's campaign advertisement in the 1966 sheriff's race (© *Selma Times-Journal*)

to go or much to do in Lowndes County at night so Stokely would come to the Chicken Shack in Selma. He was handsome—if you wanted to cast a heartthrob African prince, you'd pick Stokely— and very articulate. Sometimes he, I, and others would sit around all night talking.

Stokely and his workers didn't devote the time and effort to Selma they did to Lowndes, but they talked to people and tried to build a consciousness in black Selma that black power and separatism were the way to go. They thought it was the height of foolishness for black people in Dallas County to vote for either Baker or Clark. Both were arms of the oppressor. Dick Gregory made a speech at First Baptist in which he said the same thing.

Five black candidates filed for lesser county offices like coroner and tax collector in that 1966 election, but the Voters League talked the black candidate for sheriff into withdrawing from the race. We decided not to run a black because whites had the registration edge and a black candidate couldn't win. We had a chance to whip our number-one nemesis, kick his ass out of office, and send a powerful message to the white establishment. Baker wasn't our liberator, but he was a hell of a lot better than Clark, and without us, he would lose.

I found it pleasing that Baker would stop to tell me about his fracas with Clark, because it indicated the newfound importance of black people. Baker went on to say he was hiring Harry Gamble to represent him. He's the lawyer who gave me the old code book when I first came home. In that day, he was considered Selma's liberal lawyer. It was important to Baker that I know that. He told me McLean Pitts would be representing Clark.

"Why are you all lining up with lawyers?" I asked. "I thought this was an election. Sounds to me like a damn lawsuit."

Baker said he anticipated skulduggery. He expected to whip Clark at the polls but expected Clark's people to try to steal the election and intimidate black voters. He told me he was not going to have any blacks intimidated. Once again I thought, My God, we've come a long way. Here is Baker, the police commissioner, saying he does not intend to have black people intimidated.

This made me anxious, though. It turned out Baker knew nothing concrete. He said there were rumors and he would get back to me later about making plans to deal with problems black people might face at the polls. I talked to him then, as I had when he declared himself a candidate for sheriff, about hiring some blacks as deputies. Baker said black deputies were definitely needed and he would appoint some.

That was quite a rewarding conversation to me. Baker was saying, "I'm going to help your people and you can help me."

I'd never had any conversation like that with a white man in Selma, especially a white man running for sheriff. It was tangible proof that we were definitely inside the ballpark, and I walked away feeling pretty tall.

Several days later, I was in the sheriff's office for something and said to Clark, "Baker was telling me he came close to breaking both your arms and legs in the *Times-Journal* office." Clark said Baker was a big buffoon. He had asked him to come outside and would have wiped up the pavement with him, but Baker was scared to come out of the building. I said there was considerable concern about intimidation and interference with black people when they came to vote. Clark said if there was, it would be coming from Baker's folk because most of the "nigras" were going to vote for him, Clark.

"Do you really believe that?" I asked. He gave me a lecture on what he'd done for black people—keeping somebody's son out of jail, leaving bootleggers alone. "I know those nigras down there are sellin' a little whiskey, but what the hell? White people sell it. We ain't bothering them. The ones that got a little gambling going on, why not? They gamble out at the country club." He said he expected to get his share of black votes because black folk in Dallas County knew he didn't have anything against them. What he resented was the damn government coming down here telling him how to live. I left convinced that Clark was convinced he was going to win the race and get a sizable number of black votes.

I immediately went searching through the black community, especially the bootleg joints and pool halls. Had something developed I didn't know about? I knew a probate judge, a mayor, and a sheriff are difficult to defeat. There are so many little favors they can turn at the community level. I found no evidence, though, that blacks were going to vote for Clark and concluded this was another instance of blacks saying to whites what they thought whites wanted to hear. "Yessir, we with you, Sheriff. We didn't care 'bout that demonstration mess. We understand what you had to do."

Baker almost didn't mention race in his campaign except to say we can all work together here, this community has suffered

enough, professional law enforcement will curb federal intervention in Dallas County affairs. He had the backing of the business
community and country-club set who wanted to improve Selma's
image and get the town clicking economically. They wanted race
downplayed. Clark talked about maintaining law and order and
branded Baker as the niggers' candidate.

Neither Baker nor Clark did much direct campaigning in the
black community. That was still a little far out. Clark had his
black gamblers and bootleggers, and he sponsored a barbecue.
Baker worked through people like Edwin Moss, Reese, and me.
Reese had not forgotten Baker's part in bringing criminal charges
against him but decided that Clark had to go. In addition, Smitherman was moving around the black community, using the considerable favors a mayor can dole out to line up support for Baker.
He was building his stock as well as extending his power into the
county courthouse by getting his man elected sheriff.

If the Elks or Chesterfields, a club of light-skinned, self-styled
upper-class blacks, were having a special program, Smitherman
would give a welcome and say, "Incidentally, before I sit down,"
and get into a speech about the sheriff's race. When he got through
telling it, he and Baker were on the side of justice, the demonstrations, and black people, while Clark was the worst damn racist
to ever live.

I did not realize that Smitherman was laying the foundation of
a political machine in black Selma that would be a problem for
years to come. Here was a white man talking politics to black
people at the Elks, encouraging our participation. Here was a
white man standing with us against Jim Clark. Here was the first
mayor to put black people on the board of anything, albeit a
poverty board where black participation was required by the federal government. In that campaign, Smitherman began to establish bonds and cement loyalties that would keep him in power.

One night after he'd made his typical speech at the Elks and
everybody was applauding, I started to clap—then stopped. It
occurred to me something was not quite right. A year earlier,
this same man had stood at Brown Chapel with Clark, declaring,
"Thou shalt not march." Then he manipulated the biracial committee into oblivion. I brushed those thoughts away because I

was intoxicated with being on the side that could possibly win. For the first time in my life, I felt on the inside. We were about to whip Jim Clark. So I wasn't paying attention to the nuances and ramifications, though I was uncomfortable with the new role Smitherman and Baker were playing.

On the morning of the primary, black folk lined up an hour early at the polls. The Voters League was out in force. Naturally, Marie Foster spent all day driving people to and from the polling places. That night, Baker pulled ahead as the boxes from the black areas came in.

The next day, the skulduggery surfaced. Clark appeared before the county Democratic Executive Committee to challenge six of the predominantly black boxes, which contained enough votes to give Baker the nomination. The chairman was Alston Keith, a founder of the White Citizens' Council. The vice-chairman was former mayor Heinz, the current Citizens' Council president. It didn't take the committee long to accept Clark's objections and throw out all the boxes on the basis of "irregularities."

The Department of Justice sued in federal court on behalf of the 1,600 voters in the rejected boxes. Black poll watchers testified they'd been told by election officials to go home, they'd finish up in the morning. The next day, sample ballots and other extraneous materials were found in some of the boxes. The judge ordered the committee to count the legitimate ballots in the boxes, and Baker won.

It was the height of irony that Baker's victory was saved by the Department of Justice—in a suit filed under the provisions of the new Voting Rights Act that Baker had worked so diligently to prevent. Clark ran on a write-in in the general election and came very close to winning. Baker got virtually all the black vote. Clark got close to 80 percent of the white vote. All five black candidates for county office lost.

Clark filed or ran for some statewide office after that, but his political career was over and his swagger gone. Some months after Baker took over as sheriff, I was standing outside Sam Washington's tailor shop on Washington Street when Clark drove by, very slowly, looking from side to side. Sam noticed him and pointed him out: "There's Jim Clark." He was driving an ordinary car and wearing civilian clothes, somewhat unkempt. This was a Saturday morning. Black people, as usual, were lined up like flies, drinking whiskey, keeping up noise, and having fun. There'd been a time when Clark's presence would have cleared the sidewalk. People would have ambled on inside. That morning, they just stood looking as he drove slowly down the street.

He obviously wanted us to see him. I guess he was saying, "I'll be back. I'm down, but I'm not out." He seemed to want some reaction, but all he got was "Hell, there goes Clark." As he looked over at us, I thought I saw in his face a sad recognition that he was no longer in charge. Black people had not gone anywhere. We were still here, and we didn't give a damn about him anymore.

As time went on, the white community began to distance itself from Clark, put everything bad on his shoulders. He'd been the front man for a defeated stance. The brand of loser was stamped on him, and he left Selma. I don't know if he understood that he had not just become a scapegoat; he had always been one.

Judge Hare declared the Voting Rights Act unconstitutional and enjoined the probate judge from qualifying as voters the people who signed up with the federal registrars. This injunction, quickly overturned, was in a sense his last hurrah before he died of cancer in 1969. The white community didn't ostracize Hare as they did Clark—the Exchange Club gave the judge its annual Book of Golden Deeds Award in 1968—but some lawyers and other people tended to avoid conversation with him, perhaps because he became a sad and sour figure.

There he sat behind his desk, looking little, lost, ill. By the sheer intensity of his beliefs, Hare literally filled his office when he was at his peak. I always had the sense of him as a large man. When things began to turn, he suddenly looked small behind what for the first time appeared to be a great big desk. In his mind, he was absolutely correct, but the world was moving in another direction and there wasn't anything right-minded people like him could do about it. He was bewildered that white Northerners were protecting a bunch of misguided nigras. He was worried about what school integration, begun by then on a token, "voluntary" basis, would mean to white girls. He was upset that the Northern press was somewhat succeeding in making white Southerners feel defensive, even guilty. He didn't think they had anything to feel guilty about.

But he got quiet. Whereas before I often wished somebody would shut him off, I began to go into his office in his last years expressly to crank him up. I noticed that if you got him talking he'd be taken out of what was obviously a continuing state of misery. Debate had an effect on him similar to what it had on me. It gave him some respite, though sometimes he'd start prophesying doom and his mood would sour. I didn't like seeing him so blue. I knew what it was like to be sad and isolated, to feel the world has walked over you and spat in your face.

The day the court awarded the election to Baker, I called Baker to ask, "Now that you've won, what about those black deputies?"

"We're gonna hire 'em," he said. "We'll talk about that next week." He wanted first to test the waters, to have an opportunity to explain it to whites. He was going to keep his promise, but on his own timetable.

I talked to Reese, Edwin Moss, and several other people. It was my thinking that the longer we waited, the less likely it would be that we'd get the black deputies. Whites understood blacks voted for Baker in a solid bloc, and Baker would be smart to put the appointments behind him at the outset. I said we should have a meeting with Baker immediately.

Reese was absolutely in favor of that. Edwin said, "Well, maybe we ought to wait and see what he's going to do first." Edwin had a long-standing arrangement with Baker, starting back when Baker was a police captain, that the Elks could run a little Las Vegas gambling-type operation at their annual picnic and have slot machines in the club, though they were illegal in Alabama. Maintaining these arrangements now that Baker was sheriff was as important to Edwin as the deputies.

Reese and I kept on Baker's case until he hired two black deputies. One was chairman of the deacon board at Ebenezer Baptist Church, which Reese pastored. I pushed Baker to assign the black deputies to black Selma. There'd always been an arrangement that Selma would be patrolled by the city police and the rest of Dallas County by the sheriff. I was hoping if the black deputies patrolled black Selma, the police might pull out. Hopefully, that would end the police brutality and their unholy alliance with informants and other hustlers. Reese insisted the deputies should be treated as deputies, not as black deputies. They ought to be able to patrol all areas and arrest white people. Ordinarily, I would have been dead set against relegating blacks to black-only activities, but this police business was deep in my thinking.

For a while, Baker put the black deputies with experienced white deputies so they could learn. He said they were too green to go out by themselves. This satisfied Reese—Baker had proved he would put a black deputy with a white deputy—and with his deacon hired, he went on about his business. I kept at Baker, and I was around the courthouse every day. When the breaking-in period was over, he assigned the two deputies to black Selma.

This was a serious error on my part. By insisting that the black deputies stay in the black community, I undermined their authority, which was fragile at this stage anyway. Just because two black men became deputies, the black community didn't develop respect for law enforcement overnight and folk didn't fear the black deputies like they feared the white ones.

These first two inexperienced black deputies were told, "You cain't even go out and arrest white people, and you here harassing us 'bout some bootleggin'. You think you so-and-so. Why don't you go out and arrest white folk?" Or: "I'm goin' up there and tell Mr. Baker. I know Mr. Baker better than you do."

I made the respect problem worse by insisting they be confined to black Selma. Here the black community had turned out in droves to vote for Baker, in part because Reese and I were saying we'd get some black deputies. We came up with two, and, lo and behold, one of them is Reese's deacon and I seem to be in lockstep with the white establishment in segregating them.

To avoid the flak, the deputies didn't arrest anybody. White policemen never were withdrawn from black Selma, so the deputies didn't have that much responsibility anyway. They went out to the "pool" in east Selma and parked all day. The park had been filled with water since the Rinkydinks had played ball there, and the deputies just sat there watching people fish. Baker called them his "game wardens."

CHAPTER 15

New Life

I wish I could report that I gave up whiskey and threw away my gun the day John Lewis stared down Jim Clark and I realized neither was necessary. But I didn't.

Whenever I went to Lowndes or Wilcox or Marengo Counties, I continued to wear a gun. I knew the Klan was active out there because I got letters from them, some with a bullet enclosed. I wasn't comfortable with the gun, but I wasn't comfortable without it either. Not until the night Martin Luther King was killed did I get rid of it. I went down to the Alabama River, under the Edmund Pettus Bridge, and sat there for a half hour crying and remembering all the things King had said about the senselessness of violence and war. I reflected that my weapon hadn't saved me from or helped me achieve anything, and I threw it in the river. I felt relieved seeing it disappear in the dark, swiftly flowing water.

I tapered off drinking after the John Lewis revelation, especially during the height of the demonstrations and their immediate aftermath. But as the years went by, '67, '68, '69, '70, I became almost as regular as ever at Porter's, the Elks, the Chicken Shack, and other joints.

Getting high gave me temporary relief from the nagging, stressful recognition that even with the ballot our problems were so numerous, so widespread, and so rooted in the culture that they appeared to defy resolution. After Reese's trial and Baker's election, the Voters League gradually dissolved, leaving black Selma with no organization to keep pushing the white establishment or support the individuals still out there fighting. My efforts as the only black lawyer seemed like trying to empty Lake Michigan with a teaspoon.

Also, for somebody who really loves the nightlife of New Orleans and Harlem to be living in Selma, Alabama, day in and day out, year in and year out, was equally depressing. Some days I just didn't want to face all the problems people brought to my office. I'd think, Fuck it. Let me go to Porter's and see if I can't stir up some fun.

That was exactly my attitude one morning in 1971 when I left my office and stopped at Eddie Ferguson's café for a beer. This was a little joint down the street from the Liston and Clay Lounge, with Formica tables and the ever-present smell of frying food. I was supposed to be in court for a docket call, in which the judge and lawyers schedule cases for trial or pleas. As I sat there drinking a second beer, I decided I didn't want to be bothered with the court that day, all the phony-ass people in a racist damn system. So I didn't go.

It's not easy to convey the peculiar stress on a black lawyer, at least my type black lawyer. There's the strain of being part of and apart from the system at the same time. To be effective, you need to have some kind of relationship with the judges, the sheriff, the police. And if you genuinely like people, as I do, there's no way to deal with individuals every day and not have friendly relations.

To bridge the gap, I developed a sort of persona using humor. My jokes, stories, and funny descriptions of people and events humanized "the nigger lawyer," though some whites used this to write me off as a kind of Sambo character. One day when Sheriff Baker came upstairs to listen to me give a closing argument and overheard me joking with law-enforcement people during a break, he advised me that my performance could make certain whites think less of me and my courtroom skills. I ignored his advice. I joked and carried on in exactly the same way at the Elks and at home, and I wasn't about to stop. Laughter, like drinking, is a respite from tension.

But I remained on guard—always. If you're not, you can get

sucked in, and before you know it become another one of the minions—faceless, phony, and part of the boring, conforming, superficial, hypocritical status quo. I wasn't going to surrender. I needed to be enough on the inside to help my clients, but if I got too comfortable, I'd be in danger of thinking more like the opposition. Instead of wanting to get out and see whether some poor black fella had a claim, I'd be more apt to dismiss it, as the average white lawyer would dismiss it.

Some days, just the sheer hypocrisy of it all—the pretense that we were engaged in a system that dispensed equal justice—was too much to stomach.

That morning, I stayed in Eddie's getting on his and some of his customers' cases and letting them get on mine. I enjoyed walking into Eddie's or Wranch's place and declaring, "Wranch, you are the biggest Uncle Tom in Selma," or, "Eddie, I used to think you were the number-one Uncle Tom, but Leon here, if his boss told him to jump off the bridge, would ask, 'What time?' " Although Uncle Tomism was everywhere, neither blacks nor whites talked about it. So everybody would gather round to see how Wranch or Eddie or the customer and I would play it out. For me, these exchanges broke through the stifling superficiality of life in Selma, all the pretense surrounding the race issue.

As usual, I had more criminal cases than most of the other lawyers, and Judge Edgar Russell, Jr., Hare's successor, couldn't work out the docket without me. So he sent two deputy sheriffs to find me, with orders to bring me back with them. "The judge wants to see you," one of the deputies said when he located me at Eddie's. So I had to get up and march out of Eddie's place, trailed by two deputies, in front of everybody on Washington Street. I refused to get in their car, so one deputy and I walked the few blocks to the courthouse. Judge Russell asked where I was, and when the deputy told him, Russell said that was the last straw. This wasn't the first time I'd come to court with alcohol on my breath.

"Take him out of here and lock him up," he told the sheriff. "Contempt of court."

"Oh, don't do that, Judge," I said. But he just shook his head sadly.

They put me in a cell by myself, where they usually put the

nuts. I figured I'd wait there awhile, then call Russell and get out. Russell was the former city judge whom my mother sometimes consulted for legal advice. I waited till about noon, called, and found he'd left the courthouse. I had to stay until late that afternoon.

I came to some terms with myself in that cell. If I was going to stay and practice law in Selma, I had to stand up to the loneliness and other trials and tribulations of such a life and quit escaping. Black people had enough burdens without me being another one. But like so many people who get tied into alcohol or drugs, I rationalized that I didn't have to stop drinking all at once. I came out of that cell with a committed decision to cut down. I told myself I was not going to be defeated by alcohol or anything else.

I quit altogether a year later on one of the lowest days of my life. I'd been out late drinking, and when I came home early in the morning, I found Vivian in a panic. Her father was dying in Birmingham, and her grandmother had called to say, "If you want to see him alive, you better come right away." She'd been calling everywhere to try to find me. She didn't know how to drive.

I said, "Let me get a little sleep and then we'll go up there and see," which was an awful thing to say because it had already been hours since her grandmother had called. Vivian was so desperate, she took the keys, went out, got in the car, and started the engine. I don't know if she was going to try to find somebody else to drive her or if she was going to take off to Birmingham herself. It was obvious I had come to a pretty pathetic low, dragging not only myself down but my wife with me. I felt horrible, sick and half drunk, but I got in the car and drove.

Vivian didn't say anything on the drive or look at me. She looked so small and so still. I think she was praying her father would still be alive when we got to Birmingham. I felt most sympathetic to her plight and most unsympathetic to my own insensitivities. It was like another time when Ronnie, my oldest son, was singing in a school program and really wanted me to come hear him. I didn't show up and he cried. I said to myself and to the Lord that if I got through this, I would not drink again ever—and I haven't. We got to Birmingham in time for Vivian to see her father.

In between these two lows, a young black lawyer named Hank Sanders came by my office. He said he and his wife, Rose, who both were graduates of Harvard Law School and had just passed the Alabama bar, were planning to settle in Selma. I was intrigued by the way he picked my town—by intuition. He said he'd grown up in south Alabama, in Baldwin County just north of Mobile, and always intended to practice in Alabama. He and Rose were working temporarily for Legal Services in Huntsville in north Alabama, but Huntsville didn't appeal to Hank—not enough black people.

So he got in his car and started driving around the state looking for a town where he felt he was needed. When he got to Selma and drove over the Edmund Pettus Bridge, he happened to turn right, and there he was on Washington Street. It was a Saturday and black folk, as usual, were hanging out on the sidewalk. Something about that scene told Hank Selma was the place. He later said his feeling was similar to a man meeting a woman and just knowing she's the one he's going to marry.

Naturally, people told him to come see me, the black lawyer, but I wasn't in my office that day. Hank said folk told him I was a brilliant attorney—he didn't mention they undoubtedly added "when sober"—and he hoped we could work together.

I said I'd do everything I could to help him. "You won't have to rely on white lawyers to learn the ropes," I assured him. And I meant it. Hank is dark-skinned, heavy, serious, and he exudes sincerity. He smiles easily, but is not a naturally extroverted person. He struck me as shy, very smart, and obviously dedicated to doing something worthwhile. Up until that point, I had been surrounded by young men with little interest in law or politics, and it was a delight to talk to him.

My office then was at Preston's hair-care-products company on Broad Street just south of the Drag. After the supermarket and other ventures fell through, he'd started his own hair-products manufacturing firm, named Velberta for his wife. Preston bought containers, he and I designed the Velberta logo, and a chemistry teacher from a black high school in Perry County started mixing

Hank and Rose Sanders, back when I first met them (Courtesy of Rose Sanders)

and cooking ingredients on the stove in Preston's kitchen. I handled Velberta's legal work along with my practice of divorces, wills, and criminal cases from shoplifting to capital murder.

Hank rented an office in the Elks building, down the hall from my first office. The next time I saw him he was walking by Velberta's on his way downtown. I went out and offered him a ride.

"I need to walk," he said. "But we need to talk." He asked me to consider a partnership with him and Rose. A lawyer cannot do nearly as much alone as he can in a firm where the members work together and support each other, he argued. He ran down a litany of things a firm could do—develop civil rights lawsuits, stretch out all over the Black Belt, render considerable community services. Black people were so far behind and so much needed to be done. We ought to get together.

"Well, Hank, I'll think about it," I said. I had to decide whether I wanted to be tied down with two inexperienced lawyers or anyone at all. I worked when I wanted to work and quit when I got ready. The question was whether I wanted to give up my independence—and drinking. Also, I didn't know how I'd get along with Hank and Rose. They'd just come from Harvard Law School whereas I'd been out in the boondocks with Orzell Billingsley.

I told Hank frankly I liked to take a taste now and then and wasn't sure I wanted to be obligated to a firm. Of course, Hank already knew I drank. Various people were advising him not to associate with me because of my drinking and various people were advising me not to associate with him because I had all the experience, the contacts, the cases.

Nonetheless, I included Hank in some of my cases and showed him the ropes. Rose hadn't moved to Selma yet. Whenever we were together, Hank persisted in advocating a partnership. He won Preston over to the idea of a law firm, and I valued Preston's opinions. He sent me a letter saying my legal talent was a great gift and drinking was my Achilles' heel. I would come to see this campaign as vintage Hank Sanders—at once visionary and methodical. Hank is the type person who envisions a goal, sometimes a seemingly impossible one, and then sets after it in a deliberate, step-by-step way.

But for these qualities, this black boy from rural Alabama—one of fourteen children—would never have become a lawyer. Hank told me the teacher in his little segregated school once asked everybody what they wanted to be and he said, "A lawyer." He'd never seen a lawyer but had read about them in books. The other kids laughed, not because they questioned Hank's abilities but because that seemed like such an outlandish ambition.

Hank was very circumspect about having gone to Harvard Law School. When he told people, it was almost like a confession, which I understood instantly and which attracted me to him. It was a repudiation of middle-class pretensions. He and Rose went there in the late sixties, when Harvard and other Northern white institutions started recruiting more blacks, another by-product of the movement in the streets of Montgomery, Selma, Birmingham.

Hank and Rose came in on the tail end of a whirlwind, and they believed in that whirlwind. They got involved in the student movement—demonstrating for more black professors, a black dean—and Rose just about quit every other day. She had serious reservations about attending an elite white institution and spent as much time in Harlem, working with kids in a theater program, as she did in Cambridge.

The more I learned about the Sanderses, the more they impressed me, and Hank obviously was correct about what a firm versus an individual could accomplish. Having the independence to take a taste wasn't worth a damn, really. This was another thing weighing on my mind when I drove Vivian to Birmingham to see her father. A few weeks after that, I went to see Hank. I told him, "Let's do it. Let's go."

In June 1972, Hank, Rose, and I sat down in Hank's office in the Elks building to create a law firm. We were in full agreement on the essentials: we were not going to have the usual middle-class, fraternity-oriented-type black professional operation. Our primary objective was service to the black community and not the acquisition of wealth. We would not be turning down folks' cases and evaluating them solely on the basis of whether they would produce a profit. If battling City Hall and the county courthouse over jobs and fair representation required litigation we'd have to finance ourselves, we'd do it.

We also were determined to turn out quality work so that white judges, white lawyers, white people, and black people would have to recognize we passed any test. We were not playing around with any black law. We were going to be the equal or better of any law firm in Selma, if not in Alabama.

One of our main concerns was that this black institution survive. Black lawyers had a dismal record of organizing and staying together, beyond occupying the same offices and splitting the rent, another aspect of the crippling legacy of a people conditioned to mistrust each other. We set out to prove it could be done, especially in light of the string of recent failures—the relief disaster, B&P Supermarket, and Families Furniture and Appliance Store, a short-lived store jointly owned by black people that Preston and I had organized.

That day in Hank's office we also discussed providing leadership in any way we could. We did not foresee, though, all the activities apart from the law we would undertake or the unique hybrid that Chestnut Sanders and Sanders would become—part legal services, part legal defense fund, part civil rights organization (picketing, boycotting, marching), part youth-development agency, part political-organizing headquarters.

We signed a partnership agreement. For the first year, Hank and Rose would each draw $25 a week; I would draw $50 because I had a wife and family to support and would be the lead trial lawyer while Hank and Rose learned the practice of law.

I moved from Preston's building into one of the small paneled rooms in the office Hank rented. Hank used a small room adjacent to mine. Rose worked out of a larger space that served as our conference room and library, though calling it a library is misleading since we had few books. Barnette Lewis Hayes, our secretary, sat in a reception area up front. The only decorations were our framed law degrees and a quotation from Abraham Lincoln: "A lawyer's time is his stock-in-trade."

At this point, blacks and women had just started serving on juries in Dallas and the other Black Belt counties. Peter, Orzell, and I were the ones who filed the lawsuit against the Dallas County jury commission that finally got blacks on juries in Selma. We brought the suit back in the summer of 1965, right after the marches. By then, we and black defense attorneys all over the South had filed umpteen motions about systematic exclusion from juries in the context of criminal cases. Occasionally, we got a client a new trial, but we weren't changing the system.

In Dallas County, they saw us coming. They'd put a few blacks in the jury pool for our cases, though no more than one or two ever made it onto a jury. At Reese's trial, the chairman of the Dallas County jury commission testified that the commission was making a big effort to find qualified blacks for jury service. He said he'd sent a letter to Edwin Moss and to Phillip Green, a black man who owned a filling station, asking them to suggest names—sort of like the voucher system for voting. It became clear that if we were going to get anything other than this haphazard, token sham, we needed to file a suit in federal court that attacked the system of jury selection head-on.

Judge Thomas, as usual, took his time. But in late 1968, he ordered the jury commission to empty the jury box and institute a new system. Every two years, a pool of 3,500 people were to be selected from the list of registered voters and taxpayers on the basis of the qualifications prescribed by Alabama law—literacy and a good reputation in the community. The commissioners were required to note the race of everyone on the master list and to explain to the court the reasons for any black person rejected. Two years earlier, in 1966, a three-judge federal panel in Montgomery had overturned Alabama's law barring women from jury service.

Prior to Thomas's order, jurors were drawn from the taxpayer rolls, then handpicked by the commissioners. The same group of middle-aged or older white men—selected because they had the "right" attitudes and the time—showed up in the jury box over and over again. They were retirees and farmers whose crops had been harvested, men who prided themselves on being conservative, law-and-order types. As a rule, these jurors believed the testimony of policemen and other authorities, and they regarded maintaining order—sending a strong, swift message to anybody who got out of line—as their main duty as jurors. They looked as if they felt good when they sent somebody, usually a black somebody, to the penitentiary.

Black people brought a different perspective into the jury box. In general, a prosecutor has to prove more to them than to the old, standard white jurors, because black people are less inclined to accept as true *per se* statements from authorities, especially law-enforcement authorities.

I developed a routine to reinforce the natural doubt in black minds. If the prosecution's case depended on a confession, I asked the policeman or deputy sheriff to describe the room in which he interrogated the black defendant. How many of you were there? Were you armed? How long did you question the defendant? Do you know whether he can read or write? I'd ask not whether they hit the defendant but how many times. The DA would be on his feet to object, but the police officer would be so eager to shout No! it came out anyway, and so defensively as to be suspect. I'd stand with a practiced smirk, looking dead at the black jurors.

Another element in the black perspective was a reluctance to sit in judgment. Every black person who went to Sunday school or church heard time and again, "Judge not, that ye be not judged," and "Why beholdest thou the mote that is in thy brother's eye, but considerest not the beam that is in thine own eye?" I am convinced that black preachers relied so heavily on this particular theology because it lessened the necessity for confronting the white community regarding its treatment of black people. This religious conditioning made reaching a guilty verdict a more difficult and painful process for black jurors, a process that required some soul-searching.

The downside of "Judge ye not" was that black folk felt so uncomfortable sitting in the jury box that twice as many blacks as whites asked to be excused. Since white judges didn't want blacks on juries anyway, they usually let them go. So we had fewer blacks on juries than we should have had by the numbers. In the most serious cases, the capital cases, even fewer blacks served because more blacks than whites are against the death penalty and the prosecutor can strike any potential juror who categorically does not believe in capital punishment. Part of the reason blacks tend to be against the death penalty is the racially biased way it's used, but it's also tied to the religious thing: "Vengeance is mine, saith the Lord."

Something I hadn't exactly anticipated, though it didn't surprise me, was blacks on racially mixed juries systematically allowing the white jurors to make the decision. When you've grown up in an atmosphere where you could get whipped for not saying "sir," it's highly uncomfortable to be arguing your convictions with a white person. This turned out to be a serious problem, especially in the majority-black counties where black people were the most dependent and the least educated.

In situations where they couldn't strike all the blacks, prosecutors tended to look for older blacks of the type who'd have a hard time saying no if a white person said yes. They struck young black women first because black women, who traditionally could take more liberties than black men, were more likely to be strong and speak their minds in a black and white situation. Experienced attorneys defending black clients could look at the jury pool and almost name the state's strikes in sequence before they happened.

But blacks on juries began to change not merely justice in the South but life in the South because now black people had some genuine legal recourse. If a white person cheated them or injured them in an accident, black folk could possibly win a lawsuit. There were isolated cases before of a black winning a suit against a white, but this was rare enough that few blacks bothered to sue and few lawyers would take such a case. The unscrupulous companies and individuals who cheated black people did so in part because there was little chance of having to pay a legal price. With blacks on juries, some of that just stopped.

A problem in civil cases was the lower value systematically placed on black life, even by black jurors, where a black woman's broken arm would get $500 and a white woman's $1,500. But we were making progress, and by the time Hank and Rose came to Selma, we actually had a chance of winning cases in the courtroom.

In other ways, progress in Selma was disappointingly slow. Some streets were being paved in black Selma and some blacks were being employed by War on Poverty programs. The city and county had a few black policemen and deputies but obviously did not intend to voluntarily increase those numbers. Less than a half-dozen blacks were employed as clerks in stores or other businesses. In virtually all Selma's businesses and offices, including City Hall and the county courthouse, the black employees pushed a broom. Blacks were voting, but none had been elected to office. Reese, Marie Foster, Doyle, Reverend Anderson, and a few others kept up an aggressive dialogue, but not much happened.

In our first weeks together, as we geared up to push for jobs and fair representation, Hank, Rose, and I worked out what roles each of us should play. Watching SCLC in 1965, I saw Hosea Williams and James Bevel making all kinds of extreme statements: "Selma is racist to the core. We'll boycott and march forever if the white establishment persists in its evil ways. We'll shut this damn town down." Then Andrew Young, with his calm, reasonable demeanor, would come quietly behind them and talk to the white leaders: "If you give this, then we won't do that." Both roles were necessary. White people—probably any people—don't like to negotiate with the same individuals whose actions and threats brought them to the negotiating table.

We deliberately selected roles one afternoon. Since Hank and

Rose were younger and new to Selma, it seemed logical for them to play the abrasive role—raise the issue of racism, file the lawsuits, attack this and that, make speeches denouncing the mayor and county commission. I was older. I had a lifetime of relationships and contacts with the white establishment, so it made sense for me to play the moderate role, keep the dialogue going, work where we could in terms of compromise.

As it turned out, only Rose played the role we designated. Before I met Rose, Hank had told me she was the kind of person who grows on you—a good person, dedicated to helping the underdog, and very outspoken. When Rose sees a wrong, she attacks. She is sensitive, volatile, emotional, and idealistic. It's not easy for her to pass up anything. She has a tendency to fight every war, and awfully high standards. She ruffled feathers not only in white but in black Selma.

Rose and Hank spent a year in Africa between Harvard and Alabama, and one of the first things Rose did in Selma was organize a celebration of Kawanza, an African festival, for young people. In black Selma then, most folk pictured Africa pretty much the way Judge Hare did—as an uncivilized place where people ran around in jungles, half-clad, swinging from trees. Rose created a positive awareness of African culture. Rose often wears some kind of African hat or scarf. That's her gesture to style; she seldom wears makeup and doesn't think too much of women who do or who straighten their hair.

In a very short time, she created a pre-school, an after-school tutoring program, and a Saturday enrichment program for black youth. She founded an organization of black women called MOMs (Mothers of Many), a youth leadership group, and the Black Belt Arts and Cultural Center (B'BACC). The B'BACC youngsters performed African dances and message-type musicals, written by Rose, about black history and teenage problems like pregnancy and drugs. They still do today.

What children in Selma learned about black heroes is attributable primarily to Rose, and she constantly blasted the public schools for not doing more of this job. Rose followed in the footsteps of Claude Brown, Father Ziter, and D. V. Jemison in her deep involvement with youth, though she added black pride and activism. She sees actions, decisions, and events in terms of their impact on black youth, and she doesn't hesitate to call white people racist or black people sell-outs.

The aggressive role wasn't Hank's nature. He'd rather not be the one out front making statements or the one who negotiates and mediates with the white establishment, though he could and did do both. What Hank wound up doing was holding back to see what role was needed in any situation and then playing it. But his penchant was to work in the background shaping policy and planning strategies while giving advice to the leaders out front, a sort of director of the show.

My agreed-upon role was modified almost from the beginning. I was the one who dealt directly with white leaders. But it wasn't like me to work quietly in the background. I'm by nature a lightning rod, which draws heat, attention, and criticism. I enjoy the first two and don't mind the third. I'm happiest when all eyes are on me. So Rose and I were on the cutting edge speaking out, but I maintained relationships with the powers that be.

Hank and Rose brought new life to black Selma, certainly to me. In fact, it was as if I'd been shot out of a cannon. I withdrew from the bottle and cut loose with all the pent-up ideas of a decade, everything I thought should be done but couldn't or didn't do by myself. Within two months, we filed three civil rights lawsuits—one against the city, two against the county—and started to reorganize black Selma.

CHAPTER 16

Racial Politics

Shortly after we created the law firm, we saw an opening to place some blacks on the City Council. Selma's population had grown to a point where state law required it to change its system of electing councilmen—either to five councilmen elected at large, with a council president selected from among them, or ten councilmen elected by district and a president elected at large. At that point, Selma's ten councilmen and council president were elected at large, which meant no black could be elected. We made up slightly more than 50 percent of the population but not of the voting age population.

The city had these options: If the council changed to election by districts, four of the ten councilmen were almost certain to be black. But if it decided to remain at large and all white, six politicians would lose their seats and the city would risk a lawsuit. Edwin Moss appeared before the council with a politely worded petition: "We, the citizens of black Selma, would like to participate in the operation of our city." I came behind him with a vow to sue on the basis of the Voting Rights Act if the city chose the at-large alternative.

One of the most important developments of Voting Rights Act litigation was a prohibition against election systems that "dilute black voting strength." On the basis of this prohibition, the federal courts were striking down at-large elections in the racially polarized South. Since white people wouldn't vote for black candidates, no black person could win in an at-large election in a city or county where blacks of voting age were in a minority. If blacks made up, say, 49 percent of voters and all voted for the black candidates, their votes were diluted—in effect erased—because the white candidates always won. Often, the courts ordered elections by carefully drawn wards or districts, some black, some white, reflecting the population.

I fully expected to have to sue the city. When the all-white council voted—5–3—to go to districts, I was stunned. I felt the way I had when Lyndon Johnson said, "We shall overcome." At first, I was elated. Then I had to think about it. What is this? I decided Smitherman had convinced the councilmen we'd win a suit and the federal court would be in charge of the elections and district lines. The court might even draw the lines to make a majority of black wards and put blacks in charge of City Hall.

But what was Smitherman's angle? I looked around and there he was out in the black community taking credit for including black folk in city government. I thought, Oh, my Lord, he's locking up the black vote.

I was fundamentally distrustful of any white politician, and from what I saw of Smitherman, he was well deserving of suspicion. The man was no Sheriff Clark—he was a definite improvement over previous mayors and the Dallas County commissioners. But this gifted wheeler-dealer running City Hall created another very real problem. Smitherman learned from 1965 and from Wilson Baker. The byword of Selma's new racial order was what Baker had tried to sell in 1965: If you give just a little, you won't have to give a lot. Like George Wallace's, Smitherman's rabid racism in the 1960s proved to be more opportunism than undying belief, but his opportunism knew no bounds. That's where he was dangerous. He's also shrewd as hell. He became the master of a new kind of racial politics, and I became his chief antagonist.

Our first strategic encounter involved the new black councilmen—Reese and Doyle; J. C. Kimbrough, a postman; William Kemp, an old-line Baptist preacher; and Lorenzo Harrison, a younger Baptist preacher. We got five because the incumbent from a majority-white ward died after the qualifying date and

Doyle, the only other candidate in that ward, won by default. So, counting the council president, there were six whites and five blacks. The blacks were the first since Reconstruction and raised great hope in black Selma.

My concern was whether Smitherman would maneuver them into becoming supporters of his administration more so than representatives of black Selma. Would they be persuaded to look at the so-called big picture of the whole city as opposed to the special, long-neglected needs of the black part of the town? Would they be put in a position where the only way they could get anything done would be to go through Smitherman, thus making him the arbiter of what happened or didn't happen in the black community?

Unless the black councilmen remained independent of Smitherman, I feared the black community would wind up with the bare minimum, just enough to keep the councilmen beholden to the mayor and to ensure their and his re-election. With the exception of Reese, none of the black councilmen—or the white ones—came close to being a match for Smitherman as a political manipulator.

For the first few months, the black councilmen met in our law office before they walked across the street for the council meetings. We would go over the agenda and discuss what position the black councilmen would take. There was an agreement that they ought to have a unified position on every item of significance because the black community had so much riding on these councilmen. We didn't have the white community's many other nonpolitical sources of power and influence—bankers, industrialists, chamber of commerce, newspaper. We just had our five little councilmen to stand up for our interests.

Our meetings were an intolerable situation for Smitherman, to whom control is more important than anything else, and he set to work on drawing the councilmen to him and away from us by doing this and that in their wards. Councilmen continually go to the mayor because their constituents continually come to them, and if the mayor wants to make you big out there, he can do it—especially in a poor community desperately in need of services. If he ignores you, that can hurt.

The councilmen stopped meeting in my office, and after about a year, Smitherman was dominating the council as effectively as he had before black people had seats on it. He'd tell the black councilmen privately, "You come in and insist that I pave Minter or Small [streets in the black community]. I'll argue with you for a while, then in two weeks, I'll do it. That will build up your leadership in the black community." He was well aware that a black councilman obviously in the hip pocket of a white mayor would lose credibility and probably re-election, so he went to great lengths to allow them to appear independent.

Smitherman developed an elaborate procedure of letting black councilmen practically hold hearings for municipal services in black Selma as if they were making the decisions, establishing them as leaders of consequence who were pushing the city into making all these improvements—in the process obscuring the fact that most of the paving was being done with federal funds earmarked for the black community. Also, the mayor was ready to put friends, constituents, and relatives of the councilmen on poverty and other boards where black participation was required. Smitherman won white councilmen over in much the same fashion, the difference being that black Selma had so much more at stake with its councilmen and so many more needs.

Reese, not surprisingly, emerged to protect the black interest most aggressively. To win his allegiance, Smitherman had to give up so much that Reese became the second most powerful man in city government. Smitherman made Reese the chairman of the city streets committee; even white people had to go through him if they wanted a stop sign. So Reese joined the others as an insider, a part of the administration.

With blacks on the inside, more was done in the black wards in the city than ever before—which, of course, Smitherman capitalized on in the black community whenever he ran for re-election—and we had a voice in city government. Black folk began to be treated more politely at City Hall and began to go there with problems and requests. It was a striking thing for the deacons of a black church to call a black councilman about a needed stop sign and the next day a city crew is out there putting one up. More black policemen and firemen were hired; a few got rank.

But there was a critical limit to what five black councilmen could do. Getting the power to put up that stop sign meant staying on Smitherman's good side, and with rare exceptions, the councilmen wouldn't push anything the mayor was dead against. This was a problem because Smitherman did only what he had to do, what promoted him, and that was it. When it got down to the real thing, power and equity for black people as a group as opposed to doing something for this black and that black, we were up a damn creek.

And anyway, the white majority on the council could do or block whatever it wanted. In order to change the name of the street in front of Brown Chapel from Sylvan to Martin Luther King in 1976, we had to threaten a demonstration on a day when federal authorities were coming to Selma to decide whether to close Craig Field. Reese's bill to change the name of the street, which ran through the black community except for three blocks downtown, was racially deadlocked at 6–5 for months because the white businessmen on those three blocks didn't want to be on a street named for a black person, especially King.

The same month the councilmen won election, Hank and I filed federal lawsuits against the city and the county for discrimination in hiring and promotion. Jobs were an item at the top of the agenda of the aborted biracial committee back in 1965, and every few years after that, a delegation from the black community— usually Edwin Moss, L. L. Anderson, and other ministers—would bring a petition to the City Council and county commission asking for fairness in hiring.

The county commissioners ignored the petitions. Except for the deputies we got Baker to hire, black people held only menial positions in the county courthouse. Smitherman always said he was willing to hire black people in responsible positions when vacancies arose and qualified blacks applied. But he wasn't going to fire some people to hire other people. Radicals like Rose and I might want that, but he knew the good, decent black folk in Selma weren't in favor of anybody losing his job. Then he'd brag about the number of blacks working for federally financed programs.

In his usual clever manner, Smitherman was attempting to split the black community (the "good, decent folk") from its most aggressive leaders ("the radicals") and was skirting the issue. We rarely knew when vacancies arose because jobs weren't posted or advertised. When Hank and I looked into the situation, we discovered that not only blacks but many whites were left out because city and county jobs were the exclusive domain of a clique of politically connected people. When they had a vacancy, this little group passed the word quietly among themselves and one of them filled it. Also, "qualified" was entirely subjective since written descriptions of jobs or qualifications did not exist.

We hoped our lawsuit would give the new black councilmen more leverage in pushing for city jobs from the inside and would help break the ice for better jobs in stores and private businesses. Employment was the red-hot emotional issue in the early 1970s. The white community had come to accept using the same water fountains, restrooms, and other public facilities as black people, but working side by side with a black person on an equal footing was very controversial—supposedly an insult to the white person.

Smitherman blasted me all over the newspaper. "Chestnut is just trying to build his law practice. He's causing damage to the hiring of blacks with that lawsuit." In truth, I don't think Smitherman really objected to the suit because it gave him more room to maneuver. I saw more than one white politician, in the chambers of a federal judge, say, "Judge, I wish you'd order it," then come out lambasting the judge and the federal judiciary for messing in local business.

At that point, the *Times-Journal* didn't quote black people it considered radical, though this was about to change. But I got on the radio frequently to tell black people, "Don't buy Smitherman's political bull. He's an unbridled opportunist. He's an agent of white people. He's not our savior. He's maintaining white supremacy."

The city and county signed consent decrees, agreeing to post and advertise vacancies for ten days before they were filled, write job descriptions and qualifications, establish uniform salary structures, make a concerted effort to hire more black people, and report progress to the judge. We had to go back several times because the city didn't keep some of its agreements.

"As far as I'm concerned, Chestnut lost," Smitherman told the press after the judge threatened the city with contempt of court. "We were already doing more than what the judge ordered." A few days later, he hired a black man to head a city department—sanitation. He was doing his George Wallace—stand in the door, make strong statements to show your toughness to the white community, then bow to a court order.

Our confrontations became a pattern. I'd sue or threaten to sue. He'd denounce me, build up the issue in the press, and come off to the white community as a tough guy. Then he'd sell them on a small concession: "Chestnut's gonna have the Justice Department breathing down our necks," or, "Those damn people will be out in the streets again if we're not careful. I'm gonna give 'em such-and-such. It won't amount to a damn thing."

Then he'd go to the black community and say to the men in the Elks and Chesterfield clubs: "I've done more for black Selma than all the previous mayors combined. If J.L. would quit these damn lawsuits and carrying on all this crap, we could get a hell of a lot more done. But all he does is upset white people and they come down on me. The white people gonna run me out of here and you-all gonna have the worst somebody you cain't even talk to."

Ever since the Baker–Clark race, Smitherman had been building up support in the black middle class. He made a habit of showing up Thursday night at the credit union, where Edwin and the other officers would sit around and drink whiskey after their board meeting. Coming from the wrong side of the tracks, Smitherman wasn't stiff around black people. He didn't come off like a Judge Hare, letting you know he was up here and you were down there. Smitherman well understood the impact it would have on this crowd for a powerful white man, the mayor, to come over and drink, laugh, and talk with them.

By using the specter of black control to scare the white community and white resistance to justify tokenism to the black community, Smitherman made sure he'd never have to sell washing machines again. I don't know of any politician in the South, including George Wallace, who played racial politics more brilliantly than Smitherman, and it has kept him in office more than a quarter century.

When a white person ran against him—which most often was

the case, since the numbers weren't there for a black to win—he got virtually all the black vote and some of the white vote. He became so powerful that few whites of substance ran against him. On the occasions a black entered the race, Smitherman reminded the white community that another white candidate would split the white vote, so nobody white challenged him. Smitherman then won with all the white vote and a little bit of the black vote.

Edwin and I had many conversations about his support of the mayor.

"Joe's the best white mayor we're gonna get," he'd say.

"I don't agree," I'd say. "I think a mayor less Machiavellian and less obsessed with control would have gone further down the road to giving blacks meaningful participation in city government."

"Every time I call him about something, he's done it right away if he possibly can. He treats me like a man."

"But, Ed, we can't let him have us in his hip pocket. We need to use our vote to be the balance of power between different white candidates."

"Yeah, but in politics, if you don't support the man, you don't have the right to ask for anything. You can't be out there supporting somebody who can't win just to shake Smitherman up."

"Why not? We're not getting much anyway."

What blacks did get in the seventies came straight out of the War on Poverty, which Smitherman capitalized on to the hilt. In the early sixties, when Chris Heinz was mayor, the city turned down urban renewal money. Federal money was considered tainted because it would bring on federal control and integration. Well into the seventies, the all-white governments in some of the poorest counties in Alabama were turning their backs on federal money in the interest of maintaining local white control. Smitherman, though, looked at that War on Poverty money and saw an opportunity. His slogan was: "The only thing tainted about federal money is, t'ain't enough."

He established a relationship with the Department of Housing and Urban Development (HUD) and other federal agencies and the city got a $3 million HUD grant for an urban renewal project to clear and rebuild a slum area in black Selma and other money

Dirt streets and sidewalks like this one in black east Selma were paved during the War on Poverty (Courtesy of the Fathers of St. Edmund)

for other projects. When we looked at the city's plans, we saw serious problems—new housing projects concentrated in poor black areas, no clear-cut plans for the people who would be displaced, commercial or low-density zoning in new, developing areas that would exclude most black people, drainage and sewer projects in black residential areas that were rezoned industrial. We strongly suspected that once the sewers were in, the old shotgun houses would be torn down and white-owned industries would pop up in their place.

The biggest flaw was no black involvement. For the $3 million project, HUD required the participation of a Project Area Committee elected from residents of the affected section. A Project Area Committee was formed, but the city ignored it. Smitherman bellowed that the "radicals" on the committee wanted to "control everything." Some of them did, but so did Smitherman—and he *was* controlling it until the NAACP Legal Defense Fund sued

HUD and the city for using federal money to create and strengthen residential segregation in Selma.

That blocked $3 million plus and halted all the projects. Smitherman blamed a "small group of civil rights activists" for denying the "vast majority of sound-thinking mainstream" black people the benefits they deserved. This was in 1970, the year my friend James Robinson returned to Selma as a Roman Catholic priest and assistant director—the first black one—of the Fathers of St. Edmund mission, which had taken him up when we were teenagers and sent him to college and seminary. In the course of dealing with Smitherman on business for the mission, Father Robinson came to know the mayor. Smitherman complained constantly about the federal money held up by what he characterized as unreasonable demands, and Father saw a way to be useful to both sides.

Black Selma in 1970 still had many dirt streets, dark and unlit at night, many smelly outdoor toilets, poor drainage, and block after block of run-down shotgun houses—the physical legacy of decades of municipal neglect. "That lawsuit is the worst case of cutting off one's nose to spite one's face I've ever heard of," Father argued to us. "The black community needs the programs. Santa Claus isn't going to live forever." But what would happen if you brought all that federal largesse to town and let the white officials run it without our input? The Project Area Committee told Father they weren't about to give up the lawsuit, the only leverage the black community had.

Father succeeded in getting everybody talking. After a series of long meetings, the committee, the city, and HUD signed an agreement called the Selma Accord. In exchange for the committee dropping the suit, the city agreed to put a housing project outside the poor black area, revise its zoning, afford meaningful participation by the committee, and hire a black urban renewal director. Smitherman won the right to name which black.

This episode was typical of Selma's racial politics. Almost every step of progress for black people required either a confrontation—a lawsuit, a boycott, a march, or the threat of them—or a federal regulation requiring black participation as a condition for receiving money. Very little happened voluntarily.

The federal money flowed into Selma after that—close to $40 million before Santa Claus died. Selma was revitalized from end to end—every street paved and served with a sewer line and lights, several hundred new units of housing, a new City Hall, library, and convention center, new trees and brick sidewalks downtown, better drainage everywhere.

All the federal programs—urban renewal, Head Start, CETA— required black participation in jobs and on boards of directors. Through the early seventies, Smitherman pretty much kept white faces in City Hall and hired black people essentially for the federal programs, though he made sure he hired as many white people for these jobs, too.

One or two blacks were appointed to the city boards—planning, personnel, industrial development—that administered the federal programs. This was the beginning of a transition in black involvement in civic life from exclusion to tokenism. By the middle seventies, one or two blacks on city and county boards became the norm.

It is an irony, maybe a tragedy, that the individuals who participated in the 1960s demonstrations were not the ones to benefit. The civil rights people who went into government—Andrew Young, John Lewis, Julian Bond, Reese—were the leaders, and they got in office by votes of the black electorate. The rank and file of the Selma movement, the folk who demonstrated and went to jail, did not, with rare exceptions, march through the doors they opened. The white powers doing the picking selected blacks they could "work with"—that was the phrase—which meant middle-class, light-skinned, and moderate. I don't think the light-skinned part was something they did consciously. They just felt more comfortable with light-skinned black people, who historically have been better educated and more culturally attuned to white society, reaching back to the plantation system when house slaves were oftentimes literally part of the family. Anyway, when I checked out the blacks on the various boards, I noticed they resembled each other.

Randall Miller, the black Smitherman picked to be urban renewal director, was a funeral director with little involvement in civil rights. The first black appointed to the school board was

Marshall C. Cleveland, Jr., the pastor of my church and the personification of the old school. He was committed to the proposition that whites have the power and we have to accommodate ourselves accordingly. Charles Lett, the pastor who told Preston and me civil rights was not his business, served on several boards. Edwin got so many appointments we teased him about being "the token."

These type appointments split the black community, angering the people who had marched and got their heads beat, and sent a message that there was nothing to be gained from antagonizing white leaders and fooling around with radical blacks. My next-door neighbor told me one day he didn't need to demonstrate. When they got ready to appoint somebody, they'd find somebody like him. And they did. Smitherman put him on the city personnel board.

In the course of my many confrontations with Smitherman, I decided I needed direct contact with him rather than responding to him through others. Through Edwin, I started having conversations with the mayor and got to know him.

He's a very personable man, hard not to like. I found he has a number of good qualities—a sense of humor, an astuteness about people, a genuine empathy for the underdog, and a refreshing frankness about matters of race and politics in a community that specializes in putting on a pretty face. He flatly admits racism is central to his strategy, though he always adds it's other folks' racism, not his, he's just politickin' with it.

We started talking politics now and then on the phone. On occasion, I would get help for a client when the help was beyond the reach of other municipal politicians and administrators. Obviously he hoped to neutralize me politically in elections. He never did. But his politics were so effective I couldn't have defeated him in any event. I kept on suing the city and denouncing Smitherman and his policies. He continued denouncing me in the white community and trying to undermine me in the black community.

Some people believed that he and I fed on each other and did it deliberately for our separate purposes—he to maintain his power, I to establish myself as a black leader. To some extent, that may have been true. That's the nature of politics, and neither of us created the climate in the South and how you have to go about getting things done. But our visions of what Selma should be are quite different, and we are genuine antagonists. He wants to give black people the minimum. I want the maximum. He wants black people beholden to him. I want black people to come into their own as free people, beholden to themselves.

CHAPTER 17

Black Santa

Wilson Baker called one day and said some folk, meaning white folk, wanted to talk.

"About what?" I asked.

"Just generally," he said.

"I really don't think so."

He persisted. "I think you ought to," and I said, "Well, all right."

Baker told me to come over to the City Council chambers the next afternoon. Ten or twelve shakers and movers were there, and one black person—me. Baker, Smitherman, some white councilmen, and five or six businessmen were sitting in the first few rows of the theater-like seats on one side of the aisle. I sensed they'd been there awhile talking among themselves.

"Come in, J.L.," Baker said. I sat down in a seat in the first row on the opposite side of the aisle and faced them. They smiled and made friendly comments, but I felt some foreboding. What was this all about? Why was I the only black person there?

Baker took the lead. "Selma has suffered enough," he began. "We've been held up to ridicule by people in cities that have worse race problems than we do. We need to sit down and work together instead of carrying on all these high-velocity public charges."

He was referring to my speeches in black churches and my

remarks on the radio. Hank and Rose had been in Selma about
a year then and we were coming on strong. Though we'd originally
expected to play a supportive, legal role—filing suits, covering
the backs of folk who were fighting—we soon got cast not only
in the role of lawyers but in the role of civil rights leaders. We
were advocating direct action ourselves, threatening boycotts of
businesses and marches on the city and county government for
jobs. I was on the radio frequently, detailing wrongs and telling
black folk they were fools to think white supremacy could be
negotiated into the background. I warned white people that Selma
was a ticking time bomb, and unless crucial matters were addressed, we'd be facing confrontations worse than those in the
sixties.

Baker went on to say he understood there were problems that
needed to be solved. But I had to agree we couldn't solve them
all in a week or a month. We needed to work in good faith.

"Let me ask you something," one of the councilmen said.
"What do you think you're going to accomplish with all that
incendiary rhetoric on the radio?" I said I thought part of the
problem was inherent in his pointing out my so-called incendiary
rhetoric and making no mention about all the mayor's reckless
statements. Much of what I said was in response to attacks on me.

Smitherman then chimed in to say he was doing the best he
could in a difficult period. "I don't need all those damn snipers
out there tryin' to make names for themselves allegedly on behalf
of black people. I talk to black people every day who repudiate
all that nonsense." He agreed with Baker, he said, that progress
takes time. But all the time in the world wouldn't be enough if
I continued my irresponsible public attacks on city government,
trying to promote my law practice and re-create a civil rights
movement because I wasn't a star in the real one.

As Smitherman made his speech, I noticed a few of the businessmen exchange critical looks. The way I read it, they wanted
to prevent the city from getting into any sixties stuff again and
saw Smitherman and me headed in that direction. Selma was
volatile. It wasn't clear yet what was going to replace the old
order in terms of personal relationships, economic relationships,
or the distribution of power. With the mayor and me making

extreme statements, they were afraid we might trigger something that could develop a life of its own and hurt Selma's image and their businesses.

I said I didn't agree with what the mayor said and he obviously didn't agree with my position. "Therein lies another problem. We can't even agree on what the issues are, much less the possible solution."

"I don't think that's the case," Baker said. "I think what's happening is you and the mayor have brought the same biting and baiting you've been doing in the media to this meeting, and that's the one thing we don't want."

"What is it that you want?" I asked.

"It's not so much what we want," one of the businessmen answered, "as what Selma needs." He said Selma needed time and peace. We needed the rhetoric toned down. We needed to stop giving Selma a bad image. This led to a chorus of expressions of love for Selma—theirs and, they were certain, mine. They had great plans for the city that would benefit everyone. But they couldn't do these things overnight or in a confrontational atmosphere. I was doing more harm than good with my lawsuits and threats of further legal and direct action. Nobody likes to negotiate with a pistol cocked to his temple.

I said, "All my life black people have been quiet and all we got was spat in the face and walked on. It was only when we raised a ruckus that we began to have some rights. That's what you call agitation. I believe devoutly in what you are devoutly against. I have no interest in quieting down for the sake of peace and quiet." I said we hadn't gotten anything from them voluntarily and they weren't offering anything now. I quoted King's "Letter from a Birmingham Jail"—that "wait" to black people means "never." "At whose expense is all this time, your children or mine?"

It got hot in there. They jumped in at every pause to tell me I was off base, impatient, unrealistic. They made the same point Claude Brown used to make: Antagonizing people of goodwill wasn't going to help black people or Selma. I said if the people of goodwill wanted the black community to give up lawsuits, boycotts, demonstrations—the only effective tactics we had—then they better offer a *quid pro quo* instead of vague promises.

"What do you want?" one of the men asked. I began repeating the standard issues—jobs, more blacks in responsible positions, an elected city school board.

Baker stopped me and explained: "They"—it was interesting that he separated himself—"want to know what *you* want."

He hastened to explain that he knew my interest in economic development. I ought to be with them trying to get more government grants and industry that would create jobs for everybody. I could advise them about these boards. I could make some legal fees. I could build a good law practice and do a lot of things myself to help my people. That's where the action was. There wasn't any action on the radio arguing with the mayor about black employment or standing up in a church talking about boycotting businesses or riling up some latter-day civil rights movement that would scare industry away.

I didn't say anything right away. I was thinking about the day the Rinkydinks and I came to see the police chief in the very same building and he told us to go see Reverend Jemison. This is D. V. Jemison and Claude Brown, 1970s style, I thought to myself. You want to be the number-one nigger? You want a say in federal appointments, the poverty boards? You want that to go through you? You want to name the black principals? Do you want to be Mr. Black Selma? What is your price?

Somebody broke the silence and said, jokingly, that as soon as I got prosperous they wouldn't be hearing any more radical stuff from me. I'm sure the man believed this, and I'm equally sure he wouldn't have characterized the conversation as an attempt to buy me off. Almost all the powerful white lawyers in Selma were on the city payroll—representing the water board or the school board or whatever. Why shouldn't they strike a deal with a black lawyer? Why shouldn't I accept?

I told them I'd appreciate city legal business, but I wasn't bargaining on behalf of myself. I was trying to speak for the black half of Selma, and I couldn't see any reason for black folk to ease up or quiet down on the basis of that meeting. This wouldn't be a unilateral decision, anyway. Contrary to what the mayor thought, there were scores of black people in support of what I was doing. "As far as my public statements go, if y'all would just be fair, you won't hear a thing out of me, not a damn peep."

The meeting began to ramble and, at some point, Baker told me Jean Sullivan, the Republican committeewoman, was on the phone. I don't know if she called knowing about the meeting or if they called her hoping she could bring me around. Jean carefully cultivated black people and I enjoyed her direct, frank, and often profane approach. Ironically, her father had been the most hated policeman in black Selma when I was growing up. But Jean built up as much goodwill as he did ill will, and blacks helped elect her as committeewoman.

I took the phone and she asked, "How're you makin' out?" Suddenly a picture fell off the wall. *Bam!* I said, "I'm okay, Jean. They didn't shoot me." We all laughed and that was the end of the discussion.

"Nobody likes to negotiate with a pistol cocked to his temple." That was the standard line of the Selma business community. In the late sixties, small delegations of the more active ministers visited banks and stores that did substantial black business to ask them to hire black salespeople and tellers. Gaston's IGA, a supermarket near Brown Chapel, hired two black men to run the produce department, but other businesses offered only vague promises, if that, and told the delegations they didn't appreciate being pressured.

The situation produced a kind of Hobson's choice: nobody wanted to be forced, but nobody wanted to be first. The first businessman who got out there would catch hell from whites, probably get boycotted by the White Citizens' Council, which remained active until about 1970. If a business hired a black cashier, his black business would pick up, but he didn't know how much business he'd lose from whites or the social consequences of appearing to favor black people by being first.

Several blacks, led by Edwin, proposed to the Chamber of Commerce a joint hiring effort by a significant number of businesses. They said that if a third or a half of your customers are black, hiring blacks isn't a civil rights statement. It's a statement of economic survival and white people probably will see it that way. No joint effort happened because, I think, some merchants were stone racists and weren't going to hire a black person period.

One of our strategies for breaking the ice was going after the

chains that came to Selma in 1974 when the Selma Mall opened—
a long, low-slung structure with a Sears at one end and a J. C.
Penney at the other. When a chain store moved into Selma, a
black delegation followed on the heels of the official welcoming
committee to insist on our share of jobs and to tell the chain
executives how much money our folk were going to spend there.
Frequently, local whites became managers and we had to go over
their heads to get anything done.

The big chains had employment commitments nationally with
civil rights groups, the federal government, and unions. They
made promises and had deadlines. Preston and I went to New
York once and met with a black vice-president of Sears. We spent
the afternoon discussing Sears and its policies in Selma. We had
the brother thing going. We told him Sears had one or two black
clerks in its Selma store but they were part-time. "Brother, I'm
glad you brought that to my attention," he said. He promised
immediate changes and kept his word. Damn near overnight,
Sears acquired more black employees and a black department
supervisor.

What had the greatest impact on the local stores, though, were
the banks. When the banks hired blacks, other businesses felt
more secure. People's Bank came first, hiring a black teller in
1970. A delegation of ministers visited all the banks, but People's
had a more compelling reason to listen. Black folk did more
business with People's because People's was a little more cordial
and a little more lenient in making loans. Also, Edwin's credit
union had its funds—about $1 million at that point—deposited
there. It had expanded beyond the membership of the Elks and
now was called the Selma-Dallas Community Federal Credit
Union.

Rex Morthland, then the bank's president, grew up in California and studied at the University of Chicago. He married into
People's Bank; his father-in-law founded it. I sensed in him a
person who didn't want to rock the boat in his adopted town but
didn't feel a hundred percent comfortable with local practices like
not calling black people "Mr." and "Mrs.," a custom that died
in the wake of the sixties demonstrations.

Like the other banks, People's told the ministers they wouldn't hire a black just to hire a black. They needed qualified applicants. This word—"qualified"—became a major bone of contention. We weren't asking them to hire unqualified people. It was a putdown and a smokescreen to delay and exclude. Then a black woman applied who'd had experience as a teller in a bank in Birmingham and People's hired her.

I saw this as strictly a business decision. The board of directors risked the loss of black business, especially the credit-union deposits, if another bank came out first with a black teller. I don't think Morthland personally had any problem with hiring a black teller—he probably thought it was the right thing to do—but it was only in an atmosphere of pressure that he would or could sell this to the board of directors and the white community.

On the occasion of these firsts—the first day of the first black teller, cashier, clerk—an almost standard scenario took place. The boss forewarned the white employees with a speech along the lines of: "This won't be popular with all of you, but we've hired a Negro. You must recognize that this was going to happen sometime."

A friend hired as the first black clerk in one of the downtown department stores told me everybody walked on eggshells her first few days on the job. We couldn't pin down just what they were afraid of. It's crazy, irrational—people all riled up and actually believing a black clerk posed a threat to their well-being—and insulting as hell to the black person. Human nature, however, took over, and some of the other employees gradually began to talk and share lunch with my friend, though one woman quit.

Since the Voters League no longer existed, black Selma needed an activist organization. Hank, Rose, and I, F. D. Reese, Marie Foster, and Reverend Anderson—the core of activists—along with Edwin Moss, Father Robinson, and others cranked up a series of organizations in the seventies: the Selma-Dallas Legal Defense Fund, the Selma-Dallas Political Action Committee, the Selma-Dallas Direct Action Committee, the Black Leadership Council. The Leadership Council, an umbrella of all these groups, plus clubs and fraternities, took the lead in the employment effort.

Middle-class people, my mother's colleagues, schoolteachers who'd been scared to death of agitation, now showed up at the

(From the left) Me, F. D. Reese, and Father James Robinson in Brown Chapel on the tenth anniversary of Bloody Sunday, an occasion we used to push for parity in jobs and appointments (© Lawrence Williams)

meetings to discuss fairness and equity in jobs. I loved sitting in First Baptist or Brown Chapel or Ebenezer Baptist and seeing some black woman or black man stand up, perhaps for the first time in their lives, to express their views in a public meeting: Why can't our folk be managers? Why are we sending our children to Alabama State if we're not going to fight so they can be managers at Kress? Why should we spend money in the department stores unless they hire some of us?

A certain section of black Selma continued to hold back. I noticed in the sixties that black funeral directors weren't excited about integration. As long as they had segregation, they only had to compete with other black undertakers. If whites moved in, with their greater capital resources, out of business they'd go. The black barber had a monopoly. Matter of fact, he had something going white barbers didn't because some white people in

Me speaking at Brown Chapel at one of our mass meetings (Courtesy of J. L. Chestnut, Jr.)

the South liked having their hair cut by black barbers. He worried about integration. The same was true of black insurance companies, black cafés, and, really, the black economy across the board.

Our jobs campaign intensified these concerns. Obviously, when a white business hired more blacks, black folk would feel more comfortable patronizing that business. Black businessmen came to the meetings and raised questions. Preston said at one meeting that if we spent half as much time trying to build black business as we did trying to force our way into white businesses, we'd all be better off.

With the exception of funeral homes and barbershops, few black businesses survived integration in Selma, though there were few black businesses to begin with. Preston's hair-products business prospered, then suffered. Through my involvement in statewide black politics, Preston met President Carter's son, Chip, and the next thing I knew he received a million-dollar government loan. He set up an assembly line, hired forty people, and marketed Velberta products across the nation and in Africa. The company did great for a while but never reached its full potential. Part of the problem was Preston's unwillingness to follow the advice of experts who knew more than he did. But what hurt most were white companies like Revlon, with their giant advertising budgets and marketing networks, getting into the black hair-products business.

We continued to apply pressure on white businesses because we were interested in existing jobs. The Leadership Council met once a month, and the committee that visited stores, headed by Marie Foster, would give a detailed report—the number of black employees and black supervisors, what the manager said, whether he was hostile or polite. In the middle seventies, some stores had no black employees; others had one or two but weren't promoting them to higher positions. It was an ongoing process.

Often the white attitude was: "Well, we've hired one. Now let's go back to business as usual." The process was just too damn slow. We'd push and get one black hired and the white community acted as if we'd just won the Civil War. From our point of view, we'd just got our foot in the door. We constantly were confronted with a white perspective and a black perspective as to what was reasonable progress for black people.

Some managers asked for names to put on a list to use when they had vacancies. So Marie and the committee took the names of people who wanted the jobs and had appropriate backgrounds. When businesses kept stalling or the manager was rude or black employees complained of being passed over for promotion, the committee recommended a boycott and pickets with signs telling folk the store discriminated.

The white community detested the boycotts and put forth the same rationale about gradualism, good faith, and peace that I got at the meeting in City Council chambers. So some folk who attended meetings, placed their children's names on lists to be hired, and joined a delegation to speak with store owners were reluctant to stand on a picket line and be labeled radicals. The dedicated picketers were Rose, Hank, Marie, the women from MOMs, and

Raymond Major, a black man from New York City who had moved to Selma and opened a disco.

Our most controversial and effective boycott came over the issue of a black Santa at the Selma Mall. Two young black mothers called on the mall manager at the beginning of the 1977 Christmas season to request that a black Santa be hired in addition to the white Santa. They suggested the two Santas work different shifts so people preferring the white or the black one would know when to schedule their visits. They also reminded the merchants of a request made the previous December through the Chamber of Commerce to divide the number of Christmas jobs equally between black and white youth.

The mothers made no threats and anticipated no problems. They weren't the belligerent type. But the manager wasn't nearly as sensitive as he should have been. White Santas were traditional, he said. They treated black children the same as white children. They hadn't done anything racist so he couldn't see the problem or any reason to change the tradition. The black women tried to explain their concern, but apparently their explanations irritated him. He got somewhat hostile and abruptly cut off the conversation, saying, in effect, There will be no black Santa.

The next meeting of the Black Leadership Council drew a large crowd because the Santa thing caught fire in black Selma. One merchant made public statements that the request was "ridiculous." The publisher of the *Times-Journal* wrote a naïve column asking, "What color is Santa Claus? Does it really matter? He might just as well be purple or green or orange because Santa is the spirit of Christmas—friendship, kindness, and understanding." These remarks pissed folk off all the more.

One black woman rose up at the back of the church to declare, loudly, that she hated to take part of the joy of Christmas away from her children. "But I'll be damned if I'll let my children believe some fat white man brought their presents. I'm gonna tell 'em my husband and I bought them." Everybody roared and clapped, gave her a standing ovation. The woman had made a profound cultural statement.

We boycotted and picketed the entire mall. This was killing them, losing about half their customers at Christmas time. By then, we'd expanded the issue to employment equity across the board at the mall—in numbers, supervisors, managers. The Chamber of Commerce director called me about resolving the situation. He said the merchants recognized an imbalance and agreed to hire more young blacks for the Christmas season and to reassess their policies. They weren't going to fire or demote any white people, but they'd hire and promote blacks when openings developed. This wasn't too easy to sell to some folk who felt, Hell, we've been waiting for years. But we called off the boycott, and that year we had a black Santa.

Meanwhile, we'd been meeting with Bruce Morrison, the publisher of the *Times-Journal*, about the paper's coverage. He was a decent fella, constantly calling for "communication between the races." We said there was a built-in white bias in reporting on matters where there was a disagreement between black and white Selma and it would help if the paper hired a black reporter. He said he'd been trying to find a qualified black person, and if we named one, he'd hire that person. I told him we'd initiate a search, but in the interim I'd write a Sunday column. He agreed. We called the column "Perspective."

Straddling Two Eras

My oldest son, Ronnie, went all the way through school in a segregated system declared unconstitutional when he was three years old. Our dire predictions at Howard about "all deliberate speed" came true. By setting no deadline and allowing the lower courts to take local conditions and "good-faith efforts" into account, the Supreme Court put us in the position of having to litigate from schoolhouse to schoolhouse to make its decision a reality.

With the passage of the Civil Rights Act, though, the U.S. Department of Education started requiring school systems to submit desegregation plans if they wanted federal funds. In April 1965, the Selma school board submitted its first plan—for so-called freedom-of-choice desegregation beginning in the first four grades the next fall and adding four more grades each year after that. Within days, a group headed by Judge Hare, McLean Pitts, Chris Heinz, the White Citizens' Council crowd, founded John Tyler Morgan Academy, a private, segregated school.

Under freedom of choice, the dual system was maintained, but students and teachers could volunteer to cross over to schools of the opposite race. Of course, most of the white teachers didn't want to go to the black schools. The black teachers didn't feel comfortable asking to be transferred to the white schools. To comply with court orders for mixed faculties, boards assigned their best and most favored black teachers to the white schools and their youngest and most inexperienced white teachers to the black schools.

My mother and Aunt Lennie were the first black teachers assigned to white schools in the Dallas County system (the county system is separate from the Selma city system). They put my mother in a little outbuilding behind the school and had her teaching art. In the black schools, she'd taught social studies and English. She knew why she wasn't in the main building but she accepted it. She was more upset about a black girl who enrolled in the school, saw her, and cried, "Aw, ain't I got a white teacher?"

Teaching in the white school, my mother discovered how wide the disparity was between black and white teachers' salaries. She also learned that teachers there were provided with money for bulletin board supplies and other materials that black teachers in black schools had to buy out of their own salaries. It was characteristic of my mother that she didn't blame Frank Earnest, the superintendent of the county system. When she got a raise or a promotion, he was the one responsible and she was loyal to him for it. "Don't you go attacking Frank Earnest," she told me. "He's my friend."

Few black students attended the white schools during freedom of choice. The white authorities didn't encourage it beyond the minimum number required by a court order or the Department of Education. And how many young people want to leave their friends and go to an alien school where they aren't wanted? Rosalind and Geraldine, my oldest daughters, were at Hudson, Selma's black high school, during freedom of choice and they didn't want to go to Parrish, the white school. Gerald was a Tigerette, a sort of drum major, and they didn't have Tigerettes at Parrish. Rosalind was a cheerleader.

In October 1969, the Supreme Court threw out "all deliberate speed" and ruled that continued operation of segregated schools was no longer permissible. Two months later, a three-judge federal panel ordered Selma to abolish its dual system by the beginning of the next school year. That's when the crunch came. The Selma school board made a quiet announcement designed to do two contradictory things—reassure whites they weren't changing that much and assure blacks they were going to be fair. More white people left the system for Morgan Academy. But not all whites could afford a private education, and a core of Selma's movers and shakers, members of the old families who own and run the town, kept their children in the public schools because they knew you can't chuck public education and have a viable city.

Many elementary schools, being neighborhood schools, remained predominantly black or white. In the dual system, Hudson and Parrish had been junior as well as senior highs. When the system was unified, Parrish, the nicer, larger school, became the one, integrated high school, renamed Selma High. Hudson became Westside Junior High, and a former elementary school in predominantly black east Selma became Eastside Junior High. That first fall, the student population of Selma High was between 55 and 60 percent black, Westside was about half and half, and Eastside was mostly black.

There were a series of meetings in the black and white communities that summer. Nobody wanted Selma to explode again, and the schools opened peacefully. Gerald was a senior that year, Rosalind a junior. They brought home stories of arguments, misunderstandings, disputes, and fights, but I guess the students got along as well as could be expected. Gerald, who is very outgoing, even made a few white friends. She said they were curious. Where did she and her friends go on weekends? Why were black people all different colors? How did they fix their hair? Gerald was curious, too. Why did white girls all want to be blondes?

According to my daughters, though, there wasn't much socializing across racial lines—and very little dating, that big bugaboo of the White Citizens' Council. For one thing, the board instituted a three-tier system of learning levels that to a significant degree resegregated the students, with the majority of the white students, especially the children of the prominent families, in the top level.

There were dual homecoming queens, dual student officers, a black most popular student and a white most popular student. The year Rosalind was a senior, the school decided there should be four white and four black cheerleaders. It was taken for granted, though, that the biracial Selma High cheerleading squad would adopt the white, Parrish style. Rosalind, who was on the squad, said their style was stiffer, more programmed, less improvised than Hudson's, and the squad leader kept telling her her arms or legs were moving too much. She never did learn to move the way the white cheerleaders did.

More serious issues arose in making two systems into one. Would James Street, the white principal of Parrish High, or Joe Yelder, the black principal of Hudson High, become the principal of integrated Selma High? Who would be the head coach and who the assistant coach? Who would get the better, supervisory positions, the black or the white teachers? Eastside Junior High and the elementary schools that remained all or predominantly black retained black principals and coaches. But in the truly integrated schools—Westside Junior High and Selma High—blacks were relegated to back seats as assistant principals, assistant coaches, assistant supervisors.

Of all our battles to take a front seat in the Selma school system, the most painful involved Joe Yelder. Like Claude Brown, he was straddling two eras. He was geared by nature and experience to the old era of accommodation. Then along came integration, and he happened to be the one person in a position to stand up for black people because he had the most seniority. By rights, he should have been offered the job of principal of Selma High. But Joe Pickard, the superintendent of the Selma school system, instead offered him a newly created post as coordinator of administrative services and a raise. Reese, I, and others told him, "This is a bribe. Don't do it. Don't embarrass yourself and black people."

Yelder refused that position, but agreed to be principal of Eastside, the predominantly black junior high. Pickard persuaded him white people would take their children out of the public schools if a black became principal of Selma High or Westside. If he really cared about the system and the children in it, he would rise above any rights he had personally and ignore the radicals who were telling him to insist on his right to be principal of Selma High.

We put a lot of pressure on Yelder to sue the school board.

This was a crucial time, the beginning of a new era, and whatever pattern developed now was likely to become the norm. Unless we put up a fight, blacks would be locked into secondary positions in the integrated schools, probably for a long time to come.

Yelder balked. "I'm an educator, not a civil rights fighter," he said. Yelder is a tall man, medium-brown, soft-spoken. He's the kind of person everyone's inclined to like and call a good man, because he genuinely wants to be helpful and to be liked by everybody. He sincerely wanted to do right by black people. But Yelder was a product of his generation—born in 1910, not that far removed from slavery. It ran against his grain to buck anybody, especially white authority. White people had helped him advance; they were in charge of education. He also understood how he became principal of Hudson High—through Claude Brown, the master accommodationist.

Yelder belonged to Brown's church. In 1955, when the previous principal left Hudson, Brown lobbied for Yelder, a shop teacher, to get the job. Edwin and the Fathers pushed for Andrew Durgan, a popular science teacher who some thought would be a more effective principal. The board picked Yelder. Since no white children went to Hudson High, the white board didn't give much of a damn who the principal was so long as he was a decent fellow who would follow their instructions. So they let Brown, their most favored "responsible nigra," make the choice. Several times I overheard Brown and Yelder talking about white authority and the proper relationship of intelligent blacks to that authority. This was Yelder's world. Then the world changed and we were asking him to change with it.

Reese had been rehired by the school system in the late 1960s and at that point was assistant principal at Eastside. He felt as strongly as I did that Yelder should sue, and he stood to become Eastside's principal if Yelder moved up to Selma High. Yelder had a high regard for Reese. Even though Reese bucked him in 1965 to leave school and march with King, Reese always tried to protect Yelder's flanks. That Reese did all he did and survived heightened Yelder's respect for him. So Reese was in a strategic position to put enormous, almost unbearable pressure on the man.

I stopped by Yelder's house at least once a week. I'd say, "Joe, your stock is going down to zero." This was true. Some black people were calling him Superintendent Pickard's lapdog. I was blunt: "You've had a fine career in education and you're going to let it all go down the drain. You're going to have trouble not only speaking to your neighbors but looking at yourself in the mirror. You've been a role model for black children. Look what message you're sending! We can't be a race of assistants. We've got to have black high school principals, black board members, eventually black superintendents. You're going to stifle the motivation of people you've spent a lifetime trying to educate out of some crazy loyalty to Pickard and the school board. They don't give a damn about you. They're just using you."

He'd come back with his usual argument that he wanted time to think about it. He wanted me to realize he wasn't Martin Luther King. He wanted to "facilitate the educative process," not sacrifice it on the altar of integration or anything else. He didn't agree with me about Pickard and the board. He insisted they looked out for his welfare.

Interestingly, Brown concurred that Yelder ought to sue. One afternoon I had a conversation with Brown regarding Yelder's seeming to be up and raring to proceed one day, then almost reversing field a few days later. Brown said he'd have a talk with Yelder, that Yelder should stand his ground. I thought then about how the civil rights movement affected people in all kinds of ways, how King, a cultivator of people, sought Brown's advice and help and had an impact on the man. King hadn't made Brown a civil rights agitator, but he surely wasn't quite the Claude Brown of yesterday.

Reluctantly, Yelder agreed to sue the school board, alleging that he'd been passed over because he was black. A case called *Singleton* had established the principle that dismissals, demotions, and promotions in public schools undergoing desegregation must be based on objective, non-racial criteria. Our suit was financed by the National Education Association, and I tried it with Solomon Seay, Jr., the Montgomery lawyer who defended Drewey Aaron with me and who had become a specialist in school litigation.

We asked the federal judge to order the board to hire Yelder as principal of Selma High and give him back pay equaling the difference between his salary and Street's, counting back to 1970. If we'd had legal grounds to go back further we would have. In 1970, the year the dual system was abolished, Yelder made $10,600 a year as principal of the black high school, while Street made $12,000 as principal of the white high school, though the student bodies were of roughly equal size.

In 1975, while the suit still was pending, Street resigned as principal of Selma High. The board named Roy Wilson, the white principal of Westside, to replace him and brought in a white man from another town to replace Wilson at Westside—passing over Yelder, Reese, and Evans Rutledge, Westside's black assistant principal.

The black community was enraged. The Selma-Dallas Defense Fund picketed the school board office until the board agreed to hold a public meeting. Then four hundred black folk packed the high school auditorium, spilling out into the hallways, to express the black community's grievances with the way Selma's schools were being run under integration. Learning levels were a big issue. There weren't any clear-cut criteria for placement, and the teachers and parents said too many black children were being shunted to the lower levels and vocational courses and the better teachers were being assigned to the top level.

The composition of the school board was another complaint. The board was a self-perpetuating body of upper-class whites— doctors, lawyers, bankers, and their wives from the old, established families. When someone left the board, the group picked a replacement from one of their own. They weren't Selma's die-hards—that crowd had left the public schools—but they couldn't escape a primary concern for the education of their own and their friends' children, and they were making decisions affecting our children behind closed doors, in "executive sessions." There were hardly any middle-class whites on the board, let alone lower-class whites or any blacks—until integration, when they found it necessary to appoint my pastor and a few other handpicked blacks.

Hank and I had already filed a lawsuit to change the way the board was selected. We wanted an elected body, a cross section of people whose children attended the schools. The

Alabama legislature could have enacted a law to that effect, but we didn't have any clout in Montgomery and couldn't persuade the excluded whites to take up the cause. "I have a better chance of being appointed to the Selma school board than you do," I told some whites who weren't of the privileged class. But—the age-old problem in the South—it was more important to them to keep blacks out of power than to have representation themselves.

U.S. District Judge Brevard Hand, Judge Thomas's successor, a conservative, strict constructionist appointed by President Nixon, had no choice but to rule, in 1976, that the 1890 law establishing Selma's self-perpetuating board was unconstitutional. However, he didn't give us the relief we wanted. He delayed a formal ruling to allow enough time for Selma's legislative delegation to establish a constitutional method for selecting the board—either election or appointment by the City Council.

There were no blacks in our local delegation then, and we had little influence over the white representatives. So Judge Hand, in effect, was saying he'd let the white citizens of Selma decide how they preferred to select people to run a system that was 60 percent black. They preferred a board selected by the majority-white City Council, which appointed the same people of the same class that had been perpetuating themselves.

The public meeting we demanded over the principals and the days of negotiations afterward was the first time the Selma school board had really dealt with the public. At the end of the negotiations, the board agreed to make Evans Rutledge, the black assistant principal, principal of Westside, and a few months later, named my Uncle Preston to a vacancy on the board.

At the trial of Yelder's suit in 1976, the school system's attorneys presented two contradictory arguments. The first was: Yelder wasn't demoted. He was offered a raise and a substantial, responsible position, but chose to go to Eastside instead. However, if the court found he had been demoted, this wasn't because of race but because he wasn't competent to be principal of Selma High.

The first argument was hard to sustain. The supposedly significant post didn't exist before 1970 and never was filled when

Yelder turned it down. Also, the more the lawyers puffed up its importance, the more they undermined their second argument. So they focused on the competency issue, alleging that Yelder was a poor administrator and a weak leader. His case was combined with Andrew Sewell's, the former head coach at Hudson. Like Yelder, Sewell had the most seniority when the schools were unified, but he'd been assigned as assistant coach under a white head coach at Selma High. The school system claimed he wasn't competent to be the top coach.

Pickard, Street, two school board members, and ten teachers testified in Yelder's case. They claimed Yelder delegated too much responsibility and didn't discipline students or teachers strenuously enough. They said Hudson High's student records were poorly kept, and both Hudson and Eastside had high dropout and absentee rates.

The school system placed into evidence several letters Yelder wrote to Pickard to support the claim that Yelder volunteered to go to Eastside and that he recognized he had shortcomings. To me, the letters were painful testimony of what segregation and white supremacy could do to a man.

July 5, 1971

Dear Mr. Pickard:

This letter is only a reminder of your promise to me when I agreed to come to Eastside last summer—that I would have the same office arrangement here that I had at Hudson—a 12 month secretary— which would give me full time office service.

I should like to share with you some of the bitter and critical experiences that I have lived in for the last 12 months, only because I worked cooperatively with you in the changeover.

I did it as I told you because of my faith and confidence in you. I would do it again if it was necessary to help you and the system.

These people say that I sold the "black" people down the river by moving from Hudson and that destroyed much of the achievement of their heritage.

I have been heckled by some students and many parents and called the biggest "Tom" in town. This bothers me a little but it does not disturb me at all as long as I know that you and I are together and we are making progress in meeting the needs of education for our youth and adults.

This is just a friendly communication.

Yours truly,
W. J. Yelder

I don't know any case more classic than Yelder's of what white America has done to black people: break both our legs, then exclude us for being crippled. For black Hudson High, the school board wanted somebody like Yelder who would hold down the fort under white supervision. As Yelder reveals in his letter, he cared more about Pickard's opinion than the black community's. But the accommodating qualities that enabled him to survive—and if you want to call it succeed—in the old system were held against him in the new one. He didn't change.

Yelder, of course, was deeply hurt that Pickard and the board were calling him incompetent. He told himself and everyone else that they didn't mean it. They just felt Selma wasn't ready for a black high school principal and were trying to prevent white flight. I wouldn't be surprised if Pickard had said something like that to him privately.

Though it was painful to me, I helped him rationalize: "Joe, you know they don't want any black there. We're in a war here, and you're a casualty in it. They're so worried about white flight, they wouldn't hire Booker T. Washington to be principal of Selma High."

This was true. It also was obvious, though, in their patronizing attitudes, that they didn't consider Yelder the equal of Street or Wilson or themselves. On one level, I wanted Yelder to see this. I didn't approve of his believing in the school board's good intentions when they were walking in his face. I considered it degrading to him and to us as black people. But I'd pushed him into this suit and I couldn't bear to see his self-respect destroyed. He still cared deeply about their opinions.

While the Yelder case was pending, white people—and a few black people—argued to me: "Come on. He's not the best man for the job. For the good of all children, we should get the best principal regardless of skin color." I didn't see it that way. Yelder had presided over black schools for twenty years—was still presiding over black Eastside—and I thought he'd do all right at Selma High. Also, the school board wasn't ignoring color when it assigned white principals to Westside and Selma High.

Mine wasn't a knee-jerk reaction. I had children in the school and recognized the importance of a good principal. I wasn't unconcerned about white flight either because that's the tax base. A number of us discussed the situation and we decided most white people who were going to leave the public schools already had done so.

Basically, we decided black people couldn't draw a line at this point and say, "From now on, we'll be color-blind." Academic underachievement among black teachers was pretty much institutionalized. Virtually all the black teachers and principals in Selma in 1970 had attended separate, underfunded, and deliberately inferior public schools and teachers' colleges. Of course, there were excellent black educators. But where black teachers were better than white teachers, it wasn't because the state of Alabama or the city of Selma had given them a better education. To suddenly say, now that white children were involved, that we'll promote only "the best"—especially as measured by white-oriented tests—meant black teachers would continue to get the short end of the stick.

We viewed the matter long-range. We had to open the door somewhere. We thought it was better tactically to go ahead immediately because then there'd be more incentive for the white authorities to be fair with everybody. If they knew they weren't going to get away with relegating black teachers and principals to the predominantly black schools or as assistants in white schools, that these teachers and principals were going to be over *their* children, too, then they'd be more likely to push for decent appropriations to Alabama State, the black teachers' college, and to pay more attention to the education of black people.

We won Yelder's case because the school board was in an untenable position. In Yelder's fifteen years as principal of black Hudson High, scarcely a word of criticism had come up about him at any board meetings. Not once did anybody suggest he be reprimanded, let alone demoted or fired. Far from it. We put into evidence a pile of letters and commendations from school board members, Pickard and the previous superintendent extolling his virtues as an educator and administrator. The judge ordered the board to offer Yelder the job as principal of Selma High and give him the back pay, ruling that he'd been demoted on the basis of race.

Coach Sewell made a deal before the trial was over to take a raise and stay on as assistant coach. But Yelder stood his ground and became principal of Selma High School in 1976. I give him a lot of credit for rising to the occasion against his own nature. And he did do all right, and there was no mass exodus of white students.

But he was miserable. One day near the end of the 1976–77 school year, he called and said he wanted to talk to me. It was urgent. I told him to come by the office at the end of the school day.

"Old buddy," he said, giving me a forlorn look, "I'm not getting any younger. I've paid my dues. You and Reese insisted I stand up for all it meant. You were right and that's why I did it. But I've earned the right not to live under all this strain. I'm getting old, and my health isn't what it should be. I want to resign."

We explored the impact his resignation would have. We concluded that while some black people would consider him a quitter, they wouldn't say so openly because they knew what he'd gone through to get there. White people undoubtedly would be grateful to him, but more importantly, we'd made our point that black people couldn't be stepped over. The day the school board announced Yelder's resignation and Wilson's appointment as principal of Selma High, it announced the resignation of the white head coach to take a job somewhere else and the appointment of assistant coach Sewell as head coach.

Yelder became a preacher. He told me he had confronted hell here on this earth. I guess he'd seen the devil and it was integration.

CHAPTER 19

Contradictory
Individuals

A little black fella wearing a dashiki came up to me on a break
in a civil case I was trying in Birmingham in 1977. "I heard about
you," he said. "You stand up to the oppressor." He started talking
about the Birmingham police. They were rotten, violent, and
racist. I thought he was going to propose getting up an organization to hold some meetings about the problem. Instead, he told
me he'd formed a group of ex-convicts to police the police, and
now the police were trying to kill him or frame him. He was in
a heap of trouble and needed my help.

This was the beginning of my association with a black revolu-
tionary named Richard Lake, Jr., who called himself Mafundi.
He was short, stocky, muscular, a small man who exuded power.
He'd grown up in a middle-class family but had so repudiated
middle-class values that he got mad if I called him Richard. He'd
served thirteen years in the penitentiary for robbing a service-
station owner of $33 at gunpoint. Like Malcolm X, he educated
himself in prison, from which he emerged as Mafundi.

When I met him, he could sit in a restaurant, eat fried chicken,
and discuss oppressed people all over the world all night long.
His viewpoint was Marxist: The corporations ran the so-called
free world. Greed ran the corporations. People were fodder; black
people the cheapest fodder. The police were the occupying army
of the oppressors. Mafundi also believed profoundly that every-

thing Elijah Muhammad said about the white devil was correct. Walking down the street and seeing a black man slapping a black woman, Mafundi would walk on. But if a white man raised his voice to a black woman, he literally would be prepared to kill him. His wife, a fine person and a noted gospel singer, told me he had so much fire in his gut about race he refused to work at a job like an ordinary man. He made a vocation of risking his life to save the black race.

Mafundi was one of the most contradictory individuals I've ever met—smart, well-spoken, absolutely bent on making the world better for black people, but also capable of violence. Mafundi occasionally made speeches to black student organizations at prestigious Northern colleges like Dartmouth and Princeton. He'd lecture on the "dialecticism" of life in America. Then he'd come back to Birmingham, put a pistol in his pocket, and go out to confront the police.

The police were his obsession. Instead of just doing investigations and making arrests in the ghetto, some Birmingham policemen went out of their way to be rough and disrespectful. Others pushed drugs and took payoffs from the worst elements in the black community. Three black men had been shot and killed by white policemen in questionable circumstances within a two- or three-year period in the mid-1970s. One black man, arrested after a fight at a service station, was held down by one white policeman while another jabbed his eye with a nightstick, causing him to lose sight in that eye. The police charged the man with assaulting an officer with a deadly weapon, though numerous witnesses said he had no weapon.

Whenever Mafundi rode in my car and we passed a police vehicle in front of a house in a black neighborhood, I would have to stop the car so he could go inside and see what was happening. He was as fearless as King, though his courage sprang from an altogether different well. He was forever putting out leaflets in the black community. You talk about a pamphleteer—that was Mafundi.

Mafundi concluded that black people needed to be protected *from* the police and organized a brotherhood, a group of fellow ex-cons, some of the most dangerous damn people you can imagine. The brotherhood monitored calls on a police band radio. When a police car was dispatched to the ghetto, Mafundi and his folk picked up the call and arrived before the police, just as heavily armed. Often, by the time the police got there, they'd be in the process of interviewing people and giving advice. Invariably, some sort of confrontation would develop. Words would be exchanged, and two or three times, there was an actual shoot-out—O.K. Corral on the streets of Birmingham.

Mafundi often went to the mayor and the City Council—then six whites and three blacks. He cited name and badge number where a policeman had exceeded his authority in the black community. The police department and the then-mayor, David Vann, conducted several investigations of Mafundi's complaints of harassment and contended that most were unfounded.

Instinctively, I believed Mafundi. There was no question Mafundi and his people were engaging in some far-out activities, needlessly provocative, but he was dead right about the Birmingham police department so far as I was concerned. I saw Mafundi serving a need in the black ghetto that nobody else dared to. The police now had to think twice before they slapped a black woman or kicked a black man. Before Mafundi, they didn't have to worry about anything. They certainly didn't have to worry about Mayor Vann.

With the exception of Richard Arrington, a black educator and city councilman who pushed for the investigations, most of Birmingham's black establishment shied away from Mafundi's charges. Vann was a liberal, a good fella. Established blacks, led by A. G. Gaston, Birmingham's black millionaire, were kind of timid in what they said about the police department or any part of Vann's administration because they were so happy to have a liberal mayor. They talked to Vann behind the scenes, and he promised to do what he could. But he didn't have control of the police. Bull Connor, Birmingham's notorious police commissioner who used fire hoses and dogs on civil rights demonstrators, was gone. But he'd left behind a police department that was almost an empire unto itself.

When Mafundi asked me to represent him, he said he wanted to use his trials to raise public consciousness in Birmingham about the excesses of the police—in other words, try the system. I said, "I love it. Let's go."

Mafundi had at least twenty different charges pending against him, from jaywalking to assaulting a police officer, so I spent a good deal of time in Birmingham. Often, at lunchtime, I'd walk over to City Hall to see Peter Hall. Vann had appointed Peter a municipal judge, and he turned out to be the toughest judge Birmingham had ever seen. He was so tough some black people petitioned the City Council to dismiss him.

"I don't believe you. You're a lush. You're probably a dopehead. I'm going to put you away for six months. Now get out of my sight." That's how Peter presided. He was the same Peter who had taught me the practice of law twenty years earlier—still looking for perfection in people and still not finding it.

Sometimes Peter and I went around to black cafés and hangouts to see if we could find Orzell. Unlike me, Orzell refused to give up the bottle and sank lower year by year. Sometimes we found him; sometimes we couldn't. When we did, we'd have lunch and talk about old times.

The prosecution had a hard time convicting Mafundi. Some charges obviously were trumped up by the police or were stretching it. One time, the police charged him with possession of marijuana when they found a tiny quantity, a gram, in his jacket pocket. We got two mistrials on that charge, though the third time he was convicted.

The majority of the charges involved resisting arrest or assaulting police officers. The incidents always took place in the ghetto, and we put blacks on the stand who testified about what they saw the police doing then and in general. Ordinary working-class black folk had no problem believing the Birmingham police capable of lying and doing wrong. When we were able to get some blacks on the jury—liberal whites, too—and to bring out what the police were doing, we sometimes could get a hung jury.

Our credibility was boosted greatly by Richard Arrington, the black councilman. Arrington was by no means a radical. He had a Ph.D. in zoology. He'd taught at Miles College, a small black liberal-arts college in Birmingham, headed a consortium of Alabama's black colleges, and been a thoughtful member of the council since 1971. Arrington volunteered to testify for Mafundi. He genuinely was concerned over police misconduct and constantly called for investigations of beatings and shootings where the police version and the version of black witnesses were different. He told me he'd gotten eighteen complaints of police brutality within six months of becoming a city councilman.

Arrington testified that Mafundi constantly came to the council complaining of police harassment, that he'd checked into the complaints and found substance in some of them, that there was a vendetta against Mafundi by some policemen, and yes, racism was a serious problem in the Birmingham police department.

One way or another, we kept Mafundi out of the penitentiary. It seemed like the worst that would go down was that he might have to do some time in the city jail. Mafundi was going full steam ahead with his brotherhood, and I was no longer involved with him on a weekly basis because most of the cases were resolved. Then one day he called me in Selma and said he desperately needed to talk. When I went up to Birmingham a few days later, he told me he'd been charged with raping a black woman. He was out on bond.

In Alabama, three felony convictions make you a habitual offender and can put you in prison for life without parole. Mafundi already had two—the armed robbery that put him in prison for thirteen years and one other. He said he would be totally insane to go out and commit rape when he was a two-time loser and the whole white establishment was down on his back. I told him I could easily buy his contention that the woman was a police plant who was chasing in behind him because I wanted to believe him and I knew the Birmingham police were capable of such a setup.

The woman testified at the trial that Mafundi had pulled a knife on her in a car, threatened her, and called her all kinds of names. I tried to persuade Mafundi's wife not to come to the trial. But she loved him so much she wanted him to know he had her unqualified support. She sat through all the testimony and believed none of it.

The jury, however, believed the woman. The irony of Mafundi getting life in prison on a charge of raping a black woman when he devoted his life to protecting black people points up the contradiction that was Richard "Mafundi" Lake—good and bad all wrapped up in one little determined ball of black fire.

During one of Mafundi's trials, I looked up at a break and there was a young man standing in the back of the courtroom, waiting for me. He was neat and natty, dressed in expensive sport clothes, his face haloed by a well-trimmed Afro.

"My name is Mike Howard," he said, with an expression that suggested the name should mean something to me.

I said, "Great. I'm J. L. Chestnut."

I was leaving the building to tend to some business. He came down in the elevator with me and asked if I'd stop by his shoe store at the close of the day. "I want to talk to you about a retainer," he said. I agreed to come. Nothing in my mind clicked then as to who or what he was. I was interested that he owned a business and talked about a retainer.

His store, Foot Steppers, turned out to be a high-priced shop located in the main downtown business section. The cheapest pair of shoes I saw cost $75. The carpeting was thick, the chairs were plush, and the salesgirls were pretty—red lips, red fingernails, semi-formal dresses, high-heeled shoes.

Mike had changed into a pinstripe suit. "Come on in, brother, and sit down and let's talk," he said, and led me over to a pretty padded bench near the cash register. He told me he owned a nightclub as well as the shoe store and he had a problem with certain policemen who were trying to shake down his operation.

"I'm already paying a bundle," he said. "I can't afford to support the whole Birmingham police department." He added, "They're leaning extra hard on me because I'm black," and waited to see my reaction. Mike Howard, as I was to learn later, always tried to seduce people. So he threw that black thing out to me as bait. I said he didn't seem to have so much a legal problem as a political problem. I suggested he talk to my Howard classmate Richard "Icewater" Pearson, who was now his state senator. Mike said he had political contacts. That wasn't why he'd come to me. He anticipated some serious legal problems.

I was beginning to get a little bit incredulous. Obviously there was more to this fella than he was saying, but he seemed to enjoy being mysterious and indirect. We continued to talk, and some-

Mike Howard being arrested in front of his shoe store (© *Birmingham News*)

where in the conversation he asked me to stay and have dinner. Then he brought the four salesgirls over.

Something finally began to dawn on me in the proprietary way he introduced them and in their subservience to him. "This is Shirley. Shirley loves me. This is Sheila. She loves me, too. Girls, this is J. L. Chestnut." They smiled and did some kind of little curtsy. Mike said to me, "We can go to dinner, have some fun, whatever is your pleasure."

"Let me level with you," I said. "My partners and I are trying to do a number of things around this state. We've got all kinds of people depending on us. I have to be careful about my involvements." I wanted him to know up front that I did not intend to do anything beyond legal representation.

Mike grinned. "I don't have any problem with that," he said. I was in a rush to get back to Selma, so I didn't stay for dinner. But I agreed to meet him at his club to talk further after court let out the next day. We sat in a booth and Mike came clean about what his operation was. I'd already checked and learned that the Birmingham newspapers called him the "kingpin" of the largest prostitution ring in Birmingham. He was appealing his conviction for bribing two undercover policemen, and was reputed to be paying off a fourth of the Birmingham police force. He asked me to represent him and his girls in court, and I said I would. I just liked the fella. And I was irresistibly curious about him and his operations and connections.

Mike Howard, I would learn, had been a schoolteacher. He'd always had a way with women, and he told me he'd decided to turn this talent into a business. He could make more money in a day that way than in a year as a teacher, and Mike craved material wealth. He believed in the almighty American dollar, and so far as he was concerned, so did the rest of America. He didn't give a damn about civil rights. The dollar was the thing. If you got it, you could transcend color or anything else.

Most of Mike's girls weren't streetwalkers in the sense that they'd be out on Birmingham's prostitution strip knocking on car windows. Some of them cruised the malls, mingled in hotel lobbies during conventions and other places where white men with money gathered. Mike rented apartments all over the city, and clients often called him for "dates." Three or four carloads of his women would go to Montgomery when the legislature was in session. They'd stay a few nights in a hotel, paid for by certain big-time lobbyists. That's one of the things that fascinated me about Mike. His tentacles reached into the statehouse.

People who worked for Mike kept constant watch on the bus stations, looking for runaways. Some of them he'd take in and keep around a year before asking them to turn a trick. Meanwhile, he showered them with attention. He was unusual in that his girls couldn't sit around and not do anything but be prostitutes. He kept telling them how quickly beauty fades, so many of his girls had other jobs as telephone operators and such. One was a teacher. Many were going to junior college.

It's not hard to understand why some young girl who worked in a dime store or had just got off a bus from Demopolis would fall under Mike's spell. He lived in a lavishly decorated house on the same street as Councilman Richard Arrington, with his wife and four or five of his favorite girls. He had a stable of expensive automobiles. He thought nothing of chartering a plane and taking a group of his special girls to Las Vegas or New York when Muhammad Ali was fighting somebody.

Whenever musical acts like the Temptations came to the Municipal Auditorium, Mike would get a block of tickets from the promoter, and he and a selection of his girls would come dressed as if going to the most exclusive affair in Hollywood. Mike would be wearing a floor-length mink coat that cost as much as a house, one of those hats the Russians wear, and an expensive suit. The girls—black, white, Asian—wore outfits that probably cost a thousand dollars. In the intermission, the announcer would call them up to the stage. "Ladies and gentlemen, Mike Howard and his family." Folk would go wild as Mike strutted across the stage with his diamond-studded walking stick and his United Nations of girls.

Mike was like old Massa sitting at the head of a plantation. He knew what was best for all and he handled everything, especially the money. He was the girls' protector from the outside world. If they were jailed, he bailed them out. I think it was necessary for Mike, because of his middle-class upbringing, to be a "good" slaveholder. He claimed he didn't strike his girls or hold them against their will. He was generous to a fault with the money their labor earned, using gifts and his affections to reward and punish. I was at his house once when he commented, casually, "That Cadillac looks dirty," and three girls jumped up and rushed out to wash it.

Mike always was trying to get me to go to New York or Las Vegas for a prizefight or a show. He constantly tried to get me in bed with one of his girls. He was looking for my Achilles' heel. He bought me suits, but I wouldn't wear them. They looked like something from an Al Capone movie, with big lapels and stripes. My resistance to his offers upset him because he wanted to put his brand on me. I was equally determined I was not going to be branded. And I always had reservations about representing Mike Howard. What kept me in there was his boyish charm—he was fun—and my fascination with what this black man had accomplished in Birmingham. He had a concept of power—how to manipulate people and events to get what he wanted—that I hadn't bumped into since my days with Adam Clayton Powell. Mike could make things move in banks and in state government. Part of my cynicism about men in power came from my association with him.

Hank, Rose, and Vivian got on my case about representing Mike. One day, out of some sort of wicked curiosity, I brought Vivian and Gerald by Mike's house to see their reactions to the way his wife and girls tippy-toed around him, bringing him long glasses of lemonade and talking softly in his presence. Mike showed off his imported dining-room table and big screen television. Gerald was absolutely knocked out by all that sumptuous living. Vivian looked askance at all the girls. She spent the whole ride back to Selma talking about how awful it all was.

Rose commented, "I'm surprised at you. You must be overwhelmed by those girls." She knew that would get to me. Mike paid considerable money to our law firm, but toward the end, I stopped accepting payment, to rationalize that at least I wasn't representing him for the money.

My association with Mike Howard didn't end until after he went to prison for so-called white slavery. The man was so tied into the system that it wasn't the state that arrested him; it was the FBI. I represented Mike, his wife, and four girls, along with a white lawyer who showed up at court every day on a motorcycle. The FBI persuaded a few of the girls to testify against Mike in exchange for dropping charges against them, though one of their witnesses changed her mind at mid-trial. They testified to being taken across state lines for prostitution.

The jury convicted Mike, and the judge gave him a stiff sentence, twenty years, concurrent with the six years he was about to serve for his earlier bribery conviction. He sent Mike to a tough federal prison in Atlanta, the same prison where they once put Al Capone.

Less than a year later, I was coming out of the courthouse in Greensboro, in Hale County, and saw a familiar back across the street. I thought, Damn, that looks like Mike Howard. But it can't be. He's in Atlanta doing twenty years. I went over, the man turned around, and sure enough, it was Mike. The Alabama penal system operates a cattle farm about three miles outside Greensboro and powerful hands had gone to work to allow Mike to serve some of his time on this farm instead of in a prison. That's power. He gave me a great big smile.

The Mafundi trials brought me another client whose case became a *cause célèbre* in black Birmingham, a classic confrontation between a black nobody from the ghetto and the Birmingham establishment that intensified black unrest over the police.

The nobody was Annie Johnson, a woman in her late forties, the mother of nine children. In October 1977, she got in a fracas at a City Council meeting, knocked the deputy police chief to the ground, and broke his glasses, after complaining for six months that the police had stolen $280 from her purse in the glove compartment of her car.

Annie had been in a car with two of her children and her boyfriend, who was a preacher. A policeman stopped them for a traffic violation, searched the car, and found a pistol. Annie said the policeman was unnecessarily abusive, pointing his gun at her son's temple and using nasty language, then pulling a gun on her when she protested. They were taken to the station. When Annie was released and got her car back, she discovered that the money in her purse was gone.

Every few weeks, Annie went to the City Council to make a plea for her missing money. She said she needed it to feed her children and pay her light bill. Each time, the council would refer the matter to a committee or suggest she go to small-claims court. She was a relatively tall, solid woman, with a kind of fire in both her voice and her eyes. After several months, Mayor Vann ordered an investigation. Everyone involved—Annie and her folk, the policemen—passed lie detector tests. The mayor and the council concluded that since no proof had been found that the police took the money, the city had no obligation to Annie Johnson.

She kept coming back, getting on the agenda, and denouncing the police department and the city government. Each time, a few more folk came with her, cheered when she spoke or raised a black-power fist. Finally, the mayor suggested a compromise, offering Annie half her money back. She refused. She didn't see why she should take only half of what was stolen from her.

At its next meeting, the council gave her the usual five minutes to speak. She said the councilmen didn't know what it was like to be poor. They were big shots and she wasn't. The police were the law, but they broke the law. They stole her money. She pointed her finger at the mayor and screamed, "I want my money back!" She got so emotional, the five minutes came and went and she still was at the podium, jumping up and down and denouncing everybody.

The acting council president was Arthur Shores, the dean of black lawyers in Alabama who fought NAACP cases with Thurgood Marshall in the 1940s and taught Peter Hall the practice of law. He admonished the packed chamber that cheering and placard raising weren't allowed and told Annie several times that her time was up. She ignored him. Arthur then asked the deputy chief of police, an old fella in his sixties who served as the council's sergeant at arms, to eject her. He came over to pull her away from the podium, she resisted, and in the scuffle he was knocked to the floor.

The deputy chief filed assault-and-battery charges against Annie. Her preacher boyfriend found me at one of Mafundi's trials and asked, "Will you stand with Annie Johnson?" I said, "Of course."

Annie became a big story. A local television station covered council meetings, so film of the melee was all over TV. The Fraternal Order of Police came to the trial in force; so did black folk. Annie's boyfriend had them marching around outside with placards. As a direct confrontation between a black woman from the ghetto and the deputy chief of police, the trial intensified the division and hostility between poor blacks and the police. It also revealed the growing gulf between blacks like Annie, whose daily lives didn't change much as a result of the civil rights movement, and blacks like Arthur Shores, who moved up and became part of the establishment.

Since the television cameras caught most of the action, there were few factual differences at issue in the trial. The top prosecutor in Birmingham, David Cromwell Johnson, handled the case for the city. We really went at it. I said the law was no good without justice. He asked where would we be if everybody did what Annie did. I said she was a poor black outsider ignored by the insiders. He said she thought she was above the law.

The jury was mixed, black and white, and, not surprisingly, it hung up. Annie was convicted the second time around, fined $300, and given a 30-day suspended jail sentence.

Annie's case and the Mafundi cases got black people talking more openly about police excesses. The cases antagonized many whites but opened the eyes of some others that the Birmingham police department wasn't what it should be. They needed to take a look and stop assuming that every time a policeman says something he's right and a poor black out of the ghetto is wrong.

These cases in 1977 and 1978 were drops in a bucket. If you keep putting water in, after a while the bucket fills up. It ran over when an unarmed black woman who committed no crime was shot to death by a white policeman in front of a convenience store during an attempted robbery. Mayor Vann, caught between firing the policeman and having his police department out on strike, retained the policeman. Black folk were up in arms.

The woman, Bonita Carter, was killed in June 1979, a few months before the mayoral election. Established blacks continued to support Vann, who had won office with the help of the black vote, but no way were the grass roots going to follow their lead this time. Many people, including me, encouraged Richard Arrington to run. He was ambitious to be mayor but reluctant to oppose Vann, his longtime friend and ally. We all said, "Well, if you don't, somebody else will." Arrington finally agreed to run.

Vann received only 15 percent of the vote in the primary, which put Arrington in a runoff with a white businessman. Black people,

Richard Arrington, the mayor of Birmingham, and I
(Courtesy of J. L. Chestnut, Jr.)

who comprised about 45 percent of Birmingham voters, came to
the polls by the busload for the runoff and Arrington got enough
of the white vote to become mayor of the city that fifteen years
earlier had experienced so many bombings it earned the name
"Bombingham."

CHAPTER 20

Roadshow Two

A great loneliness and a kind of quietness had developed in the Black Belt in the years since Orzell and I rode around it in his big Lincoln. Gone were the folk in the fields. Vines and kudzu strangled abandoned houses and shacks. What once were cotton fields now were cow pastures or were leased to paper companies to grow trees. Since agriculture no longer required an army of workers and the Black Belt had almost no industry to speak of, many black and white folk had moved elsewhere. County seats like Marion, Hayneville, Greensboro, Camden—Selma, too—no longer bustled with country people on Saturdays. Stores began to be boarded up. Some of the little crossroads towns simply ceased to exist.

But poverty and subjugation were as widespread and as debilitating as ever. Certain sections of every town still looked like little slave quarters—shanties with cardboard in the windows, no running water or plumbing, toddlers wearing nothing but diapers playing in muddy front yards beside the useless hulks of ancient automobiles. For every black person who could read, three or four couldn't. Many of these folk thought the white man or woman who dispensed the welfare checks or food stamps was the absolute authority on eligibility and could cut them off at will.

A better life, if they envisioned one, was someplace else— Detroit, Chicago, Birmingham. I knew families whose only insurance was a little burial policy. They had no medical insurance if they or their children got sick. No nothing, just burial. They wanted to be buried right when the sweet chariots came to take them home.

Gaining political power in this region was a long, intense struggle, even though many counties were more than half black and three—Wilcox, Lowndes, Greene—were at least 70 percent black. Each had its active black leaders, folk deeply involved in voter registration and in getting out the vote—Theresa Burroughs, a hairdresser in Hale County, Albert Turner in Perry County, Wendell Paris in Sumter, John Hulett in Lowndes, and others. They all led or were part of some voters league or improvement association and they worked like hell, daily.

But it was an uphill battle, and in 1975, ten years after the Voting Rights Act, only one Black Belt county—Greene—had blacks elected as probate judges, county commissioners, or school board members. Only two—Greene and Lowndes—had blacks elected sheriff. The obstacles were substantial: black folk conditioned to believe that voting was white folks' business, old people afraid to come to the courthouse to register, almost everybody more intent on daily, personal survival than a better future for the group.

Besides voting in greater numbers, the white community controlled the jobs, stores, banks, law enforcement, and newspapers. All this was brought to bear in elections. Sheriffs and probate judges, hard to beat in small counties where they know everybody, had certain blacks passing out money in the black community. The newspapers and influential whites hammered away at the teachers and middle-class blacks that black people voting as a bloc was racist.

In some counties, the polling places were grocery stores where many folk used food stamps as money and the man or woman in charge sat there glaring at the black people who voted. If this was a new polling place, the local black leaders would file an objection with the Department of Justice under the provision of the Voting Rights Act that requires additions and changes in voting procedures to be pre-cleared. Dozens of pre-clearance issues came out of the Black Belt counties in the 1970s. Another widespread practice was posting the sheriff and his deputies or the town policemen outside polling places to watch the black people who went inside. On many occasions, the local black leaders requested federal observers to prevent even more blatant forms of intimidation.

All the election machinery—certifying candidates, counting the votes—was in the hands of the probate judge and the circuit clerk, both of whom stood to lose office if enough black people voted and voted for black candidates. Black candidates had to learn to dot every *i* in the certification process or be thrown off the ballot. Sometimes the reasons were questionable and we took it to court.

Another necessity was getting black poll watchers who were willing to challenge whites. Theresa, Wendell, Albert, and the others had to set up schools on poll watching. We never trusted vote counts to be accurate and constantly challenged them. I don't think there was another region in America with more election contests than the Black Belt of Alabama. Our law firm filed dozens of them.

In the middle 1970s, I went back out in the Black Belt with Roadshow Two—two campaigns for the State Senate and one for the State House of Representatives. I wasn't campaigning to win. The legislature had drawn the districts to include parts of majority-white counties with parts of the majority-black counties so the numbers weren't there to send a black person to Montgomery.

My purpose was to spark more enthusiasm for voting and politics. It was becoming a slow and painful process to add more black voters to the rolls and get them to the polls—especially when, year after year, the black candidates lost. These losses also dampened enthusiasm for running. It seemed to me that politicians like Joe Smitherman, Wilson Baker, and George Wallace, who made a pitch for the black vote in the governor's race in 1974, would be the primary beneficiaries of our vote unless black people realized what was possible and what we needed to do.

Consequently, when the white opponent of Walter Givhan, the longtime state senator from the Black Belt, dropped out in the 1974 election, I decided to run against the old senator myself. I hoped it would motivate black people to vote and others to run, and I knew I would enjoy the hell out of it.

Walter Givhan was a medium-sized landowner who had represented the Black Belt for thirty-six years. He owned the Givhan Land & Cattle Company in rural Dallas County. His son was president of the Central Bank of Uniontown; his wife was vice-president. He also earned income as the secretary-treasurer of the Alabama Farm Bureau, one of the most powerful lobbies in Montgomery. Alabama then had no rules on conflict of interest, and legislators voted regularly on issues that affected them personally. Givhan had become so entrenched he rarely had any significant opposition.

The Farm Bureau represented the interests of the large land-owners, including the paper companies, going back to the plantation days. For a hundred years, the Black Belt dominated state politics and the big landowners dominated the Black Belt—with two long-term consequences that tell so much of the story of Alabama. For most of this century, until agriculture was mechanized, industry was discouraged from coming to the rural parts of the state for fear it would increase the price of labor. Also, Alabama has the lowest property tax in the nation, financing itself almost entirely by sales taxes.

In my campaign, I said Walter Givhan not only didn't represent black people, who made up about half his constituents, he didn't look out for the interests of the average white person either. I called him the "Senator from Farm Bureau." On a white radio station, I talked about the burden the sales tax put on the average person. I advocated exemptions for medicine and food. I attacked the property-tax system that assessed the value of land owned by the paper companies and large farmers at a fraction of the assessment of the homes of individuals.

I knew there were white people out there who didn't like this or Givhan worth a damn. I had no illusion, though, that Alabama had advanced to where white people would vote for a black man. I asked two white lawyers who belonged to Selma's Rotary and Kiwanis Clubs if I could address these organizations, which had a tradition of inviting candidates to speak to them. The lawyers came back and told me the clubs "weren't quite ready" to hear a black candidate. My hope in the little campaigning I did in the white community was that white people would get so disgusted

Campaign leaflet when I ran for the State House of
Representatives in 1978 (Courtesy of J. L. Chestnut,
Jr.)

with Givhan they wouldn't vote at all. Givhan did no direct campaigning in the black community. He worked through local sheriffs and probate judges to use their influence with local blacks on
his behalf.

The Senate district included parts of Dallas, Hale, Perry, Sumter, Marengo, Greene, and Autauga Counties. The local leaders
set up meetings of their folk and I came out to speak. On Sundays,
I went around to the churches. Some met the first and third
Sundays; some the second and fourth. By this time, the acute
sense of danger that Orzell and I had felt constantly while traveling these same roads was almost gone.

In Hale County, the meeting place was an old wooden building that used to be a black elementary school. Theresa Burroughs would have the local black leaders and interested citizens there. I would come in, shake hands, and Theresa would introduce me. When I first approached these groups, they treated me somewhat as a celebrity and that was a barrier. So I started a banter between me and the audience, as in a nightclub, that was kind of a let's-get-acquainted person-to-person thing, never mind what you've heard or read.

One effective thing was the way I carried on with women: "Lord have mercy, there are some good-looking women in this county! I really don't need to run for office. What I need to do is move here." I might come down off the little platform and go kiss a woman. I made sure she wasn't a young woman. She'd have to be about seventy years old. I'd kiss and hug her, say "*Oooh* I cain't live without ya."

I also found it dramatic and memorable to single out by name and directly attack the most hated or most feared white man in the area. "So-and-So ought to treat black people the way he wants folk to treat him. He wants me to call his wife Mrs. and he wants to call my wife Vivian. To hell with him."

Everybody knew the man would hear what I said almost as soon as I left, and the fact I said it meant I didn't give a damn. To emphasize that, I said, "I know he's got his niggers right here in this room who can't wait to get back and tell him. Who gives a damn! He comes here, I'll tell him myself." This technique produced votes.

Once folk were fired up, I went into the reasons they needed to vote themselves and to get their families and neighbors to vote—the regressive tax system, high unemployment rate, high cost of medical care and utilities, and, most of all, the second-class status of black people.

"I come asking you not so much to vote for J. L. Chestnut. I come asking you to vote for every black man whose head has ever been beaten or whose neck was stretched on a lynch tree. I come asking you to vote for every black woman who's ever been violated and humiliated. I come to ask you to vote for you. It is dedicated black leadership I offer, a leadership that is not afraid but, rather, is proud to be black. I promise you I won't sell you out. I can't do it alone, but together we can do a lot. Why is it black people are the last hired and the first fired? Why is it we have millions of dollars in these white banks and can't hardly get jobs in them? Why is it we have so few elected officials or jobs or influence in these city halls and county courthouses?

"Does this have to be? I say, 'No.' I say, 'Hell no, a thousand times. Hell no! Hell no!' My opponent is not merely part of the system; he personifies the system. Look who's backing him. Let's move out from the shadows of doubt, indecision, and fear. Let's get up and be prepared to face whomever and do whatever to move ourselves forward. Nobody's going to hand us first-class citizenship. It's up to us. Let's rise up. Let's stand up. Let's think up and, by golly, stay up. Let's walk tall. Let's vote the rascals out. Let's vote ourselves in!"

Sometimes, when I had a big rally, a group called the Gospelaires came and sang for me. I waited outside in my car, listening, while a local preacher made some long, emotional prayer, asking the Lord to take our hand and lead us on. Then, as the Gospelaires raised the emotional level in the auditorium or church to an extremely high pitch, I came in, smiling, from the side. These appearances were more like revivals than typical political rallies. People left on a high and, I think, somewhat inspired. I know I was.

I came out of that campaign with my own commitment renewed. There were people out there who really wanted to see their lives and their neighbors' lives improved. There were people who, in spite of what Alabama had done to them, really loved the state and wanted to make it better. It's inspiring to talk to people like that. Even a few white people told me, "I agree with you." One elderly white woman approached me on the street one day and said, "My husband thinks you're the devil, but he doesn't control my vote. I'm votin' for you. Damn Walter Givhan."

As expected, I didn't win. Also as expected, the vote was polarized on racial lines. But the numbers were closer than I or others anticipated, and I made the point that a good fight is worthwhile. It gives you a platform, brings you attention, makes you a spokesman. Losing was no disgrace.

Two years later, Walter Givhan died. I ran again for the seat—

Another campaign photo of me on the steps of the state
capitol in Montgomery (Courtesy of J. L. Chestnut, Jr.)

against Earl Goodwin. He's a somewhat different type from
Givhan: new rich. His father was a coal miner in north Alabama.
After he moved to Selma, Goodwin and some businessmen got
together with a man who invented a machine with rotary blades
to cut weeds along highways. They started the Bush Hog Company, and it hit big. The *Times-Journal* referred to him as an
"industrialist." Goodwin, in my opinion, always wanted to be an
important force in the community. Having made some money did

not guarantee that in Selma. So politics was a natural avenue for him to take. He was president of the Dallas County White Citizens' Council in the mid-sixties.

One of my favorite tactics against Goodwin was to build up an issue on the radio or in a speech and challenge him to a debate. I'd tell the press, "Go see can't you find Earl." I knew damn well he wouldn't debate. Goodwin is the type politician who goes from courthouse to courthouse lining up blocs of votes through the sheriffs and probate judges. He wasn't a practiced public speaker, and he sure as hell wasn't going to get in a debate with a trial lawyer, especially since front-runners, tactically, have no reason to engage in debate. I then portrayed Goodwin as a white man on the run from a black man, which delighted and invigorated the black community. I must say, it delighted me. I lost as expected, but not by much.

In 1978, Hank and other people pushed me to run for a seat in the State House of Representatives. There wasn't an incumbent in the race because the incumbent had decided to run for the State Senate. But I really didn't want to campaign for office again and Vivian definitely didn't want me to do it. We were having all kinds of trouble with Terry, our eighteen-year-old son. He got involved with a bad crowd in our neighborhood on Eugene Street. Vivian tried everything she could to turn him around. I was gone a lot of the time campaigning, making speeches, and trying cases.

The problem started when he was thirteen or fourteen. The police would arrest him for stealing a bicycle and I'd have to go to the station and get him released. I had long conversations with him. "If you want a bicycle, why don't you ask for it? Or you can work for one of your uncles and earn the money"—meaning Preston's cosmetics firm or Frank's contracting business. "Why would you steal?"

Terry told me once he didn't think stealing was so much a matter of right or wrong as who had the power to define it. He brought up black folk being worked half to death for next to nothing or flat out cheated, and this being condoned by some of the biggest people in town. I have no doubt a person as shrewd as Terry knew that statement would strike a responsive chord in me, but I also think he believed it. It was frustrating to talk to him because he didn't talk back. All his life, he'd been well mannered, quiet, dutiful—but determined. He'd go right back and get in trouble, and the trouble became more serious—breaking into cars and businesses.

Several people have suggested that Terry grew up in my shadow and stole to get attention. There might be something to that. I know he always assumed I'd get him out of trouble. Having J. L. Chestnut as a father was something all my children had to deal with. Rosalind complained that some girls in school, black girls, were jealous. If she came dressed nicely—and Vivian and her daughters love to dress and shop—they'd say, "You lawyer Chestnut's daughter. You think you so-and-so." Ronnie was going to law school at Miles College in Birmingham, trying to follow in my footsteps. Terry set out on his own path, but also used the fact that I was his father to his advantage. "I'm attorney Chestnut's son. Watch out."

By 1978, he had four arrests for burglary. He told me he did some of them but not others, but I didn't believe him. I discovered later that he was telling the truth. The police tend to want to clean up every unsolved case and, when they arrest somebody, to pin everything on him. But I was so disgusted with Terry by that time I forced him to plead guilty to everything. I didn't want to put Vivian through the ordeal of a long trial.

Circuit judge J. C. "Dick" Norton sentenced Terry to three months to a year in a reformatory north of Montgomery. My inclination was to leave him in jail for a while, not help him get out. But the children are Vivian's life and she was extremely nervous, upset, and unable to sleep when Terry was in custody. She insisted I immediately go get the boy and help him. This was a dilemma I faced any number of times.

Terry wasn't in the reformatory more than a month before I filed a motion with Norton asking him to put Terry on probation. I did this after I took the family up to see Terry one Sunday afternoon. He was dressed in those oversized overalls issued by the state and big brogans. When he came into the visiting area, walking slowly with a sad look on his face, Vivian saw her child and went to pieces. I felt awful myself. There was no way I could leave him there if I could help it.

Norton said the youth center was what Terry needed and it wouldn't do the boy any good to be released so soon. I persuaded Norton that if he'd permit me to send Terry to Birmingham, his older brother would probably have a better impact than the youth center. Also, I had a wife who was suffering more than Terry. Norton put Terry on supervised probation in Birmingham. The district attorney charged in the newspaper that Norton's decision was political because the black vote had been decisive in electing him. But it really was based on Terry's youth, the small amount of property stolen, and the absence of violence. I also think Norton sympathized with my dilemma.

We enrolled Terry in Miles College in Birmingham, and he moved in with Ronnie, who, besides attending Miles Law School, was working part-time as a salesman for Preston's cosmetics company and doing quite well. He had his own apartment in Birmingham. Vivian and I hoped Terry would straighten out if he was in college and away from the bad crowd in Selma, and we hoped Ronnie would be a good influence. There was a risk in this. If we couldn't handle him, how could Ronnie? And there was more opportunity for crime in Birmingham than in Selma. But all things considered, that's what we decided to do and we were hoping and praying it would work.

Meanwhile, I bought a nicer house in a nicer neighborhood— a three-bedroom brick ranch house on Kingsley Drive at the edge of town. I could afford a better place and Vivian deserved it. We moved there with her mother and our two youngest children, Greg and Kim. Rosalind and Gerald both went to Stillman College, a black Presbyterian college in Tuscaloosa. In 1978, Rosalind was married and living in Montgomery; Gerald had moved to Los Angeles and was working for the state of California.

On Kingsley Drive, as on Eugene Street, Vivian constantly asked me to give more time to the family. My life was at odds with her determination to have a tightly knit family that stayed together, prayed together, and played together. Some weeks, the only time we all were together was on Sunday morning when we went to First Baptist.

Vivian raised questions that were hard to answer. "How can you love a community or a race more than you love me or your own family?" I'd say that wasn't true. "Well, how can you justify giving more time to elections, causes, and clients than you give to us?" I'd say I was trying to make things better for my family and all families, but this didn't get too far with Vivian. To her, there is no higher calling than to love, protect, and defend your own children.

Still, I didn't slow down my activities. I'd get to the law office, there'd be cases and clients, and off I'd go. There was always a meeting somewhere in Selma or the Black Belt, and people insisted that if I didn't come to make a speech the meeting wouldn't be for zero. And they were important meetings, dealing with various issues about black people. I felt guilty if I didn't go, but at the same time I felt guilty for being gone so much.

Hank stayed on my case about running for the state legislature in 1978, saying I had the experience and the name. I finally agreed, and back on the road I went. My opponent was Noopy Cosby, a young man, then twenty-nine, who wasn't well known. One of his claims to fame is his imitation of George Wallace. It's really good. He came from a middle-class family and married a wealthy young lady.

I was about 1,500 votes ahead of him on election night, but by the morning I had lost. Several people later told me I should have contested the election. Dale Curry, a white Yankee running against the establishment candidate for Dallas County tax assessor that same election, demanded a recount in his race and discovered that he had more votes than were recorded on the official tally. He was declared the winner. He later told me he thought he saw more votes for me, too. But I wasn't focused on winning and I didn't contest the election.

By that time, our main problem in elections for sheriff, probate judge, and other county offices was the absentee-ballot box. The decade of efforts at registration, motivation, turnout, and unity finally were paying off at the polls in the counties with large black majorities. But then, when the absentee ballots were counted, the white incumbents won.

Absentee voting is somewhat complex, involving several mailings, crucial timing, and a notary public, and black organizers at that point were concentrating on producing numbers at the polls.

The white courthouse crowd, though, knew the potential in absentee voting and developed it, working the nursing homes, the white kids away at college, the people who had jobs in other counties. You could get hundreds of votes this way because, with so few jobs, these rural counties have high proportions of elderly people and people who worked too far away to get to the polls between 8:30 a.m. and 6:30 p.m. At least a half dozen of the election challenges our firm brought on behalf of black candidates turned on absentee ballots. We charged that the white candidate not only used but abused the absentee system by soliciting and collecting ballots from people who no longer lived in the county.

I wrote, telephoned, and even went to Washington to try to persuade people in the Department of Justice to investigate the absentee-ballot situation in the Black Belt. This was during the Carter Administration. They listened and sympathized, but said that vote fraud in a county or state election was a state matter. We needed to take it up with the secretary of state or the district attorney. I said, "Shit. You're saying we should go to George Wallace," who was governor then. They told me that with so many black people in these counties, we shouldn't be leaning on Washington. We should master the absentee system ourselves.

By the late seventies, each of the little black county organizations had two or three people in charge of nothing but absentee ballots. They learned the process and requirements, and usually one of them became a notary public. They went to the old black folk in nursing homes and out in the country. They learned whose kids were away at college and who worked out of the county and got them to vote absentee. Once hundreds of black absentee votes were added to black victories at the polls, black candidates won.

The local black leaders in these counties often asked me to speak at the final get-out-the-vote push in churches on the Sundays leading up to the crucial elections. I usually talked about Paul, my favorite apostle. "Paul was not lukewarm. That's what I like about him. When he was a devil, he was one of the leading devils. When he went over to the other side, he went all the way over. Black folk can take a lesson from Paul. Let's stop being lukewarm. Let's stop straddling the fence. Most black people living under the thumb of the white society are trying to be two people at the same time—trying to do what they can for black folk without disturbing white people. There's no way under the sun that can be done in Alabama. If you take a lesson from Paul, you understand that being lukewarm is the equivalent of being nothing. Come up here and stand with these black candidates. Quit hiding under the rocks. Martin Luther King said, 'If there is nothing for which you are willing to die, then you are not fit to live.' Quit bending over. Be proud. Be brave. Be strong. Be involved."

CHAPTER 21

A Multitude
of Problems

We won political control in Perry County in 1978, Lowndes in 1980, Wilcox and Sumter in 1982. The turnovers were almost complete—from all-white county governments to all or majority black. County commissioners and school board members, as well as sheriffs, circuit clerks, tax assessors, and other county posts, were elected at large so when white people voted in larger numbers than blacks, only white candidates won. When black folk finally produced more votes, black candidates won. In Dallas, Marengo, and Hale Counties, which are less black, the county commissions, school boards, and all county offices remained all white.

Winning control of county courthouses in the onetime plantation belt of Alabama—the heart of Dixie—was a significant achievement for black people. It meant black children could aspire to be genuine leaders, a county commissioner or a school superintendent. When it came to getting county jobs, paved roads, and other services, black folk no longer would take a back seat. The election of black sheriffs promised fair treatment from law enforcement. Almost immediately, I noticed more black folk lingering around the corridors at the courthouse and coming to public meetings to express their views because for the first time they felt like citizens.

So it was a new day. But we hardly had time to enjoy the

sunrise. Black folk now had the responsibility of running some of the poorest counties in America with a multitude of problems and a scarcity of resources in a racially polarized atmosphere. For a hundred years, white leaders had been saying that if blacks won power, civilization would fall, so the white reaction to these new black governments was fear or hostility.

With the changeover, my role shifted from attacking the establishment from the outside to participating on the inside because our law firm was hired to represent some of these predominantly black school boards and county commissions. I personally became the lawyer for the Wilcox County Commission and the school boards in Sumter and Greene Counties.

In the Black Belt counties, the school board often is the largest business in the county, with the most employees and capital assets. Frequently, the county government is the second-largest employer. I quickly discovered that it's much easier to stand on the outside and throw bricks than to have the responsibility for making a thing work.

I had been focusing pretty much on equality of treatment and services to black people, but of course that's only one aspect of running a school board or government, an involved process even in the best of circumstances. Add to that ones that are virtually bankrupt and alienated from the community's economic resources and the job is even more difficult. Then add to that that black folk are inexperienced, all new to the job, and represent great expectations, some unreasonable, of the black community, and it's one hell of a monumental task.

At the turning point election in 1982, the Wilcox County Commission changed from all white to all black with the exception of Reg Albritten, the white probate judge who presided over the commission. He was sheriff before he became probate judge, and enough blacks stood by him because he got somebody out of jail or helped somebody who had a problem with the bank that he won re-election.

Wilcox County routinely shows up on the list of the ten poorest counties in America. To this day, a sizable number of folk have no running water. Its only industry is a pulpwood plant. A lot of land that used to be farms now grows timber for the paper companies or is used as hunting preserves. The year blacks took over, Wilcox County had the highest rate of unemployment—33 percent—in Alabama, which at that time had the highest unemployment rate in the nation. The state had just condemned the county jail for not meeting the fire code and the county had to cut services to pay for repairs.

Camden (pop. 2,250), the Wilcox County seat, is a forty-five-minute drive from Selma on two-lane country roads. The commission met in a relatively modern building, an annex to the old courthouse. The commissioners sat on one side of a long table, with the probate judge at the end. For the audience, there were pews like you'd find in a church. I recommended that the commission meet at night to give working people a chance to attend. The previous commissions had met in the daytime.

On any given night, we'd have about twenty-five people, mostly black, in attendance. Most folk wore work clothes, flannels, overalls, though a few teachers might be there in jackets and ties and a few preachers in shiny black suits. The sessions always opened with a prayer. These meetings sometimes lasted four or five hours because everyone wanted their say. Black people who'd been reluctant to pressure a white county commission were hardly reluctant to make all kinds of demands on a black one.

We tried to cut the personal speeches and complaints at least in half by requiring advance permission to get on the agenda. But it didn't work. Black people saw this as their government and they would say what they wanted when they wanted. So it often was midnight before we were able to complete our business.

Our first major problem was figuring out who was properly on the payroll and what they did. We found some people drawing checks but couldn't find out where they were assigned. There weren't any job descriptions. We also didn't know for certain what equipment the county owned and where it was. We were told that some road equipment with county tags had been stationed on the private property of large, influential landowners. Records were either nonexistent or missing.

In none of the rural Black Belt counties where blacks won power were the outgoing white officials helpful. Missing records were a common problem, or failing to tell the new black officials of upcoming deadlines for state or federal programs. In Sumter County, where the county commission changed from all white to all black in 1982, the outgoing white commission spent the entire $2 million in the county's general fund on all sorts of vehicles and equipment between their defeat in November and the swearing in of the black commission in January. The new black commission had to get a loan to meet the payroll.

At its first meeting, the newly elected Wilcox County Commission fired five white county employees, and there was some public sentiment for firing all of them. Some of the new commissioners felt that the employment disparity between the races should be corrected immediately; others thought it should happen by attrition. It was a damn thorny issue. There was no question that something had to give because of the wholesale built-in unfairness. There weren't any black department heads, blacks held maybe 20 percent of county jobs, while making up 70 to 80 percent of the population, and the black unemployment rate was twice that of whites. At the same time, nobody looks forward to disrupting somebody's life. Some white people had been working for these counties for years, albeit because blacks were excluded, but they were just doing their jobs and now they needed to send their kids to college.

A few white people quit because they refused to work under the supervision of black people. That freed up some jobs for blacks. Certain department heads who'd been there a long time and had a lot of expertise were kept on, but we made sure blacks were put in as their assistants or deputies so they could get the experience they needed to eventually run the department.

On the other hand, we couldn't do that across the board because it would send the wrong message—the message whites had been sending—that blacks aren't competent to be the boss. We looked at each position to see whether we had a black applicant who could do the job and how long the white person had been there. We laid off some white employees and kept others on. Our goal was that when attrition took place with the present employees, the racial balance of jobs in Wilcox County would reflect the population.

Naturally, this upset the white community. But I don't think there's any way that situation could have been handled without someone being hurt. No way could a black commission come into power after decades of struggle and then tell black folk they'd have to wait on jobs until all the white people retired. There were some black people who thought we didn't go far enough.

To put a significant dent in the desperate employment situation, we obviously needed to attract industry. But Wilcox County was not in a good competitive position. The high illiteracy rate rules out the industries that require workers with some education, and the schools—the all-black public schools and the all-white private academies—aren't up to the quality industries look for if they're sending down their key people. They don't want to bring their vice-presidents to a town without a library or do business in a county where cooperation between the white economic powers and the black political powers is shaky at best.

The courthouse squares in these rural counties symbolize the division. There sits the courthouse in the center, now with black people in charge. Ringing it are the banks and businesses, all owned by white people. The two were at a standoff and progress was at a standstill.

Economics, though, has a way of leveling the playing field. Maynard Jackson once said in a speech that what surprised him most when he was elected mayor of Atlanta was how little power the mayor had compared with the power that resided in the board-rooms of Coca-Cola and the other corporations in Atlanta. When we came into political power in Wilcox, we found the same thing on a smaller scale. There's no way to operate a city or county independent of the economic powers. So we had to try to convince white business leaders that we weren't bent on revenge and to persuade the black community that everything couldn't be changed immediately.

On the other side, even though white business people thought a black government was bad for the county and didn't want to help it succeed, they came in to bid on the contract for gasoline for the county's road equipment or printing or office equipment. Shortly after the law firm was hired, the commission went to a Wilcox County bank to borrow money using future taxes as collateral, a fairly common way of doing business. At first they told

us they wanted a voice in how the money would be spent, something they'd never tell a white government. We said, "No way.
It's probably the safest loan you'll make this year." They made
the loan because they didn't want to lose out to a bank in another
county.

That same year—1982—I began representing the Sumter
County school board. Like Selma, the public schools in the Black
Belt counties were desegregated by court order in the early 1970s.
Unlike Selma, though, where the races are more evenly divided
and a core of influential white people kept their children in the
public schools, virtually all the white children in the predominantly black counties were removed from the public schools and
enrolled in private, segregated academies.

White people often ask me what good the court cases did since
education in these counties remains segregated. This is a white
perspective. These were the counties that spent the least on black
education—many black schools had no libraries, no science or
shop equipment, no janitor service—so abolishing the dual system
was not a failure from the black point of view, though these 99
percent black systems leave a hell of a lot to be desired.

Sumter County is not quite as poor as Wilcox, primarily because
it's the site of the largest toxic waste dump in America. This says
something about how desperate folk are for jobs and industry of
any kind. Though the school system became 99 percent black in
the early seventies, the school board remained all white until 1980.
Black school board employees testified to the regional office of
HEW in Atlanta that desks and other equipment were being taken
from the public schools to the private academy, and blacks suspected that the use of open purchase orders by the white board
was designed to funnel funds to the private school. One of the
first things the black school board did was institute more detailed
purchase orders.

We were beset by all kinds of difficulties. One of the black men
elected to the board, a fella who ran a little grocery and considered
himself a businessman, wanted to put the school district's
money—almost a million dollars—in certificates of deposit in a
little country bank. He'd been doing business there and the banker
encouraged it. Another board member and I said, "You don't

put that kind of money in CDs. You have banks bid on it." He'd never heard of bidding on money and he thought we were flaunting our education and looking down on him.

The bookkeeping involved in running a school system is pretty sophisticated, and we had problems with board members or vocal members of the public who didn't understand the system and thought something crooked was going on, some kind of plot for somebody to get rich. Not only whites had been brainwashed that black people can't be trusted to handle money.

For example, the Sumter County school system—and many others—had always provided the superintendent with an automobile and access to the school gas pump. He also was given gasoline credit cards to use when he was on the road in this rural county. When blacks won control of the school board, they kept the white superintendent on until his contract expired, then hired a black superintendent. The new black superintendent hadn't been there a month before two members of the board said they wanted him to park the car in front of the central office at the close of business each day. They also wanted him to turn in the credit cards issued to his office.

"Wait a minute," I said. "You have made this man the superintendent of all the schools in this county. Now you can't trust him with a car or a credit card?"

One board member actually said, "Well, suppose he's down in Mobile gallivanting around with some woman or something." The superintendent was a married man, and there was no evidence of his being a womanizer.

We also had the problem of some black principals who now had blacks over them. These principals had been kings of the hill in their virtually all-black schools. They didn't get a lot of direction from the central office. When blacks took over the school board and made the principals more accountable, this didn't sit too well with some of them and they tried to undermine the board and the black superintendent. Frederick Douglass's statement "Power concedes nothing" goes for them, too.

Our difficulties often were magnified in the local white press. The weekly newspapers in these counties had a cozy, booster relationship with the political establishment when it was white—

they were part of it—but didn't hesitate to criticize and underline mistakes of the new black ones. You could almost say they delighted in it in a "we told you so" way.

What disgusted me about the local press and other white critics wasn't that they were necessarily wrong in their specifics, though sometimes they were, but that they were taking a snapshot in time as if nothing else had come before. Why were black folk inexperienced in government? What was the condition of the county and school system when blacks took over? Were the previous white officials anything to brag on?

A few white folk were helpful. The people at Livingston University, a state college in Sumter County, provided expertise in curriculum and public administration. Often, though, overtures from the white community were viewed with suspicion. Drayton Pruitt, the white mayor of Livingston, the Sumter County seat, suggested that the board set up a magnet school to draw some whites back to the public system. The board had two meetings to discuss it and the black community was loudly opposed. Some of the teachers thought it was some kind of trap that would be detrimental to them. The general feeling was that whites voluntarily left and they would have to voluntarily come back before blacks would agree to spending any money as enticement.

In matters involving teachers, I found I felt uncomfortable representing school boards. For a decade, I'd been representing black teachers' rights against the boards and had been happy doing it. That's a sort of natural habitat for me. Now there I was representing the establishment, though it was black, when it laid off or disciplined teachers. I also found I had a hard time providing the kind of constant petting and feeding political egos demand. A political client is the worst kind. They want to call you twenty-four hours a day. They want you to jump up, drop everything else, and give your attention to their business, which they say is the public business. If you don't constantly stroke these egos, you've got all kinds of damn problems. And I had difficulty sticking to the narrow role of legal counselor. Much as I wanted to stay out of policy areas and just advise on the law, that was highly unlikely. The problem I had from day one was that many of these newly elected officials are prima donnas and, in a sense, I may be a bigger prima donna than they are. Even if I sit off in a corner, one way or another I'll eventually jump in. The result is the elected officials then feel that you have usurped their authority, that you're trying to run the school board or county commission.

There were members of the black public who felt that blacks in power would change everything overnight for the better. When it turned out that this was not the case, they blamed the elected officials. Then another faction on the black side, plus the displaced or aspiring white politicians, tried to capitalize on the discontent. So while I felt some relief and satisfaction that we had arrived politically, I was overwhelmed by the transition I was making and we were making and by the multitude of problems out there.

CHAPTER 22

Drawing the Lines

At the same time we were unable to elect a black probate judge in Wilcox County or Sumter County or any black officials at all in Dallas County, candidates for President of the United States and governor of Alabama routinely made pitches and promises at endorsement sessions of the Alabama Democratic Conference (ADC), the statewide black political organization that Orzell and Peter had helped found in 1960. Even George Wallace came asking for ADC's endorsement when he won the Democratic nomination for his fifth term as governor in 1982, and we had a disheartening decision to make.

In the primary, ADC had endorsed George MacMillan, the lieutenant governor under Forrest "Fob" James, Alabama's governor from 1978 to 1982. (Alabama has a law restricting governors to two consecutive terms, so Wallace, who'd been governor from 1970 to 1978, had to bow out for one term.) Wallace got 30 percent of the black vote in the primary, even though Jesse Jackson, Coretta Scott King, and other black leaders came to Alabama and campaigned for MacMillan. This shocked people outside the state, though when you came inside Alabama and examined the situation, it wasn't that farfetched. I was stumping the state for MacMillan and my own mother voted for Wallace.

There was sentiment in black Alabama that Wallace had suffered enough. He said he was wrong and repented. And Wallace, in his two terms in the seventies, had put up a string of junior colleges, and many poor whites and blacks now were getting some college training. Alabama teachers, who were among the lowest paid in the nation, got four or five sizable raises while he was governor and schoolchildren started getting their textbooks for free.

A black person certainly could detest Wallace's racism, but here he was running against another white man who might well be just as racist and hadn't built any colleges or given out textbooks. The civil rights leaders and we in ADC made a distinction between Wallace and MacMillan, a younger, moderate, New South-type politician. But to some black folk, MacMillan was just another white man—and one they didn't know.

My mother voted for Wallace because of the teachers' raises and textbooks. This was no different from the way she operated all her life. If a white person helped her and her family, that did it. Also, Wallace grew up around black people and felt comfortable in black company. He often said to black folk that when he first came to Montgomery there weren't any blacks at the state capital except inmates working as servants in the governor's mansion. But now, he joked, "it looks like Uncle Tom's cabin." MacMillan—to his credit—wouldn't consider making a joke like that, but he came across as stiff and aloof.

When he beat MacMillan, Wallace came seeking ADC's endorsement in the general election against Emory Folmar, the Republican mayor of Montgomery. Joe Louis Reed, the chairman of ADC, usually called the shots on the state and national endorsements, but this was one decision he didn't want to make by himself. Joe called about twenty ADC leaders from around the state to come to Montgomery to meet with Wallace the next day in the boardroom of the Alabama Education Association, the state teachers' union where Joe works. I had just become ADC's vice-chairman. We were all sitting around the big conference table when Wallace—smoking a big cigar—came in with a black man pushing his wheelchair.

He started talking his usual stuff about how he was a populist. He and his family had been dirt poor. He'd built trade schools, raised teachers' salaries. Emory Folmar was nothing but a damn

"Republican chief of police" running around looking for some black heads to whip. He said he wanted us to make a statement endorsing him. He thought it would make a difference.

Somebody said they didn't think the race would even be close. There weren't that many Republicans in the state of Alabama except when electing a President.

"In all my years in politics, I've never taken a race for granted," Wallace responded.

Wallace was correct that we weren't going to ask black people to vote for Emory Folmar, who was so right-wing some folk in Montgomery called him the mayoratollah. He liked to strap on a pistol and ride to the scenes of crimes with the policemen. More than one black had been shot or injured by the Montgomery police under questionable circumstances, and the black community there deeply disliked him.

But endorsing Wallace? There was a feeling in the room of great reluctance to go out and say to black people, "Please vote for George Wallace." The man I replaced as vice-chairman—Chris McNair, a Jefferson County commissioner—was the father of one of the four girls killed in the bombing of the Sixteenth Street Baptist Church in Birmingham in 1963. He resigned as vice-chairman to work for the MacMillan campaign. Even though he was no longer an ADC officer and not at the endorsement meeting, he made it clear to us that he held Wallace responsible for creating the atmosphere that led to the bombing and under no circumstances should the organization endorse him.

It was an awful choice. The only redeeming element in the situation was what the presence of onetime Mr. Segregation revealed about how far inside the ballpark we now were and how successful we had been in organizing black Alabama.

From its modest beginning as a little collection of folk getting a little collection of votes for Jack Kennedy, ADC had become the most powerful black statewide political organization in America, routinely delivering a solid bloc of 275,000 black votes, a quarter of the votes cast in Alabama.

We were uniquely fortunate in that our chairman, Joe Reed, was also the associate executive director of the Alabama Education Association. Through Joe, a very close association grew between the teachers' union and our black political caucus, and it was a boon to both.

The Alabama Education Association has a large bankroll, an effective research and lobbying staff, and the loyalty of many teachers, black and white. It brought our black caucus these assets. We brought the teachers' union potentially a quarter of a million votes. Since blacks and labor want pretty much the same things from the legislature, the more blacks who voted, the more likely it was that legislators who favored labor's objectives would be elected. So the teachers' union financed black voter registration efforts. By the late seventies, our black caucus, the teachers' union, other Alabama labor unions, and the Trial Lawyers Association, whose interests run counter to big business, had become a powerful lobby in Montgomery that gave big business and the Farm Bureau some stiff competition.

And we had our chairman sitting in an office a block from the state capitol politicking every day—and Joe is a natural-born politician. He started out as a biology teacher but became active in teacher politics in VISTA, the organization of black teachers in Alabama, right at the time Alabama's schools were undergoing desegregation and VISTA merged with the Alabama Education Association, then the organization of white teachers.

ADC was a natural extension of teacher politics and Joe began coming to ADC meetings, maneuvering in a manner not altogether different from a corporate takeover. He ran for chairman one year and brought a busload of teachers from Montgomery to vote for him. He lost, but he came back the next year, 1970, and won.

Joe's problem with ADC was how to go out in the boondocks and build the organization. Joe felt most comfortable with black teachers and teacher types. If ADC was going to be able to organize and deliver the black vote in numbers large enough to have impact, it was going to have to expand its base. Some of the grass-roots leaders in the Black Belt, the area with the most black votes, were suspicious of an organization dominated by professionals who did little during the civil rights struggle or even worked against it. It also was a social class thing. To me, unity was far more important than these differences, and one of my contributions to ADC was helping to build chapters and memberships among non-teacher types.

With Joe's efforts, my efforts, and those of many other folk, voting the yellow sample ballot with ADC's endorsements became the standard practice in black Alabama. We were turning out between 250,000 and 300,000 votes statewide and turning them out as a bloc. That's a hell of a cushion for any candidate to have, and if your opponent has it, you may be in trouble.

We were helping to elect U.S. representatives and senators, state supreme court justices, secretaries of state, governors. All but one were white. For a black to win statewide required getting at least one-fourth of the white vote, and that did not happen in Alabama. The black vote, though, made the margin of difference in close races between two white candidates, and we had our price.

Jimmy Carter, whom ADC endorsed in Alabama's Democratic primary in 1976, appointed two black lawyers to federal judgeships in the state—U. W. Clemons in Birmingham and Myron Thompson in Montgomery. He made the appointments with the backing of Alabama's U.S. senators, Howell Heflin and Donald Stewart, whom ADC also endorsed. Fob James, Alabama's governor from 1978 to 1982, appointed a black lawyer, Oscar Adams, to a vacancy on the Alabama Supreme Court. In 1982, Oscar ran to keep the seat and became the first black to win a statewide race in Alabama. His colleagues on the bench campaigned for him and the state bar endorsed him. I think they got used to Oscar, liked him, and discovered he wasn't a threat.

That day Wallace came seeking our endorsement, I could sense that most of the men in the room could not forget, even if they could forgive, what Wallace had done. I also could sense that some didn't want to say that to Wallace. In one-on-one situations, Wallace can be very personable and effective, and he has an aura of power. He was really turning on the charm with that collection of black leaders.

Wallace has a skilled politician's ability to deflect folk from their original purpose and persuade them to accept what he wants to offer. I'd seen him pull this off all too well when Ace Anderson, the funeral director whose ambulance picked up the injured peo-

ple on Bloody Sunday, asked Preston, Edwin Moss, two councilmen, and me to come with him to see Governor Wallace in the
early 1970s. The Dallas County coroner had died and it was up
to the governor to appoint someone to fill the remainder of the
term. Ace had run unsuccessfully for the office—like all Dallas
County offices, the white candidate always won—and he wanted
Wallace to appoint him.

We filed into the governor's office and Wallace remarked to
me, "You ought to go ask Albert." I had campaigned for Albert
Brewer, his opponent in the 1970 election. He told me to sit down
on his left, deaf side. "J.L., you sit here." Wallace started wink-
ing, joking, and carrying on with Ace, Preston, and the councilmen and, boy, they were melting. He said he didn't see why
anybody would want to be coroner. It's a thankless damn job. If
he had known Ace wanted it, he would have been glad to appoint
him, but Senator Givhan had already asked him about appointing
somebody.

"I got something better for you gentlemen," he said.

I said, "Wait a minute, Governor," but he went right on talking.
He didn't even hear me.

"You talk about a coroner! I'm going to make each of you a
trustee at a college." He immediately named Edwin to the board
of Alabama State, Preston and another councilman to the board
of Alabama A & M, a black state college in Huntsville, and promised to name Councilman Kimbrough to the board of Tuskegee
University. I don't think he offered Ace anything. He ignored
me. I never got a word in sideways. The episode was typical of
the way Wallace operates, and I was on guard that night in the
ADC gathering.

When Wallace finished his speech about school books and junior colleges, some of us who were a little more outspoken tried
to put into words what we knew was in the minds and hearts of
the other folk and started pushing Wallace about jobs and
appointments.

"Who are some of the blacks you would consider in your administration?" we asked. He mentioned a woman we'd never heard
of. Who else? He was kind of on the spot and just said, in effect,
"Trust me. I'm going to be fair. I'm a changed man." Then he

made his Uncle Tom's cabin quip. He kept repeating how he had helped poor people and a few of us kept pushing jobs and appointments. It became a kind of verbal tug-of-war. Finally, we asked what statement he would be willing to make publicly alongside our making a public statement that we endorsed him. Wallace said he'd be willing to say that he appreciated and was grateful for our support. His attitude and demeanor conveyed that he felt he was doing a big thing by standing up in Alabama and saying, "I appreciate black voters." Some of us found that insulting.

"Governor, we need a commitment to do something for black people in exchange for black votes," we said, and he said his whole program was aimed at the underdog, but not just the black underdog. There was more discussion, but nothing moved.

Wallace left without any understanding or agreement. We stayed about an hour discussing what the hell to do. We decided to tell folk to vote a straight Democratic ticket. Since Wallace was part of the Democratic slate, he benefited from our blanket endorsement, though we didn't put an X by his name on our sample ballot. He got 90 percent of the black vote, which reveals the distasteful choices black voters sometimes must make and how forgiving a people black folk are.

That same year, Hank Sanders challenged Earl Goodwin for the State Senate seat in Dallas and surrounding counties. The district had become about 55 percent black, and Hank and I thought if we got out there and worked hard there was a chance for a black person to win. The federal courts have established that it takes a 65 percent black district to ensure the election of a black person because of the legacy of racial discrimination— fear, lack of history of voting, and the lower educational and economic status that correlates with less voting. But Hank and I decided it was worth a shot.

Initially, Hank pushed me to run again, but I told him I didn't want to. I didn't have the taste for running around all those counties again, and I really didn't want to be in the Senate. The idea of serving in public office has always fascinated me, but the price frightens me. Often what I say and do upsets middle-class blacks as well as whites, and I don't want to give up that freedom. I think I'm more useful promoting others than I would be as a gadfly in the office itself, which is surely what I would become. Hank didn't want to run, either. The daily burden of the law firm—clients, politics, trying to provide leadership in all kinds of controversies—had worn him down and he was thinking of taking a few months off. It became kind of a war of nerves. Who was going to give in first? When Hank realized I wasn't, he decided to run. Also, folk from across the district started to come in and encourage him. We knew Hank would bring to Montgomery a kind of commitment that's rare in life and even rarer in politics.

His was a well-organized campaign, with black taxicabs delivering people to the polls, waves of folk distributing the ADC sample ballot that endorsed Hank for state senator and George MacMillan for governor, then more waves going out knocking on doors on election day, seeing who had gone to the polls, checking the lists at the polling places to see what voters had not come in, and going out looking for them.

As usual, Rose had scores of young people out campaigning, along with the women in MOMs. We weren't able to do this all over the district, but we certainly did it in Selma and some other places where local folk were well organized. Mrs. King and Jesse Jackson campaigned for Hank as they campaigned for MacMillan. Goodwin—the industrialist, former head of the White Citizens' Council—campaigned as usual with organizations, the probate judges. He's not a door-to-door man, and getting out the white vote doesn't require the same effort as getting out the black vote.

By 1982, Selma's Kiwanis and Rotary Clubs were ready to hear a black candidate, and Hank spoke to them. He told me he had to pump himself up, almost as an athlete does before a game. Having to ask white people for anything makes Hank uncomfortable. There's such a long history of the black person getting the short end, and Hank is almost too honest to be a successful practical politician. He will genuinely discuss what he thinks are the legitimate issues and try to state his views as accurately as he can.

If someone at a white civic club asks a question regarding his support of the business establishment and jobs, Hank is sure to list first his disagreements with the establishment in terms of hiring practices and promotions. He won't skirt it. So it becomes an uncomfortable situation, because that's the business establishment he's talking to. Also, somebody at this type gathering invariably talks about how far Selma has come racially and Hank would feel hypocritical if he didn't put that in perspective.

A few white people contributed to his campaign, and at least two were willing to go on television and endorse him publicly. Neither of them were natives of the Black Belt, though, and it was thought that a third supporter, a member of an old Selma family, was needed to legitimize white support. But this didn't work out. I'm not sure the man was so much unwilling to do it as Hank was unwilling to ask. Hank was concerned about how the endorsement would affect the man's standing among his peers. Also, Hank knew he wasn't going to get white votes anyway, so his few appearances before white groups were something he felt he should do rather than anything that would make a difference at the polls.

In the meantime, Smitherman, who was Goodwin's key advisor, was telling the white community Hank was a black racist. Actually, it was hard to pin this on Hank, so Smitherman campaigned against Rose and me, who are more outspoken. He told people "the law firm" would go to Montgomery and do everything for black people and nothing for white people.

Hank lost—but by only 490 votes out of about 33,500 cast. He got more votes losing than winning Senate candidates got in other parts of the state, which shows the intensity of that race. As always, the vote was racially polarized.

Goodwin no sooner won than the legislature was faced with reapportionment, required by federal law every ten years after the census. This entailed a battle because there are many ways of drawing the lines. The legislature drew up a reapportionment plan, but the U.S. Justice Department, under the pre-clearance requirement in the Voting Rights Act, rejected it after intense lobbying by ADC. They especially objected to the way lines in the Black Belt were drawn to split up the huge black population so no Senate district and only one House district had a winnable black majority. The legislature drew up a second plan, which the Department of Justice also said "diluted the black vote."

Meanwhile, Joe Reed submitted a plan. Like the legislature's, it kicked the Republicans in the ass. But the lines were drawn in a way that likely would increase the number of black state representatives from seventeen to at least nineteen and state senators from three to six. The plan required a number of white incumbents to run against each other, and the legislature rejected it.

The Alabama legislature had never reapportioned itself because the incumbents always insisted on perpetuating themselves in power. Each decade, somebody sued and the courts drew new lines. Figuring the matter would once again land in court, Joe filed a lawsuit with the federal panel in Montgomery that was overseeing the reapportionment. Having a suit out there would give Joe leverage with the legislature.

He then went back to the legislature with a new plan, called the "Reed Plan," that reduced the black districts by about two and required fewer white incumbents to face each other. He drew a majority-black district in the Black Belt and added some white areas onto Earl Goodwin's district so Goodwin could keep his seat. Joe told the legislature that if it passed his new plan, he'd drop his suit and ask the court to let the incumbents remain in office for two more years. That was pudding to a bunch of politicians and it started to look like the Reed Plan would pass.

I looked at Joe's plan and said, "No way." The Black Belt district stretched from Montgomery to the Mississippi line—and bypassed Selma. Blacks in Selma were going to remain in Goodwin's district. After everything blacks in Selma had done to bring about the black vote, no way was I going to sit by and let somebody in Montgomery cut us out so he would have more control. I saw this as an attempt by Joe to put his man, Andrew Hayden, in the Senate without any serious opposition from anyone in Selma.

Hayden, a black businessman in Uniontown, in Perry County, played an accommodationist role there similar to D. V. Jemison's and Claude Brown's in Selma. In 1965, he sent a telegram to Martin Luther King at Brown Chapel telling him not to come to Uniontown. Since his election as Uniontown's mayor in the early seventies, his method has been to make deals with white people on behalf of black people—or so he would put it. I question whether black people benefited. In the 1982 Senate race, Hayden supported Goodwin, the former head of the White Citizens' Council, against Hank, and the black votes he swung to Goodwin in Uniontown were Goodwin's margin of victory. But Joe and Hayden are friends and Joe, being a classic political broker, wants people who will do his bidding. Hayden would be Joe's man; Hank was his own man.

Other folk in Selma and the Black Belt were as upset as I was, and a delegation of us went to Montgomery to tell Joe his plan was unacceptable. Joe assured me Hayden was not going to run for the Senate. I said, Whether he runs or not, we are not going to agree to a plan for the Black Belt that bypasses its hub and its leadership.

"Well, grab hold because the legislature's going to pass it," Joe said. He named the committee people he was working with and said it would be impossible to redraw the lines because if one thing were put out of kilter here, everything would go wrong over there.

I filed a motion to intervene in Reed's lawsuit on behalf of Hank, Reese, Marie Foster, and fourteen other blacks, contending that Reed's suit did not represent the interests of blacks in Selma and Dallas County. This gave us some leverage.

Reed's plan was being considered in the State Senate. I wrote a letter to each of the senators saying that even if they passed Joe's plan, the suit would not be dismissed and no federal court was going to let them stay in office two more years. Albert Turner and I made speeches along those lines and put the Senate in a riproar. They told Joe, "You need to get with these people because this damn thing is not going to fly otherwise." Joe came to me and said, "Well, maybe we can make some changes."

I went to his office. He said, "We can redraw the line and put it out there by your house." Our house on Kingsley was on the edge of west Selma, a little black enclave in a mostly white area. I said, "No, don't put it by my house. Put it by Hank's house." Hank lived on the east side of town, where most blacks lived, and he was the one who was going to run for the Senate seat. We got down on the floor with a big map, drew lines to include the majority of blacks in Selma in the black district, located where Hank lived, and drew a loop out to his front door.

The legislature passed the Reed Plan with the "Chestnut amendment," which put part of Selma in the white district and part in the black district. In November 1983, Hank ran and won in the 70 percent black district and became the first black state senator from the Black Belt since Reconstruction. Goodwin ran and won in the 70 percent white district. Folk joked that Selma now had separate but equal state senators.

CHAPTER 23

Salt and Pepper

Instead of giving up crime when we sent him to Birmingham, Terry became one of the most notorious burglars in Alabama. Ronnie soon began calling to tell me his brother was involved in something, though he couldn't put his finger on just what. In less than a year, Terry got his own apartment. When he came to Selma, he'd be driving an expensive automobile, dressed in expensive clothes and carrying a pocketful of money.

He always had some glib explanation as to how he came by such great prosperity—a job, a business—and I didn't know how to deal with it other than saying he might ride high for a while but eventually he'd be busted, and don't call me. Vivian, who wants to believe her children, would be persuaded that Terry was just smart in business, which he is. Terry has Preston's gift of brilliance; he's a quick study of almost anything, but he craved material wealth and took a shortcut to get it.

The worst day of my life—worse even than the day Vivian's father was dying—was the day I got a call from Rosalind in Birmingham that the police had Terry's apartment surrounded. One of Terry's confederates had been arrested and had told the police the extent of Terry's burglaries and where Terry lived. I drove up at breakneck speed. Rosalind had gone to stay with her brother for a while. I was against it but didn't argue as hard as I should have. On the drive, I was sick with worry that she would be hurt or implicated in what Terry was doing.

When I arrived, the place had been ransacked, but Terry was gone. The police were questioning Rosalind about what she knew but left her alone once I got there. You talk about relief! Rosalind told me Terry had walked out of the apartment, right by the police. He spoke to them, got in his car, and drove off. They didn't know what he looked like.

The cool, brazen calculation of Terry's breaking-and-entering houses and walking deliberately through police lines with a smile was in ways similar to the calculated chances Orzell and I had taken in the past. Terry heard Vivian and my mother constantly citing the risks I was taking; in part, that's what people meant when they said he was attempting to come out from my shadow and attract attention to himself.

A few days later, Terry called from Chattanooga to say he was all right. I pleaded with him to come back and turn himself in. They were flashing his picture on television, saying he was driving a late-model Datsun and asking anyone who saw him to call the police. "You are going to kill your mother," I said. I told him we wanted to talk to him face to face. He agreed to fly to New Orleans. Vivian and I drove down there and spent several days trying to talk him into surrendering. I promised I'd do everything I could to help him. He said no way. He couldn't make it in the reformatory that time, couldn't stand being cooped up. He knew he couldn't make it in the penitentiary.

For a period of months, he called from different places from time to time. It was a damn nightmare. Vivian and her mother were afraid to answer the telephone at night. When it rang, we'd all be worried that a voice at the other end of the line would tell us Terry had been shot and killed. Sometimes I got emergency calls from clients late at night and it would be impossible to go back to sleep. I could handle the tension better than Vivian, and I didn't handle it very well.

Some of the time, I knew where he was and was tempted to turn him in. But Vivian would never have forgiven me if I had. And if he ran or something happened when the police came and he got shot, I'd never have forgiven myself.

What we didn't know was that Terry was making forays back to Birmingham to commit more burglaries. Then one day he called me from the county jail in Birmingham using a fictitious name. He said he'd been arrested breaking into a house but the police didn't know who he was. He wanted me to come bail him out quick, before they checked his fingerprints. I said I wasn't going to do it. I'd do everything under the sun I could do for him as a lawyer, but he was going to have to face the music. He begged me to get him out, but I refused. Vivian was sad but relieved.

I persuaded Terry to plead guilty to a series of burglaries; then I asked the black sheriff of Perry County if he would take Terry in his jail thirty miles from Selma. A county jail wouldn't be as rough as the penitentiary, I could keep my eye on him when I was over there on cases and Vivian could visit him more easily. The sheriff agreed. So did state prison officials. The penitentiary system was overcrowded and under a court order to reduce its population. I also needed the permission of the presiding judge of the circuit and that was Judge Russell, whose connection with my family went back to my mother's borrowing money to send me to college. He signed the order without hesitation.

"Chess," he said, "you didn't even need to ask."

A number of people, including white people, called offering help. Jean Sullivan, the Republican committeewoman, telephoned Emory Folmar, the Republican mayor of Montgomery, and his police chief on my behalf. Terry had several arrests over there. Joe Smitherman said he was a father himself and anything he could do to help he would. Once again, you have the individual/group thing that makes the South so peculiar and complex. These white leaders genuinely wanted to help with my son, but where I pushed for more power for the group, they opposed me. Here lies the greatest pitfall for someone involved in fighting for social change. When people in power do a favor for you and your own, you may not be so ready to do battle against them.

The Perry County Jail, where Terry began serving his time in 1982, is in Marion, the county seat. Ronnie also was working in Marion—for the district attorney. When he graduated from law school, he worked at the law firm for about a year. But he couldn't find time to study for the bar in our hectic pressure cooker. He wanted a job that would be connected with the law and give him time to study. I thought a position on the district attorney's staff might be ideal and spoke to Roy Johnson, who was elected with black votes in 1980. Ronnie went to work there in 1983 as an investigator and administrator of the victim's-rights program. He was eager to do it. He likes having a badge and the authority that goes with it. When he came by the house, I'd joke to Vivian, "Watch what you say. The police is here."

Our law firm gradually developed a large practice—in fact, an outrageous practice. By the early 1980s, we had thousands of active cases pending—criminal, civil, property, civil rights, domestic relations. We took too many small ones that paid little or nothing because we rarely turned folk down. We always were pushed for time and searching for help. We weren't getting rich, but we were paying our bills and making some money. We hired my Uncle Frank to build us a new brick office building on Jeff Davis Avenue on a small black business strip that included a black-owned drugstore, a black insurance company, a black dentist, and Edwin's credit union.

Perry Varner, a graduate of Boston College of Law who married Rose's sister, came on board to manage the office. Barnette Lewis Hayes, our secretary, had two additional secretaries under her supervision. In 1980, Albert Turner's brother Robert joined us as a full-fledged lawyer ready to try cases. Robert had been an artillery officer in the Vietnam War and was a graduate of Dillard University. He worked as an insurance adjuster, then studied law at night at Miles College. He was older, married, and more mature than some youngster just out of law school. He said he liked the kind of law we were practicing in the Black Belt, which is his home. We now were Chestnut Sanders Sanders and Turner.

Our clientele consisted mainly of poor and working-class black people. The middle class, with some notable exceptions, tended to go to white lawyers. Certain black families had been dealing with certain white lawyers for more than a generation. Some considered anything black second-rate and second-class. A few expressed concern that somebody in our office would spread their business around. They didn't want the people they lived near and socialized with to know the details of their divorces or finances, especially if they had some sort of front out there with nothing much behind it. The reverse is uncommon, although I've had a few white people bring me matters they wanted kept from the white community.

One of the significant outcomes of blacks and poorer whites serving on juries has been an increase in the amount of money judgments in civil cases. When juries were drawn from property tax records and handpicked by the establishment, they were conservative not only racially but economically; it was difficult to win a claim against a bank, big business, or landowner on behalf of somebody sold bad stock, hurt on the job, or cheated on a contract. The new system was a boon for me because it was my natural style to make emotional Big Shots vs. Little People arguments.

Still, when blacks of any means in the predominantly black counties got hurt in an accident or other situation with the potential for making a killing, they often retained a big white law firm in Montgomery or Birmingham. These white lawyers then would hire me as an associate to deal with the mostly black juries they were sure to get in these counties. After a while, I refused to associate with all but a few of these white firms. It was so silly for black people to hire a white lawyer who then hired me.

A similar problem arose on the other side, with large white law firms hired by insurance carriers to represent them against claims in the Black Belt. They wanted to associate with me just for the trial for a set amount after they'd done the paperwork, run up big bills, and collected huge fees. I cut that out. I said, "You either bring us in at the outset or forget it."

Gradually, we picked up some middle-class black clients, but it was a slow process. One of the great services Joe Reed performed as associate director of the Alabama Education Association in charge of teacher litigation was insisting that black lawyers get a fair share of the legal work financed by the teachers' union. This brought some black teachers to the law firm who otherwise might not have come. Some were impressed by our services and retained us for other matters.

On occasion, we represented white clients for insurance companies, but few white people walked through the doors of our office and retained us as lawyers. Those who did usually had cases against the local white establishment no white lawyer wanted to touch.

This situation began to change somewhat in 1982, when I got a call from Wyman Gilmore, a white attorney in Clarke County. He wanted me to help him represent Bain Henderson, the richest and most powerful landowner in Wilcox County.

My initial reaction was "You must be kidding!" Bain Henderson and his father before him were the epitome of the Old South. At one time, more than a hundred black families lived in little shacks on their place. They operated a general store on the property and paid their black sharecroppers in scrip instead of money. I considered Bain Henderson racist and arrogant, and my view was reinforced by what I'd read in the newspaper about his alleged crime—shooting to death a working-class white man from Birmingham he caught looking for deer on his land.

"He's not such a bad fella, J.L. You really need to get to know him, anyway," Wyman said, referring to the fact that blacks had just won control of the county government in Wilcox and I was about to become the county commission's attorney.

"I already know him," I told Wyman, saying that Bain Henderson was on the opposite side of black efforts to win power and to raise taxes to help the black schools. "It would be a plus for the county if he was convicted," I said. "I hope they put his white ass in the penitentiary."

"That's a racist, cold damn position for you to take," Wyman said. "You're supposed to be a defense attorney. You sound like a prosecutor. I'm surprised at you."

He persuaded me to at least consider it. Wyman was an unusual man, different from any other white Southern lawyer I knew. I met him in the early 1970s when I was representing three black teachers against the white school board in Choctaw County. These black teachers, who'd been fired to make room for white teachers, were members of the Alabama Education Association and I was sent to represent them. Wyman was representing another black teacher and a black principal.

I walked into the courtroom about thirty minutes late because I'd had a flat tire. There was this giant of a white man, weighing over two hundred pounds, a few years older than I, rugged and even handsome in a John Wayne sort of way, arguing several preliminary motions. He was as much in charge of the courtroom as Peter Hall used to be.

Wyman was asking for a summary judgment because his clients obviously were fired for political or, as he put it, "reasons even worse." He said these black educators had spent their professional lives in the public schools of that county, and as long as there had been a dual system, they'd been praised. They had mortgages and children in college, but the school board didn't seem to give a damn about that. They ought to come down out of their "privileged pews." He used arguments and even words that I used in such cases.

I said to myself, "Damn!" I'd heard white attorneys for the government, the ACLU, or the Legal Defense Fund make such arguments on behalf of blacks in federal courts. But here was a country attorney in private practice—one of their own—attacking the white establishment in a state court in a backward little county. I was fascinated.

We tried other cases on the same side—usually civil cases where we were bound to wind up with a racially mixed jury and were trying to cover all bases. More often, we were on opposite sides— also, usually, civil cases—and these were hard-fought legal battles. Wyman was a fierce competitor who would almost rather die than lose. Over time, we developed a good courthouse friendship. We enjoyed each other's company. His views of courthouse characters and other lawyers paralleled mine, and our views about power and privilege were similar up to a point. Wyman's father was a dirt-poor farmer from Clarke County, about halfway between Selma and Mobile. His wife grew up in a little crossroads town in Dallas County just outside Selma. She was a farm girl. Wyman told me once that the elite of Dallas County thought they were more than she was and acted accordingly. I don't know what had happened, but I got the impression this was something he'd witnessed. I do know Wyman threw a brick at the establishment every chance he got, representing black and white clients against the Farm Bureau, the paper companies, and other monied interests.

Wyman tried hard to persuade me to socialize with him outside the courthouse. He pestered and pestered me about coming down some Friday or Saturday afternoon to eat chitlins and Brunswick stew, the kind made in big black iron pots, which he and I both knew as boys. He lived in Grove Hill, the seat of Clarke County, but owned two large farms where he relaxed with his friends. He had a smokehouse there, a large pond stocked with catfish, and several deep freezes filled with deer and other game.

I knew he'd have his hunting buddies there on a Friday or Saturday afternoon and I didn't want to be bothered. I'd had no experience socializing with white people in their homes and it wasn't high on my list. Much as I enjoyed talking and joking with Wyman while working on a case, I wasn't anxious to sit down with him and his friends in a purely social situation, especially where they'd be drinking and telling jokes. He or they could very well say something, being white, that I must take issue with, being black. On the other hand, to sit down and make a deliberate effort to avoid a clash would be to create a phony, tense, unrewarding situation. I'd rather be spared that, and I didn't want to jeopardize a satisfying courthouse relationship by trying to put it on another level.

But one day I went. When I drove up to the farm, where Wyman had two mobile homes side by side under a grove of trees, about ten middle-aged white men were sitting or standing around a fire and an enormous pot filled with rich bubbling Brunswick stew. They looked so much like juries used to look when I started practicing law, I was reluctant to get out of my car.

Then a young black man who was tending some hams being barbecued over a pit recognized me, hollered "Lawyer!" and opened the car door. Wyman often got young black men released from the county jail to his custody and gave them jobs on his farm. This young man was one of them. I gave him the black handshake. Wyman came over to me, grinning.

He introduced me as the second-best lawyer in Alabama. He went on to describe cases we'd tried together and suggestions I'd made to him about some of his cases. His Southern white friends sat there almost spellbound, listening to these words about a black man coming from a white man they liked and respected.

Wyman and his buddies were drinking Johnnie Walker, and we got into a conversation about why I wouldn't drink. I told them about my long and almost losing struggle with alcohol. One of them wanted to know why a black man who had made it through college and law school would wind up drinking too much whiskey. It seemed to him the hard part was over. Wyman answered before I could. It was interesting to hear a white man try to outline to another white man what it meant to be black and practicing law in Alabama. It was clear that Wyman felt he understood that better than I did. Of course, he didn't. But that was Wyman.

I thoroughly enjoyed myself and so did everyone there. I wondered, however, how much effect the Johnnie Walker had. The only thing that hung heavy by the end of the afternoon was the difficulty reconciling our relationship to each other and their relationship to the four young black men who were dipping out the Brunswick stew, slicing the hams, and serving everybody's wants and needs. Ordinarily, being served by black people was a comfortable and familiar arrangement to them. Having a black man sitting next to them being served, too, not only was at odds with Southern customs; it somehow silently threw the arrangement into question. The mere fact that I was sitting on the white side made me uncomfortable. This was not spoken but was clearly present in everyone's mind.

Wyman obviously was amused by all this. He had long since convinced himself that race played no part in his relationships with anybody. Therefore, he saw no need to be uncomfortable. I wanted him to explore the possibility that he was white in ways he didn't see, so I told him about my Uncle Frank and Harmon Carter on horseback and another black man opening gates for them. I asked if he thought the situations were parallel. He quickly said no way. The men serving the food were ex-cons and were lucky to get the job. They could just as well have been white. And while there may have been something unequal in the situation of Frank and Carter, there wasn't between us. We were two lawyers, underdog lawyers, defense lawyers.

I went back three or four times. That homemade Brunswick stew—fresh corn, okra, smoked meat—and the barbecued hams were an irresistible epicurean delight. I genuinely liked and en-

Wyman Gilmore (Courtesy of the Gilmore family)

joyed one of Wyman's friends, a lawyer from Baton Rouge. He was a wild man. He begged me to come visit him in Baton Rouge, but I never did. Visiting white people's homes or getting together with them in purely social situations remains difficult and unappealing to me.

Meanwhile, Wyman kept inviting me to come to his home and meet his wife. With many white Southern men, a wall goes up where a white woman is involved. That's a world they want to keep you out of. Not Wyman. He kept saying, "Vivian wants to see you." His wife was named Vivian, too. When I was in Grove Hill on legal business one day, he drove me to his house and insisted I stay for dinner. A black woman who'd worked for the Gilmores for years served the meal. She obviously was pleased that Wyman and Mrs. Gilmore had a friendly relationship with me based on equality, and that pleased me. Eventually, Wyman almost transcended color with me. He became not so much a unique white man as just Wyman.

That Wyman telephoned me on behalf of Bain Henderson didn't surprise me. Wyman was a complex man with many types of relationships. Bain inherited wealth; Wyman grew up poor and earned a lot of money. But both were macho outdoor types who loved hunting, sports, and other masculine diversions. They drank whiskey with gusto. Though Bain probably could buy and sell most members of the average country club, he wasn't likely to join one. He isn't the type to sit around a swimming pool or play golf. You'd more likely find him hunting or sitting around a pot of Brunswick stew, telling lusty sexist jokes, wearing overalls and Western boots. Wyman didn't share Bain's political views, but surely had more impact on Bain than Bain had on him. In addition, Bain was a valuable and powerful client.

On the telephone that day, Wyman told me the details of the shooting. He made a case that it was self-defense, though Bain's guilt or innocence mattered little to me. I represent many guilty people and see the job of defense attorney as making sure prosecutors prove guilt beyond a reasonable doubt. While lecturing me about racism, Wyman made certain I knew the victim was white. He said he needed my help.

"You know there are some pitfalls out there on the landscape," he noted. Wyman knew how to appeal to black jurors; he was successful at it. But he wasn't sure how black jurors would react to Henderson shooting the young man. If the district attorney portrayed the deceased as a regular guy and family man—his wife and two children were with him when he was shot—and Bain as rich, powerful, and arrogant, a black jury might well convict. Also, there were blacks in Wilcox County who, though they'd been playing a game with the Hendersons, didn't like them and might well use the opportunity to convict him for past sins. So it was important which blacks got on the jury.

"I don't know if I want to deal with the pitfalls for the sake of Bain Henderson," I said. "He's on the opposite side of everything I'm about."

"Well, there's one way you can get even," Wyman said. "Your fee can be anything you want."

I thought about it and agreed to do it—for the money, for Wyman, and for the law firm. I knew representing Bain Henderson would boost our credibility. Many white people were surprised, and most black people were proud. In some kind of way, it signaled that we had arrived. Had the victim been black, though, I would not have defended him.

At first, Bain was self-conscious around me because he wasn't used to dealing with blacks as equals. For a long time, it was Mr. Chestnut. I could hardly get him to say J.L. or Chess. He loosened up a little when he saw how Wyman and I carried on with each other. I kidded them about the macho nonsense of stalking a beautiful, helpless deer, tying its carcass on a truck, and driving slowly down the main street so everybody could see the blood and gore. They told me to go somewhere and put on my ballet shoes.

I had no illusion that Bain had changed or that his attitudes had changed. The world had changed, and he was acting out of what Hank calls "the squeeze of necessity." With me, Bain took on the complex dimensions all human beings have when you see them up close and was no longer just the white opposition— though he remained the opposition.

Duck Sadler, a seventy-five-year-old white Wilcox County lawyer, also was part of the defense team. We got a jury list early on and met to discuss who we should strike. They concentrated on the whites and I concentrated on the blacks, who made up about 75 percent of the jury pool. I took the list to Reverend Thomas Threadgill, a preacher, politician, and black activist in Wilcox County. I had to work on him as hard as Wyman worked on me to persuade him to help. I told him Bain would owe blacks one. I asked him which blacks on the list would give Bain the most benefit of the doubt. He said our chances were best with the least educated and the most dependent, who were fond of and close to the white powers in Wilcox County. I said, "Put an X by everyone who qualifies," and he did. The jury impaneled had seven blacks and five whites.

The trial was the talk of Alabama. The courtroom on the third floor of a relatively new building in Camden was crowded with curious black people, concerned local white people, and a contingent from Birmingham. The press ran a story every day. The *Birmingham News* was incensed that one of its citizens had been murdered, as an editorial put it, by some land baron over a deer.

A reporter from the *Montgomery Advertiser* dubbed Wyman and me the Salt and Pepper Team.

The shooting happened at night on a rural road that circles part of Bain's property. Bain and his wife, returning from an Auburn football game, came upon a truck traveling slowly and flashing a light as if looking for deer. Bain cut in front of the truck, came over, and tried to take the keys from the ignition. Inside the truck were Herman Adams, an assistant superintendent of the sanitation department of a Birmingham suburb, his wife and children. Adams had been drinking and so had the Hendersons.

Adams's daughter testified that her father and Bain cursed each other and that Mrs. Henderson approached with a gun saying she would "kill us if we came back." Her father pulled a pistol from the glove compartment, kicked Bain, and drove off, with Bain and his wife in pursuit. Then Adams's truck overturned on the roadbank. Bain approached it and began fighting with her father. Bain, then fifty-six, is a large, tall man, about 250 pounds. Adams wasn't quite as big but was younger, thirty-nine.

The last thing Adams's children remembered was looking back and seeing Bain pinned down by their father, who was telling them, "Go on! Go on!" The children and their mother were running when they heard shots. Two sheriff's deputies testified that when they got to the scene, Bain told them he'd shot Adams as they struggled over a pistol, saying, "I have killed the son-of-a-bitch, and if anybody else messes with me, I'll kill them, too."

Bain testified that his wife handed him a pistol when he approached the truck. He said Adams grabbed the pistol as they struggled; he grabbed it back and shot Adams twice as they rolled around, once in the back. Bain and Wyman rassled on the floor in front of the jury with an unloaded gun to demonstrate how the shooting happened.

The district attorney argued that the shooting was a cold-blooded murder, that Bain came up to the truck half drunk and angry, that Adams got the best of him and Bain shot him when it was clear he couldn't whip him. He argued that the entrance and exit wounds of the bullets couldn't have occurred in the manner we claimed.

The jury found Bain not guilty. Almost immediately, more

Our law firm office (© Penny Weaver)

white people came to our law office. Prior to that case, it would have been inconceivable that any white person of means would have retained a black lawyer in Wilcox County, even to stay out of the penitentiary. Breaking the ice required somebody in Bain's position. Ironically, this case also gave us more legitimacy with middle-class blacks. Some of the cases folk were taking to big white law firms they started bringing to us. Hell, if Bain Henderson had hired us, why shouldn't they?

CHAPTER 24

Intense Politickin' Time

When Jesse Jackson started talking about running for President in 1984, Joe Reed was in the "Jesse don't run" camp. We in the Black Belt were saying, "Run Jesse Run." Joe and those who hoped Jesse wouldn't run were people who viewed politics in mainstream terms of winning elections. We saw a Jesse Jackson campaign as a kind of civil rights vehicle for pushing the race forward. Jesse's candidacy could do nationwide what I'd set out to do locally when I ran for office—energize black people into greater political participation and add dimension to the debate.

These differences collided at ADC's presidential endorsement session three months before the Super Tuesday Southern presidential primaries. All the 1984 Democratic contenders were there at the Hilton Hotel in Mobile—Jesse, John Glenn, Walter Mondale, Ernest Hollings, Gary Hart.

The morning of the endorsement session, a small group of ADC leaders met with Jesse in his room at the hotel. He was propped up in bed, with silk monogrammed pajamas on. We all sat down and Jesse told us he thought ADC's endorsement should be his because he was not a mere candidate, he was one of us. Joe told him he would be "treated with the same cordiality and consideration as all the other candidates." Jesse looked disappointed, but I don't think surprised.

The others left, but I stayed to talk. I've known Jesse since he came to Selma as a go-fer for King. Since then, he's been back to Selma for demonstrations, important political campaigns, and every memorial march. I don't know how many times Jesse has walked across the Edmund Pettus Bridge. I consider him gifted, tireless, and shrewd. I've never known anyone with a keener sense of the dramatic and a better ability to milk a situation for everything it's worth.

I told Jesse we in the Black Belt were pushing Joe for at least a co-endorsement of him and Mondale. We were making the argument that ADC couldn't lead folk where they didn't want to go and folk were going with Jesse. He was a black man who dared to run for the highest office and he was more than holding his own in debates and public appearances. That he didn't have government experience and couldn't win was irrelevant. Jesse made speeches about people who "take the early bus"—the maids going to work in white homes or motels, the janitors going to start up

Jesse Jackson and I at a memorial service for Jimmie Lee Jackson in Perry County in 1984 (Courtesy of J. L. Chestnut, Jr.)

the furnace at some office building or school, the invisible Americans. Why shouldn't they be for Jesse? He was the only candidate who even noticed them.

I was worried that ADC would lose credibility if the organization endorsed Mondale. Joe had been close to the Carter-Mondale Administration, and I knew the furthest he might go with Jesse would be a co-endorsement. But Joe said a co-endorsement was no endorsement. Joe is 100 percent politician, an inside manipulator to whom power, influence, and winning are everything. The civil rights perspective, which is long-range and not obsessed with short-term victory, is alien to him. Since a black man couldn't win the nomination, Jesse's candidacy made no sense to Joe.

In Jesse's room that morning, I said it was reasonable to assume ADC would not endorse him, but I thought that would hardly be fatal to his campaign in Alabama.

I left and went back to my room. A Secret Service man knocked at my door and told me the Vice-President wanted to talk to me. I guess Joe had told him I was lingering with Jesse. So I went to his room and there was Mondale in his undershorts and a T-shirt. It was about the middle of the morning, but everybody had been up late the night before. This was an intense politickin' time.

"J.L., come here with me," he said. I stood in the bathroom doorway while he shaved and we talked. He said he understood the sentiment people felt for Jesse, but winning the nomination and running the Republicans out of the White House was not a matter of sentiment. The endorsement would help him build momentum, and he wanted me to do everything I could to help him get it without ruffling feathers to the point that folk would leave divided.

I told him frankly I thought the endorsement should go to Jesse—with Jesse's delegates switching to Mondale at the convention—but that Joe was for him so he was going to get it. I said I didn't know what I could do about ruffled feathers, but I certainly hoped we wouldn't leave divided because I damn sure didn't want four more years of the Republicans.

At the screening session, Jesse came in, made a rousing speech, and left the room. Mondale made a speech similar to what he'd told me in his room. Richard Arrington, the mayor of Birmingham, made a motion that we endorse Mondale for President and Jesse for Vice-President, and the speeches began. The ones for Mondale were civil and reasonable. No black man was going to be nominated. The stakes were too high for us to go off on a frolic, as much as we wanted Jesse. We needed to be realistic and not mislead our people with false expectations.

On the Jesse side, the speeches were emotional. How dare black men ask us to nominate a white man over Jesse! It was intense, with real anger, profanity. Two or three times Joe had difficulty gaveling the meeting back to order. Meantime, Albert Turner of Perry County and a group of other folk Joe didn't put on the screening committee were banging on the door, yelling that Joe was a dictator. The motion carried by a considerable number because Joe had picked the committee.

A few days later, Hank and about forty other black leaders in Alabama held a press conference at Brown Chapel saying they didn't agree with the endorsement or with the undemocratic way it was decided. They were supporting Jesse Jackson. Hank and Michael Figures, a young black state senator from Mobile, became Jesse's campaign managers in Alabama. Rose organized a group of teenagers, Youth for Jesse, who worked with Hank and Michael.

I didn't participate in the press conference. I stuck with Mondale—not for Mondale, but for ADC. I helped build the organization and I wasn't going to chuck twenty years over one election. It went back to Orzell in the roadshow. The institution was more important to me than Mondale or Jesse.

About a month before the Super Tuesday primary, Coleman Young, the black mayor of Detroit, came to Selma on behalf of Mondale and asked me to organize a rally. Under ordinary circumstances, this wouldn't have been hard to do. Coleman was reared in Selma and Tuscaloosa. His aunt lives in Selma. Like Joe, Coleman is a dyed-in-the-wool Democrat and also an officeholder, and he was not about to buck the ticket for a man he described as a preacher who never had a church or congregation or even a job.

We arranged to have a mass meeting and a press conference

at historic Brown Chapel. But we couldn't produce the people, so we wound up with just a press conference. Even for that, nobody wanted to be on the platform with Coleman. This was the period leading up to the local election—Reese had just declared himself in the mayor's race and Jesse was campaigning for him and other local black candidates at joint rallies. So the only people who got up on the platform with Coleman were me, Edwin Moss, Joe Rembert, the Brown Chapel pastor and chairman of the local ADC chapter, and Smitherman, who came to welcome a fellow mayor.

Notably absent was Earl Goodwin, who was chairman of the Democratic Party in Dallas County. He not only didn't appear at the press conference but refused until the eleventh hour to even open a local office on behalf of the national Democratic ticket because his white constituents were going to vote for Reagan. It was obvious right there in Brown Chapel that Mondale and the Democratic Party were in trouble.

Jesse's candidacy, though, soared in the Black Belt and took on more of the character of a movement than a political campaign. Marie Foster and others pushing voter registration began to step up their efforts, and the excitement encouraged Reese to run for mayor against Smitherman. Though the city election was not until July, Reese declared himself in the race in early February, and Jesse campaigned for Reese as he campaigned for himself.

The January and February before Super Tuesday, 600 additional black people registered to vote in Dallas County. Whites continued to hold the registration edge—1,400 in the county, less in the city of Selma—but the gap was closing more every day. Suddenly the Dallas County voter registration office became the focal point of the racial battleground once again.

Cecil Williamson, a white Presbyterian minister, called a press conference to announce a white voter registration drive. He called it Project SAVE (Selma Area Voter Enlistment). What was fair for the goose was fair for the gander, he said. He claimed he didn't have "anything against black people," but white people would leave town and industry wouldn't come if blacks were in charge of City Hall.

Next, Smitherman summoned to his office the two white members of the Board of Registrars, along with Senator Earl Goodwin and Representative Noopy Cosby. He deliberately bypassed the lone black registrar, Edwin Moss. The meeting obviously concerned the narrowing gap between black and white voters and the role deputy registrars were playing in closing it. Deputy registrars can go out in the county and register people at any time and place. Our lobby in Montgomery—ADC, the teachers' union, other unions, and the trial lawyers—had gotten a bill through the legislature that required Boards of Registrars to appoint deputies, which led to the registration of more black people.

Three days later, Goodwin showed up at the regular meeting of the Board of Registrars and detailed alleged problems with the applications brought in by the deputy registrars—cards sent to people registered by the deputies that came back "Doesn't live here," underage registrants, and the use of Xeroxed rather than original forms. The board voted 2–1 to "rescind" all the deputy registrars.

Edwin objected strenuously to the discharge of the deputies and to being excluded from the meeting in the mayor's office. He even called the action racist, which was quite a stand for him. Ironically, Edwin owed his appointment on the board to Smitherman and Goodwin. In 1981, then-Governor Fob James put out word through Senator Goodwin that he was willing to appoint a black to the board to replace a white man who had died. Reese, Edwin, and I met with Smitherman and Goodwin in the mayor's office and recommended Marie because of all her voter registration work. Edwin already was on two boards and said he didn't need to be on another one.

Goodwin agreed to abide by our wishes and recommend Marie, but then he came back later and said James wouldn't appoint her but had appointed Edwin. I doubt if that's what happened. I think the governor asked Goodwin, "Who do you want?" and Goodwin said Edwin. But we let it pass because, hell, we got a black on the board.

We filed a complaint with the Department of Justice that the firing of the deputy registrars was a change of procedure that hadn't been pre-cleared. The Department of Justice said the board had to reinstate deputy registrars but didn't have to reappoint the same individuals. The board named a few new deputies and all the former ones except Marie and our office manager, Perry Varner, the two most active deputy registrars. Goodwin claimed they'd made the most mistakes on the forms.

Smitherman had a dual purpose in orchestrating this show—to slow down the registration of blacks and to make sure whites knew blacks were getting dangerously close to a voting majority. There still was time for other people to sign up as candidates, and Smitherman was guaranteeing no white person would oppose him and split the white vote. Since he already had black opposition, he could afford to turn off black people. He predicted in the newspaper that blacks would march because Perry and Marie were not reinstated. I'm sure he hoped we would march and further scare the white community. It probably would have been wiser not to play into his hands and reinforce the notion in the white community that Joe has some uncanny knack of knowing what blacks will do. But folk couldn't overlook the insult to Marie. So on the nineteenth anniversary of Bloody Sunday, we were marching in the streets again.

The Reese-Smitherman race turned into a classic example of how Southerners avoid honestly addressing the reality of race. Both candidates talked about improving garbage collection, stopping crime, recruiting industry, and increasing jobs. They made almost no mention of race and applauded each other for not running "racial" campaigns. When the national media came to town to cover the race between a black man and a white man who once stood on the opposite sides of the barricades, Smitherman called Reese a gentleman, shook his hand, and bragged about how much racial progress Selma had made.

Reese's campaign manager was James Perkins, Jr., a computer consultant with no political experience. Early in the campaign, Hank and I met with Reese and Perkins to talk about strategy. Reese and Perkins said they'd decided to downplay race because they didn't want to turn off white voters. Their strategy was to get between 10 and 15 percent of the white vote and between 40 and 45 percent turnout of the black vote. They felt there were plenty of white people in Selma who'd had their fill of Smitherman.

White moderates, including the editors at the *Times-Journal*, were saying that Selma had progressed beyond crude racial politics. They wrote editorials saying voters would be objective and choose on the basis of non-racial qualifications. They implied that if Reese didn't make the campaign a racial thing, he would get white votes. I think Reese and Perkins genuinely believed this. Reese had been on the City Council for twelve years. Operating day to day in the predominantly white world downtown, you hear constantly that racism is not a problem and only extremists raise the matter. You also hear constantly that white people will vote for a reasonable and qualified black person.

We said they were dreaming. In the almost twenty years that blacks had been running for office in Selma and Dallas County, not one had ever gotten more than 3 percent of the white vote, whatever their qualifications or campaign messages. There was no reason to assume the mold would be broken with Reese. Indeed, his past civil rights record and the fact that he is a strong, independent-minded black man made the assumption almost outlandish.

We advised Reese to forget about 10 percent of the white vote and concentrate on turning out 55 percent of the black vote. Even in a black-white race, Smitherman at best would turn out about half the white voters. Reese and Perkins were not persuaded by our analysis of the situation and ran a campaign aimed at capturing 10 or 15 percent of the white voters.

In racially polarized Selma, what it takes to turn out black voters often turns off white voters, and vice versa. A black candidate going around pretending racism isn't a major problem will have a credibility problem in the black community. When a black candidate talks about racial harmony before racial justice, black people become skeptical. Does this mean the candidate won't do anything for black people if it upsets or causes disharmony with white people?

A look at black Selma in 1984 was unassailable evidence that we were a ways from parity with white Selma. A sort of quota system was in place for city boards, including the school board, and city departments. Blacks occupied positions on all of them, but every board in the city had a white majority, which meant that every decision about public policy was made by the white community. Only two city departments were headed by blacks;

one was sanitation. The other, personnel, was headed by Randall Williams, the funeral director Smitherman had appointed urban renewal director in the seventies.

To get a good black turnout, a black candidate must deal with racism in a forthright manner. Campaign speeches telling black people "the time has come to end the plantation system where Joe Smitherman is the head honcho and we get the crumbs" would have stirred up the black community and turned out many more voters than merely echoing Smitherman about crime, industry, and garbage.

The implausibility of trying to straddle the fence was evident when Reese was asked in a newspaper interview about city jobs. He was at pains to say he wouldn't fire or lay off any white people. As they moved away or retired, he would look for qualified blacks to fill the posts so that city jobs and top positions eventually would be 50–50, like the population. Smitherman immediately spread the word that Reese was going to institute a quota system. To the white community, this was unfair "reverse discrimination." At the courthouse, I heard white people say, "Well, Reese is for a quota system." They weren't going to vote for him anyway, but this gave them their reason. The black community was almost as turned off by Reese's comments as the white community. What I heard in black Selma was "Hell, he's saying white people are going to have to die before we get a fair share of jobs down there."

When the citizens of Selma went into the voting booths and pulled the levers, race was the only issue. Reese got at most 2 percent of the white vote and a miserable turnout of black votes. Smitherman won 60–40. He got 4 percent of the black vote after a campaign both candidates applauded as non-racial.

Two weeks after Reese lost, Jackie Walker, a thirty-five-year-old black woman involved in youth activities with Rose, filed to run for Dallas County tax collector. Smitherman's margin of victory had been embarrassing and discouraging and Jackie ran to try to prevent defeatism from setting in. Most black people started out thinking she couldn't win. Though we made up 55 percent of the population of Dallas County, we made up only about 48 percent of registered voters. No black person had won office in

Dallas County for more than a hundred years. As far as I know, no woman ever had. In 1984, all county officials were white men, with the exception of an elderly black woman, Dr. Catherine Bozeman, appointed to the Dallas County school board when a board member died. Jackie's opponents in the September primary were two white men. One of them, Tommy Powell, was chief clerk in the retiring tax collector's office.

Hank thought Jackie had a chance and managed her campaign. He figured white turnout would be low in the September primary because there weren't any major races. He made the decision to run an almost secret campaign, arranging small meet-the-candidate gatherings in black people's homes rather than holding mass meetings. She talked to folk one-on-one and made a good impression.

Jackie, a native of Huntsville, was married to Nathaniel Walker, a young man from Selma. They met at college in Huntsville, lived in New York City while Nathaniel studied law and she finished college, then came South in 1977 to make Selma their home. Jackie quickly became known and loved in black Selma because she got deeply involved in community activities with Rose. When she ran for tax collector, she was executive director of the Black Belt Human Resources Council, an umbrella organization for youth and community efforts. She was short, brown-skinned, cute, kind of shy but easy to laugh and smile.

In the house meetings, she told folk, "We need a black person in the county courthouse. Sometimes black folk aren't even treated cordially. We need to be on the inside." I took her around to black churches all over the county on the two Sundays before the primary. Because her campaign was low-key and the white community and black community are so separate, neither the white community nor the *Times-Journal* took note of it. I don't think they figured Tommy Powell was in any trouble from this black woman few had heard of. In her picture in the newspaper, she looked younger than her years—a small woman with big round glasses. But black people turned out for her. Powell got more votes than she did, but not a majority, so Jackie, who came in second, faced him in a runoff two weeks later.

At this point, Jackie surfaced as far as white people were concerned. What they saw in her interviews on television and in the newspaper was a young, soft-spoken, articulate, intelligent college graduate. I think she probably got some white votes, probably women. There certainly was nothing threatening about her, and once again, I think the white community assumed that Powell would win. He led in the primary and presumably the losing white candidate's votes would go to him. But Hank and Rose mounted an impressive effort, with all kinds of folk going door to door on election day, and increased black turnout by almost 50 percent. And again the black-owned United Cab Company had their cars out all over the county driving people to the polls free of charge.

The election was so close we had to wait for the last box to come in before the winner was declared. Jackie won by 42 votes out of 10,000 cast. Rarely in Alabama are there Republican candidates in local races, so winning the Democratic primary runoff means winning the election. We had a jubilant celebration at the courthouse. Nathaniel, Jackie's husband, put her on his shoulders so she could touch the sign over the tax collector's office.

Our celebration was premature. Powell mounted a write-in campaign, something I'm certain he wouldn't have done had he been defeated by a white man. But black folk came out once more for Jackie in the general election in November, and once more, she won.

Before she could take office, Jackie was killed in a car accident on an icy bridge. Hundreds of folk came to her funeral. It then fell to the all-white county commission to appoint a replacement. We gathered petitions asking them to appoint Nathaniel or, if not him, another black person. It was a custom in Dallas County for spouses to be appointed when elected officials died. At least twenty names were submitted—teachers, an IRS auditor, several administrators of agencies.

The commission ignored the black community and, in May 1985, voted 4–1 to appoint Tommy Powell as tax collector. They didn't discuss it or explain their reasons to the group of black citizens waiting to hear their decision.

"To hell with them." That's what I said when we walked out en masse. A few nights later, several hundred black people packed

Brown Chapel and some stayed until 6:30 in the morning. It was hot! When after a hundred years we succeeded in electing a black, the historic nature of it alone should have been enough to select one of the people we put forward. And to appoint the man she defeated, a man who ran a write-in campaign against her, was spitting on Jackie's grave. This phrase was used by I don't know how many people who got up to speak that night.

We formed an organization called COPE, Committee to Oust Political Enemies, to work on voter registration to put out the incumbents in the next election. This was long-range, though. Some speakers insisted on closing down the mall immediately with picket lines and boycotts, or removing black children from school. There was talk of forming a human chain around the courthouse. One example of the depth of feeling was my father sending a letter to the newspaper protesting the insensitivity of county government to the feelings of its black citizens. He is not a public man and that is the only time I've ever known him to take such a stand.

We feared an explosion could come from almost anywhere and might not be nonviolent. We needed to take some direct action to let off steam—and quickly. So Hank, Rose, Edwin, Perry Varner, Dan Rutledge of the Black Leadership Council, and I came early to the next week's commission meeting, took the commission's seats before they got there, and symbolically appointed Nathaniel tax collector. The commission had to meet somewhere else.

The newspaper called our sit-in a "childish stunt." Somebody filed a complaint against Hank, Rose, and me with the Alabama Bar Association, which initiated an investigation and brought formal charges against us for engaging in conduct unbecoming lawyers. Mort Stavis, an associate of William Kunstler at the Center for Constitutional Rights in New York, came down and defended us at the hearing. The bar decided to take no action against us.

There were white people in Selma who thought a black person should have been appointed. More than a few told me so after Powell was named. At least one white person wrote a Letter to the Editor to that effect. But none organized a petition drive among white voters or joined our drive. In my view, they were afraid of what their white friends would say if they joined with black people in pushing something controversial. Sometimes I think white people in Selma have no backbone. Then I have to reflect that few people of any color take actions their peers disapprove. In any case, Tommy Powell remains the Dallas County tax collector.

A few weeks after our sit-in, a young white man called my office and said he and a friend wanted to come to talk to me.

"About what?" I asked.

"Improving race relations," he said. "We have an idea that might work." He told me about a biracial supper club in Montgomery.

I put no stock in biracial committees. Two or three of them had come and gone since 1965 without accomplishing anything. Typically, they were formed *after* something happened that outraged the black community and were used by white leaders to substitute talk for doing anything about black grievances. The committees met for a few months, discussed ideas, and expressed good intentions. Then they faded away as angry feelings subsided. None of the important gains made by black people in Selma—integration, voting, jury service, employment—came as a result of white people sitting down with black people and deciding it was the right thing to do.

But this fella sounded seriously concerned and I told him to come on over. He and his friend were young, late twenties. One owned a video store; the other worked for him. They told me the Friendly Supper Club in Montgomery was started by an anonymous person who sent letters inviting a group of black people and white people to eat together and asked each of them to invite a guest of the opposite race. They met and ate together monthly, making an effort to invite new people. These young men wanted to start something similar in Selma.

I figured, Hell, it couldn't hurt and might be fun. I said I'd supply the black names and make the announcement in my column in the newspaper. I asked the young men if they had any political ambitions. One flatly told me he'd like to get elected to the county commission at some point. I was impressed with his honesty. We decided to urge on the group at the first meeting that no politicians become members. Previous biracial gatherings were semi-official discussions between black and white leaders, about half of whom were politicians. We thought maybe ordinary folk could do better. We called it the Salt and Pepper Club.

We met the first time at the Tally Ho Restaurant, a place that became a private club after integration to keep black people out. Father Robinson, who by this time had left Selma for a parish in Detroit, integrated it in the early 1970s with some black airmen from Craig Field.

I agreed to be the emcee. About forty people came—housewives, teachers, a bank president, ordinary citizens. They looked apprehensive so I cracked a few jokes on myself to break the ice.

"I told Vivian I was concerned about being able to find a white friend to bring along. She said I didn't hardly have a black friend."

As we ate, people talked about the hostages on the hijacked TWA airplane in Beirut, mortgages, their children. After supper, I called on a few people to stand and give their opinions about the club. Their speeches were quite emotional, full of phrases like "a new beginning," "tearing down the walls of prejudice and fear," "working together because we all love Selma."

We met once a month. The club grew as other people came in. Most of the black people were middle-class. The white people were middle-class but mostly not the upper middle class that runs Selma. We talked about a long list of civic projects—noncontroversial, of course—and raised some money. One time a white preacher made a conservative speech against welfare. I was quite pleased when some white people lit into him.

Then the two fellas who started it got in trouble. The one who owned the video store said he'd fired the other one for stealing money. The other man denied all the charges and said he had permission to take the money. Both called me and accused the other of being racist and using the club for some other end. It was embarrassing. Attendance at the gatherings was declining anyway, but this kind of killed it. It lasted about eight months.

The Salt and Pepper Club didn't change a damn thing. But I guess it established that regular black and white people could sit down together and not have to play games. When I had cases out of town, I'd rush back for it. I didn't want to miss it. I stayed there on a couple occasions after the dinner was over shooting the bull with some of the white participants. One night I told them about Orzell and me out on the road, and they were amazed that stuff like that went on. I love an audience and I got a kick out of it.

CHAPTER 25

Ironies All Around

For the first meeting of the Salt and Pepper Club, on June 18, 1985, I rushed from Mobile where we were selecting jurors for the highly controversial vote fraud trial of Albert and Evelyn Turner and Spencer Hogue. The trial itself began a few days later in the somber gray stone federal building in Selma across the street from the Dallas County Courthouse.

The Turner case had ironies all around. On the Edmund Pettus Bridge on Bloody Sunday, Albert marched in the second row, behind John Lewis, and Albert marched in Marion the night state troopers killed Jimmie Lee Jackson, the incident that led to the march to Montgomery. Since the Voting Rights Act, Albert had been Mr. Voter Registration in Perry County.

But now, in 1985, he stood accused of cheating black folk of the vote he literally risked his life to gain for them. The government said he'd altered the absentee ballots of twenty-six elderly black voters—picked the ballots up from these voters, crossed off the voters' choices, and unlawfully marked the ballots for the candidates he was supporting. His accuser was the U.S. Department of Justice, which until then had been his ally. Since the passage of the Voting Rights Act, the Department of Justice had refused to pre-clear any number of new, discriminatory voting procedures in Perry County and routinely sent election monitors to prevent intimidation of black voters. Now the Department of

Justice had joined with local white officials to prosecute Albert.

All over the Black Belt, the FBI was knocking on doors and taking affidavits. Just before Albert's trial, the Department of Justice indicted four black voting activists in Greene County on similar charges, including Spiver Gordon, an SCLC leader whose civil rights activities, like Albert's, went back to the 1960s. Vote fraud investigations were underway in Lowndes, Wilcox, and Sumter, all majority-black counties where blacks had recently won political control. The investigations were directed at local black leaders who championed the struggle that led to political gains for black people. The Justice Department spokesman told the press that as many as forty more indictments might come.

In the tense weeks before the trial, black leaders in Alabama and Washington publicly accused the Reagan Administration of using the prosecutorial might of the government against Albert and the others to discourage black people from voting and to intimidate black activists—in effect, to destroy the black political machine in the Black Belt. We argued that black Alabamians vote solidly for the Democratic Party and that our growing margin of votes, unless checked, could defeat the 1986 re-election bid of Alabama's Republican senator, Jeremiah Denton, a right-wing conservative and a staunch supporter of the Reagan Administration. The Justice Department denied these charges. They countered that the government was only enforcing the law, that the investigations and indictments came in response to complaints from some Alabama blacks against other Alabama blacks.

The election at issue in Albert's trial—the one in which he'd allegedly changed absentee ballots—was the September 1984 Democratic primary, in which two slates of local candidates, all black, competed for county offices. Albert and his organization, the Perry County Civic League, supported one slate of blacks, including Albert's brother, Wilbert, who was running for the county commission. Candidates on the opposing black slate complained of vote fraud, and the Justice Department said it was simply responding to their complaints.

It was hardly that simple. In Perry and Greene Counties, a new phenomenon had developed by the early 1980s. Once the white courthouse crowd could no longer elect whites, they began to promote for office black people who thought the way they did or whom they could control. Instead of white candidates running against black candidates for county commission, school board, and other county offices, you now had white-sponsored black candidates against black candidates.

Some of the "coalition" blacks were of the old school—almost bowing, looking to a white person for direction. Some were younger people I consider opportunists. None took a risk to get black people the vote or anything else or ever criticized white wrongs. They waited for their own best shot and took it. The coalition blacks and their white sponsors say, "The time has come for blacks and whites to work together," which sounds fine. But when you looked at what they did once elected, it was obvious the coalition wasn't Martin Luther King's dream of whites working *with* blacks; it was a 1980s version of the old arrangement I'd seen as a child of whites working *through* blacks for white ends. Following white direction, some black coalition officials even lobbied against taxes for the 99 percent black schools.

More often than not, those "coalition" candidates old enough to have been adults in the 1960s had opposed Martin Luther King and local blacks who were actively involved in demonstrations and marches. Albert and the others indicted or under investigation were the premier demonstrators and marchers. Albert, a Perry County native, was the state coordinator of SCLC in Alabama in the 1960s. When King was killed, he led the mule train that pulled King's coffin on an old wagon.

Albert went to Alabama A & M, but he deliberately affects a manner opposite that of a typical college graduate. He's hefty, dark-skinned, and has a slow, country way of talking. For at least a decade, he worked with the Southwest Farmers Cooperative Association and later became an insurance agent. But the Perry County Civic League, an organization similar to the Dallas County Voters League, was his real vocation. The business of voting became his obsession—getting people registered, getting them to the polls, getting them to vote for local candidates the league endorsed.

Marie Foster has a book, almost fifteen years old, listing the elderly people in Dallas County and the people who work at jobs outside the county. She got them registered to vote; then later, as they got old or ill, encouraged them to sign applications for absentee ballots. At election time, she goes back and discusses with them how they should vote. These folk feel more loyalty to Marie than to any candidate on the ballot. What they want to do is vote the way she votes or, as they often put it, "the way y'all are voting," which meant ADC's endorsements.

Albert plays a similar but expanded role in the northern part of Perry County. His wife, Evelyn, became a notary public. Albert knows who's in the hospital or nursing home, whose children are away at college, who lives in Perry County but works in Tuscaloosa or Selma. At election time, he can tell you just about how many people are going to vote absentee and name two-thirds of them.

Somewhat like Mayor Daley's political machine in Chicago, the Civic League didn't just come around at election time. They helped people get on the rolls of social-security, food-stamp, and poverty programs. They helped folk when a son needed a bond to get out of jail or somebody had to go to the hospital but didn't have insurance. The Civic League would take up contributions to help. A number of the elderly people who voted absentee could not read or write. But even those who could often relied on Albert and his people in deciding which candidate to vote for. For some folk, there wasn't but one candidate in every race, and that was Albert.

In a sense, their reliance on Albert was an extension of the old plantation thing—like Lucius's mother's reliance on the white man in the case Orzell and I tried in Perry County in the early 1960s. Life moves in stages. It evolves; it rarely leaps. Claude Brown wasn't altogether wrong when he said, "You cannot free an ignorant unskilled man." Martin Luther King in a way was a crutch. When he said "Let's march," it wasn't a matter of the rank and file debating the issue. This preacher and father figure knew what was best. The crucial difference is that Martin and Albert weren't seeking to exploit but to help.

Roy Johnson, the local district attorney, sought unsuccessfully several times to persuade a Perry County grand jury to indict Albert in connection with ballots and voting. He's the DA blacks helped elect; my son Ronnie still works for him. I objected to Roy's trying to dig up evidence against the Civic League to satisfy dyed-in-the-wool whites. Roy insisted he hadn't prejudged anything, but blacks had brought him complaints about Albert's operation. I told him I could name the blacks who brought the allegations to him and we both knew what that was all about. The Civic League wasn't doing anything different from the "coalition," the White Citizens' Council, or other white groups promoting candidates and collecting absentee ballots. Hell, Albert learned it from whites.

The grand jury refused to return any indictments. Roy made public statements that the predominantly black grand jury was afraid to indict a prominent local black. He wrote to the U.S. Department of Justice, asking them to assist or take over his investigation. Two years later, the Justice Department gave approval for Jefferson Beauregard Sessions, the U.S. Attorney for the Southern District of Alabama, to join Johnson in a joint local-federal investigation. This was a departure from prior policy. Federal investigations previously had been limited to fraud matters that affected the outcome of federal contests. The only federal contest in Albert's case was the Senate primary contest, and none of the alleged ballot changes related to that race.

The FBI and local law enforcement monitored a meeting of the Civic League on September 3, 1984, the day before the election. Later, FBI agents hid in the Marion post office and watched Albert and Spencer Hogue, an active member of the Civic League, place the absentee ballots they collected into a mail slot. The agents opened the mail box, seized the ballots, and took them to Mary Auburtin, the white circuit clerk and absentee ballot manager.

Roy advised the "coalition" candidates, who were opposed by the Civic League, to file a lawsuit against Mrs. Auburtin that was a sort of election contest in advance. The coalition blacks said they believed election fraud was being committed by their opponents and the absentee ballots should be numbered in case of a recount. Absentee ballots come in two envelopes—the outer envelope addressed to the circuit clerk and an inner envelope with the voter's notarized signature. Normally, once the signature is verified, the ballot is removed and is no longer identified with a particular voter; it becomes a secret ballot.

Mrs. Auburtin didn't object to the suit; she was a supporter of the coalition slate. The white circuit judge granted permission to number the absentee ballots collected by the Civic League to match a corresponding number on the inside envelopes, so investigators would know whose ballot was whose. A three-judge federal panel later ruled that this voting change, which violated the secrecy of the ballot, was illegal because it had not been pre-cleared by the civil rights division of the Department of Justice. The Justice Department got its hands crossed; its criminal division then used the illegal order. Also, the issue of a recount became moot because the changes had no effect on the outcome. The "coalition" candidates won.

After the election, FBI agents took the ballots around to the little houses and shanties of the voters, all of them black and most of them elderly. Is this your ballot? Is this how you voted? The Civic League collected 504 absentee ballots out of the 750 absentee ballots filed in that election. The FBI concentrated on ballots where a coalition candidate had been scratched out and changed to someone favored by the Civic League. Did you make this change? Who picked up your ballot?

Sessions's office in Mobile subpoenaed some of the voters to come to the courthouse in Marion. There, surrounded by FBI agents and other law-enforcement people, they were put on buses for the three-hour trip to Mobile to testify to a grand jury. Albert called our law office and said the FBI was in Perry County asking questions and wanted to interview him. Hank and I said we didn't think he ought to be making statements, but Albert said he wanted to talk, he had nothing to hide.

"At least wait till we get there," I said. "You know how complex Alabama voting laws are. You can say something that will get you in trouble without even knowing it." Albert agreed to wait, but by the time Hank and I got over to Marion, he was talking a mile a minute.

We also advised him not to testify before the grand jury, but he didn't listen to us there, either. Off he went to Mobile to tell the grand jury in detail his system of obtaining absentee ballots—

encouraging folk to apply, collecting the ballots at their homes, mailing them. He said the changes were made on the ballots at the voters' direction or with their permission, and he didn't deny persuading some to change their ballots. He was proud of the trust voters had in him. He bragged about it.

Judging from the questions the grand jurors asked Albert, they were turned off by his statements that people voted the way he and his organization wanted. This, to them, was abuse. But the abuse of these old black folk took place a long time ago and not at the hands of Albert Turner. Albert was using their vote to make county government more responsive to black people, so there wasn't anything stupid or foolish about black people following his endorsements.

At the time of the Turner investigation, the Justice Department announced a new policy of prosecuting individuals for "more subtle" forms of election fraud. This policy targeted "political participants" who "seek out the elderly, the socially disadvantaged, or the illiterate, for the purpose of subjugating their electoral will." In my view, the Reagan Department of Justice, like the grand jurors, wanted to disenfranchise all but their type voters. People who don't possess, in their way of thinking, a certain minimum knowledge or independence of judgment shouldn't vote. But who's going to decide what is independence of judgment? Should Miss Ann at the top of the hill, with her college degree and notions of independence, have a right denied Aunt Jane at the bottom of the hill, who chooses to allow Albert or Marie Foster to guide her choices?

Albert and Spencer were indicted for unlawfully changing 26 of the 504 absentee ballots collected and mailed by the Civic League. Evelyn was charged with being part of the conspiracy and for notarizing ballots out of the presence of the voters.

Hank formed a defense committee to get more lawyers involved and to focus national attention on what was happening. We needed trial lawyers experienced in taking on the government in unpopular causes. In addition to Robert Turner and me, he enlisted Howard Moore, the Oakland, California, lawyer who successfully defended Angela Davis; Mort Stavis of the Center for Constitutional Rights in New York, one of the best constitutional lawyers in the country; James Liebman, Patrick DuVal, and C. Lani Guinear from the NAACP Legal Defense Fund; Dennis Balske from the Southern Poverty Law center, a white civil rights group in Montgomery; Margaret Carey, an attorney from Greenville, Mississippi, on the staff of the Center for Constitutional Rights; and John England, an attorney from Tuscaloosa.

The "Marion Three" became a *cause célèbre* in the civil rights community, a symbol of the way the Reagan Justice Department was turning on black people. On the day the trial opened, there were picketers wearing *Free the Marion 3* T-shirts on the steps of the federal building. Clarence Mitchell, president of a national association of state legislators, and Walter Fauntroy, Washington, D.C.'s congressional delegate, stirred national interest. Nevertheless, there was a kind of wait-and-see attitude in much of black Alabama. The Justice Department was making statements both in Washington and in Mobile that they had a strong case: just wait till you hear the evidence.

We opened with a flurry of motions, few of which we won from U.S. District Judge Emmett Cox, who was newly appointed by the Reagan Administration. During the discovery process, we obtained from the government absentee ballots gathered by other political groups in the same election where votes were crossed off and changed in favor of coalition candidates. None of these voters was questioned nor were their ballots numbered, and we made a motion claiming selective prosecution. Cox denied the motion and barred us from using selective prosecution as a defense; he also ordered us to keep race out of the trial. This was strictly a matter of vote fraud, he said.

Race was hard to avoid, and it caused Howard Moore to be judged in contempt of court. He was questioning Mrs. Auburtin, the circuit clerk and absentee ballot manager, about two absentee ballots she voluntarily sent to Tuscaloosa County. We were attempting to show she knew that these voters, a white couple, no longer lived in Perry County. The husband was the county's former superintendent of schools. I leaned over and told Howard, "Ask her, Are they white?" Howard did, and Judge Cox found him in contempt. Mort later appealed to the Eleventh Circuit and the contempt citation was overturned.

Our defense team—seven blacks and three whites—took up two long tables. Robert, Howard, and I represented Albert. Dennis, Lani, Patrick, and James represented Spencer. Mort, Margaret, and John represented Evelyn. It is a rare thing to have that much legal talent pulled together in one case and I found it invigorating. Lawyers don't come any better than Mort Stavis and Howard Moore, and I loved to tease Lani Guinear, a smart, sophisticated black woman educated at Radcliffe.

We were involved in a case that at one level pitted black accommodationists against civil rights types, and I would have thought a black woman who went to Radcliffe would be more on the accommodationist side. When we went to lunch, I was fascinated to see whether Lani wanted to go to Lannie's BBQ Spot, a black place, or some white restaurant downtown. How black was she? She liked many places, but I think she liked the BBQ Spot a little better. While she was in Selma, she called her boyfriend every day, and I wrongfully assumed he was white. When I went to an NAACP conference six months later, she pointedly introduced me to her black boyfriend. She surprised me, and I came to have great admiration for her.

The majority of the government's twenty-some witnesses—black absentee voters—were over sixty years old. One old woman came in a wheelchair. The prosecution hired a nurse to accompany some others. Several of the witnesses surprised the prosecutors by testifying that they gave Albert or Spencer permission to change their ballots. They said they'd already marked their ballots when Albert or Spencer came to collect them. When told that some of the people they voted for weren't the ones the Civic League was "going with," they said, "Well, fix it for me." There had been an unusual amount of confusion during that election because the Civic League, for tactical reasons, decided not to put out a sample ballot or announce their preferences on the radio.

The prosecutors put FBI agents on the stand to say these witnesses had told them their ballots were changed *without* permission. They suggested someone had "gotten to" the witnesses. Most prosecutors take the position that a first statement is correct. Any subsequent statement is a deliberate change for a deliberate purpose and is made under pressure.

We argued that the first statements were made under pressure. The average black person in Perry County, especially an elderly black person, is frightened when an FBI agent knocks on the door, flashes a badge, and starts asking about "irregularities" on a ballot. They understandably do not assume white law enforcement would be coming to their door to help them. Robert talked to many of the witnesses, and they thought they'd broken some law. Maybe changing a ballot was illegal. The natural inclination is to say, "I didn't do it. I didn't change it."

The oldest witness, Willie Lee, ninety-two, was afraid to admit he even voted. In his case, the absentee ballot wasn't changed; he claimed somebody else must have voted it and submitted it for him. The government had his absentee application, and he said he had been persuaded to apply for one. But he said he never got it; the ballot submitted in his name and notarized by Evelyn Turner wasn't his.

Some witnesses gave contradictory testimony. An elderly woman, Eva Lou Smith, told prosecutors she didn't vote in the primary. "I ain't gonna lie," she declared on the witness stand.

"You know nothing about this ballot?" the prosecutor asked.

"No, I don't," she answered.

When Robert asked if she had voted in the September primary at issue, she said, "Yes, I think I did." She said she authorized Spencer to help her "decide how to vote." Robert then asked if her ballot indicated the same choice she made when she voted. She paused and said, "I can't see too good."

Many of the folk said on the witness stand the same thing they told the FBI at their houses: They hadn't changed their ballots or authorized any changes. On cross-examination, though, several said they couldn't read or write and told Spencer or Albert to "pick their ballot." But no, they didn't know anything about any changes, they said.

Others, while insisting they didn't make the changes, gave endorsements for Albert and Spencer. "They're nice boys. I been knowin' Albert all my life. I know his daddy. I know his mama and that's his little brother sittin' there beside him. Albert's been pickin' my ballot for sixteen years." Few could remember who they did vote for, if they didn't vote the way their ballots indicated.

The government's strongest witnesses were six members of one family, some of whom were young and adamant in insisting that their ballots were changed without permission. But they contradicted each other in other aspects of their testimony and some admitted that they lied on their absentee ballot application, stating they would be out of town when, in fact, they were voting absentee as a convenience.

Confusion increased because the FBI had taken two or three different statements from some of the witnesses. The statements did not necessarily conflict on the main point of changing ballots but were contradictory in other ways that raised credibility questions. The government was overzealous. When the FBI learned that Robert had talked to some of the witnesses, they went out behind him to be sure folk weren't going to change their stories. Each time, they wrote up a statement. In the trial, the prosecutors chose the statement most favorable to their case. Didn't you say this? They tried to withhold the other statements from us, but we knew about them. A couple times the judge had to stop the trial and order the government to produce a statement they hadn't shown us. This hurt the government's credibility.

When the prosecution completed its case, the judge reduced the counts against Albert to sixteen. We brought in character witnesses, including Andrew Young, the mayor of Atlanta. Andy, once the pastor of a church in Marion, testified about working with Albert in SCLC. "Dr. King was very much impressed with Albert Turner," he said. "I have trusted Mr. Turner in many difficult situations over the last twenty-five years."

The prosecution read into the record Albert's grand jury testimony in which he explained the operation of the Civic League and insisted that ballots were changed only at the voters' direction. While maintaining that the voters did not give such authorization, the government also attempted to argue that voters cannot ask other individuals to fill out or change their ballots. We asked the judge for a ruling, and he gave a charge to the jury—seven blacks and five whites—that proxy voting is legal.

Judge Cox wanted to move the trial to a conclusion because the jury was sequestered and he, the court staff, and the prosecutors were from Mobile, so the closing arguments came on July 4. All the lawyers made some reference to the Edmund Pettus

Bridge. E. T. Rollison, the assistant U.S. attorney who prosecuted the case, said no man was above the law no matter who
his friends are or who he marched with. Albert had lost sight of
his purpose. He was bent on getting power by any means and
taking advantage of people who couldn't read or write.

Howard Moore said the case would be a turning point for black
voting rights, either signaling that the federal government can
intimidate black voters or reasserting the rights fought for by
Turner and others. Mort said the jurors would have a great deal
of impact on democracy in the region. "What happens to the
democratic process if the people who win elections and have
control of law enforcement can routinely go into court and kill
off the opposition by criminal prosecution?"

We decided beforehand that the other lawyers would deal with
the specific evidence relating to particular ballots. I would come
last with an emotional appeal aimed particularly at the blacks on
the jury. I developed a double refrain: "The government would
not come; it did not come" and "Who is this Albert Turner?"

"The government did not come when the Ku Klux Klan drove
blacks from the polls. It did not come when black men in Alabama
were hung from trees for daring to think politics. It did not come
when white politicians legislated a whole race into political oblivion . . . Now, a scant twenty years after blacks fought, marched,
bled, and died to gain the vote, the government comes to criminal
court to prosecute three black people. The government comes
allegedly to save black voters from other blacks. It comes to argue
about sixteen votes out of thousands cast, sixteen votes that did
not even affect the outcome of the election.

"The government has singled out this black man in Alabama.
I ask, 'Who is this Albert Turner?' He is a man who risked his
life so blacks in Alabama could vote; a man who faced police
dogs and armed state troopers when the government would not
come. It did not come." I argued that it didn't make sense that
a man who had sacrificed as much as Albert would cheat black
voters or that he had to change folks' ballots without their permission. They thought enough of him to give him permission.

The jury returned a not guilty verdict in less than three hours.
We were overjoyed; the government was stunned.

Not long after the trial, a group of Alabama blacks went to

Evelyn Turner (with hand up) and Albert Turner (next to her) and I as we emerged from the federal building in Selma after a jury found them not guilty (© *Montgomery Advertiser*)

Washington to see Edwin Meese, the U.S. Attorney General. Joe Reed arranged it through the National Education Association. We were ushered into a large room in the Justice Department building. We sat down at a massive table and in came the Attorney General followed by about twenty Justice Department lawyers and staff, all male, all white. After the introductions, Meese commented, "Gentleman, there's one thing we all can agree to. Women do not constitute a minority." It was intended to be funny and his aides laughed on cue. Nobody on our side of the table cracked a smile. We sat there stone-faced until the laughter on the other side died down.

We told Meese we thought the prosecutions were politically and racially motivated. Meese said he'd heard those charges but they didn't make sense to him. These were complaints by blacks against other blacks for vote fraud. I explained the history and context, the coalition, the fact that the Department of Justice had not intervened when we brought evidence of absentee vote fraud by white officials in the 1970s. Meese said, "Well, now, that's before my time." I said we had to deal with the government as an ongoing entity. Why, when blacks won power, did the policy change?

We showed Meese absentee ballots from the Perry County election, some collected by Albert, others collected by other political groups that showed erasures and votes changed to "coalition" candidates. Why were only ballots collected by the Civic League questioned? Meese began writing furiously on a yellow legal pad and turned to the lawyers with him. They said the government received complaints only about the Civic League. We pointed out that the government, nonetheless, had the ballots; We got the ballots from the government. Meese stayed with us more than an hour, listening and writing. He said we had raised some serious matters and he would be in touch with us. We never heard from him.

Spiver Gordon and the two other voting activists in Greene County were tried in Tuscaloosa in October 1985. The jury pool there was more white, and the government used its preemptory strikes to eliminate all the blacks, so Spiver and the others were tried by an all-white jury. The jury deliberated for five days—at one point, the judge practically ordered them to reach a verdict— and found Spiver guilty of four counts out of twenty-three. The two others were acquitted; a third had pled guilty earlier to a misdemeanor.

The Eleventh Circuit Court of Appeals overturned the verdict in Spiver's case and returned it to the district court. The appellate judges found that we had presented enough evidence that other Greene County groups, white and "coalition," had committed the same alleged offenses as Spiver to be entitled to a hearing on selective prosecution. They ordered the government to provide the defense with information on all the vote fraud cases it pursued and evidence of fraud it did not pursue.

Also, the prosecution was ordered to give racially neutral reasons for striking the blacks from the jury. Six months after Spiver's trial, the U.S. Supreme Court ruled in *Batson* v. *Kentucky* that prosecutors could not strike blacks from a jury pool on racial grounds. Heretofore, they were not required to make any explanation as to why blacks were stricken. In areas where there are no large concentrations of blacks, *Batson* now guarantees the presence of at least a few black jurors.

I got a call from an assistant U.S. attorney saying that if I filed a motion to dismiss the charges against Spiver, the government would not oppose it. That was the end of the vote fraud prosecutions. None of the other investigations and promised indictments came. It was all over.

While the investigations were going on, Hank came in my office one day with some books on the post-Reconstruction era in Alabama, when all the black elected officials were removed from office and black people disenfranchised. This happened soon after the politicians in Washington found it advantageous to make a deal with the South and removed the federal troops, while the abolitionists went on to other causes. Hank was concerned that something similar was happening again. Did the door open for black people once every hundred years, stay open for a decade or two, then close again?

There's some truth in this. The difference is, it was relatively easy for the South to disenfranchise black people in the 1870s; it's not so easy today. In 1986, U.S. Representative Richard Shelby defeated Jeremiah Denton in the Senate race with black votes providing the margin of victory. Also, blacks successfully persuaded Alabama Senator Howell Heflin and other key members of the Senate Judiciary Committee that Jeff Sessions, the U.S. attorney who prosecuted Albert and whom Reagan had nominated for a federal judgeship, should not be confirmed.

Judge Brevard Hand, in his chambers in Mobile, told me I had stuck a knife in Sessions's back. I responded, "He did it to himself."

PART FIVE

1985 - 1990

Black elected and appointed officials in Selma and Dallas County in November 1989. Marie Foster is standing in the front. In the second row, third from left (and next to me), is Bernard Lafayette, who came to Selma to make a speech at a Men's Day service honoring these officials (© Lawrence Williams)

Introduction

When Jesse Jackson came to Selma a few weeks before Super Tuesday, 1988, to speak to a crowd of citizens and schoolchildren— mostly black—in the gymnasium at Selma University, Mayor Smitherman welcomed him to town, saying, "It is an honor to have you in Selma as a candidate for President of the United States. Some twenty-three years ago, you marched with others to give all Americans the right to vote, not just blacks, but Hispanics, poor whites. Course, I was on the other side then, but it has helped all of us." He gave Jackson a key to the city.

Many in white Selma do not share this positive assessment of the changes brought about by the civil rights movement. Earl Goodwin, Selma's white state senator, said in an interview on the MacNeil-Lehrer NewsHour during the 1988 Democratic Convention that school desegregation was a mistake and that "the separation of the races has been for the good of the country."

He was speaking for a number of his constituents. It's hard to put a figure on how many, but a sizable group of white residents believe that Selma has changed too much, and mostly for the worse. Some attribute everything from the way young people act today to the decline of the city's economy to integration and the growing power and freedom of black people. These are the people who send their children to one of the two private all-white schools (there's now a private Christian school as well as Morgan Academy) and who attend all-white churches and belong to all-white clubs.

Another sizable group of white residents seems genuinely pained and embarrassed about at least some of the community's and their own actions and views in the 1960s and earlier. "A lot of the views I espoused in the sixties came from my father, deeply ingrained views on segregation, jury service, voting," said Henry Pitts, son of the late McLean Pitts, who was Jim Clark's attorney and the attorney for the city and county who fought on the other side of many civil rights suits filed by Chestnut and others. "I look back on arguments I made against voting by black people or blacks serving on juries and they seem asinine. But I was caught up in them and I didn't know why."

Pitts, who is an attorney, made these comments one day while he and Chestnut were having lunch together during the 1988 trial of Joe Duncan, a white state trooper they were co-defending on charges of murdering his fiancée. (As Pitts lunched with his black co-counsel, his black retainer, Walter Chambers, a very dark man in his forties who drives Pitts around, carries his briefcase, does errands, and keeps him company, waited for "Mr. Hinry" at the bar.)

Today, Selma (pop. 27,000), like other places in the Black Belt, is struggling to find jobs to replace its former agricultural economy. The main sources of employment now are small manufacturing plants, and the town constantly seeks to recruit more industry, especially since Craig Field closed in the late 1970s.

Selma's main selling points are cheap labor, an attractive community, a decent public-school system, and a relatively low crime rate, though crime is increasing as crack has come to town. Few homes, however, have barred windows or high fences, and Selma residents, black and white, keep furniture on their porches. The drawbacks, the recruiters say, are the relatively high rate of illiteracy and Selma's national image as a place with racial trouble.

Downtown Selma often wins awards for its preserved old storefronts, but nearly a third are vacant. The old black downtown— the Liston and Clay Lounge, Eddie Ferguson's café, Sam Washington's tailor shop—is almost gone, boarded up and abandoned.

The Drag is no more. All the streets in black Selma are paved now. Small complexes of one-story brick houses—some government-subsidized—have been developed on the outskirts of town or in former slum areas of black Selma cleared during the 1970s. But many of the old wooden shotgun houses remain and the physical difference between white and black Selma remains striking.

Some of Chestnut's classmates from Knox Academy, returning to Selma for the first time in many years for their fortieth class reunion in 1988, went by the houses where they used to live and found them unchanged. "Folk were still living in the little shotgun I grew up in. It looked like it hadn't even been painted since I left," one said. The returnees were equally struck by how much of Selma was available to them in 1988 compared to the 1940s.

Selma, now about 55 percent black, is governed by five white and five black councilmen elected from districts and a white council president and white mayor elected at large. There are black policemen—the highest-ranking is an assistant chief—black firemen, and two department heads, personnel and sanitation. Seven whites and six blacks serve on the Selma school board, which oversees a system that is about 70–30 black to white. In 1986, the board named a black superintendent of schools, Norwood Roussell, a school administrator from New Orleans. When Roussell moved to town in 1987, the question arose as to whether he would be invited—or allowed—to join the all-white Rotary Club and Selma Country Club. A group of young white business people encouraged Roussell to apply for membership in the Rotary and successfully fought for him to be admitted.

Roussell did not join the country club. Vaughn Russell, a young white attorney and city judge, said that a few years earlier when Oscar Adams, the black justice on the Alabama Supreme Court, was in Selma and expressed an interest in playing golf, Russell and a few other young men who belong to the country club called some officers to ask about bringing Adams as a guest. Russell said he was told he could bring Adams if he wanted. The club had no rules about whom members could bring as guests. But, Russell was told, "We can't assure you of your continuing membership" or the social consequences.

"We were ready to go forward anyway and called Oscar," said

Russell, a member of one of Selma's prominent families who said his perspective was broadened when his mentor at the University of Alabama Law School had him researching cases for the American Civil Liberties Union. "Oscar said he just wanted a relaxing afternoon. He didn't want to be in the spotlight." Superintendent Roussell hasn't pushed for membership, saying, "I don't want to pay $2,500 to play golf, and I didn't come to Selma to claw down racial barriers."

Social pressure not to break tradition or rank remains strong in white Selma, but it's not nearly as organized or devastating as in the days of the White Citizens' Council. It now takes the form of disapproval of one's peers rather than loss of business or ostracism, and what is considered acceptable is gradually expanding.

A few churches now have a racially mixed membership—notably the Catholic church, which merged its black and white congregations in 1971. Two of Selma's most prominent white churches, First Presbyterian and St. Paul's Episcopal, have no black members but say they would welcome them. Both hold occasional joint programs with black churches. When the daughter of Jean Martin, a reporter on the Times-Journal, *was married in St. Paul's in 1988, Chestnut, his wife, and about a dozen other black people attended the wedding. On the other hand, the white Central Baptist Church barred a black divinity student from Selma University who, on a dare from a professor, attempted to attend a Sunday service with two black women in September 1989. He wrote about their experience in a letter to the newspaper, and by the next Sunday, the church had revised its policy and allowed them in the sanctuary.*

On the Sunday before Martin Luther King Day, 1989, in the hallway of one of Selma's largest white churches, a junior-high-age white teen, obviously a student at one of Selma's all-white private schools, told another junior-high-age teen, obviously a student in public school, "We don't have tomorrow off. We don't have any niggers in our school."

In that same church that same day, however, the associate pastor used King's daughter, Yolanda, as the subject of the children's sermon. Several dozen white children in suits and dresses sat at the foot of the sanctuary as the pastor told them about how much Yolanda, when she was six, wanted to go to Funtown, the public amusement park in Atlanta. But her father had to tell her she couldn't go because the park didn't allow black people.

"How would you feel if you couldn't go someplace you really wanted to go because of your color?" the pastor asked.

"Sad," the children responded.

The Probability
of Miracles

One Sunday, my Uncle Preston came along with me to Greene County, where I was making a speech in a little rural church. This wasn't unusual; Preston and I have remained very close over all the years, going back to when I deviled him to teach me the tricks of gambling. He showed up at my house with a great big cowboy hat on. On the drive, he got on my case that I hadn't been giving his hair-products business enough attention. He was worried that his sons didn't have the maturity to run it if something happened to him. I agreed that the next day I'd give him as much time as he wanted.

Preston's worries vanished once the church service began. He loved to carry on like I do in church, holler back at the preacher, "I hear ya!" "Say it!" "Watch it, now." He enjoyed listening to me speak as much as I enjoy speaking, and because he was there, I gave an extra measure and really preached for about thirty minutes. Folk were jumping out of their seats. Preston grinned, hollered, and moved from pew to pew until he got down to the front row. Afterward on the church grounds, I could see his big Western hat moving around as he laughed and talked about business and politics.

As soon as we got in the car to go home, he began talking about his business again. He had plans he wanted me to work on. He had a brochure he wanted me to critique. He wore my

Our home since 1987 (© Penny Weaver)

ears out. I dropped him off at his home, but thirty minutes later he was at my house with the brochure. Less than an hour after he left, his son called and said Preston had keeled over and they'd called an ambulance. I rushed to the hospital. We waited. The doctor came out and told us Preston was gone.

I said at his funeral that Preston had taken a sixth-grade education, borrowed a million dollars from the federal government, and created a business with international outlets. But he never reached his full potential or realized his dream of cooperative black business ventures in the Black Belt. Blacks in Selma own a few retail stores and small businesses, but that's about it. And no black person sits on the board of any Selma bank.

Though I lost Preston, I finally gained my son Terry. He was released on parole in 1987 and went straight to Dillard University. He put aside his criminal career, works three jobs, and will graduate in 1992. Vivian is more at ease than in the last thirty years, but continues to complain that I'm not home enough or involved enough with the family. Rosalind works as a case manager for the clerk of the U.S. District Court in Montgomery. Ronnie still works for the DA's office. Gerald works for a corporation in California. My two youngest children are in college.

My dear mother has not mellowed in the least and remains a strong supporter of her white friends. My father keeps busy in the large garden behind my house. They live in a modest brick house five blocks from the law firm, and I visit them every day after work. We sit and watch the *MacNeil-Lehrer NewsHour* and my mother and I trade commentary.

The law firm continues to grow. We're now Chestnut Sanders Sanders Turner Williams and Pettway. Quite frequently now, we're associated in major negligence and malpractice litigation with large white law firms. Not long ago, I argued a case on behalf of a white man who was driving on a road in Sumter County, hit a hole in the road, ran into a bridge, and was impaled on the steering wheel. He lost a leg. David Johnson, the Birmingham prosecutor in the Annie Johnson case who now heads one of the most successful law firms in Alabama, associated our firm in that case. We bring David into some of our cases which require large sums of money to develop. We have one with him now against a railroad company on behalf of the family of a black woman who was run over by a train and killed.

At another level, we've maintained the firm in a manner that the Annie Joneses and Leroy Browns and all the rest are at home. They come daily and fill up the waiting room, and we give them as much time and effort as ever. Today in civil court we win more often than we lose, and in criminal court the innocent are less likely to be convicted. The criminal justice system has changed substantially since a cross section of citizens began sitting on juries, though no white person has ever been executed in Alabama for a crime against a black person.

I gave up personally representing county governments and all but one of the school boards, but the firm still represents many of them in the Black Belt. These officials want you to be there at every meeting to hold their hands, and I was late all the time, rushing to get to the meetings from someplace fifty miles away where I was trying a case. Wilcox County let me go and hired another law firm.

Hank sometimes puts a thousand miles a week on his car, going

The law firm (back row from left: Carlos Williams, Perry Varner, Hank Sanders; front row: Robert Turner, Rose Sanders, and I). Collins Pettway wasn't there for the picture (© Penny Weaver)

from county to county in his district, listening to complaints, attending meetings, and mediating disputes. He got legislation passed in 1985 that changed elections in the majority-black counties in his Senate district—the ones that had all or majority black governments—from at large to districts so a few whites could be elected directly rather than operating through the subterfuge of "coalitions." This has helped some. But whenever we're asked for a status report on the Black Belt, we say it's in a "transitional period" economically, politically, and socially. There remain a multitude of problems in this desperately poor region.

Knowing the many difficulties somewhat tempers my joy at new political gains. On occasions when a black wins office in a place that seems unthinkable, looking back at the sixties, national reporters come and sometimes ask me, "Aren't you excited?" My response is "Yes and no." I always have to look down the road.

I had exactly these feelings of pride and concern in September 1988, when I went to Hayneville, the seat of Lowndes County, to make the keynote speech at the swearing in of Hayneville's

first black mayor, John E. Hulett. The black community had a
parade through town with decorated cars, the high school band,
and children walking. The new mayor and council members—
three blacks, two whites—and those of us on the program sat on
a truck flatbed in front of the county courthouse where a banner
read, INAUGURATION 88: PROGRESS THROUGH COOPERATIVE
LEADERSHIP.

As always, a choir sang. A white minister prayed for leadership
and cooperation. A new black councilman said, "For the first
time in Hayneville, we have truly representative government—
black, white, and female. I know some of you out there may be
a little dismayed. Don't be. We don't come to destroy but to
build." The audience, mostly black, sat in folding chairs or stood
on the grassy square facing the courthouse. This is the same square
where other black folk were standing when I emerged from the
courthouse the day the then-white sheriff held the ax handle over
my head. John's father, also John Hulett, is now the sheriff. He's
a local fella who got involved with Stokely Carmichael when
Stokely set up shop in Lowndes. This also is the county where
the Klan shot Viola Liuzzo and Jonathan Daniels in 1965.

I spoke about what John's father and I were doing twenty-five
years earlier when John, the new mayor, was only eleven years
old. "I don't think we looked forward to this day. I don't think
we thought this day was possible. We only sought a better life
and were determined to have it." I talked about the possible and
the impossible; how so much that seemed impossible turned out
to be possible. I found the occasion extremely satisfying, but at
the same time, I knew damn well that John and the black councilmen weren't going to have an easy time of it.

When the ceremony ended, who should come up to say hello
but Drewey and Mary Aaron, who live in Lowndes County.
Drewey served close to nineteen years for his conviction for raping
the white woman in Montgomery. Mrs. Aaron took the bus once
a week to visit him, raised their children, and never lost faith that
he would get out, though he was on death row for years while
we appealed. I've never met anyone whose faith in God was
stronger than Mary Aaron's. Drewey became a model prisoner.
He worked in the library, and other inmates and guards looked

Mary and Drewey Aaron (© Al Benn)

up to him. They have grandchildren now. Just seeing the two of them made me feel good.

A few years before Drewey was paroled, William Fikes's grown son came over from Texas to see me. He was just a young boy when his father was convicted of raping the wife of an airman from Craig Field and attempting to rape the mayor's daughter. He said he wanted to get his daddy out of jail before his daddy died. I went to see Fikes at the penitentiary. He was pitiful, subservient to the point of embarrassment. Tears came to my eyes looking at what was left of him. I argued in federal court that his life sentence was based on an illegal confession thrown out in the rape case, but for tactical reasons, Peter Hall had only appealed the death sentence. The judge agreed. The state wasn't going to try Fikes again. He'd already served twenty years. So Fikes walked out and his boy took him to Texas.

Inevitably, Hank, Michael Figures, Dick Arrington, and other black elected officials in Alabama formed a new organization— the Alabama New South Coalition—which split off from ADC and Joe Reed in 1986. Since I helped build ADC, it was more

401

painful for me to leave, but I did. Problems that engulf black Alabama don't all have political solutions and I thought a state-wide black organization should broaden its approach. Joe was too politically oriented to be interested in anything but politics.

New South is deliberately different from ADC. Nobody heads the organization in perpetuity. Endorsements are made more democratically. The organization isn't a caucus within the Democratic Party, and though predominantly black, it's biracial. New South has committees dealing with minority economic development, the environment, and women's rights. It sponsors leadership camps for young people several times a year. I was asked to be chairman of the board. Dick Arrington was the first president. Later on, Hank became president and Dick and I became co-chairmen. New South now has more members and chapters than ADC and has considerable weight at the national and state level.

In Selma, blacks now are players. But the white community owns the ballpark, sets the rules, and calls the shots. So I was surprised when the Selma school board—still appointed by the majority-white City Council, still majority-white, still elite—appointed a black superintendent of schools. Joe Yelder's stand established that blacks could not be bypassed for top positions, but my attitude about the new superintendent, Norwood Roussell, was wait and see. Surely the board interviewed the man and apparently was satisfied he would protect white interests. What about black interests? Was he some kind of Trojan horse?

Roussell was in Selma for months before I met him. I felt some foreboding, afraid he might be an opportunistic Uncle Tom type who would do anything to keep his job and make our work more difficult because the board would now have a black superintendent to hide behind. He didn't turn out to be what I anticipated. He is opportunistic, but he nevertheless rocked the boat.

Roussell wasn't at work long before an organization of black parents called Best Education Support Team (BEST) sent a letter to the board asking it to do away with the system of three learning levels, where children essentially are tracked, and institute honors and remedial classes in some subjects instead. At Selma's genu-inely integrated schools—notably Westside Junior High and Selma High—the top level was almost entirely white, the bottom level almost entirely black, and the middle level a mixture, but more black than white. Records indicated that, at Selma High, 90 percent of the white students—and only 3 percent of the black students—were placed in the high-ability track.

At a series of BEST meetings, parents got up and talked about their children or other black children being trapped in low levels. Several mothers said their kids scored the same as white kids but weren't put in the top class because the teacher said they weren't mature enough. Rose said her younger daughter was put in a lower level in elementary school and complained that the reading was too easy. Rose had her tested and she came out gifted. Folk also said the better teachers were teaching the kids in the top level.

About a year went by without any response. Then, in early 1988, Roussell made a modest proposal to establish objective criteria for the three levels and to open honors classes and algebra to more students. He said he could find no criteria for the current system, that it varied from school to school and seemed primarily based on teacher recommendations and, in some cases, the desires of the parents. This subjective system favored the white community because many more white than black parents had the clout and the sense of entitlement to call a principal or teacher and insist that their children be placed in the top level.

The white community panicked. It was rumored that the black superintendent was going to do away with levels. At a public meeting, white politicians and parents talked about standards being lowered and white flight.

As always, there was disagreement between white and black Selma over whether race had anything to do with levels. Virtually all white people said they didn't see anything racial about learning levels; levels were a matter of educational preparedness. Virtually all black people, with the exception of the usual few at the top, saw leveling as, if not racist, at least racial. In our view, how could race not have anything to do with a system, instituted when integration came, that put most white children over here and most black children over there? The white community spoke exclusively of concern that classes would be watered down for children on the top. The black community's concern was whether children in the lower levels were being adequately placed, taught, and challenged. When white parents are saying one thing and black parents something else, that alone should indicate that race is a central factor—in perceptions if nothing else.

This is an ongoing dispute in Selma. The white community invariably latches on to the non-racial reasons in every controversial matter and accuses outspoken members of the black community of "making a racial issue out of it." I write about race and racism often in my newspaper column—the *Times-Journal* still has no black reporters—and many white people are infuriated. Not long ago, I was trading funny stories with some white law-enforcement people while we waited for a jury to return a verdict, and one of them commented, "J.L., you like us. Why do you write all that shit in the newspaper?" Some people have concluded either that I don't mean my friendliness or that I don't mean my columns and activism.

Of course, I mean both. I have learned to separate the personal from the battles I fight both in and out of the courtroom. When I'm engaged in courtroom combat over an issue, no holds are barred. I think I'm right and will do everything I can to win. That is not nearly so personal to me as it is a matter of objectives sought and purposes served. I may have coffee with the opposing lawyer afterward. It goes back to 1958, when I had to have some relationship with Judge Hare and the rest of the bar. If I let the personal spill over into the professional, I would be upset and angry with everybody all the time. I can't live that way.

The difficult part is being impersonal about personal things. I'm fighting for things that affect my children and grandchildren, yet I try not to get caught up emotionally to the extent that I lose perspective or get angry personally at ordinary white individuals. If you lose perspective, you don't know when to compromise or what's an honorable compromise. What I attack in my columns is a system, a way of thinking, and the hypocrisy of this community and America about race. My point often is, Let's at least be honest.

Superintendent Roussell had other problems in addition to his leveling proposal. He transferred or demoted several teachers and coaches, black and white, and they were disgruntled. He awarded contracts to a black printer and contractor, and the white people who used to have these contracts were upset. He snubbed the Chesterfield Club of middle-class black men. He showed up an hour late to a cocktail party at the home of a prominent white moderate. The white members of the school board were talking about firing him, saying he was "abrasive" and "moving too fast" and "acting too much on his own." In my view, this elite group, accustomed to having their way, couldn't stomach a somewhat arrogant, independent-minded superintendent, especially a black one who was rethinking the placement of students and time-honored practices like naming school kings and queens on the basis of how much money their parents raised for the school. In May 1988, the *Times-Journal* ran an editorial calling on the board to "back him or boot him."

That day I received a call from Sullivan Jackson, Marie Foster's brother. He wanted me to come to his dental office and meet with him and Edwin Moss. Both he and Edwin had read the editorial as a prelude to firing Roussell and thought the black community needed to show support or the black superintendent would be "run out of town," as Edwin put it.

Interestingly, Jackson, like Edwin, is very much part of the black middle class, with many white friends and contacts. Also like Edwin, you can push him only so far. King often stayed at his house in 1965. We decided to call a public meeting a few nights later at Brown Chapel to plan an appreciation banquet for Roussell and to discuss the school situation.

The night we met at Brown Chapel the board issued a one-sentence statement that it "supported" Roussell so the immediate crisis was over. The thirty or so black folk voted to have a banquet anyway and to send the board a letter of support for Roussell's leveling proposal. Then folk got up and angrily expressed grievances with the school system and white Selma. I gave my usual speech about the unelected school board—the City Council appoints the same crowd every time; not even the blacks on it are picked by the black community.

The next day, the *Times-Journal* carried an account of the meeting. Charlie Morris, a white lawyer and city councilman, called me and said he and his wife wanted to come over and talk.

Mrs. Morris said she was just sick to read about the uproar. "It would be one thing if it came from you," she said. "But it came from Mr. Moss and Dr. Jackson, people I respect."

Charlie said he and others were concerned about public education and didn't want the community to be polarized. I said, "You mean further polarized." He said, "Well, yes." I said it might be a good idea for some white people to get on the steering committee for the banquet for Roussell. Charlie said the Roussell situation was over and we should do something else to show biracial support for the public schools. I said I couldn't speak for the group at Brown Chapel, but I'd get some people to come to a meeting and he could get some white people to come.

The fact that Charlie and his wife approached me and not the black people they "respect" speaks volumes. White leaders can no longer name black leaders. A biracial meeting that included only the blacks the white community prefers would have little credibility with blacks and no impact on potential black protests.

The conversation with Charlie launched six months of biracial meetings over public education. The first was in my office; the others were held in the boardroom at People's Bank. Rex Morthland's son, Dick, now president of the bank, was in the group. So was Harry Gamble, Jr., the son of the lawyer who gave me my first law book; Mallory Reeves, a doctor from an old Selma family whose wife is on the school board, and Alston Fitts, the public-relations director for the Fathers of St. Edmund. On the black side were Alice Boynton, president of BEST; Joe Rembert, pastor of Brown Chapel; Chudy Okoye, a black doctor whose wife is on the school board; a high school teacher; and others.

"We're here for a healing," Charlie said at the start of the first meeting. Willis Wright, the retired black president of Concordia College, said he hoped for a "fruitful enjoyable evening that will avoid confrontation."

"What's wrong with confrontation?" I asked. "That's how Selma's progressed."

The white participants said they believed in public education, or their children would be in the private schools. They also pointed out the serious flak they often face for standing by the public-school system. Every time blacks create a public stink, propose some change accompanied with threats, some white people leave or talk about leaving and the private schools use the opportunity to recruit.

We said we were tired of being held hostage to white flight because it means a disproportionate allocation of resources and concern to those in the top levels. The price is paid by black children who historically have gotten second best and often need the most help. Some of us doubted that, at this late date, white flight was a serious problem. The private schools aren't paragons of academic excellence; they don't have the money or resources to offer the salaries and programs available in the public schools.

"White flight was the main argument made by the school board in the fifties and sixties against desegregation," I said. "Y'all haven't changed."

Mallory Reeves said he'd changed. "I remember when I was in medical school in 1958 in New Orleans. I went to see George Wallace in the Superdome. He said, 'The wall is cracked but it will never fall.' I remember cheering. Now here I am sitting with J. L. Chestnut." Later, Mallory told me he wanted to be fair to black people, but didn't want to give up any advantages enjoyed by his children. I appreciated his honesty.

Joe Smitherman won re-election once again in 1988. His black opponent, Councilman Cleophus Mann, repeated Reese's losing campaign strategy in 1984 and met a similar fate. A black mayor in Selma will take office when a black candidate forgets white votes and concentrates on turning out 55 or 60 percent of the black vote. The votes are there now; the strategy isn't.

Cleophus challenged the vote count, and the black councilmen refused to certify Smitherman the winner. The black councilmen were facing runoff elections in their black districts and I advised them to let the court declare the winner or their black opponents would certainly use the certification issue against them. I was asking them to do as some white leaders did in the sixties when they asked a federal judge to order them to take certain actions that would hurt politically if done voluntarily. The court certified Joe the winner.

Joe made some livid remarks in the media about black councilman Lorenzo Harrison, his closest black ally, who joined in refusing to certify. He fired Lorenzo's daughter from a city job. I stopped by Joe's office just as a TV crew were putting cameras away. We talked about the politics of his public attacks on Lorenzo. I said that by firing Lorenzo's daughter he was sending a message to whites that he (Joe) stands up and a message to Lorenzo about who's in charge.

"I can get Lorenzo back this afternoon. Just pave a sidewalk in his district," Joe said.

"Yes, but by attacking him you're helping get him elected," I said. Lorenzo's closeness to the mayor is a political liability in black Selma. "You're damn right," Joe said. "I don't want to have to deal with his opponent. I hear she's a Pentacostal who speaks in tongues."

Joe said he'd just told the press that "no politician is more self-serving than Lorenzo Harrison. Hell, he's not only on City Coun-

Hank Sanders and I with some shakers and movers in the office of Congressman Claude Harris for a 1987 meeting about trying to save jobs at a local plant. (From left after me, Selma City Councilman Charlie Morris, Probate Judge Johnny Jones, City Council President Carl Morgan, Mayor Joe Smitherman, Hank, Senator Earl Goodwin, banker Rex Morthland, banker Dick Morthland, *Selma Times-Journal* publisher Shelton Prince, Chamber of Commerce director Jamie Wallace) (© *Selma Times-Journal*)

The new biracial Dallas County Commission being sworn in on Martin Luther King Day, 1989 (© Penny Weaver)

cil, he works for the board at Craig Field [industrial park], his daughter had the city job. His brother's on something."

"What you didn't tell the press," I said, "was you put them there." Joe grinned. That's Selma politics.

In September 1988, after more than a decade of litigation, the Eleventh Circuit Court of Appeals ordered the all-white Dallas County Commission and school board (of the county system, not the city of Selma's) to be elected by districts rather than at large. Hank and I had filed the lawsuit in 1977 so some blacks could serve in county government, then persuaded the Department of Justice to assume the handling of the case.

The case took a decade to be decided because Judge Brevard Hand, the strict constructionist Nixon appointed, consistently ruled against a change to election by districts, and it would take months to get the matter reversed in the Eleventh Circuit in Atlanta. Then Hand waited awhile and ruled against districts on another basis, and up to Atlanta the Justice Department would go again. It was costing Dallas County taxpayers, including black taxpayers, hundreds of thousands of dollars to fight the suit so the county government could stay all white.

Finally, though, the county's appeals were exhausted. Under

the plan drawn by the court, two districts were 70 percent black; two were 70 percent white; the fifth was a so-called swing district. The probate judge would no longer be a member of the county commission.

We were looking not only at the certainty of electing some blacks but the possibility of black control of county government. The racial proportions were based on the 1980 census, and since then, the swing district had become more black. ADC, New South, and other black organizations jointly screened and endorsed candidates. The white as well as the black candidates came to the basement of First Baptist to seek our endorsement. We endorsed Perry Varner, who manages our law firm, as the candidate for county commission in the swing ward. We endorsed the black candidates we preferred in the black wards and white candidates in the white wards.

As usual, the conference room at our law firm became campaign headquarters for all the endorsees. An army of volunteers covered the county. The Sunday before the primary I introduced Perry at about eight churches in Selma. Hank spoke at other churches. A doctor's wife ran a phone bank. Rose had a troop of young people going door-to-door. Marie Foster collected absentee ballots. Through Hank, Marie was appointed to the Dallas County Board of Voter Registrars in 1987, so she now serves on the body she's been battling for twenty-five years.

Most of our endorsees made the runoff. The shock was District 1, a huge rural district out in the county, where a white candidate for the county school board won outright in a 70 percent black district. The white incumbent county commissioner from that district also did well and looked as though he might defeat the black candidate in the runoff.

Samson Crum, a black activist who lives in that district, heard reports that a black preacher was giving money to folk to vote for the white commission candidate. We went out to see the preacher before the runoff. He knew why we were there and immediately sought to establish his black credentials. "My father was a white man and I couldn't stand the son-of-a-bitch," he said. This preacher himself was a slick son-of-a-gun. When we asked a direct question, he whomped us with the Bible. We told him we had fought too long for a better life in this county to give it back to white politicians. He said he didn't think black people were going to do anything, so he might as well make a deal with white people, who usually win. He agreed to support our candidate, but we didn't believe him.

Smitherman came to our office several times politicking for his man, Bill Porter, who was running against the incumbent white commissioner in one of the 70 percent white districts. He argued that Porter's opponent was more conservative than the Republicans. Joe was always battling the county commission over how little money it allocated versus the city to joint enterprises, and he was interested in extending his influence from City Hall to the county courthouse. Porter, a former city councilman, was the perfect vehicle. I preferred any white over the incumbents, who had fought blacks so long and so hard, and I said we'd do all we could for Porter with the 30 percent of blacks in the district.

On election day, we stationed people with sample ballots at the polling places where any appreciable number of blacks voted. This included a few polling places in Porter's district. Porter called in the middle of the day to request that we withdraw our people from his district because he felt their presence would be used against him by his opponent. We moved our people out.

Nationally, Dukakis was following an identical process. He wanted black votes but was unwilling to be seen directly in pursuit of them. That is the unrewarding political status of black America today: One party takes us for granted. The other ignores us at best and, at worst, uses racist tactics like George Bush's Willie Horton ads, which raised the old bugaboo of black men and white women.

Racial politics produces peculiar and disheartening postures even in black politicians. Oscar Adams, the lone black justice on Alabama's Supreme Court and still the only black elected to statewide office, was running for re-election that same November and maneuvering like hell. His colleagues on the court were all supporting him. His Republican opponent was rated unqualified by over half the lawyers responding to a survey. But still, Alabama being Alabama, the race was close. Oscar heard that Jesse was coming to Alabama to campaign for the Democratic ticket, and he was concerned this might produce a white backlash against him. Hank and I didn't agree, but to satisfy Oscar, Hank called Jesse to ask him not to come to Alabama.

On the other hand, I was watching C-Span one night and there at the annual convention of the black National Baptist Convention USA, up on the podium next to each other, were Dick Gregory, Jesse Jackson, Michael Dukakis, and T. J. Jemison, the son of D. V. Jemison, the preacher the police chief sent the Rinkydinks to see about playing ball. T.J. now is president of the convention, as his father was before him. Jesse, in his remarks, alluded to the fact that Jemison had led a boycott in the 1950s in Baton Rouge, where he lives. Jemison has been one of Jesse's staunchest supporters.

Jesse introduced Dukakis, and Dukakis lit into an emotional speech. "*In sixty days*, the doors of the White House will open not just for me and Kitty but for all of you. *In sixty days*, we will have an attorney general who will not embarrass you but will inspire you. *In sixty days . . .*" He went right down the line to this black audience with this black-style refrain. At one point he stopped and said, "You can see how much I've learned from Jesse," and the audience roared. Dukakis also quoted Scripture to the crowd, which was made up mostly of black preachers and church people. This was an amazing scene to me. Here was a man who could be the next President of the United States adapting to the black religious style, and there was D. V. Jemison's son presiding over the event.

I almost fell out of my chair when Dick Gregory got up and said black folk eat a lot of strange things—pigs' ears, chitlins— but we will not eat Quayle. That brought to mind Dick Gregory coming to Selma in 1963 and letting loose with his sharp humor. The symbolism here was deepened for me because my church financed the expenses of two of our members to attend the convention. One was Rowena Cleveland, the widow of our long-time pastor who at first was reluctant to open the church to Bernard Lafayette. Now politics had become a legitimate issue before the national black Baptists, its president, D. V. Jemison's son, was leading the Jesse crusade and Mrs. Cleveland was in the audience listening to it all. Then I thought about Jesse back in those days, with all his damn bushy hair, trying to sit next to King and talk like him. Now he'd arrived at a summit nobody could have predicted.

I sat in my den enmeshed in all this symbolism and trying to fathom what it represented. The scene was a far cry from what America was twenty-five years ago. I came away with what I generally conclude when the past and present collide—that the status of black America today is a very mixed bag. To claim nothing has changed is as ridiculous as claiming we have arrived. I just sat there smiling at the television.

We won in Dallas County—three of the five seats on the formerly all-white Dallas County Commission (though only two of five on the county school board). One of the two winning whites was endorsed by us, but Porter lost to the incumbent.

The new commissioners were sworn in on Martin Luther King Day, January 16, 1989, in the large courtroom in the Dallas County Courthouse. The room was packed, mostly with black people, though 15–20 percent of the audience was white. Some of the black women wore furs. Little girls wore white dresses and ribbons in their hair. It reminded me of the Fikes trial in the same room when black folk brought their children to see the black lawyers. The acting head of the civil rights division of the U.S. Department of Justice and the white attorneys who tried and won the case participated in the ceremony. One of them had tears in his eyes when a young black woman sang "The Battle Hymn of the Republic." I was moved.

The new commission appointed Bruce Boynton, Sam and Amelia Boynton's son, as county attorney. He now practices law in Selma. A black woman was promoted to clerk of the commission, and the white woman who had been clerk and her boss was demoted. Naturally, the *Times-Journal* attacked the commission for making the appointments "on the basis of color rather than qualifications." Also, certain white people who used to be at the top of the list for county services are complaining that the new commission isn't "color-blind." The commissioners often vote on racial lines, but not always. They seem to be doing all right.

The same week the new commissioners were sworn in, Superintendent Roussell's plan on levels came before the Selma school board. Several whites said the criteria for the top level were too low. A black board member offered a compromise of raising the cut-off line by a part of a grade point; then the board voted to accept the compromise. All the black board members voted for it, along with one white, so it passed.

That spring, some black students wore African medallions to Selma High. A brouhaha developed when a few white teenagers took issue and shouted, "Niggers, go back to Africa." There were several incidents that culminated in a fight at a local drive-in. BEST was upset that more grade points were given for debate than for band, which meant a smart and popular black student did not become valedictorian. There were meetings, letters in the paper, and the policy was changed after the fact.

In the summer of 1989, the white principal at Selma High resigned. Reese had the most seniority, but whites were concerned about white flight if he was named principal. I said the board could expect a lawsuit if it bypassed him. In September, Reese was appointed Selma High principal and a white principal replaced a black principal at Westside Junior High.

Then in December, five days before Christmas, the white board members—the majority—voted not to renew Superintendent Roussell's contract, scheduled to expire in June 1990. They said he was dictatorial and a poor manager, though the school system had just received a good report from a state evaluation team. The black board members all walked out in protest. We held a series of meetings, the most heated since the county commission appointed Tommy Powell instead of a black to be tax collector. The issue galvanized the entire black community. We boycotted the businesses of some of the most influential board members, and many black parents kept their children out of the school for a day in an effort to get Roussell reinstated, to change the way the board is selected, and to address our other ongoing complaints about the way the schools are run.

Our protests escalated in February, when the white board members—the black members had not returned—announced that they intended to fire Roussell immediately. Throughout the controversy, Roussell attempted to walk on both sides of the street, and his experience illustrates, once again, how difficult, if not impossible, this is in racially polarized Selma. When black leaders called for the one-day boycott of the schools, Roussell opposed it. A black doctor and I told him privately that we understood a superintendent could not sanction a school boycott. But Roussell went further, making all kinds of public statements admonishing the children as to what would happen if they didn't go to school. Obviously, this was geared to please the white community but was disgusting to black people, who were calling for the boycott to save his job.

The board used Roussell's opportunism to try to manipulate black public opinion. In early February, Roussell overrode Reese's suspension of some white Selma High students on the debate team for partying on a trip. Suspensions of some black students on the track team for similar infractions were left standing. Reese announced, "Well, if the white students aren't suspended, neither are the black students." This was when the board decided to fire Roussell, apparently figuring the black community would be mad at him. Figuring we'd be pleased with Reese, they appointed him acting superintendent (he would stay on as Selma High principal) while a search was conducted for a new superintendent. The black community didn't go for Roussell currying favor with the whites, but we damn sure didn't fall for this transparent scheme. You talk about anger! Reese's church almost put him out as pastor, and he resigned as acting superintendent within days.

A group of blacks then went to see Smitherman, who was up to his neck in the effort to get rid of Roussell. Roussell isn't one of Smitherman's black supporters, and Smitherman resents the fact that the superintendent is paid more than he is. Every time I ever heard Smitherman talk about Roussell, he mentioned his salary and his expensive car. So I wasn't surprised that when a white photographer from *Newsweek*, a young man who looked like a redneck, asked what the school flap was really all about, the mayor responded, "An overpaid nigger from New Orleans."

Smitherman kept the black delegation waiting for several hours and called the police. When Rose attempted to open the door to the mayor's office, a policeman dragged her off. She was hospitalized for cuts and bruises, and Perry Varner and Carlos Williams of our office were arrested. That night we had the largest mass meeting in Selma since the 1960s. I thought First Baptist would explode. More than 2,000 folk marched to the auditorium where the school board was meeting. I stood on the steps and told them I had one partner in the hospital and two in jail and we would not be turned around.

A few days later, fights broke out at Selma High and about 150 black students started a sit-in in the cafeteria. The board said it would keep Roussell on for the remainder of his contract and closed the schools until tensions subsided. The white community was up in arms over the black protests and school disruption, and more than two hundred families put their children in private academies. When the schools reopened five days later, they were surrounded by the national guard, state troopers, city police, the national media. The next week, the black city councilmen walked out of a council meeting after the white majority voted down Edwin Moss's proposal to have the racial majority on the school board alternate every year.

So life goes on in Selma—controversy, confrontation. I doubt it will be much different in my lifetime. Everyone in Selma is warped by race in some way. The white people who run the town see themselves as superior and uniquely suited to rule. While they view Hank and other black officials as representing the black community, they see themselves as representing the whole community. They think they know what's best for everybody. They remain dedicated to maintaining white control because they believe black people can't run things as well as they can. They're warped that way.

It's hard to persuade me that any white person in power wants to be fair and work on an equal basis with black people. I assume otherwise. In my experience, they want you to agree with them and let them continue to be in charge of everything. It takes a lot for me to overcome my built-in suspicion. I suppose I'm warped that way. I know of few black people in Selma who escape this cultural baggage.

The Sunday before King's birthday, 1989, I delivered the speech I've given many times in the past few years: "The Probability of Miracles." I told an emotional crowd in a black church in Opelika

My parents and I (© Penny Weaver)

in east Alabama that in black America it is common to hear what can't be done. Too many of us are obsessed with the impossible. Four hundred years of slavery and segregation have had an awesome impact on the black mind. There is a powerful negativism in every black community and pressing problems of dope, crime, children having children, illiteracy, and hopelessness. There is some Negro and some slave in every black American you meet.

"But we have only been free since 1965. The fact that we have survived is a miracle, and some of us have thrived. Black people ought have no problem believing in miracles. In India, a baby bull elephant is tied by the leg to a tree. He tries to free himself, can't, and eventually gives up. A grown elephant is a massive creature, strong enough to uproot a tree, yet he can be restrained by a little rope tied to a sapling. It is the elephant's mind, not the rope, that enslaves him. We need to unshackle our minds and rise above the limits others impose on us and the limitations we impose on ourselves.

"I am not worried, though, my friends, because I know that when black people finally decide to get up, when black people finally decide to reach up, when black people finally decide to see up, when black people finally decide to move up, we can make mountains move, rivers stand still, trees tremble, angels sing, and devils cry! Why don't you believe in the probability of miracles?"

At times, I find it difficult myself to see progress, let alone believe in miracles. When you're involved in an ongoing struggle, it often seems as if you're fighting the same old battles all the time, hitting the same old barriers. Sometimes I feel so discouraged and worn down by the persistent white resistance and the loser psychology of too many black people who don't think we have what it takes to make it. When the white powers make decisions, like firing Roussell, that blatantly disregard the black community, and leave us no recourse but a return to sixties-style protest, I think, Shit, nothing has changed in this damn town at all.

On the ride home from Opelika that Martin Luther King's birthday, though, I felt pretty good. I slowly crossed the Edmund Pettus Bridge at sunset. There was Selma. The *Times-Journal*. City Hall. Our law firm. I reflected back on my return to Selma on the same road in 1958. From the vantage point of how things used to be, the present is not so discouraging. When I stop and look back, I see the many barriers that have fallen and the great distance we have traveled. Remember, I started out thinking we'd be making substantial progress if we could just get a string of black-owned supermarkets in the Black Belt. It's disappointing that we don't have them, but, in context, this was a modest goal. We've gone beyond where I even dared imagine—black people and white people.

We are far from the world envisioned by King in his "I Have a Dream" speech. We are closer to it, but getting there will continue to be a struggle. People forget that King said near the end of that speech, "I [now] go back to the South"—meaning to implement the dream of freedom and justice for all by marches, boycotts, and other means the establishment detested. I see King, at the expense of his life, striving to realize the dream, not just pleasantly dreaming.

I see my own life as helping to realize the dream in my world in Alabama. Though I never imagined I'd spend my whole life in little Selma, I don't know of any better place I could have taken a stand. Selma is my home. I love Selma. It's my life.

My family (front row: Vivian and I; second row: Terry, granddaughter Shawn-tya, granddaughter Shequitta; third row: Kim, Ronnie holding his daughter Danielle, Greg; fourth row: Rosalind and Geraldine) (© Penny Weaver)

Acknowledgments

The word "charmed" comes to mind about the course of creating this book. Right from the beginning, when I started telling people about this man in Selma whose life I thought was a book, I scarcely heard a word of discouragement. And each step along the way proved to be richer and more successful than I had imagined. There are many people to thank for this.

My parents, Kenneth and Arline Brown of Mankato, Minnesota, were excited about the project and were insightful readers of the manuscript. I thank my good friends Lucinda Fleeson, Jeannette Hardy, and Fred Cusick for reading the manuscript or book proposal and providing moral support. Louise Tiranoff, my friend and creative sounding board, made many valuable suggestions about the manuscript and incalculable contributions to the book in progress. I don't know how many phone conversations Louise and I had about this book as I was researching and writing it.

I thank Eugene Roberts, executive editor of the *Philadelphia Inquirer*, for sending me to the South as a reporter, for allowing me a year's leave of absence to write the book, and for his keen interest in the South as a story. And I am very grateful to my agent, David Black, and my editors, Jonathan Galassi and Rick Moody, for their great enthusiasm and helpful suggestions about the book.

For making my year in Alabama more enjoyable, I thank Virginia Durr, one of the great women of the South. Her household in Montgomery had been a safe haven for students, reporters, and others during the 1960s, and she told me, "Honey, if anything happens to you in Selma, you come over here and stay with me." I never fled to Montgomery—I never felt in danger—but I visited Virginia often. She frequently organized dinner parties with people she thought I'd like to meet. I'm also grateful to Penny Weaver, who took many of the photographs in this book, and her husband, Kendall Weaver, the Associated Press bureau chief in Montgomery, for their help and hospitality. Ditto to Ireys and Charles Nelson for some enjoyable weekends at their home in New Orleans, and to Winifred Green in Jackson, Mississippi.

In Selma, there are many people to acknowledge for their friendliness and helpfulness. The members of the First Presbyterian Church, which I attended, went out of their way to make me feel at home. In particular, I thank the pastor, Grady Perryman, and Claire Hutchinson, a Sunday-school teacher. Becky Nichols and her staff at the Selma Public Library were extremely helpful, as was Jean Martin at the *Selma Times-Journal.* I thank Alston Fitts III, Hannah Berger, Pat Blaylock, Kathryn Windham, Shannon Laramore, and the late Edgar Russell, Jr., and his wife for taking an interest in me and my project and including me in social occasions. I'm indebted to Alston, an expert on Selma history, for being generous with his books and his knowledge.

I'm also indebted to the many people in Selma and elsewhere who took the time for interviews: Drewey Aaron and his wife, Mary Aaron, the Reverend Lewis Lloyd Anderson, Richard Arrington, Pat Blaylock, Bruce Boynton, Theresa Burroughs, J. L. Chestnut, Sr., and Geraldine Chestnut, Vivian and Ronnie, Geraldine, Rosalind, Greg and Kim Chestnut, Frank and Lennie Chestnut, Emma Craig, Samson Crum, Ernest Doyle, Marie Foster, Harry Gamble, Sr., Bill Gamble, the late Wyman Gilmore, Earl Goodwin, Spiver Gordon, Barnette Lewis Hayes, Bain Henderson, Sam Earl Hobbs, John Hulett, J. D. Hunter, Bobby Jo Johnson, Roy Johnson, Johnny Jones, Bernard Lafayette, the Reverend Charles Lett, John Lewis, Muriel Lewis, Worth Long, Jean Martin, Henry Mayfield, Carl Morgan, Rex Morthland, Edwin Moss, Wendell Paris, Henry Pitts, Frederick D. Reese, Billy Reeves, Amelia Boynton Robinson, Father James Robinson, Norwood Roussell, the late Edgar Russell, Jr., Vaughn Russell, Hank and Rose Sanders, Arthur Shores, Loskar Smith, Joe T. Smitherman, Mort Stavis, John Tabor, Benny Tucker, Albert Turner, Robert Turner, Perry Varner, Nathaniel Walker, Willy White, Carlos Williams, Frank Wilson, Kathryn Windham, Harris Wofford, and Andrew Young.

Also helpful were books on Selma and chapters on Selma in books on the civil rights movement: *Bearing the Cross: Martin Luther King, Jr., and the Southern Leadership Conference* (William Morrow and Company, 1986) by David J. Garrow. *Eyes on the Prize: America's Civil Rights Years* (Viking Penguin Inc., 1987) by Juan Williams. *My Soul Is Rested: The Story of the Civil Rights Movement in the Deep South* (G. P. Putnam's Sons, 1977) by Howell Raines. *Selma: Her Institutions and Her Men* (Selma, 1879) by John Hardy. *Selma, Queen City of the Black Belt* (Clairmont Press, 1989) by Alston Fitts III. *Selma 1965: The March That Changed the South* (Charles Scribner's Sons, 1974) by Charles E. Fager. *Selma's Peacemaker, Ralph Smeltzer, and Civil Rights Mediation* (Temple University Press, 1987) by Stephen L. Longenecker.

I especially want to thank Hank and Rose Sanders, Barnette Lewis Hayes, Roberta Bryant, Josephine Coleman, and everyone else in Chess's law firm for supporting the project and being gracious about my frequent presence in their midst. I am very grateful to Vivian and to Chess's parents for including me in their lives and activities while I lived in Selma.

Above all, I am grateful to Chess himself. Interviewing him about his life was not like pulling teeth—that is, a difficult or painful extraction. It was more like striking oil—so much there just flowing out. I thank him for making the process enjoyable. I also thank him for his generosity with his time, his openness about himself, and his trust in me to do his life justice.

J.C.

Index

Page numbers in italics denote illustrations.

Index

Naibreth, James, 67
National Association for the Advancement of Colored People (NAACP), 69, 74, 83, 84–85, 133, 174, 179; banned in Alabama (1962), 128; Legal Defense Fund, 67, 70, 74–75, 78, 107, 109–10, 117, 191, 192–93, 206, 267, 351, 381; at odds with SCLC, 192–93; Selma chapter, 51, 74, 78, 128
National Baptist Convention U.S.A., 38, 412
National Education Association, 289, 386
New South Coalition, 401–2, 410
Nixon, Richard M., 130, 291
nonviolence, 148–50, 199, 215, 219
Norton, Judge J. C., 319–20

Okoye, Chude, 406
Olds, Cleophus, 170–71
Ouellette, Father, 184–85
Owens, J. H., 153–54

Paris, Wendell, 311–12
Parrish High School, Selma, 47, 285, 286, 287
Peabody, Endicott, 210
Pearson, Richard "Icewater," 87, 301
People's Bank, Selma, 277–78, 406
Perkins, James Jr., 365–66
Perry County, Alabama, 110, 113–17, 120, 205–6, 311, 314; under black control, 324; vote fraud charges and trial, 374–87
Perry County Civic League, 375, 376–80, 382, 384, 387
Pettway, Collins, 398, 399
Pettway, Wranch, 172, 247
Phillips, Johnnie Mae, 24
Phillips, Lewellen, 22–25, 29
Phillips, Nat, 29
Phillips, Nathaniel Jr., 234
Pickard, Joe, 200, 287, 289, 292–93, 295
picketing, 223, 226, 253, 281–83, 290, 370
Pitts, Arthur, 34
Pitts, Henry, 392
Pitts, McLean, 76–77, 83, 238, 284, 392
Plessy v. *Ferguson*, 68
police, South, 97, 208; excesses in Birmingham, 118, 160, 188–89, 296, 297–300, 306, 308; of Selma, 30–36, 42–43, 44, 47–49, 170, 194–95, 243–44, 393; sheriff's posse, Dallas County, 127, 174, 194, 205–6; state troopers, *205*, 205–7
poll taxes, outlawed, 233
Porter, Bill, 411, 413
Porter, James, 128–30, 170–71, 192, 212
Powell, Adam Clayton Jr., 60, 69, 71–72, 179
Powell, Tommy, 368–69, 370–71, 414
presidential election campaigns: of 1960, 123–24; of 1976, 337; of 1984, 359–63; of 1988, 391
Prince, Shelton, *408*
private schools and white flight, 284, 286, 329, 391–92, 407, 416
Project SAVE (Selma Area Voter Enlistment), 363
Pruitt, Drayton, 331

Pryor, Calvin, 87
public accommodations, 21; integration of, 173–74, 182, 188, 212, 220, 264
public employment, blacks in, 226, 243–44, 256, 262–64, 269, 327–28, 366–67, 393, 413; discrimination in Selma schools, 285, 287–90, 291–95; quotas, 366, 367; salaries, 6, 285, 290

Quarles, Benjamin, 64

Reagan, Ronald, 363, 388; Administration, 375, 380, 381, 386–87
reapportionment of 1983, Alabama, 341–44
Reeb, Rev. James, 211, 222
Reed, Herbert, 67
Reed, Joe Louis, 334–37, 341–44, 349, 386, 401–2; and Jesse Jackson campaign, 359–62
Reed Plan, 342–44; "Chestnut Amendment," 343–44
Reese, Frederick, x, 134–35, 149, 168, 189, 191, 194, 200, 226–28, 240, 243–44, 256, 269, 278, *279*, 295, 343, 364; in biracial meetings, 226–28; on Bloody Sunday, 205–6; city councilman, 260–61, 262–63, 366; embezzlement charges and trial, 231–33, 245, 253; mayoral candidate (1984), 363, 365–67, 407; Selma High principal, 414–15; as a teacher, 134–35, 287–88, 290
Reeves, Mallory, 406–7
Reformed Presbyterian Church, Selma, 6, 40, 47, 157, 184–85
Rembert, Joe, 363, 406
Reynolds, Judge Bernard, 83, 88–89, 98–99, 220
Rhodes, Isaac, 85
Rinkydinks baseball team, 41–44, 49, 275, 412
Robertson, Willie C., 153
Robinson, Father James, 41, 268, 278, *279*, 373
Rollison, E. T., 385
Roosevelt, Franklin D., 51
Rotary Club, 313, 340, 393
Roussell, Norwood, 393–94, 402–6, 413–16
Russell, Judge Edgar Jr., 5, 93–94, 112, 247–48, 347
Russell, Vaughn, 393–94
Rutledge, Dan, 370
Rutledge, Evans, 290, 291

Sadler, Duck, 356
St. Paul's Episcopal Church, Selma, 221, 394
salary differentials, racial, 6, 29, 285, 290
Salt and Pepper Club, 372–73, 374
Sanders, Hank, 249, *250*, 250–53, 256–58, 263–64, 273, 278, 281, 290, 305, 318, 321, 365, *399*, *408*, 409–10, 412; campaign management roles, 362, 368–69, 370; State Senate races of, 339–41, 343–44; as state senator, 344, 398–99, 401–2, 416; and vote fraud case, 379, 380, 388

Index

Sanders, Rose, 249, *250*, 250–53, 256–58, 263, 273, 278, 281, 305, 340–41, 343, 348, 362, *399*, 403, 410, 415; and Walker campaign, 370

SAVE (Selma Area Voter Enlistment), 363

school desegregation, 119, 127; "all deliberate speed" directive, 70, 284, 285; Dallas County, 285; early futile attempts in Selma, 83–85; other Black Belt counties, 329; Selma, 284–95, 329, 407; Selma freedom-of-choice ruse, 284–85

school segregation, 6–7, 67–68, 70, 81–85, 284

Seay, Solomon Jr., 87, 289; Aaron case, 103–6

segregation and discrimination, 6, 21–22, 46, 61–62, 81–85, 94–95, 187, 219–21; crippling effect of, 22, 417; residential, 21, *52*, 268, 343–44

Selma, Alabama, 392–95; black leadership of 1950s, 44–45, 48–49, *128*; blacks in government, 260–62, 268–71, 366, 393; black-white population ratio, 393; city hiring and promotion, 263–64, 269, 366–67, 393; compared to other Black Belt cities, 4, 6–7, 111, 310; history of, 3–7; map of, xvi; in 1983 reapportionment and districting, 342–44; Northern white civil rights influx, 209–10, 211; population statistics, 3, 392; urban renewal, 266–69, 393; white power and black accommodation, *see* accommodationism; white vs. black neighborhoods, 21, *52*, *267*, 268, 343–44, 393

Selma: Her Institutions and Her Men (Hardy), 4

Selma Accord (1970), 268

Selma Country Club, 393–94

Selma-Dallas Community Federal Credit Union, 277–78

Selma-Dallas County Chamber of Commerce, 92, 196, 223–24, 226, 276, 283

Selma-Dallas Direct Action Committee, 278

Selma-Dallas Legal Defense Fund, 278, 290

Selma-Dallas Political Action Committee, 278

Selma Emergency Relief Fund (SERF), 229, 231

Selma High School, 286–87, 402–3, 414, 415; issue of black vs. white staff, 287–90, 291–95; sit-in of black students, 416

Selma Mall, 277, 282–83

Selma school board, 275, 290–91, 294–95, 402, 413–16; appointed by City Council, 291, 402, 405; blacks on, 269–70, 291, 366, 393, 414, 416; and desegregation, 84–85, 284–90, 407

Selma *Times-Journal*, xi, xii, 81–85, 165, 223, 236, 239, 264, 282, 317, 365–66, 368, 394, 404–5, 413; concessions to blacks, 283; pro-segregation ads in, *167*, *237*

Selma-to-Montgomery march, *see* Montgomery

Selma University, 6, 38, 131, 139, 156–58; students and civil rights, 153–54, 160, 163

separate but equal doctrine, 67–68

separatism and black power, 238

Sessions, Jefferson Beauregard, 378–79, 388

Sewell, Andrew, 292, 295

Shelby, Richard, 388

sheriff's race of 1966, Dallas County, 236–41

Shields, John F., 43–44, *44*, 45–51, 53, 60, 61–62, 125, 135, 154, 164, 183, 198

Shores, Arthur, 75, 87, 96, 124, 307, 308

Shorty, Jim, 15–18, 114

shotgun houses, Selma, 32, *33*, 268, 393

Singleton case, 289

sit-ins, 169, 173–74, 187, 189, 370–71, 416

Smeltzer, Ralph, 220–21

Smith, Eva Lou, 383

Smith, Rev. Kelly Miller, 148

Smitherman, Joe, x, 84, *195*, 195–97, 221, 222–24, 312, 341, 347, 363–65, 391, *408*, 411; biracial meetings of, 226, 228, 240; Chestnut's confrontations with, 264–65, 270–71, 272–73; manipulation of black councilmen by, 261–63; opportunism of, 260, 264, 408–9; racial politics of, 228, 240–41, 260–66, 268–71; and Reese case, 232; and Roussell controversy, 415; and urban renewal, 266–68, 367; *see also* mayoral races, Selma

Southern Christian Leadership Conference (SCLC), 148, 160, 174, 188–89, 223, 229–32, 375, 376; at odds with other civil rights groups, 192–94, 204, 231; Selma activities, 189, 191, 192–94, 199, 204, 206, 214, 231, 234, 256

Southern Poverty Law Center, 381

Southern Regional Council, 147

Stallworth, Kemp M., 85

States Rights Party (1948), 61

Stavis, Mort, 370, 380, 382, 385

Stewart, Donald, 337

Stewart, Edgar, 200

Stone, Roy, 49–50

Street, James, 287, 290, 292, 293

Student Nonviolent Coordinating Committee (SNCC), 46, 147–49, 164, 173, 214; in Lowndes County, 236; and SCLC, 194, 204; Selma activities of, 149–50, 152, 164, 168–69, 173, 174, 189, 198–99, 206; *see also* Lafayette, Bernard

Sullivan, Jean, 276, 347

Sumter County, Alabama, 110, 311, 314, 333; under black control, 324, 327, 329–331, 375; school board, 325, 329–31; vote fraud investigation, 375

Suttles, Green B., 28–29, 58–59

Tabernacle Baptist Church, Selma, 24, 38, 161–62, *162*; mass meetings at, 161, 163–65, 170

Talladega College, 60–62, 63–64

tax collector race, 1984, Dallas County, 367–71

Thomas, Judge Daniel, 137, 175–76, 185–86, 192, 193, 214, 253–54, 291

Thompson, Daniel, 64

Thompson, Judge Myron, 337

Threadgill, Rev. Thomas, 356